Approaches to the Evolution of Language

This book is one of the first systematic attempts to bring language within the neo-Darwinian framework of modern evolutionary theory, without abandoning the vast gains in phonology and syntax achieved by formal linguistics over the past forty years. The contributors – linguists, psychologists and palaeoanthropologists – address questions including: What is language as a category of behaviour? Is it an instrument of thought or of communication? If the latter, how does it differ from other systems of animal communication? What do individuals know when they know a language? What cognitive, perceptual and motor capacities must they have to speak, hear and understand a language?

For the past two centuries, scientists, as children of societies preoccupied with technology, have tended to see language function as largely concerned with the exchange of practical information about the mechanics of the physical world: toolmaking, hunting and so forth. By contrast, this volume (a product of the age of mass democracies) takes as its starting point the view of human intelligence as social, concerned with one's own and others' desires and motives, and of language as a device for forming alliances, making friends and thus achieving successful feeding and mating through a complex social network. From this perspective, phonologists and syntacticians may explore the origins of the sound patterns and formal structures that characterize all language.

JAMES R. HURFORD has been Professor of General Linguistics at the University of Edinburgh since 1979. Prior to that he held posts at the University of California, Los Angeles; the University of California, Davis; and the University of Lancaster. His publications include *The Linguistic Theory of Numerals* (1975), *Semantics: a Coursebook* (with Brendan Heasley) (1983), *Language and Number* (1985) and *Grammar: A Student's Guide* (1994).

MICHAEL STUDDERT-KENNEDY is a past President of the Haskins Laboratories, New Haven, Connecticut; Professor Emeritus of Psychology at the University of Connecticut; and Professor Emeritus of Linguistics at Yale University. He has published numerous articles on speech perception and speech development and edited or co-edited several books including *Psychobiology of Language* (1983).

CHRIS KNIGHT is Reader in Anthropology at the University of East London. His research explores the origins of cultural symbolism, and has recently focused particularly on language and its evolutionary origins. His publications include two books: *Blood Relations* (1995) and *The Human Conspiracy* (forthcoming 1999), as well as book chapters and journal articles.

Approaches to the

Edited by James R. Hurford,
Michael Studdert-Kennedy
and Chris Knight

Evolution of Language

Social and Cognitive Bases

CAMBRIDGE UNIVERSITY PRESS
Cambridge, New York, Melbourne, Madrid, Cape Town, Singapore, São Paulo

Cambridge University Press
The Edinburgh Building, Cambridge CB2 8RU, UK

Published in the United States of America by Cambridge University Press, New York

www.cambridge.org
Information on this title: www.cambridge.org/9780521630498

First published 1998

A catalogue record for this publication is available from the British Library

Library of Congress Cataloguing in Publication data

Approaches to the evolution of language: social and cognitive bases /
edited by James R. Hurford, Michael Studdert-Kennedy, Chris Knight.
p. cm.
Includes index.
ISBN 0 521 63049 5 (hardback) ISBN 0 521 63964 6 (paperback)
1. Language and languages – Origin. 2. Grammar, Comparative and
general – Phonology. 3. Grammar, Comparative and general – Syntax.
4. Human evolution. I. Hurford, James R. II. Studdert-Kennedy,
Michael. III. Knight, Chris.
P116.A68 1998
401–dc21 98–42162 CIP

ISBN 978-0-521-63049-8 hardback
ISBN 978-0-521-63964-4 paperback

Transferred to digital printing 2008

Contents

Contributors

Jean Aitchison, Worcester College, Oxford OX1 2HB, UK. <jean.aitchison@worcester.oxford.ac.uk>

John Batali, Department of Cognitive Science 0515, University of California at San Diego, 9500 Gilman Drive, La Jolla, CA 92093–0515, USA. <batali@cogsci.ucsd.edu>

Robert C. Berwick, Centre for Biological and Computational Learning, Massachusetts Institute of Technology, Cambridge, MA, USA. <berwick@ai.mit.edu>

Derek Bickerton, Department of Linguistics, University of Hawaii, Honolulu, Hawaii 96822, USA. <derek@uhunix.uhcc.Hawaii.Edu>

Andrew Carstairs-McCarthy, Department of Linguistics, University of Canterbury, Private Bag 4800, Christchurch, New Zealand. <a.c-mcc@ling.canterbury.ac.nz>

Jean-Louis Dessalles, Groupe 'Modèles Informatiques pour le Langage et la Cognition', Dep. Informatique, Ecole Nationale Supérieure des Télécommunications (ENST), 46 rue Barrault, 75013 Paris, France. <dessalles@inf.enst.fr>

Merlin Donald, Department of Psychology, Queen's University, Kingston, Ontario, K7L 3N6, Canada. <donaldm@pavlov.psyc.queensu.ca>

Robin Dunbar, Department of Psychology, University of Liverpool, Eleanor Rathbone Building, PO Box 147, Liverpool L69 3BX. <rimd@liverpool.ac.uk>

James R. Hurford, Department of Linguistics, University of Edinburgh, Adam Ferguson Building, 40 George Square, Edinburgh EH8 9LL, Scotland, UK. <jim@ling.ed.ac.uk>

Simon Kirby, Department of Linguistics, University of Edinburgh, Adam Ferguson Building, 40 George Square, Edinburgh EH8 9LL, Scotland, UK. <simon@ling.ed.ac.uk>

Chris Knight, Anthropology Subject Area, University of East London, George Brooker Building, Longbridge Road, Dagenham, Essex RM8 2AS, England. <C.Knight@uel.ac.uk>

Klaus Kohler, Institut für Phonetik und digitale Sprachverarbeitung der Universität Kiel, D-24098 Kiel, Germany. <kk@ipds.uni-kiel.de>

Björn Lindblom, Department of Linguistics, Stockholms Universitet, 10691 Stockholm, Sweden. <lindblom@ling.su.se>

John L. Locke, Department of Speech Science, University of Sheffield, Sheffield, UK. <J.L.Locke@sheffield.ac.uk>

Peter F. MacNeilage, Department of Linguistics, Calhoun Hall 501, University of Texas, Austin, Texas, 787122–1196, USA. <macneilage@mail.utexas.edu>

Frederick J. Newmeyer, Department of Linguistics, University of Washington, Seattle, Washington 98195, USA. <fjn@u.washington.edu>

Camilla Power, Department of Anthropology, University College London, Gower Street, London WC1E 6BT, UK. <ucsaccp@ucl.ac.uk>

Luc Steels, VUB AI Lab, Pleinlaan 2, 1050 Brussels, Belgium. <steels@arti14.vub.ac.be>

Michael Studdert-Kennedy, Haskins Laboratories, 270 Crown Street, New Haven, Connecticut, 06511–6695, USA. <msk@lenny.haskins.yale.edu>

Mária Ujhelyi, Semmelweis University of Medicine, Institute of Behavioural Sciences, 1089 Budapest, Nagyvarad tér 4, Hungary. <ujhmar@net.sote.hu>
Ib Ulbaek, Department of Languages and Culture, University of Roskilde, Denmark. <ibu@jane.ruc.dk>
Robert Worden, Charteris Ltd, 6 Kinghorn Street, London EC1A 7HT, UK. <rworden@dial.pipex.com>

Acknowledgments

This volume grew out of a conference in Edinburgh in 1996 on the evolution of human language. We gratefully acknowledge the support of Edinburgh University Interdisciplinary Symposium fund, Edinburgh University Northern Scholars Committee, Edinburgh University Arts Faculty Research fund, Edinburgh University Linguistics Department, the Linguistics Association of Great Britain, the Royal Anthropological Institute, *The Times Higher Education Supplement*, the Edinburgh International Science Festival, and the organizing genius of Diane Nelson. The editorial work was assisted by a fellowship at the Collegium Budapest for Jim Hurford and by a sabbatical fellowship at the Ecole Nationale Supérieure des Télécommunications, Paris, for Michael Studdert-Kennedy. Michael Studdert-Kennedy thanks Haskins Laboratories for their support, and Chris Knight acknowledges the support of the University of East London and, in particular, the dedication of his research assistant, Catherine Arthur.

Introduction: new approaches to language evolution

MICHAEL STUDDERT-KENNEDY, CHRIS KNIGHT
AND JAMES R. HURFORD

Several strands of thought in linguistics, evolutionary biology and cognitive psychology have come together in the past few decades to encourage a new approach to language and its evolution. Rather than taking an indirect approach based on inference from supposed correlates of language, such as hominid tools and artifacts, or lateral biases in hominid brain morphology and handedness, the new approach confronts language directly. What was the nature of the hominid social matrix within which language arose, and what was the function of language in that matrix (Part I)? How did its biologically unique hierarchical structure of phonology (Part II) and syntax (Part III) evolve?

Consider, first, the biological status of language. Within a few years of the publication of *The Origin*, philologists were applying Darwinian principles to the taxonomy of Indo-European languages. Darwin (1871) himself judged 'The formation of different languages and of distinct species [to be] . . . curiously parallel . . . We find in distinct languages striking homologies due to community of descent, and analogies due to a similar process of formation' (pp. 465–466). Indeed, by extending principles of zoological taxonomy to languages, August Schleicher (1821–1868) and other nineteenth-century philologists traced a path back to what we now call Proto-Indo-European, and plotted its family tree.

Implicit in this work and in the work of much historical linguistics that still goes forward is a view of language as a property of a group rather than of an individual. In fact, Ferdinand de Saussure, in a famous course of lectures at the University of Geneva (1906–1911), distinguished *langue*, language as a system, a cultural institution, from *parole*, language as spoken and heard by individuals. For Saussure (1966), 'language is not complete in any speaker; it exists only within a collectivity . . . only by virtue of a sort of contract signed by members of a community'

(p. 14). Language was thus an abstract property of a group, related to its speakers somewhat as a species is to its members.

However, historical changes within, and divergences among, languages, are largely cultural matters, biologically constrained, no doubt, but quite distinct from the evolution of language as a species-specific capacity. Here, the language–species analogy, language as a property of a group, is not by itself sufficient. To be sure, certain conditions essential to the emergence and maintenance of language in individual speakers clearly do derive from their being members of a group. For example, speech-act theory (e.g., Austin 1962) demands a background of shared understandings as a condition of the illocutionary force of an utterance. On the other hand, we cannot slight a central tenet of neo-Darwinian theory: in the evolution of 'adaptive complexity' (Dawkins 1986; Maynard Smith 1969), of which language is surely a prime example, the unit of variation and selection is the gene (or the individual), not the group. What we need therefore is an account of language evolution, sensitive both to language as 'a sort of contract signed by members of a community' and to language as a hard-wired (individual) competence generated under standard processes of Darwinian natural selection. We need to place language among those many group behaviours of social animals – from the reproductive processes of eusocial insects to the hunting routines of a wolf pack – that can only emerge through interactions among individuals. What had to get into the genes, among other things, was the capacity and motivation to enter into the processes of social interaction that led, and still lead, into language.

For the biological evolution of language we must turn therefore to another, not incompatible tradition within linguistics that focuses on the individual. The tradition stems from the work of seventeenth-century grammarians and of such nineteenth-century figures as the German physicist, Herman von Helmholtz, the French neurologist, Paul Broca, and the English phonetician, Henry Sweet. Ironically, perhaps, in light of his well-known scepticism concerning the power of natural selection (e.g. Chomsky 1986: 274, fn. 22), it was Noam Chomsky (1965, 1972) who picked up this tradition by recognizing that 'external language', or language as a property of a group, was not readily amenable to psychological and biological study. He therefore reformulated the *langue–parole* distinction as *competence* (what a speaker–listener 'knows') and *performance* (what a speaker–listener does in implementing knowledge). He thus set the locus of human language capacity in the individual brain, launching a revolution in the study of language that is still in progress.

We do not have to subscribe to Chomsky's theories to acknowledge their impact. For linguistics, the shift from the taxonomic tradition was as though ornithology had switched from describing and classifying the flight patterns of the world's 8,000–9,000 species of birds to analysing the basic principles of flight as they must be instantiated in the anatomy and physiology of every hummingbird and condor. New questions came into view: What is language as a category of behaviour? Is it an instrument of thought or of communication? If the latter, how does it differ from other systems of animal communication? What do individuals know when they know a language? What cognitive, perceptual and motor capacities must they have to speak, hear, and understand a language? What is the course of their ontogenetic development? And so on.

The last question is of particular interest for a theory of language evolution, because the course of ontogeny provides our most plausible model for the course of phylogeny. No area of language study has been more radically affected by Chomsky's work than language acquisition. Indeed, it is fair to say that until Chomsky's writings began to be widely disseminated among psychologists in the early sixties, the field did not exist. Yet today language acquisition is one of the largest and most active areas in developmental psychology.

A consequence of this proliferation, and of concurrent booms in psycholinguistics and in linguistics itself, has been recognition that language is a system of such complexity that its selective value may be difficult to imagine. Premack (1986), for example, writes: 'It is not easy to picture the scenario that would confer selective fitness on, specifically, syntactic classes and structure-dependent rules . . . I challenge the reader to reconstruct the scenario that would confer selective fitness on recursiveness . . . Human language is an embarrassment for evolutionary theory because it is vastly more powerful than one can account for in terms of selective fitness' (pp. 132–133).

At least some of Premack's difficulties arise from his evident assumption that language evolved for the exchange of information about the male activities of hunting and tool-making (cf. Dunbar, this volume), the former a communal activity to which the latter, even if an individual skill, would contribute. What is needed, rather, is a more subtle view of evolving human society in which the capacity to speak and listen (including, say, the recursive capacity to handle relative clauses) might afford an individual, male or female, and its close kin a selective advantage over conspecific rivals in forming coalitions, discussing plans of action, and otherwise negotiating a path to higher social status, and so to more successful feeding and mating. What was needed for such a view to emerge was recognition of the 'social function of intellect' (Humphrey 1976), of the 'political' life of primate groups (De Waal 1982), and of primate 'theories of mind' (Byrne & Whiten 1988).

The shifts in linguistics and psycholinguistics to language as a property of an individual, in biology to the gene as the unit of variation and selection for the evolution of adaptive complexity, and in cognitive psychology to the social functions of intelligence were important moves toward studying the biological basis for both the biological and the cultural evolution of language. These developments made possible the direct approaches to language evolution taken in this volume.

Broadly, then, the topic of the chapters that follow is the emergence and maintenance of a symbolic culture, grounded in the individual's capacity for speech and language. How did a domain of collective rules emerge from, and come to constrain, the epigenetic course of individual development? How did the dual hierarchy of phonology and syntax emerge from prior perceptual, motoric, cognitive and social capacities? How, perhaps most problematic of all, should we conceive the interactive evolutionary spiral through which both individual language capacity and a communal system of symbolic communication must have more or less simultaneously emerged?

References

Austin, J. L. (1962). *How to Do Things with Words*. Oxford: Oxford University Press.

Byrne, R. & Whiten, A. (eds.) (1988). *Machiavellian Intelligence, Social Expertise, and the Evolution of Intellect in Monkeys, Apes, and Humans*. Oxford: Clarendon Press.

Chomsky, N. (1965). *Aspects of the Theory of Syntax*. Cambridge, MA: MIT Press.

(1972). *Language and Mind*. New York: Harper & Row.

(1986). *Knowledge of Language: Its Nature, Origin, and Use*. New York: Praeger.

Darwin, C. (1871). *The Descent of Man*. London: John Murray.

Dawkins, R. (1986). *The Blind Watchmaker*. Oxford: Oxford University Press.

De Waal, F. B. M. (1982). *Chimpanzee Politics: Power and Sex among Apes*. London: Cape.

Humphrey, N. K. (1976). The social function of intellect. In Bateson, P. P. G. & Hinde, R. A. (eds.) *Growing Points in Ethology*. Cambridge: Cambridge University Press: 303–317.

Maynard Smith, J. (1969). The status of neo-Darwinism. In Waddington, C. H. (ed.) *Towards a Theoretical Biology*, vol. II. Chicago: Aldine: 82–89.
Premack, D. (1986). *Gavagai!* Cambridge, MA: MIT Press.
Saussure, F. de (1966). *Course in General Linguistics*. (Translated by Wade Baskin.) New York: McGraw Hill.

Part I Grounding language function in social cognition

1 Introduction: grounding language function in social cognition

CHRIS KNIGHT

How unique is speech? What are its cognitive and social prerequisites? Did complex, syntactical speech emerge in a relatively sudden 'leap'? Or can gradualist models explain its evolution? These chapters address the continuity/discontinuity debate, specify selection pressures driving the emergence of speech, and offer a general view of language function as grounded in social cognition.

The theme of mindreading and tactical deception – Machiavellian intelligence – links several interdisciplinary contributions in this section. Darwinian signal-evolution theory invites us to abandon traditional assumptions about honest communication and instead ask questions about competition and co-operation, selfishness versus altruism, manipulation as opposed to communication. In this perspective, an animal is expected to emit a signal not in order to pass on valuable information but to manipulate the recipient's behaviour in its own interests.

This theme allows Jean Aitchison, in revisiting (or discontinuing) the continuity/discontinuity debate, to highlight an important distinction between human and other primate signals. Some primates arguably possess mindreading skills, on the basis of which they may engage in tactical deception. Whereas non-human primates 'always use this ability for selfish purposes, to achieve gains for themselves', humans can use this same capacity to communicate about absent objects and events, sometimes for selfish, sometimes unselfish purposes. Selfish deception, in this view, is only one possible outcome of the ability to deploy signals whose referents are fictions; another is the co-operative handling of displaced reference.

But if the evolutionary function of language was the co-operative sharing of 'displaced' (not currently perceptible) information, particularly social information – as Robin Dunbar persuasively argues – this leaves us with a paradox. Why are humans so co-operative? Why divulge valuable information to other individuals who may be in direct behavioural competition with the communicator? Ib Ulbaek sees the solution in the evolution of a specifically human, as against primate, sociality. There must have emerged conditions favouring strategies of reciprocal altruism, which were sufficiently stable to support the emergence of speech.

In recent years, reciprocal altruism models have been central to Darwinian discussions of language evolution. But can we make these models more specific? Exactly what strategies are implied? Does an iterated Prisoner's Dilemma game of trade-offs between cheating and cooperation match our observations of the way we actually use language in everyday life? Not according to Jean-Louis Dessalles who, along with Ulbaek, points to the paradox of speech as an apparently altruistic communication system. In a lively and engrossing chapter, he examines the key pragmatic constraint of language – that it be relevant.

To be perceived as relevant, writes Dessalles, a speaker's utterance must address some problem. Information is deemed relevant if it contributes to a solution. Being 'relevant', then, means co-operating in mental or practical problem-solving. Why, then, asks Dessalles, do speakers not guard against freeloaders exploiting such co-operation while on a future occasion declining to reciprocate? Why is there such willingness to share information? Most conversations appear as contests in which speakers vie with one another in divulging relevant information – the reverse of Darwinian expectations. Dessalles concludes that speakers are in fact advertising – trading relevant information for status accorded to them by listeners.

Dessalles tentatively proposes that the relevance-for-status system could be rooted in primate coalition formation. Chris Knight endorses the logic, but asks why primate coalitions in fact seem not to allocate status in this way. Far from enhancing its status by the free broadcasting of valuable information, a primate may do better by concealing knowledge from its actual or potential competitors. Why divulge to a potential rival information of value in exploiting a feeding or mating opportunity? In a 'Machiavellian' social environment, coalitions tend to be unstable, current allies remaining potential rivals. In this context, Knight argues, it is understandable why primates should hold back, declining to compete in the generalized broadcasting of problem-solving information and instead keeping their thought-processes, in the main, to themselves.

If this is accepted, then we are left to explain why status-allocation altered so dramatically in the evolution of hominid social life. In addressing this issue, Knight notes that to be considered 'relevant', a speaker's utterance must contribute to the solution of a *shared* problem. The question then arises: shared between whom? Coalition *boundaries* appear critical, not only in defining relevance but also in structuring those constituencies involved in the allocating of status.

A coalition may be seen as the outcome of a reciprocal altruism strategy. Reciprocal altruism models focus on a condition vital to the relevance-for-status exchange system: trust. Comeback mechanisms against cheaters are apparent in people's concern for their reputation, their good name, their ability to 'keep their word'. Information cannot be valuable to listeners unless they are currently ignorant of it. 'Displaced' information must be accepted, at least initially, *on trust*. Yet in modelling the evolution of language from primate antecedents, such trust cannot simply be assumed.

Robin Dunbar and Camilla Power address the issue of trust by modelling primate, and evolving human, social life. The rapid expansion of the brain over the last 2 million years of *Homo* evolution – primarily neo-cortical expansion – indicates increasing group sizes and social complexity. Under such circumstances, as Dunbar argues, individuals striving to maintain alliances via manual grooming would have faced impossible burdens. Using vocal calls to maintain social bonds was less costly and time-consuming, and for this reason increasingly replaced manual grooming. According to Dunbar, 'vocal grooming' became increasingly informative, the outcome being speech as 'gossip' or social information exchange. Having previously (with palaeontologist Leslie Aiello) estimated fossil human neocortex ratios from cranial capacities and then used primate equations to predict past group sizes and hence grooming time requirements, Dunbar gives grounds for dating this development to between 500,000 and 250,000 years ago – coinciding with the evolution of our own species, *Homo sapiens*.

Although Dunbar sees fully symbolic speech as a subsequent and late development, he treats earlier, pre-symbolic speech or 'gossip' as already useful 'for acquiring information about the behaviour of prospective or existing partners when these are not physically present'. As Aitchison notes, there are grounds for believing that a condition for such 'displaced reference' was the prior development among hominids of skills in tactical deception. Dunbar appears equivocal as to whether 'language evolved to facilitate and/or handle deception'. In any event, displaced reference – which by definition is reference to things not immediately verifiable – would seem to presuppose high levels of listener trust.

Why place such trust in others? Camilla Power sees the issue of reliability as crucial to Dunbar's entire hypothesis. To groom a conspecific, primate-style, is time-consuming and costly. The recipient trusts the signal because it is intrinsically convincing: the signaller's investment of time and energy demonstrates commitment, hence reliability as an ally. If the replacement of manual by vocal 'grooming' amounted to a form of cost-cutting in signalling, then to that extent trustworthiness would have been undermined. Moreover, Dunbar sees this cost-cutting as occurring while communication was increasingly taking the form of 'gossip' – that is, information concerning third parties, received second-hand. Listeners would now have been highly vulnerable to deception. In view of all this, it is unclear how the new, low-cost vocal signals in themselves could have fulfilled the function of maintaining group cohesion.

In seeking a solution, Power and Knight suggest that the high-cost bonding function performed by manual grooming among primates continued to be performed within the *Homo* lineage, but increasingly by the emergent category of costly signals known as 'ritual'.

To explain the emergence of ritual, Power outlines a general model of human social origins based on the neo-Darwinian expectation that males and females will pursue divergent reproductive strategies. Encephalization in the *Homo* lineage placed special pressure on one segment of the population: reproductively active females burdened with the costs of rearing large-brained infants. Mothers especially needed to reduce social time budgets while maintaining strong social bonds. Power identifies the key problem for females as countering male philandering strategies. Females had to ensure that energy derived from male provisioning went not only to cycling, potentially fertile females (who would tend to be targeted by philanderers), but also to lactating mothers. In Power's model, cosmetic or body-painting 'ritual' emerged in this context – embodying a strategy to prevent would-be philanderer males from discriminating against pregnant/lactating females. By scrambling menstrual signals, females in coalitions developed a form of super-efficient 'grooming' – a high-cost demonstration of commitment to one another, ensuring that male mating effort inspired by the presence of fertilizable females became equally available to pregnant and nursing mothers. Vocal gossip, Power suggests, relied on the coevolution of such ritual signals capable of sustaining the necessary ingroup trust. Power's model endorses Dunbar in seeing female coalitionary strategies as decisive in driving the emergence of speech.

Chris Knight extends the argument on ritual/speech coevolution to address the emergence of syntactical complexity. For Worden, the skills through which intelligent primates and hominids internally *represent one another's representations* provide the cognitive basis for the later development of recursion and other fundamentals of syntactical complexity in speech. The two-way (self-to-other, other-to-self) procedures of mindreading, in this perspective, turn out to constitute the computational basis of sentence generation and interpretation. 'Mindreading' cognition, in this account, already displays syntax-like structure – an idea which, if accepted, would solve the paradox of syntactical speech as a recent innovation, at most 250,000 years old, whose cognitive prerequisites would have taken much longer to evolve. If Worden's theory is accepted, we are left to explain how and why such pre-existent competences came to govern not only thought but also, more unusually, the rapid sequencing of low-cost vocal signals and hierarchical structuring of associated communicable representations.

Dunbar's approach to this question is emphatically gradualist. While conceding that grammar is an important feature of speech, he stresses that 'animals naturally code the events in the world in what amounts to grammatical form'. In arguing that grammar is already present in primate cognition, Dunbar receives support from Robert Worden's computational model of language evolution from primate social intelligence. Worden's radical contribution is to suggest that, given sufficiently sophisticated mindreading competence, 'essentially no new cognitive faculties or links were needed for the emergence of language'. Success in demonstrating such cognitive continuity would indeed solve a range of theoretical problems. Note, however, that the posited functional and mechanical continuities are cognitive: Worden says nothing as to how or why *speech as such* arose. Linguistic competence may in this light have involved the acquisition of *two* abilities: firstly, cognitive competence in forming complex internal representations; secondly, a *specifically linguistic* competence in transforming such representational structures into linear sequences of symbols. Acceptance of primate/human continuity on the first level need not extend to the second.

Dunbar's continuity approach is more far-reaching. Language, Dunbar argues, 'must have evolved piecemeal as more and more complex layers were added onto the existing primate communication system'. Challenging Chomskyan and other schools of theoretical linguistics, Dunbar sees the vocalizations involved in primate contact-calling or 'grooming-at-a-distance' as prefiguring and evolving continuously into syntactical speech.

Merlin Donald contests the view – supported by Dunbar among others – that the antecedents of syntactical complexity in speech are to be found in the complexity of primate and ancestral human vocal calls. However, in defence of 'the continuity principle', he equally rejects the Cartesian notion of a uniquely human, qualitatively novel 'grammar module' or 'language organ'. Donald sees competence in handling expressive gesture or 'mimesis' as the crucial neurocognitive preadaptation for speech. 'Mimesis' in this view emerged with *Homo* about 2 million years ago, driven by competition between groups. Simpler and slower than speech, 'mimesis' prefigured language in being an adaptation both cognitive *and cultural*. Drawing on a preexisting repertoire of 'limbic' or involuntary gestures, body attitudes, facial expressions, and vocal sounds such as laughter or crying, mimetic evolution involved a steady increase in cortical control leading to the first fully intentional representations. In this account, domain-general 'executive' skills in handling a language of dance, display, pantomime and song become harnessed, late in human evolution, to a new function – the generation of syntactically complex speech. On this basis – by rooting novel communicative function in preexistent competences – Donald complements Worden and Aitchison in offering a resolution to the continuity/discontinuity paradox: 'There might have been a dramatic discontinuity of *function* in the evolution of language, but there could not have been any discontinuities of *mechanism*.'

Ulbaek sides with Worden and Donald in arguing for continuity in the evolution of syntactical competence from a more general cognitive domain of social competence and intelligence. However, he stresses that, whereas primate evolution testifies to selection pressures steadily driving up *complex cognition*, corresponding pressures for *complexity in primate communication* are not discernible. This is also noted by Knight: chimp vocalizations appear scarcely more complex or referentially informative than those of the much smaller-brained vervet monkeys. How might we explain this apparent paradox? Ulbaek suggests an answer: whereas competence in directly gaining knowledge about the external world is always in principle adaptive, reliance on others' signals need not be. Where cognition is sophisticated, 'Machiavellian' deception will be an ever-present threat. In this context, it is understandable why primates should hold back from placing excessive reliance on one another's *volitional* signals.

On this basis, Ulbaek and Knight see exploitative and competitive social relationships as fundamental blocks to the emergence of speech-like complexity in primate call systems. Given internal conflict and a 'Machiavellian' social dynamic driving listeners to mistrust one another's intentions, signallers will have little incentive to divulge private knowledge or externalize their intimate thought processes. Instead, external cues to internal events will be under pressure to remain costly, repetitive and non-volitional as a condition of remaining credible. *Homo sapiens* eventually escaped from this system of constraints thanks to a process of profound social change culminating in the establishment of essentially egalitarian 'hunter–gatherer' relationships. Once sufficient social stability and ingroup trust had come to prevail, listeners were no longer driven to respond to costly, irrepressible signals at the expense of cheap, conventional, volitional ones.

Knight links the consummation of this process with the emergence in sub-Saharan Africa of a ritually structured sexual division of labour associated with anatomically modern humans. Previously, the demand for signal reliability on a call-by-call basis had blocked the emergence of syntactical complexity on a higher, combinatorial level. The demand that each signal perform a bonding, trust-generating function had likewise precluded 'symbolic' usage such as metaphor. In the new situation, by contrast, humans were in a position to leave group-wide bonding and the generation of trust to the ritual domain. Meanwhile, within ritually defined ingroups, listeners could for the first time confer status in exchange for cheap, vocally transmitted, conventionally encoded information received on trust. Group members now had an incentive to encourage metaphorical expression and participate in one another's intimate processes of thinking. A consequence was that the human species' complex structures of cognition escaped their former confinement within the private thought-processes of individuals, finding novel public expression as syntactical speech.

These chapters converge, then, in applying Darwinian thinking to the problem of the origins of speech. Aitchison's opening chapter deftly highlights the basic themes, advocating a move beyond exhausted dichotomies toward new, more fruitful questions. While Donald's and Worden's contributions are more cognitive and psychological than social, they appear mutually supportive and dovetail nicely with the chapters based on primate social models. Ulbaek and Knight agree in distinguishing between primate *cognition* and primate *communication*, seeing syntactical complexity in speech as continuous only with the former. Ulbaek, Dessalles, Power and Knight all converge in highlighting the paradox of speech as an apparently altruistic system which violates Darwinian expectations.

There remains disagreement as to whether speech evolved from vocal or gestural antecedents. Dunbar's model endorses the gestural hypothesis in one sense: manual grooming once played an important bonding role. But speech as informative 'gossip', in Dunbar's view, evolved not from an earlier language of gesture but from a less complex vocal system. Donald, Power, and Knight take a contrasting position, locating early selection pressures for syntactical competence in a pre-linguistic protoculture of gesture, dance and song. The debate is certain to remain a lively one.

2 On discontinuing the continuity–discontinuity debate

JEAN AITCHISON

1 Introduction

'The origin of human language is truly secret and marvellous', wrote Jacob Grimm in 1851 (Grimm 1851/1984: 24). The marvellous secret has proved an irresistible challenge for centuries. Bizarre ideas abounded: Chinese was the primitive language of humankind, happily preserved by Noah and his family in the Ark, according to the seventeenth-century writer, John Webb (Webb 1669, in Yaguello 1991). Humans learned to sing and speak from birds, just as they learned to spin and weave from spiders, claimed the eighteenth-century Scottish lawyer James Burnett (Burnett 1773). The oddity and unprovability of early speculations led in 1866 to a ban on papers about language origin by the Linguistic Society of Paris, the foremost linguistic society of the time, and in 1893 William Dwight Whitney reflected the view of many reputable linguists in his statement that 'The greater part of what is said and written upon it is mere windy talk' (Whitney 1893: 279). The whole topic came to be regarded as a playground for cranks, and was avoided by most serious scholars for over a century.

All this changed in 1990, when Steven Pinker and Paul Bloom published an influential paper entitled 'Natural language and natural selection' alongside a commentary by over thirty peers in the journal *Behavioral and Brain Sciences* (Pinker & Bloom 1990). This paper 'demolished some intellectual roadblocks in progress in understanding the relation between evolution and language' (Hurford 1990: 736). Pinker & Bloom emphasized that language evolved by normal evolutionary mechanisms, and commented that 'there is a wealth of respectable new scientific information relevant to the evolution of language that has never been properly synthesized' (Pinker & Bloom 1990: 727).

The Edinburgh 1996 conference on 'Evolution of Human Language' represented an important step forward both in the synthesis of existing materials, and also the presentation of new information. Rightly, it concentrated on certain limited topics, such as the continuity–discontinuity debate. This dichotomy provided a useful focus for discussion, but, I would like to argue, it should be a temporary staging-post only. In this chapter I support the notion that progress can be made by discussing dichotomies, but suggest that the continuity–discontinuity dichotomy should be abandoned, and that we should go beyond this to further controversies, which are in turn dissolving as research proceeds.

2 Long-standing dichotomies

Dichotomies often provide a useful way of focusing attention within wide-ranging topics. Perhaps the best-known linguistic dichotomy is the 'nature–nurture' controversy, a long-standing debate on whether language is 'natural' (birds fly) or 'nurtured' (pigeons can be trained to peck at letters of the alphabet). This debate has rumbled on for centuries, though in recent years it has acquired trendier names. It is sometimes characterized as a distinction between 'hard-wired' and 'soft-wired' abilities (e.g. Medin *et al.* 1990) or between 'instinct' and 'learning' (Gould & Marler 1987). Yet the controversy is gradually fading away. Around thirty years ago, Eric Lenneberg pointed out that language is neither natural nor nurtured behaviour (Lenneberg 1967). Instead, children acquire it 'naturally' at a particular stage in their development, provided they are properly 'nurtured', that is, exposed to sufficient linguistic data at the relevant time: Lenneberg labelled the phenomenon 'maturationally controlled behaviour'. More recently, Gould & Marler (1987) have characterized language as 'innately guided behaviour', which humans 'learn by instinct'. Their instincts guide them to pay attention to certain features, much as bees instinctively concentrate on first the odour, then colour and shape of flowers. The history of the nature–nurture controversy therefore shows how a dichotomy usefully focuses attention during the early stages of research, but fades away as the nature of a phenomenon becomes better understood – a point emphasized also by Müller (1996: 626), who comments that 'dualisms such as innate versus learned . . . dissolve the closer the mind is approached from a neurobiological perspective'.

The continuity–discontinuity question represents another longstanding debate. Did language develop out of animal communication systems in a continuous line of development, or was there a break? Linguists became aware of the question mainly in the 1970s, when Jane Hill discussed the dichotomy in a paper in *Language* (Hill 1974). Now, in the 1990s, I argue that the question has served its purpose. Language, like many other aspects of human behaviour, is a case of 'mosaic evolution' (Gregory 1951), in which some aspects of language have strong continuity, others moderate, others little. I shall therefore discuss some of the findings which have made the question intractable, then go on to outline more recent dichotomies which are helping us to move forward in our understanding of language evolution – though I point out that these too are in the process of dissolution.

3 Degrees of continuity

Language, like an orchid, has been 'jury-rigged from a limited set of available components' (Gould 1980: 20). At its simplest, it involves three main constituents: auditory mechanisms, articulatory mechanisms, and a brain which co-ordinates these. Yet each of these displays a different degree of continuity. Auditory continuity is strong: basic properties of the ear are common to humans and other primates, and non-human primates can reliably distinguish more sounds than they can produce. A large body of literature confirms that rhesus monkeys and chinchillas share with humans the property of categorical perception – the ability to perceive consonantal sounds as located firmly within one category rather than another (Kuhl 1987; Miller & Jusczyk 1989).

Brain continuity is moderate. The human brain is larger than that of other primates, and so has more interconnections, but some qualitative adaptations have taken place as well. Broca's area, traditionally associated with speech production, is now regarded as a cover term for several overlapping areas which involve different abilities. Some of these are found in non-human primates, others are largely restricted to humans, such as a forward portion which appears to serve word association (Deacon 1992). In general, our understanding of brain areas involving language has become considerably more sophisticated in recent years (e.g. Wilkins & Wakefield 1995), and 'the language areas may be understood as zones in which neurons participating in language-related cell assemblies cluster to a much higher degree than in other areas' (Müller 1996: 629).

The greatest discontinuity is in articulatory mechanisms (Aiello & Dean 1990; Lieberman 1992). Syllables are related to chimp pant-hoots, but primates cannot sustain distinct vowels. Humans possess a lowered larynx, which allows them to seal off the nasal cavity and so produce a range of distinct non-nasal sounds, especially the key vowels [i] [u] [a], as well as a wider range of consonants.

Degrees of continuity therefore vary, but they can be roughly specified for the language constituents outlined above. The question is less easy to answer in some other cases. These will be discussed below.

4 Ambiguous continuity: implicational leaps

Continuity in language evolution is harder to assess in cases of implication, when one step appears to be a precursor of another. The first step is a necessary condition for the new development, but not a sufficient condition: it enables a qualitative leap to be made, but does not inevitably cause it. In the following cases, other primates have taken the first step, but not apparently the second.

Primates, especially those closely related to humans, possess a theory of mind, in that they are able to make hypotheses about the mental states of others. This allows them to practise tactical deception (Byrne & Whiten 1992). Non-human primates always use this ability for selfish purposes, to achieve gains for themselves. Humans, on the other hand, use it sometimes for selfish, sometimes unselfish purposes. The overall consequence is a huge but by no means inevitable leap to a communication system which can handle absent objects and events. This property of displacement is valuable especially for negative information, such as: 'Fred will not be coming', and also for imaginative purposes, such as story-telling.

A further qualitative leap is from the use of symbols to the 'naming insight'. Symbolization is found among primates, though not necessarily in their natural communication system. The much-publicized alarm calls of the vervet monkey and squirrel monkey, which distinguish different types of predators, may represent an intermediate stage en route to symbolization (Scherer 1992). Chimps, on the other hand, who have been taught a language-like system, can use signs as symbols, yet do so mainly when they require something, such as *orange, nut*. Only intermittently do they 'name for the sake of naming', as when the chimp Washoe famously made the sign for 'toothbrush' on seeing a toothbrush: she was definitely not asking for this object, she hated having her teeth cleaned (Gardner & Gardner 1969). But the naming insight, the realization of the potential power of names, and the subsequent desire to label everything apparently does not occur to chimps. Yet it comes naturally to human children, usually between the ages of one and two (Kamhi 1986) – even though the naming insight may not be the instantaneous happening it was once reported to be (e.g. Schaller 1991).

These implicational leaps are ambiguous between continuity and discontinuity: the first step is necessary for the second, but the second involves a leap which is not predictable from the first.

5 More ambiguous continuity: convergence

Convergence is another situation in which continuity is hard to assess: a bound forward sometimes occurs which is more than the sum of the seemingly small steps which contribute to it. The falling together of language as a replacement for grooming, and neoteny, the extended infancy of humans, is a possible example. Language replaces the friendly manual grooming which is found among other primates, primarily because group size precluded old-style grooming, it has been argued (Dunbar 1993, 1996). Neoteny – the extended childhood of humans – ties in with this grooming theory. Humans are born immature, because bipedalism and an enlarged brain made it necessary to give birth early. Soothing noises made to infants during this extended infancy probably encouraged vocal interaction at a time when vocal grooming was becoming widespread (Locke 1995).

The ability of humans to suppress vocal reactions which in other primates are largely automatic may be a further example of convergence. The suppression possibility may have coincided with an increase in the ability to make multiple differentiated sounds, due to a lowered larynx and L-shaped vocal tract.

These examples of convergence show how apparently unrelated factors can, when they coincide, promote accelerated development in one particular direction, so much so that the resultant leap might appear to be a case of discontinuity.

Implicational leaps and convergence both show the difficulty of distinguishing between continuity and discontinuity theories of language, and suggest that no firm divide will ever be found. Trying to sort out the distinction is somewhat like asking whether steam-engines which lay on their sides and pumped water out of mines were continuous or discontinuous with trains whose engines run along rails and pull coaches: the answer is both 'yes' and 'no'.

In short, the continuity–discontinuity dichotomy has provided us with a useful staging-post in discussions of language origin. We now know enough, however, to realize that the divide is oversimple, and that it is time to move on.

6 Newer dichotomies

If continuity versus discontinuity is no longer a useful issue, then further dichotomies need to be identified, which can provide further stepping-stones in discussions of language origin. Three of these surface increasingly.

The first is the 'slow haul' versus the 'pop hypothesis'. Language might have developed slowly over multiple millennia, or, alternatively, it could have 'popped' into existence relatively fast. (The term 'pop hypothesis' originated in a discussion on the electronic bulletin board, *Linguist*.) A slow development is supported by, for example, the neurologist Deacon (1992) who argues that brain re-organization must have occurred slowly.

On the other hand, two quite different groups of people promote the 'pop hypothesis'. Language emerged when humans suddenly discovered an extra use for their already complex brains, according to the first group. In an oldish and now famous paper, Gould & Lewontin (1979) argued that language is like the murals which adorn the spandrels in St Mark's cathedral in Venice. These tapering triangular spaces between the roof and the pillars appear to some visitors to have been designed to bear the eye-catching murals. Yet in fact, the spandrels are the inevitable by-product of supporting a dome on pillars: the murals, like language, simply made use of an existing space.

The second group of 'pop hypothesis' supporters is led by Noam Chomsky. He has argued that a genetic change triggered language, primarily because he cannot imagine how a partial language could exist: 'In the case of such systems as language or wings it is not easy even to imagine a course of selection that might have given rise to them. A rudimentary wing, for example, is not "useful" for motion, but is more of an impediment' (Chomsky 1988: 167).

Yet language is highly complex, and is unlikely to have emerged suddenly. Pinker & Bloom (1990) point out that in cases of exaptation (new use of existing structures), the new uses are simpler than existing ones: a wading bird uses its wings as a sunshade, but a sunshade could not suddenly become wings.

Chomsky's argument in favour of fast emergence is unconvincing. 'What use is half a wing for flying?' he implies. Yet half-wings probably allowed birds to parachute slowly out of trees before they acquired the ability to fly upwards. Similarly, even small sections of language could have been useful, much as a few local words in a foreign city are more useful than no words.

Yet the slow version is not the only alternative. The solution is probably a compromise between the two. An S-curve, a slow-quick-quick-slow scenario, is the most likely, as in many other aspects of human life: slow beginning, sudden take-off, then gradual slowing down. Individual words possibly accumulated slowly. Once a critical mass had been reached, possibly a largish store of vocabulary items, then the main structure of language perhaps became established fairly quickly (Aitchison 1996) – though further work is needed on the order in which 'take-off' occurred.

A second dichotomy is that of single emergence versus multiple. Did language arise only in one area, invented perhaps by a clever tribe, or did it emerge in several places simultaneously? Increasingly, Africa is accepted as the birthplace of humans and human language (e.g. Lewin 1993), but within Africa the problem of single versus multiple emergence still needs to be solved. The scenario envisaged by William Golding in his novel *The Inheritors* is highly plausible (Golding 1955/1961). He proposed that a limited type of language arose as a first stage. Then one tribe which had learned this basic variety built on it, and developed it further. This enabled the pioneers of the newer system to extend their power over others (Aitchison 1996).

But an 'instruction' versus 'selection' dichotomy is potentially the most informative, as will be discussed below.

7 Instruction versus selection

Did language begin simple, and then become elaborated (instruction)? Or was it essentially chaotic, and then neatened up (selection)? This dichotomy is interesting, because it ties in with discussions on evolution taking place in other disciplines (e.g. Gazzaniga 1992; Piatelli-Palmarini 1989).

Derek Bickerton is possibly the best-known proponent of the instruction viewpoint. He has long argued for the emergence of an inevitable 'bioprogram' both at the origin of language in the human race, and at the birth of creoles: certain verb markers are predestined to arise, he suggests (e.g. Bickerton 1984, 1990). Yet Bickerton's bioprogram may be not so much the automatic starting point, as the likely endpoint of a long period of development. At an earlier stage, language evolution is possibly like a 'spaghetti junction', a cloverleaf intersection with numerous exit routes, though with one or two finally predominating (Aitchison 1989, 1996).

Language began 'messy', and only gradually neatened itself up. This is indicated by several strands of evidence. First, ordinary language change shows that alterations mostly occur when optional tendencies become obligatory: the reverse is less common (Aitchison 1996). Typically, *post hoc* reasoning tidies up an originally haphazard situation, as when young Texans imposed the interpretation of 'habitual' onto once variable *be*, as in: 'He always *be* fighting' (Bailey & Maynor 1988). This directional nature of language change is likely to have existed from its onset.

Second, creoles (pidgins which become a first language) provide useful pointers as to how a new language may become established. Stabilization of creoles is often a lengthy process, as in the case of Sranan (spoken in Suriname): 'Long after the transition from the . . . pidgin stage, [creoles] are still amenable to large scale restructuring . . . Viewed this way, creolization would not be a discrete, one-generation process, but rather one which is gradual, extending over a number of generations' (Arends 1986: 117).

Third, preferences which become habits, and habits which may potentially become 'rules', are found in the behaviour of other primates. Although artificial systems taught to apes are far from natural communication, and far from human language, the incipient rules which chimps sometimes devise for themselves are instructive. In the 1970s, the male chimp Nim Chimpsky was taught a language-based sign language. He produced a plethora of signs, sometimes involving repetition: *banana me, grape eat Nim, nut Nim nut*. Yet amidst the apparent chaos, one fact is clear: Nim was extremely fond of food, and almost always put a food word at the beginning of the sequence. He also showed a mild tendency to put his own name at the end, as in *Play me Nim, grape eat Nim, Nim eat Nim* (Terrace 1979). More recently, the bonobo chimp Kanzi was taught a 'lexigram' system in which diagrams represented words. He devised at least one personal rule, a 'lexigram–point' ordering. This involved, first, the symbol for an action, such as *chase, tickle*, then a pointing gesture to indicate whom he wanted to do the action (Savage-Rumbaugh & Lewin 1994). These primate examples therefore show the potential link between preferences, habits, and incipient rules.

Fourth, occasional disadvantaged humans also devise preferences for themselves, showing this is a natural human tendency. Vincent, the hearing child of deaf parents, was taught sign language as a first language. He began to acquire spoken language only from the age of three, when he invented a strange ordering for himself amidst multiple word repeats. When repetitions were ignored, many sentences conformed to a basic ground-plan: a pointing-out word (often a pronoun), a verb-like word, then a noun-like word, as in *You broken car* 'The car got broken.' His spoken system is instructive, because it conformed neither to his parents' sign language, nor to the order of the English spoken around him. Vincent therefore also showed a progression from preference to habit to potential 'rule' (Todd & Aitchison 1980).

Of course, 'real' language rules presuppose different word classes (of a type which were incipient in Vincent's speech). Evidence from pidgin languages suggests that reanalysis is the basis of such distinctions. For example, Tok Pisin (spoken both as a pidgin and a creole in Papua New Guinea) has sequences *mi danis* 'I dance', *mi pait* 'I fight', *mi wok* 'I work', *mi brum* 'I sweep/broom'. In these cases, a noun has possibly been reanalysed as a verb. Reanalysis of nouns to verbs, then nouns or verbs to adjectives and prepositions, is found widely not only in pidgins, but also in the other languages of the world (Aitchison 1996).

The important point, however, is this: when distinctions are made between lexical items, the next step is for order preferences to emerge, which gradually become habits, which form potential rules. At first, only a few preferences may have been evident, amidst much repetition and variation. Gradually, stabilization probably increased.

The next section will briefly consider how preferences might have emerged.

8 Constraints and preferences

At one time, linguists hoped to identify firm constraints on human languages. Yet they have been less successful in identifying these than they once hoped, perhaps because many apparent constraints turn out to be strong preferences, which allow occasional exceptions.

From the point of view of language origin, an understanding of preferences is all-important. These account for how humans narrowed down the huge number of potential options, and arrived at a manageable system. The narrowing down is effected by various interacting factors, as in the three examples below.

First, ways of perceiving the world may affect the linguistic system, though need not be firmly incorporated into it. For example, humans prefer to locate 'small on large', as in 'The cat sat on the mat', or 'On the mat sat the cat' rather than 'The mat lay under the cat' (Landau & Jackendoff 1993).

Second, semantic affinity is a factor. Certain words appear to be drawn to one another. For example, verb-object closeness is now well established as a tendency in the world's languages (e.g. Tomlin 1986).

Third, generality is important: 'Only highly general meanings can become obligatory' (Bybee 1985: 202). It is not chance that most languages have a formal means of expressing 'pastness', because very few verbs exist which cannot be used with a past marker, whereas an 'obligation' marker, for example, is not found with so many: 'He must fall down' seems unlikely.

Such tendencies are increasingly being explored in works on grammaticalization, standardly defined as: 'the attribution of a grammatical character to a previously autonomous word' (Meillet 1912/1948: 131). The end result is that various recurrent routes emerge (e.g. Bybee, Perkins & Pagliuca 1994), and presumably emerged at the origin of human language. Existing routes predict and constrain future routes, though no two pathways are identical. The hope is that eventually we shall know both about the routes taken by language from its origin, and the reasons for taking them. In short, the instruction versus selection dichotomy is withering away, as have other well-explored dichotomies.

Then some new dichotomy will take its place, as a guideline in further research.

9 Conclusion

Progress is made in complex research topics by exploring dichotomies. Such dichotomies, however, naturally fade away as researchers unravel the complexity of the issues involved. This paper first argued that we should discontinue the continuity–discontinuity debate on language origin, since enough is now known about the matter to show that it can never be resolved. It then looked at further dichotomies: the 'slow haul' versus 'pop hypothesis', single emergence versus multiple, and, in particular, the instruction versus selection opposition. Exploration of this dichotomy brings linguistics in line with discussions in other disciplines. However, this debate, as with other dichotomies, is in the process of being solved: selection predominates, though selection from a limited number of options. In the long run, the final result looks like instruction – but instruction represents a summary of what happened, rather than the process which led to it. So this dichotomy too has virtually faded away. In the future, maybe newer dichotomies will arise, which will helpfully channel the thoughts of researchers, and lead to a greater consensus and understanding of the issues involved. Language origin is still marvellous, but it is no longer so 'truly secret':

> In Nature's infinite book of secrecy
> A little I can read. [Shakespeare, *Antony and Cleopatra* I.ii.11–12]

References

(When two dates appear together, e.g. Grimm (1851/1984), the first is the date of the original publication, the second the date of the edition or reprint referred to in this paper.)

Aiello, L. C. & Dean, C. (1990). *An Introduction to Human Evolutionary Anatomy*. London: Academic Press.

Aitchison, J. (1989). Spaghetti junctions and recurrent routes: some preferred pathways in language evolution. *Lingua*, 77, 151–171.

(1996). *The Seeds of Speech: Language Origin and Evolution*. Cambridge: Cambridge University Press.

Arends, J. (1986). Genesis and development of the equative copula in Sranan. In Muysken, P. & Smith, N. (eds.) *Substrata versus Universals in Creole Genesis*. Amsterdam: John Benjamins.

Bailey, G. & Maynor, N. (1988). Decreolization? *Language in Society*, 16, 449–473.
Bickerton, D. (1984). The language bioprogram hypothesis. *Behavioral and Brain Sciences*, 7, 173–221. (Includes peer commentary.)
(1990). *Language and Species*. Chicago: University of Chicago Press.
Burnett, James (Lord Monboddo) (1773). *The Origin and Progress of Language*, vols. I–VI. Edinburgh: A. Kincaid.
Bybee, J. L. (1985). *Morphology*. Amsterdam: John Benjamins.
Perkins, R. D. & Pagliuca, W. (1994). *The Evolution of Grammar: Tense, Aspect and Modality in the Languages of the World*. Chicago: University of Chicago Press.
Byrne, R. W. & Whiten, A. (1992). Cognitive evolution in primates: evidence from tactical deception. *Man*, 27, 609–627.
Chomsky, N. (1988). *Language and Problems of Knowledge: The Managua Lectures*. Current Studies in Linguistics 16. Cambridge, MA: MIT Press.
Deacon, T. W. (1992). Brain–language coevolution. In Hawkins, J. A. & Gell-Mann, M. (eds.) *The Evolution of Human Languages*. Santa Fé Studies in the Science of Complexity II. Reading, MA: Addison-Wesley.
Dunbar, R. I. M. (1993). Coevolution of neocortical size, group size and language in humans. *Behavioral and Brain Sciences*, 16, 681–735. (Includes peer commentary.)
(1996). *Grooming, Gossip and the Evolution of Language*. London: Faber & Faber.
Gardner, R. A. & Gardner, B. T. (1969). Teaching sign language to a chimpanzee. *Science*, 165, 664–672.
Gazzaniga, M. S. (1992). *Nature's Mind*. New York: Harper Collins.
Golding, W. (1955/1961). *The Inheritors*. London: Faber & Faber.
Gould, J. L. & Marler, P. (1987). Learning by instinct. *Scientific American*, 256(1), 62–73.
Gould, S. J. (1980). *The Panda's Thumb*. London: Penguin.
& Lewontin, R. C. (1979). The spandrels of San Marco and the Panglossian paradigm. A critique of the adaptionist programme. *Proceedings of the Royal Society of London*, 205, 281–288.
Gregory, W. K. (1951). *Evolution Emerging: A Survey of Changing Patterns from Primeval Life to Man*. 2 vols. New York: Macmillan.
Grimm, J. K. L. (1851/1984). *On the Origin of Language*. Translated by R. A. Wiley. Leiden: Brill.
Hill, J. H. (1974). Possible continuity theories of language. *Language*, 50, 134–150.
Hurford, J. (1990). Beyond the roadblock in linguistic evolution studies. *Behavioral and Brain Sciences*, 13, 736–737.
Kamhi, A. G. (1986). The elusive first word: the importance of the naming insight for the development of referential speech. *Journal of Child Language*, 13, 155–161.
Kuhl, P. T. (1987). The special-mechanisms debate in speech research: categorization tests on animals and infants. In Harnad, S. (ed.) *Categorical Perception: The Groundwork of Cognition*. Cambridge: Cambridge University Press.
Landau, B. & Jackendoff, R. (1993). 'What' and 'where' in spatial language and spatial cognition. *Behavioral and Brain Sciences*, 16, 217–265. (Includes peer commentary.)

Lenneberg, E. H. (1967). *Biological Foundations of Language*. New York: Wiley.

Lewin, R. (1993). *The Origin of Modern Humans*. New York: Scientific American Library.

Lieberman, P. (1992). On the evolution of human language. In Hawkins, J. A. & Gell-Mann, M. (eds.) *The Evolution of Human Languages*. Santa Fé Studies in the Science of Complexity 11. Reading, MA: Addison-Wesley.

Locke, J. L. (1995). Development of the capacity for spoken language. In Fletcher, P. & MacWhinney, M. (eds.) *The Handbook of Child Language*. Oxford: Blackwell.

Medin, D. L., Ahn, W.-K., Bettger, J., Florian, J., Goldstone, R., Lassaline, M., Markman, A., Rubinstein, J. & Wisniewski, E. (1990). Safe takeoffs - soft landings. *Cognitive Science*, 14, 169–178.

Meillet, A. (1912/1948). *Linguistique historique et linguistique générale*. Paris: Champion.

Miller, J. & Jusczyk, P. W. (1989). Seeking the neurobiological basis of speech perception. *Cognition*, 33, 111–137.

Müller, R.-A. (1996). Innateness, autonomy, universality? Neurobiological approaches to language. *Behavioral and Brain Sciences*, 19, 611–675.

Piatelli-Palmarini, M. (1989). Evolution, selection and cognition: from 'learning' to parameter setting in biology and in the study of language. *Cognition*, 31, 1–44.

Pinker, S. & Bloom, P. (1990). Natural language and natural selection. *Behavioral and Brain Sciences*, 13, 707–784. (Includes peer commentary.)

Savage-Rumbaugh, S. & Lewin, R. (1994). *Kanzi: The Ape at the Brink of the Human Mind*. New York: Doubleday.

Schaller, S. (1991). *A Man Without Words*. Berkeley and Los Angeles: University of California Press.

Scherer, K. R. (1992). Vocal affect as symptom, symbol and appeal. In Papousek, H., Jürgens, U. & Papousek, M. (eds.) *Nonverbal Vocal Communication*. Cambridge: Cambridge University Press.

Terrace, H. S. (1979). *Nim*. New York: Knopf.

Todd, P. & Aitchison, J. (1980). Learning language the hard way. *First Language*, 1, 122–140.

Tomlin, R. S. (1986). *Basic Word Order: Functional Principles*. London: Croom Helm.

Webb, J. (1669). *An Historical Essay Endeavouring the Probability that the Language of the Empire of China is the Primitive Language*. London.

Whitney, W. D. (1893). *Oriental and Linguistic Studies*, vol. I. New York: Charles Scribner's Sons.

Wilkins, W. K. & Wakefield, J. (1995). Brain evolution and neurolinguistic preconditions. *Behavioral and Brain Sciences*, 18, 161–226.

Yaguello, M. (1991). *Lunatic Lovers of Language: Imaginary Languages and their Inventors*. Translated by Catherine Stater. London: Athlone. Originally: *Les fous du langage: des langues imaginaires et de leurs inventeurs*. Paris: Editions du Seuil (1984).

3 The origin of language and cognition

IB ULBAEK

Two kinds of theories have dominated recent discussion of the origin of language (see Pinker & Bloom 1990): a continuity approach and its counterpart, a discontinuity approach (see Table 3.1). The continuity approach has often labelled itself Darwinian and looked for predecessors of language, typically in animal communication systems. It claims that language is such a big system, that it could not have evolved out of nothing (*de novo*). Just as we cannot conceive of the eye jumping into existence, so we cannot conceive of language as having no precursors.

The opposite position argues that language is unique among the communication systems of the biosphere, and that to claim continuity between, say, bee language and human language is to claim 'evolutionary development from breathing to walking' as pointedly remarked by Chomsky (1972: 68). Language is a task- and species-specific module in the human mind, a 'language organ' (Chomsky 1980a: 76; see also Chomsky 1980b). Chomsky has been one of the few to question a Darwinian explanation of language: 'Darwinian theory is so loose it can incorporate everything', he claimed recently (Horgan 1995: 154).

Beside the Chomskyan position another anti-evolutionary and discontinuity position exists, which could be called *culturalist*. Sociological theories often separate human biological nature from human social nature. The culturalists reject Chomsky's strong innatism, arguing that, basically, humans are unconstrained learning machines who create a culture from which all relevant properties of the human mind (including language) derive. Neither Chomsky nor the culturalists have developed a detailed account of language origins, perhaps partly because their central concerns lie elsewhere. Chomsky has suggested a mutation or plain accident, whereas culturalists have sometimes hinted that a 'leap' from the natural order to the social order must have taken place (e.g.

Table 3.1 Theories of language origin, classified by their assumed evolutionary models and modes of language acquisition

Evolutionary model ***Acquisition mode***	***Continuity***	***Discontinuity***
Innate	Bickerton, Pinker, the present author, and others	Chomsky
Learned	'Behaviourism'	Culturalism

Engelsted 1984). Neither explanation is satisfactory and neither will be discussed further.

As indicated in Table 3.1, some continuity theorists also emphasize learning as a fundamental aspect of human mind and language. The reasons for this are, first, their strong anti-Chomskyan attitude – some of them are learning psychologists – and second, the simple fact that language is undeniably learned. The position of these theorists was revealed most clearly in the *ape language controversy* in the 70s and early 80s. Their position was supported by experiments in which different kinds of non-spoken languages were taught to various apes, mostly chimpanzees. Researchers emphasized that even though apes do not speak in the wild, they have a mind capable of learning. By means of a sign language, apes can symbolize external (and internal) states of affairs, and can communicate about these things – primarily with the researchers and lab staff, but also with fellow chimpanzees and their own offspring (the controversy is documented in several places, including Linden 1986). In Table 3.1, I have labelled this position 'Behaviourism'. This is partly a misnomer because nobody really is a behaviourist these days, but the position shares with behaviourism the emphasis on learning (rather than innate structures) in language acquisition. At the same time, one has to remember the strong anti-evolutionary commitment of classical behaviourism – conditioning is the same universal mechanism thoughout the whole animal kingdom, whether Pavlovian or operant.

As can be seen, one cell in Table 3.1 remains for comment. I have not left it till last because it is contradictory to claim both continuity and innateness. These are vague (and relative) terms after all. How continuous does the continuity have to be? Some kind of discontinuity must exist if things are different and not the same. And innateness comes in degrees. Even Chomsky does not claim that language is wholly innate:

to do so would fly in the face of the diversity of the world's living and extinct languages. What Chomsky *has* claimed is that without a strong innate component, language cannot be learned. To my mind his arguments are convincing. I will not defend the position extensively here. But if the child had only inductive strategies for constructing the rules of language, it would either be stuck in an enormous search space looking for consistent rules, or (perhaps) would come up with a language structure different from its parents. Some prestructuring in the child's search lightens the burden of induction and explains why parents and children speak the same language after all. One can also point to the failure up till now, even in principle, of connectionist accounts of language learning (cf. the controversy over the Rumelhart–McClelland simulation of learning the past tense of verbs: Rumelhart & McClelland 1986; Pinker & Prince 1988). So, in conclusion, I follow Chomsky in claiming a strong innate component in human language.

I do not follow Chomsky, however, in his rejection of continuity. Here is how I accept continuity. If language is within the reach of a Darwinian explanation, whatever exactly it may be, then that is enough continuity for me. So, I will evade the question of how continous continuity has to be by simply remarking that if, by Darwinian means, we can construct a path from a state without language to a state with language, then we have an explanation of how language came about, and need not care whether language developed out of simpler forms of communication (cf. Ulbaek 1990). We then have a fully Darwinian explanation without being committed to the notion that language descended from simpler forms of communication, thereby claiming some essential connection between language and bird songs, cricket songs – or whale songs, for that matter.

The cell in Table 3.1 not yet fully discussed is, then, occupied by my position, and in the following I will further defend the position and show how it gives a general account of language origin without the flaws of the traditional antagonists (but with flaws of its own, no doubt). Unfortunately for my originality, I am not able to claim sole responsibility for this position. Others have similar positions, although none of them is exactly the same: each has put his own fingerprint on the general outlook. Of scholars sharing this position, Bickerton (1990) and Pinker (1994) should be mentioned. What is remarkable about both is that they have ignored the still-effective ban within linguistics on considering language origin worthy of scholarly study: they are heretics from within the Chomskyan camp. Also in the top left cell of Table 3.1 is Darwinian psychology or *evolutionary psychology*, as its practitioners call it. Leading figures are Cosmides and Tooby (Horgan 1995; Cosmides & Tooby 1987). The importance of their position for the present discussion is that their Darwinian view makes them look for prewired and universal mechanisms behind the surface variety of cultural phenomena.

1 From cognition to language

The correct theory of evolution of language, in my opinion, is this: *language evolved from animal cognition not from animal communication*. Here lies the continuity. Language grew out of cognitive systems already in existence and working: it formed a communicative bridge between already-cognitive animals. Thus, I not only reject the seemingly natural assumption that language evolved out of other communication systems, but I adopt the far more radical assumption that cognitive systems were in place before language (cf. Bickerton 1990). Although times are changing this has not been the most popular point of view in this century – quite the contrary. The so called 'linguistic turn' in philosophy has a broad basis within scientific culture. The traditional stance is that the hallmark of human rationality, thinking, is not only strongly influenced by language, but is even determined by language, or exists solely in language. The Sapir–Whorf hypothesis expresses this strong determinism. Wittgensteinian philosophy demands that inner processes be revealed by outer criteria manifested in language use. These are just two among many converging schools of thought. Also, structuralism and its later developments, in various shades, hold this influential view. I cite Saussure because he is clear: 'Without language, thought is a vague, uncharted nebula. There are no pre-existing ideas, and nothing is distinct before the appearance of language' (Saussure 1966: 112).

Animal thinking is *a fortiori* an impossible, ruled out by the simple fact that animals do not have language. Clearly, a Peircian semiotic is not committed to such a narrow point of view. Nor is a cognitive science for which thinking is calculation across symbolic tokens or mental representations. These mental representations can be wholly in the mind, and (unlike Saussure's *langue*) do not have to be shared by a community of cognitive animals.

In short, we need a theory that does not rule out animal thinking *a priori*. Animals are not just instinctual machines or learning machines. They *are* those things, too, as demonstrated by classical ethology and classical behaviourism. But at least some animals are more: they are thinking creatures. Ironically, the battle-cry 'Language is everything, thinking is nothing' drowned the very experiments that could have made scientists, philosophers, and scholars think again half a century ago. Wolfgang Köhler demonstrated elaborate problem-solving behaviour in the chimpanzee as early as the beginning of this century. Even rats evidently do more than just learn a route when running a maze. According to Edward Tolman's account of his experiments (Tolman 1932, 1948), the rats established organized knowledge, cognitive maps, on the basis of which they made inferences, that could not be accounted for by 'habit formation', or any other concept from the behaviourist toolbox. But that was only the beginning. Now a whole subfield of ethology, cognitive ethology, is gathering evidence of behaviour controlled by cognitive processes seen (or, rather, inferred) in a broad variety of species (its first textbook is by Roitblat (1987)). Especially in the apes, many findings point to their high intelligence, and therefore support a view of these animals as cognitive creatures beyond instinctual releasing mechanisms and behavioural modification through learning. I do not have space to go through the data in detail, and so simply note some of the relevant areas.

1.1 *Tool-using and making*

Apes not only use tools, but also make them. They prepare sticks for fishing for termites (and are seen carrying around 'good sticks'). They use leaves as sponges for soaking water out of trees, and stones for cracking nuts, by arranging flat stones as anvils and using round ones as hammers.

1.2 *Cognitive maps*

Apes show a sophisticated knowledge of their territory and use this knowledge to plan routes between food areas (Menzel 1978).

1.3 *Learning through imitation*

Primates are virtually the only order that learn by (social) imitation (Passingham 1982: 176). Ladder-climbing in an enclosure spread rapidly in a group of captive chimpanzees; the spreading of potato-washing from one individual, Imo (a Japanese macaque), to its group is another example (Passingham 1982: 182).

1.4 *Social knowledge*

Monkeys and apes conform to a pecking order in their groups, with a dominant alpha male and lower-ranking males and females, and they know each other's place within the hierarchy. (This is not in itself a cognitively advanced thing to do – chickens do the same (that is where the concept of pecking order came from in the first place!).) Playing back cries of a vervet monkey infant makes the others in the group look toward the child's mother (Seyfarth 1987: 448). Other experimental demonstrations of social concepts in monkeys (mother–offspring, sibling) come from Dasser (1987). Apes also evidently gain knowledge by watching their fellows: 'Chimpanzees may be able to glean a great variety of information about the world by studying the actions of others' (Passingham 1982: 200).

1.5 *Deception*

Cheating, or feigning, is known throughout the animal kingdom by the name of mimicry and camouflage. Birds of some species will feign a broken wing to get rid of an unwelcome predator, but this is probably a non-conscious, non-cognitive program, rather than problem-solving behaviour. Anecdotal evidence does exist, however, pointing to deliberate, intentional lying among apes and monkeys (Whiten & Byrne 1988).

1.6 *Theory of mind*

One question is whether the ape itself is an intentional animal, creating and acting on goals; another is whether it treats its fellow apes as intentional. David Premack has answered the second question in a series of experiments by showing that a chimpanzee can treat others as having intentions (Premack & Woodruff 1978). His chimp, Sarah, could watch a videotape of a person trying to solve a problem and then find among alternatives the right tool to solve the problem. Here it is important to remember that the problem could not be described in purely physical terms, so that the chimpanzee could not solve it merely by looking. It had to 'imagine' the person (not another chimpanzee) as having a problem and trying to solve it. Since it did so, we can conclude that the ape has a theory of mind.

1.7 *Capable of learning a language-like system?*

Apes in the wild do not speak, but several experiments have tried to teach them language (see the short review in Donald (1991: ch. 5)). Although chimpanzees have not been able to learn any sophisticated language (say, beyond the stage of a two-year-old child) they have demonstrated a degree of language capacity by using arbitrary symbols to denote physical objects. Evidently apes can encode mental content into physical tokens (manual signs, plastic symbols, pictograms) but do not have the syntactic machinery for stringing words into sentences. If human language does indeed comprise an innate module for processing syntactic information, it is hardly remarkable that apes cannot do syntactic processing. Otherwise, they would have a complete language faculty that they never use – which is scarcely plausible.

On the basis of these diverse indications of ape intelligence, I conclude that, if language developed from cognition, the ape has the means to fulfill the role, and *so had the last common ancestor between ape and man.*

2 The function of language

The scenario is this: in some distant past (approximately 6 to 8 million years ago) an apelike primate existed which became the last common ancestor between apes and humans. The two lines separated. In one, language evolved, in the other it did not. Why? In the *Homo* line several things happened, while the apes remained relatively static. The ape's brain, for example, seems to have changed and grown very little since the split, suggesting that the ape was already well adapted to the pressures of its habitat. Not so for the line of *Homo*, where many things changed, even though they took several millions of years to happen: upright walking, freeing of the hand and changing manual function (especially of the thumb), handedness, lateralization and rapid growth of the brain, conquest of fire, toolmaking, weapons, changing social structure, culture. All these things surely contributed to the origin of language, and a total account of language origins would have to take all these things into consideration. I have not tried to do that and will not do so here. Instead I have asked why humans, but not apes, have language. This question can be given a plausible answer if we understand correctly the biological role of language. What is its survival value? My answer is that language had – at the time it began to evolve or get a foothold – the function of communicating thoughts among group members. To use language is to share information as deliberately as the sharing of food is deliberate, and contrasts with the involuntary giving away of information of, say, a monkey displaying that it is scared when approached by an aggressive male.

Not everybody agrees that language has such a function now, or had it then, when it first evolved. Chomsky opposed any fixed function for language, in discussion with Searle (Chomsky 1975). Here I side with Searle, and with the pragmatic and functionalist schools of linguistics (Harder 1996). Language can certainly be seen as a mechanism of thought, but I do not think that function is primary, because it would be much better taken care of by an interior language. Such an internal language, a language of thought (Fodor 1975), may indeed already be in place as a precondition of thinking even in non-human primates (or in every animal able to make inferences?).

If we can substantiate the above functional view, some of the answers to the question of language origin may fall into place. We can ask: why did chimps not get a language? We now know that they have enough intelligence to use simple symbols. Either they did not need a language or they were prevented from getting it. My guess is that they were prevented, because if they had had tasks that would be furthered more easily by having language, such as planning, reporting, discussing, and so on, then the need was there. The need is indeed there today, as is shown by apes patrolling, hunting, moving to new food sites, and so on. We may expect the same need in prehistoric times. So they were prevented – by whom or by what?

3 Sharing of information from a Darwinian perspective

Presumably, language was blocked in the chimpanzee by the impersonal forces of Darwinian evolution. Every trait that enhances one's fitness enhances (by definition) one's chances of survival and chances of reproduction and so of passing one's genes to the next generation. Prima facie, language would seem to be such an improvement for us that we are tempted to extrapolate into thinking that language would be an advantage for every species. Taken out of context – not entirely fairly – Cook (a Chomskyan linguist) says: 'the possession of language itself clearly confers an immense advantage on its users over other species' (Cook 1988: 23). Chomsky, too, at one time at least, presupposed the advantage of language: 'In some ill-considered popularizations of interesting current research, it is virtually argued that higher apes have the capacity for language but have never put it to use – a remarkable biological miracle, *given the enormous selective advantage of even minimal linguistic skills*, rather like discovering that some animal has wings but has never thought to fly' (Chomsky 1975: 40, my italics).

It is easy to see that this should not be generalized: a bee talking would have such a big head that it could not fly! In other words, having a language is a question of cost and benefit, or, in Darwinian terms, of losing and gaining fitness. We are so used to focusing on the benefits that we tend to forget the costs.

Loosely speaking, some of the costs are: extra brain tissue, reorganization of the brain, changes in the respiratory system, and many more. What are the benefits? The one benefit that we tend to take for granted is that language enables us to co-operate, to speak to and help each other. From a Darwinian perspective, this is also, paradoxically, its main cost. In fact, on the face of it, language as a means of giving information away, would scarcely seem to be an *evolutionarily stable strategy* (Maynard Smith 1982). Why should we share information in the first place, if evolution demands that we enhance *our* fitness, not our neighbors'? If we look at animal communication, it seems that most of it has a selfish purpose. If territorial songs are an easier way of keeping competitors away, it seems preferable to patrolling and beating up other male conspecifics (Krebs & Dawkins 1984). Mating calls have a similar selfish purpose. Warning calls, on the other hand, seem to break the rule. Yet even here, without having investigated the matter thoroughly, we may suppose that the concept of *inclusive fitness* can explain the phenomenon. Helping offspring and related family is more important for fitness than the loss of fitness due to helping competitors in the same group. Perhaps indeed selfishness has kept animal communication at a minimum. Wilson (1972) finds the static nature of animal communication striking: 'By human standards the number of signals employed by each species of animal is severely limited. One of the most curious facts revealed by recent field studies is that even the most highly social vertebrates rarely have more than 30 or 35 separate displays in their entire repertory' (p. 56). It is striking indeed: both compared to human language and to the evolution of intelligence.

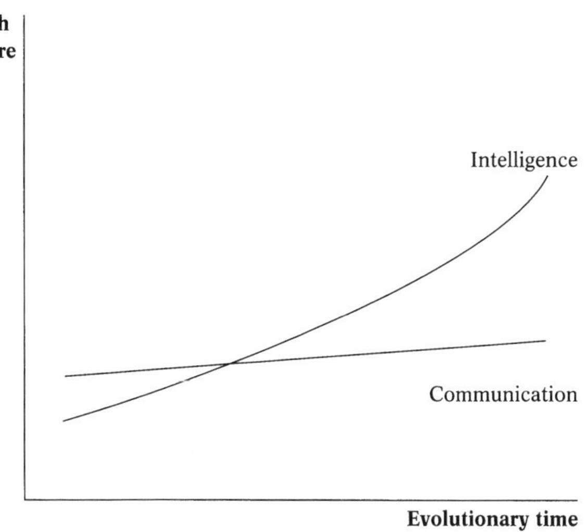

Figure 3.1 The evolution of animal communication and intelligence across species.

My conclusion from this is sketched in Figure 3.1. Evidently the advantage of intelligence is such that a selective pressure toward its increase has been steadily maintained over evolutionary time. Not so for communication, which has been static and without extraordinary selective pressures. So perhaps, we may speculate, communication has been constrained within narrow limits because a selfish animal has very few things that he wants to communicate. But with intelligence it is the other way around: extracting important information from the environment (including the social surroundings) can be increased without limits because cognition can be inherently selfish. Insofar as intelligence entails coping with information it would seem to be the 'natural' course of things that animals should become increasingly intelligent. Language, from the same perspective, is not part of the 'natural' course of things: sharing information is an altruistic act and should not occur according to standard Darwinian theory. How can this paradox be resolved?

4 The last obstacle

To co-operate, as we all know, is often more efficient than letting each work on his own. But working together and cheating the others out of their fair share is even better – except for those who are cheated. For them, once bitten, twice shy – which argues against doing co-operative work after all. This dilemma is known as the *Prisoner's Dilemma*, a dilemma imposed by the principles of Darwinian selection. Perhaps indeed this is why language is not so widespread across species: if it is better to lie than to tell the truth, why do all this elaborate coding of thoughts into speech against which an effective strategy is just not to listen?

Luckily, we have a loophole: *reciprocal altruism* (Trivers 1971). Through reciprocal altruism, co-operation becomes possible, but at a price, the price of keeping track of cheaters and freeriders. Once a cheater, always a cheater, seems to be the harsh law that animals impose. The good side is that a favour is returned by another favour, a friend can always trust a friend. The point is that, although some form of reciprocal altruism is found in many species, including primate species, it is of particular and fundamental importance to the working of a social system based on co-operation. Trivers says this on the evolution of reciprocal altruism:

> During the Pleistocene [3 million years ago], and probably before, a hominid species would have met the precondition for the evolution of reciprocal altruism: long lifespan; low dispersal rate; life in small, mutually dependent, stable, social groups; and a long period of parental care. It is very likely that dominance relations were of the relaxed, less linear form characteristic of the living chimpanzee and not of the more rigidly linear form characteristic of the baboon. [Trivers 1971: 45]

If one looks at today's Bushmen or other stone-age societies, one sees that they are even more egalitarian than a group of chimpanzees (Turnbull 1964). In fact, if it was not for the social structure of the chimpanzees, perhaps they would have language, too. But the impetus for sharing information is small in chimpanzee society, except for occasional sharing and reciprocal altruism based on friendship. As Jane Goodall observed, young chimpanzee males have the patience and ingenuity to open boxes of bananas laid out by researchers, but the older and stronger males take the bananas, leaving little incentive for the youngsters to go on (Goodall 1972).

So this is the whole story: language is cognitive whereas animal communication is not. Cognitive intelligence is an earlier and more widely spread property of mind than language because evolution selects for effective information gathering. Language's proper function is to communicate, which here means sharing of information. But information-sharing would seem to be prohibited by natural selection, except in extraordinary conditions. Only under the extraordinary conditions of reciprocal altruism can information-sharing take place without loss of fitness to the speaker. In the human lineage, social co-operation based on obligatory reciprocal altruism has evolved, a system which rewards people for co-operating and punishes them (morally and physically) for cheating. In such an environment language is finally possible.

5 Conclusions

1. Language evolved, by a wholly Darwinian process, out of animal cognition, not out of animal communication.
2. The function of language in modern *Homo sapiens* and in the species' language-using ancestors is to communicate thoughts.
3. In so far as language entails sharing information, it might be considered disadvantageous to the individual, while cognitive intelligence is clearly advantageous. Accordingly, intelligence is the rule across species, language the exception.
4. Language evolved in the *Homo* lineage not because of superior hominid intelligence, but because of special social conditions: the development of reciprocal altruism as a way of gaining fitness by sharing and helping.

Acknowledgments

I hereby express my gratitude to Michael Studdert-Kennedy in the editorial group for his many helpful corrections which have turned this paper into readable English.

References

Bickerton, D. (1990). *Language and Species*. Chicago and London: University of Chicago Press.

Chomsky, N. (1972). *Language and Mind*. (Enlarged edition) New York: Harcourt Brace Jovanovich.

(1975). *Reflections on Language*. New York: Pantheon.

(1980a). Discussion. In Piattelli-Palmarini, M. (ed.) *Language and Learning. The Debate between Jean Piaget and Noam Chomsky*. London: Routledge and Kegan Paul: 73–83.

(1980b). *Rules and Representations*. New York: Columbia University Press.

Cook, V. J. (1988). *Chomsky's Universal Grammar: An Introduction*. Oxford: Basil Blackwell.

Cosmides, L. & Tooby, J. (1987). From evolution to behavior: evolutionary psychology as the missing link. In Dupré, J. (ed.) *The Latest of the Best. Essays on Evolution and Optimality*. Cambridge, MA: MIT Press.

Dasser, V. (1987). Social concepts of monkeys. Ph.D. Zurich: Zentralstelle der Studentenschaft.

Donald, M. (1991). *Origins of Modern Mind: Three Stages in the Evolution of Culture and Cognition*. Cambridge, MA: Harvard University Press.

Engelsted, N. (1984). *Springet fra dyr til menneske* ['The leap from animal to man', in Danish]. Copenhagen: Dansk Psykologisk Forlag.

Fodor, J. A. (1975). *The Language of Thought*. Hassocks, Sussex: Harvester Press.

Goodall, J. (1972). *In the Shadow of Man*. London: George Weidenfeld and Nicolson.

Harder, P. (1996). *Functional Semantics*. Berlin: Mouton de Gruyter.

Horgan, J. (1995). The new social Darwinists. *Scientific American*, 273(4), 150–157.

Krebs, J. R. & Dawkins, R. (1984). Animal signals: mind reading and manipulation. In Krebs, J. R. & Davies, N. B. (eds.) *Behavioral Ecology: An Evolutionary Approach*. (2nd edition) Oxford: Blackwell Scientific Publications: 380–402.

Linden, E. (1986). *Silent Partners. The Legacy of the Ape Language Experiments*. New York: Ballantine Books.

Maynard Smith, J. M. (1982). *Evolution and the Theory of Games*. Cambridge: Cambridge University Press.

Menzel, E. W. (1978). Cognitive mapping in chimpanzees. In Hulse, S. H., Fowler, H. & Honig, W. K. (eds.) *Cognitive Processes in Animal Behavior*. Hillsdale, NJ: Erlbaum: 375–422.

Passingham, R. (1982). *The Human Primate*. San Francisco: W. H. Freeman.

Pinker, S. (1994). *The Language Instinct*. New York: Morrow; London: Penguin.

& Bloom, P. (1990). Natural language and natural selection. *Behavioral and Brain Sciences*, 13, 707–784.

& Prince, A. (1988). On language and connectionism: analysis of a Parallel Distributed Processing model of language acquisition. *Cognition*, 28, 73–193.

Premack, D. & Woodruff, G. (1978). Does the chimpanzee have a theory of mind? *Behavioral and Brain Sciences*, 4, 515–526.

Roitblat, H. (1987). *Introduction to Comparative Cognition*. New York: W. H. Freeman and Company.

Rumelhart, D. E. and McClelland, L. J. (1986). On learning the past tenses of English verbs. In Rumelhart, D. E., McClelland, L. J. and the PDP Group (eds.) *Parallel Distributed Processing: Explorations on the Microstructure of Cognition*. Cambridge, MA: MIT Press.

Saussure, F. de (1966). *Course in General Linguistics*. Translated by Wade Baskin. New York: McGraw-Hill Book Company.

Seyfarth, R. M. (1987). Vocal communication and language. In Smuts, B., Cheney, D. L., Seyfarth, R. M., Wrangham, R. W. & Struhsaker, T. T. (eds.) *Primate Societies*. Chicago: University of Chicago Press: 440–451.

Tolman, E. C. (1932). *Purposive Behavior in Animals and Men*. New York: Century.

(1948). Cognitive maps in rats and men. *Psychological Review*, 55(4), 189–208.

Trivers, R. L. (1971). The evolution of reciprocal altruism. *Quarterly Review of Biology*, 46, 35–57.

Ulbaek, I. (1990). Why chimps matter. [Commentary on Pinker, S. & Bloom, P.: Natural language and natural selection] *Behavioral and Brain Sciences*, 13(4), 762–763.

Whiten, A. & Byrne, R. W. (1988). Tactical deception in primates. *Behavioral and Brain Sciences*, 11, 233–273.

Wilson, E. O. (1972). Animal communication. *Scientific American*, 227(3), 52–60.

4 Mimesis and the Executive Suite: missing links in language evolution

MERLIN DONALD

There is considerable disagreement about the nature of the deep neurocognitive systems that generate human language, and how they might have evolved. The main bone of contention is whether the underlying generator of human language is continuous with the machinery of the primate brain, or something completely new. There are two diametrically opposed schools of thought on this issue. The Cartesian school insists on a special status for language, and adopts what might be called a traditional noncontinuity stance. To Cartesians, language is a truly novel adaptation, irreducible and unique. Consequently the language generator must be a qualitatively new device, and the governing mechanisms of language must be fundamentally different from the neurocognitive machinery that preceded them in evolution. These *a priori* dicta are supported by the fact that our closest relatives, the apes, are quite helpless in the distinctively linguistic realms of story-telling and narrative description, and remain so even when they are given a lexicon of symbols by human trainers. Their linguistic helplessness contrasts dramatically with the extraordinary linguistic talent of human children. This suggests a deep cognitive divide between apes and humans.

The second school of thought, which might be called the neurobiological approach, places continuity first, and remains sceptical about the special status of language. It affirms that natural selection, like diplomacy, must practise the art of the possible, and can select only from raw material already in existence. Pre-existing primate capacities must have provided the evolutionary wedge or 'foot in the door' that culminated in human language. There might have been a dramatic discontinuity of *function* in the evolution of language, but there could not have been any discontinuities of *mechanism*. A parallel might be found in the emergence of flight in birds, which is also a major functional discontinuity in evolution. The continuity principle is not threatened in this case, because the mechanisms of flight in birds are continuous with the mechanisms of terrestrial locomotion in their reptilian predecessors. There is no compelling reason to expect that other functional discontinuities, including language, are different in this regard.

Cartesians might reply that continuity theory cannot account for the specialness of human language. That criticism had some validity in the past. Behaviouristic theories of language were not successful. But, perhaps because of this highly visible failure, many modern cognitive scientists accept too easily the necessity of a discontinuous language acquisition device. This acceptance is unproductive, because objections levelled at behaviourism do not necessarily apply to a more inclusive neurocognitive approach to language. Unless we are willing to abandon the theory of evolution altogether (as some diehard Cartesians apparently are) we must maintain the continuity principle. This imposes a heavy obligation on theorists in this field to build credible bridges between primate cognition and human language, and to purge any implied saltation or evolutionary miracle from their proposals.

1 Modular versus domain-general models of language evolution

In addition to the difficult question of establishing continuity, language evolution involves an architectural issue: modularity. The architecture of the mind has sometimes been presented as a system of interconnected modules, each of which performs a specific cognitive operation. Modules are relatively autonomous brain systems that gather and analyse input, resolve patterns, store memories and generate specific classes of action. These systems are, by definition, specialists, dedicated to one cognitive function. In contrast, the supposedly nonmodular components of mind are generalists, open-ended, amodal and concerned primarily with co-ordinating the activity of the whole organism. Fodor (1983) and many others have called the nonmodular region of the mind the 'central processor'. Baars (1988) has called it the 'global workspace'. Others have labelled the same central processor the 'supervisory system' of the brain, and others have referred to 'domain-general' central processes. Whatever they may be called, these nonmodular components of mind draw on data generated by various modular specialists, creating an overall response, plan, or strategy. I prefer to call these processes, which constitute a cluster of functional subsystems, the executive processes of the mind, because they are in a position of control. In any architectural diagram of the mind, they are typically placed at the peak of the cognitive hierarchy.

It may seem obvious that language is too broad a process, involving too many subsystems, to be considered a module in Fodor's sense. But this is not necessarily the case. Modules are not necessarily dedicated to narrow functions. There are gradations of modularity, and some larger modules of the brain are dedicated to quite complex cognitive functions that employ several lower-level modules to their ends. A good example of this is a specialized primate cortical subsystem that relays retinal disparity information (which gives good stereo vision within a three-foot radius) to the frontal premotor centres for fine hand control. This is evidently a complex module that supports the unique visual–manual skills of primates. It is a fairly open system, but still basically encapsulated, and dedicated to one special function. Thus, it meets the definition of a *bona fide* module. It is probably typical of the more complex cognitive modules in the nervous system in that it feeds into, and receives inputs from, a number of high-level modules related to vision and hand control. Assuming that language could somehow be detached from other aspects of higher cognition, the possibility of a similar high-level modular subsystem for language cannot be ruled out in principle.

The Cartesian approach leads inevitably to a modular evolutionary scenario for language. Cartesians insist that scenarios of language evolution must, at the very least, account for the existence of a unique human grammar module that, by its very nature, would be placed quite high in the architecture of mind, and depend upon a number of lower-level modules for its function. Both Bickerton (1990, this volume) and Pinker & Bloom (1990) have argued that the basic elements of Universal Grammar cannot be accounted for by any known feature of human serial motor behaviour, and must therefore be produced by a preprogrammed language module built right into the human brain. They seek empirical proof of their theories in 'language genes' and dedicated brain structures, such as the so-called language regions of Broca and Wernicke.

Although language capacity must obviously reside in some feature of the human brain, the search for a fixed, localizable brain module for language has been a failure. After a century of searching, there is still no identifiable cortical subsystem, no special Brodmann area, no commissure or fasciculus, no characteristic laminar organization, no distinctive cellular or columnar structure, no special linguistic neurotransmitter system, indeed no known feature of the cortex or any other part of the brain that can be identified universally and exclusively with language. Moreover, the patterning of language breakdown in neurological cases, especially in those with syntactic deficits, does not support a straightforward modular solution for grammar. The genetic evidence for a language or grammar module is even more problematic, given the enormous epigenetic plasticity of the human neocortex during language development.

The most common neurobiological alternative to a Cartesian module for language takes the form of a quasi-modular, rather than a nonmodular, solution. The mainstream form of such a proposal is that language originated in a mechanism that was not initially dedicated to language *per se*, and is thus somewhat 'leaky', and domain-general, but nevertheless specialized for communication. Many of these proposals are variants on the motor-origins theory of language evolution. The motor-origins theory proposes that the evolutionary adaptation for language is really the end-result of a series of evolutionary modifications to the serial motor control systems of the primate brain. The strongest evidence in support of this idea is the close association between human praxis and language, which is evident in the genetic linkage between handedness and language dominance, and in the clinical correlation between aphasia and apraxia. Lieberman (1973, 1975, 1984), Kimura (1976, 1979) and Calvin (1993) have suggested that human language might have originated in the serial-ordering capabilities of the primate motor system, coming under intentional control in hominids, and eventually generalizing this property to a more recently evolved hominid vocomotor system. There might also be a link between gesture and language origins; this position has been expanded and articulated in detail by Armstrong, Stokoe & Wilcox (1995), who argue that, at the governing level, language is a nonmodular adaptation that originated in the human capacity for gesture.

Corballis (1989, 1991) and Deacon (1988, 1995) are in basic agreement with the motor-origins approach, but they have added a computational twist to the theory: namely, that a common property, 'generativity', underlies both praxis and speech. Generativity is the ability to build an infinity of recombinatorial sequences out of a finite set of discrete components. Greenfield (1991), Calvin (1983), MacNeilage (1992) and

Studdert-Kennedy (this volume) have all suggested closely related variations on that central idea, trying to bridge the gap between primate and human expressive skills in terms of changes to the computational principles governing the movement system. Although these proposals do not necessarily insist on the emergence of a discrete language module, they do propose a left-hemisphere motor-sequencing adaptation for the special kind of recombinatorial control that supports both praxis and language. All these theorists adhere to the continuity principle.

A second class of quasi-modular proposal has ensued from the literature on social cognition. Tomasello, Kruger & Ratner (1993) have proposed that language could only have emerged after hominids had evolved the social skills that are evident very early in human development, and that are normally the precursors of language. These social skills include a capacity for mindreading – that is, for understanding the intentionality of other minds – which forms the basis for the later development of both imitation and intentional expression. Thus the origins of language are tied to expanded conceptual capacity, rather than motor skill *per se*. Tomasello *et al.* concede something to the motor-origins theories inasmuch as they believe that the human capacity for imitation is important in evolving language; but even in the case of imitation, they see the primary cognitive adaptation as conceptual, rather than motoric, in nature. In the view of these authors, people can only imitate the actions of others if they can grasp their intentions; this allows them to unify conceptually an otherwise perceptually complex and confusing episode. Dunbar (1993) and Aiello (1995) have also supported the importance of social cognition in language evolution. They have suggested that language emerged as part of a more inclusive hominid adaptation for sustaining larger social groups. Their theory, vague about cognitive details, seems to place language squarely in the realm of a domain-general conceptual skill, or a communicative skill with strong ties to social cognition.

Most authors in this field, including myself, will concede that language has some degree of modularity in its evolution. The human vocal apparatus, and the extraordinary capacity for high-speed phonology associated with it, are obviously based on a modular adaptation. Human vocal skill represents a significant break with the primate pattern, and in itself constitutes a major functional discontinuity in primate evolution, as well as an empirically verifiable new module. Humans simultaneously evolved a corresponding phonetic memory capacity for sound-based lexical addresses. But, granting that vocalization and its spinoffs are regarded as an essential part of the evolutionary emergence of language, they must be seen as a side-story to the main evolutionary question, because vocal phonology is neither necessary nor sufficient for language. The primary evolutionary story centres on representation itself, and it is not at all clear that representational skill is modular in the sense of being restricted to its use in language.

I have proposed a synthetic approach (Donald, 1991, 1993a, 1993b, 1993c, 1995, 1997) in which both elements, social cognition and the need for improved praxis, play a role in evolving a cognitive capacity that I have called mimesis. Mimesis is a nonverbal representational skill rooted in kinematic imagination – that is, in an ability to model the whole body, including all its voluntary action-systems, in three-dimensional space. This ability underlies a variety of distinctively human capabilities, including imitation, pantomime, iconic gesture, imaginative play and the rehearsal of skills. My hypothesis is that mimesis led to the first fully intentional representations early in hominid evolution, and set the stage for the later evolution of language. The emergence of mimetic capacity involved changes that were primarily in the brain's domain-general or executive capacities. Mimesis, and language itself, are therefore traceable to a modification of the hominid executive brain, or Central Processor. This chapter will expand on that idea.

2 An additional consideration: language does not self-install

One additional point, and one that has generally been neglected, is relevant here. The language brain does not act like a preprogrammed capacity in one very important way. Even when it is given rich material on which to exercise its powers, it does not automatically self-install or self-trigger. This can be seen in people who are linguistically isolated from birth, such as the nonsigning deaf. They do not invent languages, even when they are exposed to an environment rich with describable experiences. One might expect that, given an event-structure to describe, a preprogrammed, fully equipped language acquisition device would dive into the task of labelling and describing the world. This would at least afford the individual brain some internal means of classifying the environment, and perhaps even of thinking symbolically. Such a capacity would undoubtedly have great adaptive advantage.

But the brain does not do this, ever. Without extensive cultural programming, the mind *does not suspect the possibility of language, not even of inner language*. The supposedly automatic process of language assembly is therefore not at all automatic; it depends heavily on extensive social interaction. It is hard to imagine how a fully preprogrammed language module could exist in such a form that it would not spontaneously self-trigger simply by being exposed to the episodic event-structure of the world, just as the visual system triggers vision, simply by being exposed to normal levels of patterned light (curiously, mind-reading skill self-triggers in the nonsigning deaf, and seems more easily defensible as a module than language itself).

Perhaps we have not faced the neurocognitive consequences of Saussure's famous assertion that languages are inherently collective and consensual communication systems. Languages apparently have no independent possibility of existence in individual brains. Single brains simply do not invent languages or symbols, and in isolation *do not appear to have the capacity to do so*.

What, then, is language capacity? Where might it reside? If it resists localization, and fails to self-trigger during development, then it must be assembled in the brain very differently from the way sensory–motor modules are assembled. It depends on complex epigenetic programming that does not take place without intensive cultural interaction. This implies that much of the replicative information needed to perpetuate language is stored in culture, not in the genes. While the human brain obviously has a capacity for language in a general sense, it might take the form of a broad potential for communication and representation, rather than a preset language system with precise specifications, such as Universal Grammar, built right in. The question then becomes an epigenetic, rather than a genetic one. The central issue is to determine the nature of the brain's interaction with the communicative environment. How does the individual brain 'couple' with culture to create language, and how could such a process have begun?

3 Cognitive fundamentals and the role of the executive brain

The idea that the evolution of language was heavily dependent on the expansion of a domain-general executive brain may appear odd at first, especially to linguists. But the executive brain makes possible many of the complex cognitive functions that exist not only in humans, but also in other mammalian species. It provides the cognitive fundamentals of most higher mental activity. These fundamentals allow the individual brain to 'couple' with the labyrinthine representational mazes that constitute the building-blocks of culture. Cognitive engagement with culture stands at the heart of our uniquely human forms of representation, and *the executive brain directs this process.*

The human executive brain thus provides the basis for cultural engagement, and, indeed, of cultural invention in the first place. It is fundamental to all our unique communication skills, including language. It is not simple in structure. In fact, the executive brain is an extensive complex of brain subsystems that collectively supports a class of domain-general capacities, including various kinds of working memory, at least two or three different kinds of attentional selection, the basis for autocuing or self-triggered recall, abstract self-representation, and much of the basis for social cognition. These skills were the evolutionary wedge from which language was fashioned by selection pressure, because of their close relationship to primate executive skills.

Before developing this notion any further, some common misconceptions must be corrected. One objection made by Tooby & Cosmides (1989) to the possibility of general-purpose adaptations in cognitive evolution is that it is difficult to imagine what kind of selection pressures could cause such (presumably) diffuse adaptations in any given species, given that the gene-pool is always responding to very specific environments. But this objection is based on a complete misunderstanding of what is involved in a domain-general cognitive adaptation. Domain-general aspects of the mind and nervous system are not unstructured or unspecialized in their evolutionary origins and biological function. They are not general-purpose, or diffuse, in that sense. On the contrary, domain-general executive skills are a specialization in themselves, like any other. There are many potential forms that a domain-general evolutionary change might have taken. The particular solution in the case of humans was successful because it responded directly to the specific selection pressures that were at work in human evolution. *Even though, in architectural terms, this solution was domain-general, it was not 'general-purpose' in terms of adaptation.*

Even from the more restricted perspective of cognitive architecture, the executive systems of the brain are not necessarily as amorphous as Fodor (1983) suggested in his important treatise on modularity. Executive systems perform very specialized functions, such as retrieving and holding relevant knowledge in working memory, switching between ongoing tasks, temporarily interconnecting various cognitive subsystems (as in many multimodal tasks), building and updating an ongoing model of the current environment, initiating searches of long-term memory, maintaining a hierarchy of priorities and so on. The elaborate component structure of the executive brain reflects that complexity.

The mammalian executive brain has a traceable evolutionary history. The gradual elaboration of executive brain functions is one of the signal features of mammalian evolution. This elaboration was related to the emergence of a unifying cortical mantle and the subsequent need to manage the traffic of the emerging mammalian central nervous system. The executive brain in humans is simply a modification, a particular variation, of the ancient mammalian core brain system that includes (in humans) much of prefrontal cortex, the tertiary areas of the parietal-temporal cortex and most of the insula, cingulate gyrus and hippocampus, in addition to many subcortical structures, including parts of the midline thalamus and basal ganglia. All these structures are known to play an important role in working memory, attention, voluntary movement, explicit recall, social cognition, planning and conscious function in general. They work together in the regulation of what is usually called controlled cognitive function. Relative to the rest of the brain, the relevant brain areas are larger in humans than in apes. Thus, it must be concluded that, during human evolution, these specific brain regions expanded much more than other neural structures, such as the brainstem or the primary sensory areas.

The executive brain is necessary, and complementary, to the specialized modules it helps to regulate. It is consistent with a general pattern of neural adaptation to the escalating unpredictability of the mammalian world, as mammals evolved a greater capacity for learning, thus leading to greater ontogenetic variability. As selection pressures moved hominids toward social complexity, their societies created even higher degrees of unpredictability that had to be dealt with in terms of memory demands, divided attention and so on. By the very nature of its functions, the human executive system had to become increasingly domain-general in its architecture. As an evolutionary adaptation, however, it was highly specialized.

4 Where humans excel: the Executive Suite

The expansion of the hominid executive brain corresponded to a change in our core capacities. This change is evident in a variety of behavioural and cognitive domains for which humans are specialized. In this section I will describe a series of task-paradigms on which, relative to apes, humans excel. All these paradigms tap our executive skills directly. A mastery of language is not necessary for the performance of any of them. Apes, and sometimes monkeys and other mammals, have the ability to perform most of these paradigms either poorly, or to a limited degree. Differences between apes and humans on these tasks are usually quantitative, not qualitative. These paradigms were selected by researchers because they were on the very edge of what primates can achieve, and situated, as Vygotsky (1978) might have put it, in their 'zone of proximal development'. It follows that these functions could have been subjected to natural selection early in hominid evolution.

Hominid executive skills, complex as they are, must have evolved almost simultaneously, forming what is sometimes called a suite of interrelated adaptations. These might therefore be called the Executive Suite.

4.1 Metacognition, or self-monitoring

Metacognition is the ability to monitor one's own performance. It is essential in the rehearsal of skill, inasmuch as a degree of self-evaluation is demanded if performance is to be improved by repetition. It is also important in maintaining a communication linkage over time – that is, monitoring the success of one's own performance as a communicator. Humans have a highly developed, and primates a limited, metacognitive capacity. Smith, Schull & Washburn (in press) have shown this with a behavioural test consisting of what they call the 'bailout' option. Animals are trained to respond to a stimulus with a 'yes', 'no', or 'bailout' option. The bailout option indicates that the animal wants to skip the present trial, and advance to the next one, thus avoiding punishment for a wrong answer. Monkeys can do this task. Thus they can, to some extent, monitor their own likelihood of success or failure on a given trial. Rats cannot perform this task,[1] but there may be other mammals that can.

1 However, rats are apparently able to achieve a limited kind of self-report; see Beninger, Kendall & Vanderwolf (1974).

4.2 *Imitation*

Apes and monkeys are capable of some imitation, but Tomasello *et al.* (1993) have argued that the imitative skills of apes fall far short of those of humans. In particular, they are not as good as humans at precise, detailed reproduction of sequences. It is as if they were lacking in the essential attentional and/or mnemonic power to focus on, and remember, the specifics of the imitated sequence.

4.3 *Multitasking (consciously managing two or more operations)*

Savage-Rumbaugh and her colleagues (1991, 1993) have suggested that chimpanzees and bonobos have most of the cognitive components for language, with one major exception: multitasking, or the ability to consciously manage more than one thing at a time. Multitasking is common among humans, and essential to intentional communication, since speakers must keep track of both their own behaviour and that of their audience, splitting their attention between two or more channels.

4.4 *Autocuing, and explicit memory*

There is a great methodological divide between the literatures on human and animal memory (see Sherry & Schacter 1987). Animals, including apes, have a very limited capacity for recall. Like that of most other mammals, the ape's memory is best addressed passively, and this limits the kinds of symbols that apes can be taught to use (they are much better at using prepackaged symbol-boards than they are at signing, for example). Humans, in contrast, can easily self-trigger, or autocue, their memories. Explicit recall in humans depends heavily on what Karmiloff-Smith (1992) calls the 'representational re-description' or 'explicitation' of reality.[2] This skill is fundamental; hominids could not have invented lexicons unless they already had some capacity for creating retrievable morphology, a precondition for the emergence of protolanguage.[3] Once language had evolved, it greatly enriched our capacity for explicit recall at higher levels of representation.[4]

2 This traces back to Bartlett's (1932) concept of 'reconstructive' memory and is also related to Edelman's (1992) notion of 'recategorical' memory. In all three cases, memory is part, or a reflection, of the modelling intellect.

3 For a more detailed discussion of this topic, see Donald (in press).

4 See also Nelson (1990, 1996).

4.5 *Self-reminding (mnemonic uses of action)*

The acquisition and maintenance of a complex skill require an ability to repeat an action in order to self-remind, so that long sequences can be acquired and remembered. Human children often use their own actions as mnemonic devices, but apes do not, at least not systematically. Self-reminding is related to autocuing skill, as well as to metacognition. It is an intermediate step to long-range intentional guidance behaviour.

4.6 *Self-recognition*

Apes can recognize themselves in a mirror, whereas monkeys and other mammals cannot (Gallup 1970). Thus apes possess the capacity not only to construct an objectivized image of themselves in the environment, but also to consciously examine and recognize rotations and transformations of that image. Humans are generally much faster at self-recognition than apes, and this capacity is central to praxis. Actors and athletes use this kind of kinematic imagination, or self-visualization, in training.

4.7 *Purposive rehearsal*

One of the most essential components of advanced skill is the capacity to rehearse action purposively. This complex self-supervisory capacity is unique to humans. Human children endlessly rehearse and refine their own actions, sometimes without any obvious reinforcement; for example, they might practise throwing stones at a tree, or balancing on one foot. Although apes play repetitive games, they do not appear to spontaneously rehearse and refine their skills. This involves many of the skills listed above – self-monitoring, autocuing, visual and kinetic imagination, advanced self-representation, and so on – which exist in limited form in primates, and could have evolved as a result of the convergent evolutionary expansion of these other elements. Purposive rehearsal requires the individual brain to evaluate its own outputs and conceive of *idealized* actions as a template for judging outcomes. Rehearsal involves a form of intentional representation; the act is used to represent itself (a kind of self-demonstration). This ability seems to be based on *implementable imagery*.

4.8 *Action metaphor (iconicity in expression)*

The repetition of an action to communicate what the act naturally conveys is the most elementary kind of intentional iconicity. This might be called action metaphor, and constitutes a rudimentary form of gesture. There is no evidence for the existence of this kind of intentional behaviour in apes, but there are some reports of pseudo-gestures, which means that they may be quite close to having gestural skill. Thus, iconic skill in primates, or in early predecessors of humans, such as the australopithecines, may have been subjected to selection pressure.

4.9 *Mindreading (imagining and understanding intentionality in others)*

This capacity is domain-general in the sense that it is abstract and amodal. Inasmuch as they are capable of deception, mindreading is already present in monkeys and apes. However, their mindreading skills are evidently not sufficient to support the spontaneous appearance of a conventional system of gestures (cf. Tomasello, in press). This is mainly due to the absence of the other cognitive fundamentals listed here.

4.10 *Reciprocal intentionality (proto-pedagogy)*

This is two-way mindreading, or what might better be called mindsharing. It is fundamental to pedagogy, in which one person consciously regulates the learning process in another, while the learner tracks the teacher's intent. The teacher–apprentice relationship is central to human culture. It involves not only understanding the intentionality of others, but also engaging in intentional exchanges, and understanding how the mind of the other has been affected by the communicative act. This capacity exists in people who lack language (see Schaller 1991) but seems to be absent in apes, although some signs of it are present in their subtle social event-perceptions.[5] Their perceptions, however, are much better than their productions, and even extensive enculturation has failed to ignite much by way of spontaneous reciprocal intentionality.

4.11 *Spontaneous symbolic invention*

This has never been convincingly demonstrated in apes, even enculturated ones, although there have been a few reports of symbolic invention in the form of small variants on existing expressive custom (cf. Wrangham, McGrew, De Waal & Heltne 1994). Human children, in contrast, are very expressive with gesture as early as one year of age. Gestural skill is domain-general inasmuch as it can harness any input or output modality.

5 Boesch & Boesch (1984) claim that a quasi-pedagogical relationship exists between mother and infant chimpanzees, with regard to learning how to use certain tools. This could be due to imitation or emulation by the infant, rather than systematic instruction by the mother. Nevertheless, it is close enough to basic pedagogy to provide something for natural selection to act on.

This brief summary makes no claim to be exhaustive. But it does show that there is a fairly broad class of executive skills that distinguish humans from apes. These functions are heavily dependent upon the executive brain; extensive experimental evidence on the properties of the executive system is summarized in Baars' book (1988) on this subject.

The whole executive complex – both brain anatomy and the executive capacities themselves – evolved during hominid evolution, and this raises the question of their origin.

Could all this not have co-evolved with language? I regard this as highly unlikely, for the following simple reason: language is the most complex of human skills; the simpler ones probably came first. Even protolanguage could not have evolved before the central executive apparatus had reached a certain point. Intentional communication demands a great deal of executive management. The moment-to-moment difficulty of acquiring and managing language in the real world is very high, because the cultural environment that encompasses language is constantly changing, and in need of very rapid updating. Moreover, human speakers often carry out several complex operations at once, in several modalities, simultaneously maintaining parity with the often several recipients of their communications. All these achievements demand central attentional control to a degree that is unheard-of in other species.

Human language is characterized by improved access to memory. Speakers gain voluntary access to their own memory systems, a skill that is singularly powerful. But this is not unique to language; it applies to other special human abilities. For instance, an actor can carry a repertoire of literally hundreds of conventional gestures, postures, sounds, facial expressions and attitudes. This skill pales in comparison to language, however, where the explicit retrieval of words and idioms must be achieved much faster and more accurately; no small matter when a lexical search must separate out a single item from a repertoire of tens of thousands.

Thus the distinguishing cognitive features of language, when compared with other highly skilled tasks, are its complexity and speed, and its demands on attention and working memory. Language is really a gigantic meta-task, requiring the co-ordination of an entire hierarchy of subtasks and sub-subtasks, regulated from working memory. Speakers hold in their working memories a model of their own past communications, and a model of what other participants have already said, tagged as to source; otherwise a two- or three-person conversation would cease to make sense very soon after having begun. This multichannel updating skill cannot be modular in any meaningful sense of the term; it must remain open to all sorts of inputs, including nonlanguage ones. Moreover, the working model must be immediately available for constant updating; one might say that the model *is* the speaker's effective working memory. It guides the overall contour of communication for considerable periods of time. This kind of model-building, including its role in working memory, is a major component of human executive capacity.

The inevitable other face of controlled performance is a capacity for automatization on a massive scale.[6] The *acquisition* of any special human skill, including language, depends on executive control. But the efficient *routine use* of those same skills depends more on an ability to automatize them, leaving conscious capacity free to deal with more urgent matters, such as the novel, the complex and the unexpected. Thus the basic cognitive operations underlying language, such as lexical search, sentence assembly and the generation of linguistic morphology,[7] must become automatized so that the speaker is free to take a complex communicative context into account. By increasing their executive capacity – including an expanded capacity for automatization – humans have effectively become self-programmable organisms.

5 Episodic competence in primates and humans

There were other demands placed on the executive brain in primate evolution, especially in the social domain. Acquired social skills are among the most esoteric achievements of primates. Remembering and responding to social situations is a complex multi-channel task that demands the integrated use of several basic brain functions. One of

6 The best evidence of automatization comes from the study of trade-off effects while doing several things at once, in which one task, say, driving a car, interferes with performance in another, say, carrying on a conversation in Italian. Inexperienced performers, for instance someone who is simultaneously learning to drive and to speak Italian, find it impossible to perform two non-automatized tasks at once. Once skills are sufficiently automatized, multitasking becomes possible without significant tradeoffs. Automatized skills can be nested in quite complex hierarchies, as in piano-playing, for instance.

7 The best summary of the evidence for these operations in language is found in Levelt (1989).

these functions is social event-perception, and its corollary, event-parsing, which includes an implicit understanding of the agents, their interactions, their effects on the contingencies of action, and the consequences of perceived episodes. These are the product of highly abstract amodal capacities.

I have called this sophisticated style of event-representation *episodic cognition* because it is concrete or episode-bound. Apes are among its most skilled practitioners, and are very clever problem-solvers within any brief experiential episode. Episodic skills sit at the top of the cognitive hierarchy. Episodic competence demands considerable executive skill, including an ability to attend selectively (the parsing of episodes is, after all, a matter of registering the event selectively and interpretatively), the capacity to sustain vigilance over fairly long periods, and a prioritizing capacity that allows strategic decisions as to the best course of action, when several courses are possible.

Above all, episodic cognition makes great demands on working memory. Various facts and implications that are inherent in social episodes must be kept in mind when negotiating, for instance, the subtleties of chimpanzee social behaviour. These might include one's place in the dominance hierarchy, territorial interests, past interactions with other players and past interactions between the others involved in the episode, as well as one's immediate objective (for instance to be groomed by a particular individual). These facts need constant updating, since social relationships can change suddenly.

Humans also apply their executive capacity in the regulation of social behaviour. In many ways, social behaviour is the most conscious of our behaviours, because it is unpredictable and complex, and thus requires constant updating and vigilance, careful attention to multiple simultaneous channels of input and a good memory for past social interactions. Above all, social behaviour involves the constant construction and updating of mental models of events and actions, a process that is highly conscious and controlled, precisely because it must remain well matched to a constantly changing social and cultural environment. In this, social behaviour is like many other human skills, including language.

Language is undoubtedly much more abstract in its structure than episodic cognition, and in human interactions it can dominate our thinking about social relationships to the point of obscuring the more basic episodic capacity that drives it. But it is important not to underestimate the complexity of episodic processes. Most importantly for evolutionary considerations, language – and intentional communication in general – seems to rely on the same kinds of executive skill as episodic cognition.

6 Mimesis: the linkage between primate event-cognition and intentional cultures

The primary reason for proposing an expansion of executive skills early in hominid evolution is that such a change would have maintained evolutionary continuity, while forming the basis of a cognitive adaptation that can account for the achievements of early *Homo* (this is where a close consideration of evidence from physical anthropology and archaeology is essential). The most credible form of early hominid culture, appearing with species *Homo* about 2 million years ago, is a mimetic style of thought and communication. Mimetic skill is the foundation for a variety of hominid achievements, including advances in toolmaking; co-ordinated collective endeavours such as fire use; sophisticated hunting and gathering; and the division of labour. This was a significant step away from the primate mainstream, without invoking anything so refined or powerful as language.

My hypothesis of the early evolution of mimesis achieves four important theoretical objectives. First, it accounts, as well as can be expected at this time-distance, for the archaeological evidence on the achievements of early hominids. Second, it explains the presence of a very salient (especially in the neuropsychological literature) analog mode of representation in modern humans, that represents our major alternative to language. Third, it accounts for a self-contained level of human culture that still operates on mimetic principles, and forms the basis for many expressive arts, such as dance and athletic display, pantomime, theatre, painting and many basic crafts.

Finally, it establishes the fundamentals of intentional expression in hominids, without which language would not have had an opportunity to evolve, since there would have been no existing communicative environment on which natural selection could act. There could not have been selection pressure to evolve such a sophisticated, high-speed communication system as modern language unless there was already a simpler, slower one in place. Mimesis fulfils that condition: it provides the preconditions out of which language, improbable an adaptation though it may seem, might have evolved, simply as the need for disambiguation grew. Mimetic culture is considerably closer to language than primate expressive cultures.

The evolutionary process is not teleological; there could have been no foresight, no anticipation of language. This is also consistent with the early evolution and stability of mimetic culture. The archaic social adaptation of hominids was self-sufficient enough to last for a very long time. This is evident from the archaeological record. In both brain anatomy and associated cultural artifacts, *Homo erectus* was a rather stable species for well over a million years. There was clearly no need for it to evolve any further toward language to ensure its survival. To reiterate my rejection of teleology, there is no anticipatory element, implicit or explicit, in proposing the early evolution of mimesis. Mimesis would have been a successful adaptation in its own right, forming a satisfactory basis for the refinement and diffusion of praxic skills, for the development of much more intricate expressive scenarios and for the maintenance of some degree of social complexity.

Its early appearance as an archaic adaptation would not have ruled out further *mimetic* evolution at the time language emerged. Mimesis was, and remains, the basis for an analog style of communication and thought that is common in humans,[8] but absent in apes. It is a highly sophisticated capacity, easily underestimated as to its importance in modern human behaviour. It would have made hominids formidable foes in any area in which competition was an issue, because the entire range of voluntary behaviours was brought under voluntary control.

Table 4.1 lists some common mimetic behaviours. They make up a loose representational hierarchy, including both the simpler forms of mimetic expression, such as pointing and intentional gaze, and the more complex forms, such as re-enactment and pantomime. The representational style of mimesis is variously describable as fuzzy, iconic and/or analog. It is consistent with what Burling (1993) has called an 'iconic' style of communication. The principle of similarity that links mimetic actions and their referents is perceptual, and the basic communicative device is best described as *implementable action metaphor*. Mimetic skill is a powerful device for communication: it can convey requests and

8 The universality of this analog mode of thought is nicely documented in Paivio's (1986) massive review of dual-coding theory. Mimetic cognition also seems dissociable from language on neuropsychological grounds. See Donald (1991, 1993a).

Table 4.1 Some representational forms in the mimetic mode

Form	***Meaning***
Intentional pointing (incl. gaze)	Sharing of attention, requests, commands
Demonstration	Contact, reiteration, sharing
Reciprocal games	Participation, contact, display, skill
Self-demonstration	Explicit act-reference
Play-acting	Explicit act-reference
Rehearsal	Explicit act-reference
Re-enactment	Explicit event-reference
Pantomime	Explicit event-reference
Gesture (solo, dyadic or group)	Explicit event-reference
Ritualized group action	Explicit event-reference

commands, capture and hold the attention of others, show or declare, establish and maintain contact, refer explicitly to actions or events, demonstrate, oversee the actions of others and convey emotion. It also allows basic instinctual behaviours, for instance, pair-bonding and mating, to be made more elaborate and culturally specific in their forms.

In fact, the role of primate expressive instincts should not be overlooked in discussing human mimesis. It is highly likely that mimetic expression was initially built from preexisting primate emotional and social expressive algorithms. Humans have an unequalled expressive repertoire of limbic or involuntary gestures, body attitudes, facial expressions and sounds, including such uniquely human behaviours as laughter (itself a very powerful device for both bonding and social ostracism), extended and very intense grief reactions and many other universal behaviour patterns, which have been documented by Eibl-Eibesfeldt (1989) and colleagues in cross-cultural studies. Such stereotyped emotional reactions and interactions project deep into the hominid past, and do not in themselves constitute mimesis. It is only when such reactions are used or elaborated *intentionally* that we have evidence of mimetic skill.

In addition to its role as a form of thought and representation, mimetic capacity serves a crucial subsidiary role in modern language, creating the communicative envelope of language, including such things as eye contact, facial expression, prosody and gesture, all of which

Table 4.2 Proposed sequence of expressive behaviours and cultural forms during the transition to mimetic culture. Note that each successive category incorporates and enlarges the previous ones.

(1) Rehearsal of action-sequences (throwing, toolmaking, emotional displays)

(2) Sharing of action (basic pedagogy, shared expressive patterning, custom)

(3) Action-metaphor (increased reciprocal use of facial, ocular, manual and vocal gesture)

(4) Shared event-models (elaborate games, proto-ritual, group action-patterns)

(5) Fixed cultural rhythms (greater intragroup conformity and intergroup variation)

help in establishing and maintaining parity between various agents in a communicative setting. The close relationship of mimetic expression and culture to language development in modern human infants has been documented by Katherine Nelson in a recent book (Nelson 1996).[9] Mimesis is the key to the earliest stages of human cultural engagement, and to the most basic repository of custom and many other forms of cultural memory. The common knowledge mediated by mimetic cognition eliminates the need for various kinds of explicit markers in oral communication. Additionally, many uses of language are basically mimetic, and in young children the use of spoken language is essentially secondary to their mimetic expressive agenda. Oral language typically emerges as an independent level of representation after four years of age (Nelson 1996).

Table 4.2 illustrates a hypothetical sequence in which mimetic communicative behaviours might have emerged. The most immediate fitness advantage for the evolution of hominid executive skills was probably a general improvement across the whole range of their voluntary repertoire, driven by intraspecific competition. A group of hominids with better communication and memory skills would have had a great advantage in most survival-related tasks, including toolmaking, hunting, scavenging and gathering.

The preexisting emotional expressions of hominids, including laughter, extended grief and other special facial, vocal and manual expressions, formed an important foundation for mimetic expression. The ease with which humans can employ these various response modalities, alone and in combination, testifies to the amodal position of mimesis in the communicative hierarchy. A domain-general capacity for modelling

9 This type of theory is not necessarily recapitulatory in nature (cf. Nelson 1996; Donald 1995).

one's own action is integral to mimesis and, by definition, whatever the initial reasons for its emergence might have been – whether better food-gathering, hunting, or toolmaking, or social innovations such as the division of labor – its emergence would automatically have generalized to better voluntary control over intentional expression in general. This has a variety of immediate social consequences: reciprocal gesturing, shared action-models, more elaborate games and signature behaviours that characterized specific groups. Even a small amount of intentional experimentation with these behaviours would have greatly complicated hominid social life. A small change in expressive ability would also have greatly increased opportunities for the use of deception, Machiavellianism, conspiracies and alliances, as well as inter- and intra-group competition. Mimesis would make social hierarchies more complex, and lead to greater differentiation of custom. With the arrival of mimesis, all the intricate social arrangements of primates were suddenly vulnerable to elaboration and differentiation. Natural selection had the opportunity to act on these, shaping a new form of hominid culture.

Mimetic vestiges persist in human affairs. Surely the most convincing evidence for the time-depth of the mimetic adaptation in hominids is the persistence of mimesis into the era of modern *Homo sapiens*. The vestiges of mimesis are especially evident in our irrepressible tendency toward conformity. A unique feature of human social life is an incessant pressure to conform to group norms, and to be accepted by one's peer group. Another is the tremendously subtle cultural variations that occur outside the realm of language. The pressure to conform to those unwritten, unspoken cultural norms is virtually irresistible, whether it takes the form of imposed totalitarianism or the superficially voluntary conformity manifest in great public spectacles and demonstrations. Moreover, the threat of social ostracism is so profound that it can drive individuals to suicide. Mimesis is the driving force here; the pressure to conform reflects a profound instinct in humans to imitate the group, to absorb and internalize its cognitive models of reality.

Mimesis is thus as deeply instinctual as language itself. It is an adaptation in its own right, and the continuing importance of mimetic communication should not be underestimated. People can still be moved to act in a co-ordinated manner by a few gestures and utterances, and they cannot resist miming one another's behaviour in large-group demonstrations. Language has only a minor role here. Mimetic culture has provided the cognitive foundation of human conventionality. It has also provided humans with a public communicative space that is a necessary, if not sufficient, precondition for normal language acquisition. Most important, the fundamentals of articulatory gesture, from which all languages are built, were put in place when mimetic capacity emerged.

References

Aiello, L. (1995). Hominine preadaptations for language and cognition. In Mellars, P. & Gibson, K. (eds.) *Modelling the Early Human Mind*. Cambridge: McDonald Institute, University of Cambridge.

Armstrong, D., Stokoe, W. & Wilcox, S. (1995). *Gesture and the Nature of Language*. Cambridge: Cambridge University Press.

Baars, B. (1988). *A Cognitive Theory of Consciousness*. Cambridge: Cambridge University Press.

Bartlett, F. C. (1932). *Remembering*. Cambridge: Cambridge University Press.

Beninger, R., Kendall, S. B. & Vanderwolf, C. H. (1974). The ability of rats to discriminate their own behaviours. *Canadian Journal of Psychology*, 28, 79–91.

Bickerton, D. (1990). *Language and Species*. Chicago and London: University of Chicago Press.

Boesch, C. & Boesch, H. (1984). Possible causes of sex differentiation in the use of natural hammers by wild chimps. *Journal of Human Evolution*, 13, 415–440.

Burling, R. (1993). Primate calls, human language, and nonverbal communication. *Current Anthropology*, 34, 25–53.

Calvin, W. (1983). A stone's throw and its launch window: timing precision and its implications for language and hominid brains. *Journal of Theoretical Biology*, 104, 121–135.

(1993). The unitary hypothesis: a common neural circuitry for novel manipulations, language, plan-ahead, and throwing? In Gibson, K. R. & Ingold, T. (eds.) *Tools, Language, and Cognition in Human Evolution*. Cambridge: Cambridge University Press.

Corballis, M. C. (1989). Laterality and human evolution. *Psychological Review*, 96, 492–505.

(1991). *The Lopsided Ape: Evolution of the Generative Mind*. Oxford: Oxford University Press.

Deacon, T. (1988). Human brain evolution: 1. Evolution of language circuits. In Jerison, H. J. & Jerison, I. (eds.) *Intelligence and Evolutionary Biology*. Heidelberg: Springer-Verlag.

(1995). Why a brain capable of language evolved only once: prefrontal cortex and symbol learning. In Velikovsky, B. (ed.) *Social and Biological Origins of Language*. Hove: Erlbaum.

Donald, M. (1991). *Origins of Modern Mind: Three Stages in the Evolution of Culture and Cognition*. Cambridge, MA: Harvard University Press.

(1993a). Précis of *Origins of the Modern Mind*. *Behavioral and Brain Sciences*, 16(4), 737–791.

(1993b). Human cognitive evolution: what we were, what we are becoming. *Social Research*, 60, 143–170.

(1993c). Hominid enculturation and cognitive evolution. *Archaeological Review from Cambridge*, 12, 5–24.
(1995). The neurobiology of human consciousness: an evolutionary approach. *Neuropsychologia*, 33, 1087–1102.
(1997). The mind from a historical perspective: human cognitive phylogenesis and the possibility of continuing cognitive evolution. In Johnson, D. & Ermeling, C. (eds.) *The Future of the Cognitive Revolution*. Oxford: Oxford University Press.
(in press). Preconditions for the evolution of protolanguages. In Corballis, M. C. & Lea, I. (eds.) *Evolution of the Hominid Mind*. Oxford: Oxford University Press.
Dunbar, R. I. M. (1993). Coevolution of neocortical size, group size and language in humans. *Behavioral and Brain Sciences*, 16, 681–694.
Edelman, G. (1992). *Bright Air, Brilliant Fire*. London: Penguin.
Eibl-Eibesfeldt, I. (1989). *Human Ethology*. Berlin: Aldine de Gruyter.
Fodor, J. A. (1983). *The Modularity of Mind*. Cambridge, MA: MIT Press.
Gallup, G. G. (1970). Chimpanzees: self-recognition. *Science*, 167, 86–87.
Greenfield, P. M. (1991). Language, tools and brain: the ontogeny and phylogeny of hierarchically organized sequential behaviour. *Behavioral and Brain Sciences*, 14, 531–595.
Karmiloff-Smith, A. (1992). *Beyond Modularity: A Developmental Perspective on Cognitive Science*. Cambridge, MA: MIT Press.
Kimura, D. (1976). The neurological basis of language *qua* gestures. In Whitaker, H. & Whitaker, H. A. (eds.) *Current Trends in Neurolinguistics*. San Diego, CA: Academic Press.
(1979). Neuromotor mechanisms in the evolution of human communication. In Steklis, H. D. & Raleigh, M. J. (eds.) *Neurobiology of Social Communication in Primates*. San Diego, CA: Academic Press.
Levelt, W. (1989). *Speaking*. Cambridge, MA: MIT Press.
Lieberman, P. (1973). On the evolution of human language: a unified view. *Cognition*, 2, 59–94.
(1975). *On the Origins of Language: An Introduction to the Evolution of Human Speech*. London: Macmillan.
(1984). *The Biology and Evolution of Language*. Cambridge, MA: Harvard University Press.
MacNeilage, P. (1992). Evolution and lateralization of the two great primate action systems. In Wind, J., Chiarelli, B., Bichakjian, B. & Nocemtini, A. (eds.) *Language Origin: A Multidisciplinary Approach*. Amsterdam: John Benjamins.
Nelson, K. (1990). Event knowledge and the development of language functions. In Miller, J. (ed.) *Research on Child Language Disorders*. Little, Brown.
(1996). *Language in Cognitive Development: Emergence of the Mediated Mind*. Cambridge: Cambridge University Press.
Paivio, A. (1986). *Mental Representations: A Dual Coding Approach*. Oxford: Clarendon Press.
Pinker, S. (1994). *The Language Instinct*. New York: Morrow; London: Penguin.
& Bloom, P. (1990). Natural language and natural selection. *Behavioral and Brain Sciences*, 13, 707–784.

Savage-Rumbaugh, E. S. (1991). Multi-tasking: the pan-human Rubicon. *Seminars in the Neurosciences*, 3, 417–422.

Murphy, J., Sevcik, R. A., Braake, K. E., Williams, S. L. & Rumbaugh, D. (1993). *Language Comprehension in Ape and Child*. Monographs of the Society for Research in Child Development 233, v. 58, nos. 3, 4. Chicago: University of Chicago Press.

& Rumbaugh, D. (1993). The emergence of language. In Gibson, K. R. & Ingold, T. (eds.) *Tools, Language and Cognition in Human Evolution*. Cambridge: Cambridge University Press.

Schaller, S. (1991). *A Man without Words*. Berkeley and Los Angeles: University of California Press.

Sherry, D. F. & Schacter, D. L. (1987). The evolution of multiple memory systems. *Psychological Review*, 94, 439–454.

Smith, J. D., Schull, J. & Washburn, D. A. (in press). Uncertainty monitoring in humans and animals.

Tomasello, M. (in press). Social cognition and the evolution of culture. In Langer, J. & Killen M. (eds.) *Piaget, Evolution and Development*. Hove: Lawrence Erlbaum.

Kruger, A. C. & Ratner, H. H. (1993). Cultural learning. *Behavioral and Brain Sciences*, 16, 495–552.

Tooby, J. & Cosmides, L. (1989). Evolutionary psychology and the generation of culture, part I. *Ethology and Sociobiology*, 10, 29–49.

Vygotsky, L. S. (1978). *Mind in Society*. Cambridge, MA: Harvard University Press.

Wrangham, R., McGrew, W. C., De Waal, F. B. M. & Heltne, P. G. (eds.) (1994). *Chimpanzee Cultures*. Cambridge, MA: Harvard University Press.

5 Ritual/speech coevolution: a solution to the problem of deception

CHRIS KNIGHT

1 Introduction: the Darwinian paradigm

Darwinism is setting a new research agenda across the related fields of palaeoanthropology, evolutionary psychology and theoretical linguistics (Dunbar 1993; Hurford 1989, 1992; Pinker & Bloom 1990; Steele & Shennan 1996). It is now widely accepted that no other theoretical framework has equivalent potential to solve the major outstanding problems in human origins research. Rival paradigms from the human and social sciences – Freudian, Piagetian, Chomskyan, Lévi-Straussian – cannot explain evolved human mentality because they already assume this as a basic premise. Tried and tested as a methodology applicable to the social behaviour of all living organisms (Dawkins 1976; Hamilton 1964; Trivers 1985), Darwinism makes no such assumptions, thereby avoiding circularity.

Modern Darwinism seeks to harmonize research into human life with the rest of scientific knowledge. This project depends, however, on accounting for the emergence of symbolic culture, including speech, a system of communication unparalleled elsewhere in biology. While Darwinians confidently expect an explanation (Pinker & Bloom 1990), it has to be admitted that, to date, no compelling account has been advanced.

In this chapter, I treat speech as a revolutionary development made possible by the establishment of novel levels of social co-operation. In this, I follow Maynard Smith and Szäthmáry (1995), who provide a Darwinian game-theoretic perspective on the origins of human social co-operation, including speech. They view the momentous process as one of a limited number of 'major transitions' during life's evolution on Earth. Each such transition is revolutionary in that it involves a relatively sudden and dramatic restructuring, like the breaking of a log-jam. The preceding barrier to the new level of complexity, discernible with hindsight, arises because, despite any emergent potential for self-organization on the higher level (that of the multicellular organism, for example, or the speech-based co-operative community), the necessary co-operative strategies repeatedly lose out to more stable strategies of 'selfish' gene-replication on the lower level.

Previous, gradualist, models of language origins ignored such problems, taking speech to be in some absolute sense 'better' than a primate gesture-call system. Speech, it is frequently said, allows access to a communal pool of knowledge, saving duplication of effort in trial-and-error direct discovery (Pinker & Bloom 1990: 712). But a primate-style 'Machiavellian' social dynamic (Byrne & Whiten 1988) would weigh heavily against reliance on uncorroborated second-hand information. Vulnerability to deceit is costly. Every adaptation has costs as well as benefits; a novel adaptation spreads only if the benefits outweigh the costs. Previous thinking on speech evolution has simply ignored the costs.

2 Darwinism and symbolic culture

Speech differs from a primate gesture-call system in presupposing a wholly new *representational* level. Through exposure to art, music, dance and other 'external memory stores' (Donald 1991), humans from infancy learn to internalize a set of representations essential to the self-organization of a cultural community. The representations central on this level are morally authoritative intangibles or 'collective representations' (Durkheim 1965). 'God', 'Unicorn' and 'Totem' are among the possibilities. 'Symbolic culture', to quote archaeologist Philip Chase (1994), 'requires the invention of a whole new kind of things, things that have no existence in the "real" world but exist entirely in the symbolic realm. Examples are concepts such as good and evil, mythical inventions such as gods and underworlds, and social constructs such as promises and football games.' It would be surprising if this new representational level did not bring with it a new level of complexity in communication.

Linguistic reference is not a direct mapping from linguistic terms either to perceptible things or to intentional states; the mapping is from linguistic terms to communal constructs – representations established in the *universe of discourse*. This universe is structured by people's ritual and other symbolic experience. While hunting eland in the Kalahari – to take just one example – Zu/'hoãsi will refer to their prey using the 'respect' term *tcheni* – literally 'dance'. 'People', 'fatness', 'menstruation', 'gender-ambiguity' and 'fertility' are associated meanings (Lewis-Williams 1981; Power & Watts 1997). A complex representation of this kind is not perceptually constrained. The god-like 'Eland' of these hunter–gatherers is a communal fiction, connected only in the loosest way to anything existing in the real world.

Not being perceptually verifiable, representations of this kind – the kind to which words are attached – are bound up with anomalous levels of trust and social co-operation; these require 'special' explanation (cf. Maynard Smith & Szäthmáry 1995). Theoretical linguists have traditionally avoided the problems by simply *assuming* the existence of a homogenous speech-community, committed to the co-operative, honest sharing of information. The anthropologist Pierre Bourdieu (1991) terms this the 'assumption of communism', noting its centrality to formal linguistics since the discipline's inception. While speech indeed presupposes social co-operation (Grice 1969, 1975), such models distract attention from precisely the problems which, to a Darwinian, most cry out to be addressed. Why, in the human case, can such anomalous levels of co-operation be assumed?

The value of Darwinian theory is that it forces us to consider the barriers to the establishment of co-operation on the necessary scale. In a Darwinian world, individuals who deceive others to make selfish gains, or who 'free-load' – enjoying the benefits of society while evading the costs – are likely to have higher fitness than co-operators (Axelrod & Hamilton 1981; Trivers 1971). Attempts to solve this problem by modelling ever-higher benefits from co-operation are self-defeating: the greater the benefits, the greater the gains made by any free-loader who can still reap these while avoiding the costs. Neither can it be objected that lying and cheating, in undermining co-operation, would threaten the extinction of whole groups. Evolution is blind and individualistic. If individual genetic fitness is best pursued through such strategies, selfishness is to be expected regardless of negative consequences at the population level.

3 How animal signals evolve

Politics and power relations are inevitably involved in communication. Krebs & Dawkins (1984) broke new ground by abandoning assumptions about truthfulness and defining animal communication as the means by which one individual, the actor, exploits the muscle power of another, the reactor. Where animals have conflicting interests, they will seek to exploit and deceive rather than share good information, prompting receivers to develop corresponding 'sales resistance'. As conflict intensifies, signals become restricted to displays of fighting or other competitive ability. Such signals are uninformative except in one narrow respect: they reveal the signaller's ability to meet the costs of the display. The more discernibly costly the signal, the more impressive it is (Zahavi 1987). As receivers incur fitness penalties for being too impressionable, all but the most costly, elaborate, repetitive and 'ritual'-like signals are simply ignored. The dynamic culminates in extravagant advertisements such as peacock displays or the roars of rutting caribou bulls.

Where interests converge, however, this dynamic is set into reverse. Instead of resisting and checking out all incoming signals, receivers can now afford to minimize response times, acting on trust. Signals then evolve to become less repetitive and 'ritualized', more cryptic, quiet and efficient. Signals may now take more effort to detect and decode, but if the information is valuable, receivers should be motivated to invest that effort. This allows signallers to offload costs of communication onto receivers – minimizing redundancy, lowering amplitude and narrowing the range of utilized channels. The outcome is what Krebs & Dawkins call 'conspiratorial whispering'. Social insects communicating within well-defended colonies offer examples of such highly informative 'whispering'.

In the animal world, however, the process of cost-cutting comes up against constraints. Where whole local populations are concerned, interests rarely converge except in relation to a narrow range of challenges such as external threats. Even in this context, any build-up of mutual trust will simultaneously offer scope for cheating. The discrete, species-specific anti-predator alarms of vervet monkeys, for example, are occasionally used deceptively against conspecifics. On hearing an alarm, correspondingly, vervets do not behave as if wholly trusting; they scan the horizon 'as if they were searching for additional cues, both from the source of the alarm call and elsewhere' (Cheney & Seyfarth 1990: 107). Admittedly, vervet alarms are honest by default: they would not work otherwise. But it is precisely where listeners expect reliable signals that they are most vulnerable to being deceived.

In the human case, speech as a low-cost, low-amplitude system meets the specifications of 'conspiratorial whispering', but by the same token it exposes listeners to the most extreme risks. Linguistic signs are related in an 'arbitrary' way to their referents; it is learned convention alone which links a word with its semantic meaning. Such decoupling of signals from emotions and associated real-world stimuli renders listeners highly vulnerable to deception. We would expect 'Machiavellian' strategists to resist signals of this kind, setting up negative selection pressures against their evolution.

A thought-experiment may illustrate the problem. Suppose certain unusually intelligent chimps in a wild population develop a repertoire of volitional vocal signals, each with a conventional meaning. Enterprising animals will soon be using these in tactically deceiving each other (Byrne & Whiten 1985). Emission costs will be low, making even small gains worthwhile, putting pressure on all to deceive where possible. On that basis, ingroup trust will rapidly be exhausted, to the point where no-one is listening any more; the system will now be useless for any purpose, honest or dishonest. Zahavi (1993) concludes that, since potential conflicts of interest exist throughout the animal world, even between close kin, resistance to deception has always selected against conventional signals – with the one puzzling exception of humans.

4 Apes: too clever for words?

The problem, then, is that conventional signals depend on trust, whereas those animals intelligent enough to use such signals will also be clever enough to exploit that trust competitively. This may help explain why, despite their cognitive capacities (cf. Ulbaek, this volume), chimpanzees have no natural use for conventional signals. In particular, it clarifies why, in common with other primates, chimps do not vocalize dispassionately, lacking those capacities for cortical control which appear natural in other contexts such as manual gesticulation (Hayes 1950). Such lack of control should not be seen as maladaptive: at stake is the maintenance of credibility. Chimps, like other primates, need reliable signals on which to base their behaviour. Only to the extent that their vocalizations remain governed by the limbic (emotional) system can listeners trust them as reliable cues to internal states.

Admittedly, apes may volitionally suppress their calls. For example, on discovering food, a chimp may with difficulty conceal its excitement, suppressing the associated food-call and succeeding thereby in keeping all for itself. Still more impressively, a group of chimps may maintain silence for hours while patrolling near a neighbouring band's range. This reflects a group-wide temporary convergence of interests, the suppression of sounds being backed with reprimands (Goodall 1986: 490–491). Once the danger is over and calls can be resumed, however, these are as usual highly emotional. Where calculating manipulation is concerned, the most impressive chimp signals are not their calls but their silences.

For use in deceiving one another, however, primates have resources beyond the purely vocal. In one often-cited incident, an adolescent male baboon was threatened by an approaching group of adults. Instead of running, it stood on its hindlegs and stared into the distance, as if it had noticed a predator. Its pursuers turned to look – and although no danger was present, the distraction enabled the adolescent to escape (Byrne & Whiten 1985). In another incident, a female gorilla, moving with her group, noticed a partly concealed clump of edible vine. Pretending to have seen nothing, she stopped as if to groom herself. As the others moved on, she was able to consume the food undisturbed (Whiten & Byrne (1988: 218), citing Fossey). Now, it is true that tricks of this kind would not work unless most such signals were reliable. But it would be a mistake to conclude that 'primates are usually honest'. The truthful versions of the deceptive signals noted here – genuinely seeing a predator, genuinely stopping to groom oneself – would be examples of *incidentally informative* functional behaviour, not truthful deliberate signalling. The trust exploited by deceivers has nothing to do with expectations of intentional honesty. On the contrary, the cues habitually trusted as sources of information are valued precisely in proportion as their informational content appears *unintentional*.

Humans, unlike chimps, can vocalize dispassionately. This is clearly a key capacity essential to the evolution of a convention-based system of vocal communication. Under what selection pressures did it emerge? We know that it is in deceptive use of signals that cortical control most decisively takes over from the limbic system. The literature on primate tactical deception shows how, in being co-opted for deceptive use, functional routines are in a sense 'displaced' under cortical, volitional control (e.g. Savage-Rumbaugh & McDonald 1988). It is known that, among humans today, lying typically requires more cognitive effort than truth telling (Knapp & Comadena 1979). Machiavellian manipulations were by inference central to the selection pressures driving neocortex evolution and enhanced cortical control over signals among group-living primates, including evolving humans (Byrne & Whiten 1988). But our problem is to explain how, in the human case, vocalizations became cortically controlled without becoming self-evidently manipulative and so resisted.

Although speech is not intrinsically reliable, conversationalists in fact routinely give one another the benefit of any doubt. The philosopher Paul Grice (1969) has identified mutual intentionality as the heart of human linguistic communication. We humans rely not merely on unintended truthfulness in one another's signals: where we are on speaking terms, we expect intentional honesty. It follows that without the establishment among humans of a new kind of honesty as a default – habitual honesty in volitional signalling – speech could not have got off the ground. In the human case, then, precisely the most unreliable kinds of signals – namely, the volitional, intentional ones – must have become adapted for honest use. Somehow, in the course of human evolution, what were once frequency-dependent tactical deceptions must have become increasingly routine while becoming simultaneously harnessed to a reversed social function – the group-wide sharing of good information.

Imagine a population in which volitional signals are becoming commonplace, thanks initially to skills in deception. How can a new honest strategy invade the deceptive one and become evolutionarily stable? An immediate problem is that any increase in the proportion of trusting listeners increases the rewards to a liar, increasing the frequency of lying. Yet until hearers can safely assume honesty, their stance will be *indifference* to volitional signals. Then, even lying will be a waste of time. In other words, there is a threshold of honest use of conventional signals, below which any strategy based on such signalling remains unstable. To achieve stability, the honest strategy has to predominate decisively over deception; yet the evolutionary route to such honesty seems to pass inescapably across a point at which deception is so rampant that trust in volitional signals collapses. How can this conundrum be solved?

There are those (e.g. Konner 1982: 169) who argue that the main function of speech was and remains lying. Such claims may appear persuasive; humans routinely tailor their utterances and the information divulged according to their audience and the effect desired. Yet this view poses as many problems as it solves. Speech is not only a convention-based, radically arbitrary means of communication; it is also (by comparison with primate calls) minimally redundant, low in amplitude and heavily demanding of listeners. Darwinians view these as the tell-tale design-hallmarks of 'conspiratorial whispering' – indicating a system designed for communicating good information to trusting listeners at speed (cf. Krebs & Dawkins 1984).

This implies that speech has been co-operative from its inception. In accounting for the necessary honesty, it is tempting to draw on Darwinian reciprocal altruism theory (Trivers 1971): if you lie to me, I'll never again listen to you – so be honest. But even accepting this, we need to explain why the dynamic did not lead to volitional, conventional signalling among those apes which appear cognitively capable of reciprocal altruism. It would seem that in their case, the logic of tit-for-tat – if you lie to me, then I'll retaliate – perpetuated the equivalent of a financial crash, in which all paper currency is worthless. What stopped this from happening in the human case?

Reciprocal altruism presupposes a local network of communicators known to each other and likely to meet repeatedly over time. In larger, open populations, deceivers could theoretically escape retaliation by exploiting one gullible victim after another, each in a different locality. Our problem is that a human speech-community is not a personal mutual aid network but is typically an extended group transcending the limits of affiliation on the basis of residence, economic co-operation or kinship. Given an initial situation of primate-style Machiavellian competition and manipulation, it is difficult to see how an honest strategy could successfully invade and take over so open a population.

5 Individual versus collective deception

In seeking a solution, we may begin by noting that fictions need not be exploitative – in principle, they may be deployed co-operatively, by a coalition. As we have seen, primates on occasion signal deceptively – such imaginative usage arguably prefiguring 'symbolic' behaviour. But they do so only for selfish, competitive gain. A primate deceptive representation, therefore, is never valued by others; resistance to it prevents the fiction from being collectively perpetuated or elaborated. Symbolic culture, consequently, cannot even begin to emerge.

The key point, then, is that primates do not engage in *collective deception*. Humans by contrast deceive collectively, recurrently establishing group identity in the process. Told by his Dorze (southern Ethiopian) informants a patently unbelievable 'fact' – that the local leopards were devout Christians, for example – the social anthropologist Dan Sperber (1975: 3) suspected 'symbolism'. Sperber found this to be borne out regularly enough to suggest a rule-of-thumb: ' "That's symbolic." Why? Because it's false.' Nigel Barley (1983: 10) glossed Sperber's rule as 'This looks crazy. It must be symbolism.' Note the implication: far from embodying self-evident truth, symbolic culture may be better understood as a world of *patent fictions* held collectively to be true on some deeper level.

Myths, dramatic performances, art and indeed all expressions of human symbolic culture may in this light be understood as 'collusion in deception' (Knight, Power & Watts 1995; Rue 1994) – collaboration in the maintenance of fictions which have social support. Trust in the founding fictions is not given lightly. Durkheim (1965) indeed showed long ago that a community will place ultimate confidence only in those fictions which are emblematic of itself. If all collude, then on another level the deceptive signal may constitute a performative, *constructing* its own truth. Ritual specialists may assume the burden of sustaining such circular 'truths' on which group identity depends (Rappaport 1979). Note, however, that ingroup/outgroup polarity is central here: one group's most sacred truths may be another's transparent deceits. 'Lies', to quote Lattas (1989: 461), 'must be hidden from some and available to others, and as such lies are ordering phenomena, constitutive of groups in their opposition to others.' A symbolic community is always on some level a secret society, its knowledge inseparable from others' ignorance and hence its own power in relation to them.

An ability to handle fictional representations, then, is the essence of human symbolic competence. Distinguishing between surface and deeper meanings poses a major cognitive challenge; involvement in 'pretend-play' during childhood is crucial to the development of the necessary cognitive skills. Pretend-play is the imaginative use of one thing *as if* it were another. One child may take, say, a pencil, and move it through the air like an aeroplane. Despite knowing that the 'plane' is a fiction, the same or another child may *still enjoy the pretence*. This ability to hold in mind both 'true' and 'false' implications, handling them *on different levels*, is central to human mindreading and symbolic competence. A young child who fails to play in this way may be showing early signs of autism or 'mindblindness' (Baron-Cohen 1995). Such a child will prioritize literal truth – insisting, for example, that a pencil is just a pencil. Faced with a playmate's patent fiction, the child shows little inclination to collude.

Effective, creative speech depends on imaginative mindreading skills and hence on collusion in a much wider domain of symbolic behaviour. The concept of *co-operative pretend-play* is central to our current understanding of how children acquire speech (Bates, Bretherton & Snyder 1988; Bruner 1977; Trevarthen 1979); it is equally central to 'speech act' theory (Austin 1978; Searle 1969). Take a seemingly propositional utterance – for example, *There are three bison over the hill.* As a factual statement, this may appear unconnected with performative invocation or communal pretend-play. Yet in reality, a constellation of ritual assumptions and expectations underpins its force. Faced with scepticism, the speaker might preface the statement with an oath: *I swear by the Great Spirit that* . . . This could involve taking a knife and drawing blood. If listeners need no such costly demonstration, such swearing may be abbreviated or left implicit. But in that case, the speaker must already have paid the ritual costs of getting to a position where his or her utterances have such weight.

According to anthropologist Pierre Bourdieu (1991: 107): 'The power of words is nothing other than the delegated power of the spokesperson, and his speech . . . is no more than a testimony, and one among others, of the guarantee of delegation which is vested in him.' The words of some derided 'nobody' have no weight; we may accuse such a person of 'talking through his hat' or 'talking off the top of his head'. Words emanating from such a source lack what Austin (1978) calls 'illocutionary force' – that efficacy which attaches to words when they are accepted as trusted, authorized. If a known liar says 'I promise', it is not just that no-one believes; rather, no promise is in fact made. To promise is to enter into a communally sanctioned contract; one individual cannot do this alone. To 'do things with words' is to *play by the rules of the whole congregation*, as if mandated by 'the gods'; only thus authorized does any utterance work (Bourdieu 1991).

Speech-act theorists (Austin 1978; Grice 1969; Searle 1969, 1983) have established that all effective speech works on this basis. Utterances have force only through collusion with a wider system of ritual or ceremonial. It is this wider system which sustains the communal fictions (gods, spirits, etc.) upon whose authority oaths, promises and comparable declarations depend. The relevant 'morally' authoritative intangibles are products of communal ritual (Durkheim 1965): they are ingroup self-representations, frequently 'misrecognised' (Bourdieu 1991) as other-worldly beings. Deployed to certify statements as reliable, they reflect communal resistance to deception. In the final analysis, people are on speaking terms only with those who 'share the same gods'. The magic of words is the collusion of a ritual ingroup. Withdraw the collusion and nothing happens – the speaker's words are empty sound.

Unlike Machiavellian primates, whose creative fictions prompt countermeasures from those around them, human conversationalists routinely *encourage* that very resort to imaginative story-telling which in primates is socially resisted. Humans reward one another in the currency of status, conferred by listeners in proportion as utterances appear relevant in addressing some shared concern (Dessalles, this volume). Such status-seeking may appear individualistic and competitive (Burling 1986), but we should remember that there are limits to this. Speakers, whatever their differences, must remain in effect co-religionists – those 'in the know' must be trusted to use the discourse for shared purposes, concealing it where necessary from outsiders. Where these conditions are not met, then the relationship of status to relevance may be reversed. When conspiring to rob a bank, for example, the important thing is *not* to divulge the plan to the authorities. Preparations for war, or for a ritual contest against the enemy team, equally demand discretion. Such cases remind us that 'relevance' is defined by a problem shared, and that social boundaries are likely to be decisive. Far from raising one's ingroup status, being relevant to the wrong people will lower it.

A status-conferring ingroup admits members only at a price. Traditionally – as in the case of Aboriginal Australian male secret societies – the initiatory ordeals tend to be bloody and painful (Knight 1991). Willingness to pay the costs displays commitment; in principle, the heavier the costs, the better. Ritual is the one signal which, in being visibly costly, carries its own authentication – requiring no external corroboration because in principle it cannot deceive (Aunger 1995; Rappaport 1979). Ingroup confidence in other signals, such as cheap vocal ones, can now be based on this ultimate 'gold standard'. Effective speakers are those who, having paid the costs, are authorized to act 'in God's name' (Bourdieu 1991). Such authority can at any time be withdrawn. Under such circumstances, only an incompetent Machiavellian would be tempted to lie.

All this is far removed from primate-style 'Machiavellian' politics. Chimpanzees may play, but their playful fictions are not collectively shared. Given such isolation on the imaginative level, intangibles such as 'promises' stand no chance of emerging as publicly available fictional representations – no chimp ever swore on oath. Note, moreover, that for a chimp to freely broadcast relevant information would be maladaptive: opponents would simply take advantage and status would be lost. Chimps, not surprisingly, are as concerned to conceal relevant information as to reveal it. Experts at being poker-faced, they have no interest in having their minds read too easily (De Waal 1982).

6 The origins of ritual

How and why, then, did social life change so dramatically in the human case? Current models (e.g. Dunbar 1993) associate the rapid evolutionary expansion of the hominid brain with increasingly Machiavellian cognitive demands. Darwinian strategies of 'Machiavellian status escalation' – coalitionary resistance against physical or sexual dominance by individuals – may account for the emergence of egalitarian social norms of the kind characteristic of modern human hunter–gatherers. Recall the obsequious sexual and other submission-displays central to the signalling repertoire of the social great apes; these contrast sharply with the 'don't mess with me' norms of human hunter–gatherers. If everyone is king, then no-one is. Hunter–gatherer females as well as males show strong aversion to submission (Knauft 1994: 182). Hunter–gatherer egalitarianism, in this Darwinian perspective, becomes established as the capacities of dominant individuals to exploit subordinates become increasingly matched by group members' 'counterdominance' capacities. Under such conditions, a strategy of 'playing fair' – resisting dominance by others while not attempting dominance oneself – becomes evolutionarily stable (Erdal & Whiten 1994).

A more detailed speculative model (Knight *et al.* 1995; Power & Aiello 1997) locates the emergence of symbolic behaviour in counterdominance strategies driven by the needs of females undergoing reproductive stress as brain-size underwent rapid expansion between 400,000 and 100,000 years ago. Unable to afford monopolization by dominant male philanderers, child-burdened mothers were increasingly driven to meet the costs of encephalization by making use of all available males, mobilizing coalitionary support from male kin in extracting from *out-group* males increasing levels of mating-effort in the form of provisioning.

Kin-coalitions of females, backed by male kin, brought to a head such strategies by periodically refusing sex to all outgroup males except those prepared to hunt at a distance and bring 'home' the meat. Periodic collective withdrawal of sexual access, prompted whenever provisions run low, is conceptualized by Knight (1991) in terms of 'strike'-action.

One way of testing this model is to ask what kinds of signalling behaviour it would predict. Courtship 'ritual' in the animal world is central to a species' mate recognition system; the basic pattern is one in which females signal to prospective male partners: *I am of the same species as you; of the opposite sex; and it is my fertile time.* On this basis, we would predict sexually defiant females to reverse the signals to *Wrong species/sex/time.* This, then, is the predicted signature of 'sex strike'.

On Darwinian grounds, we would not expect such a message to be transmissible in whispers or in code. For human females to indicate *We are males!*, *We are animals!* and *Anyway, we are all menstruating!* is on one level absurd and implausible. The target audience of outgroup males will have no interest in collusion with such a collective fantasy. To overcome listener-resistance, signallers will therefore have to resort to the most explicit, loud and spectacular body-language possible. A costly, multimedia, deceptive display is now being staged by an ingroup to impress and exploit outsiders.

We now have a Darwinian model of the origins of collective deception through symbolic ritual. Although speculative, it is detailed and specific enough to be testable in the light of archaeological and ethnographic symbolic data. An extremely conservative level of cultural tradition is that of magico-religious symbolism. Southern African archaeologists widely agree that significant continuities in San hunter-gatherer material culture extend back about 25,000 years – the duration of the Later Stone Age (Knight *et al.* 1995). Checking the model's predictions against the data on ritual, we find that during the 'Eland Bull Dance' of the Kalahari San, held to celebrate a girl's first menstruation, women motivate males to hunt by defiantly signalling 'maleness' and 'animality'. Specifically, women signal *We are Eland!* This explains why linguistic reference to this antelope embraces meanings which include 'people', 'dance', 'fertility', 'gender-ambivalence' and 'menstruating maiden' (Lewis-Williams 1981; Power & Watts 1997). The 'Eland Bull' of Kalahari discourse is not a perceptible entity but a morally authoritative construct – a 'Totem' or 'God'. The gender-ambivalent, woman-loving 'Rainbow Snake' of Australian Aboriginal tradition equally matches the model's 'wrong sex/wrong species' predictions, as do representations of ritual potency/divinity cross-culturally (Knight 1991, 1996, 1997).

Ritual maintenance of such paradoxical constructs requires elaborate communal pretend-play. Imagine a group of outgroup males faced with a performance such as the 'Eland Bull' dance. The women's ritual identification with this animal of male gender will appear to them implausible – yet unanswerable in being forcibly asserted. Dancers are here asserting counterreality through counterdominance – a strategy of sexual resistance. Challenges would amount to harassment. But while the audience must neither probe nor question, literal belief is equally impossible. Consequently, 'mindreading' takes over; belief is displaced to another level. Behind the vivid, dramatic lies, listeners are invited to discern a simple idea: 'No' means 'No'. On this 'metaphorical' level, the message indicated by the dancers is certain truth.

Communal self-defence is now inseparable from maintenance of the founding ingroup fiction (cf. Hartung 1995). Such defiance/defence might logically be expected to generate intense and diffuse internal solidarity, including the extension of each coalition to embrace 'brothers' and 'sisters' across the landscape (for hunter–gatherer patterns of 'fictional kinship' interpreted in this light, see Knight (1991)).

7 The origins of speech

If we are to understand the origins of speech, it is essential to understand first the factors obstructing its evolution in other species. 'Machiavellian' primate politics, we have seen, prompts mistrustful listeners to resist all signals except those whose veracity can be instantly and directly corroborated. This immediately excludes (a) volitional conventional signals; (b) displaced reference; (c) signals literally false but metaphorically true; (d) signals meaningful not in themselves, but only in combinatorial contexts. Primate-style resistance to deception, in other words, obstructs the emergence of the characteristics of speech not just on certain fronts but on all fronts simultaneously.

Suppose that whenever I opened my mouth to begin speaking, I found myself instantly challenged, my audience demanding on-the-spot corroboration of the very first sounds, refusing to listen further until satisfied. Denied the chance to express one transparent fiction, modify it by another, modify that in turn and so on, I could hardly display any skills I might have for handling such sequences. Faced with refusal to suspend disbelief even momentarily, I could hardly venture to refer to phenomena beyond the current context of 'here-and-now' perceptible reality. How could I express a fantasy, elaborate a narrative or specify with precision a complex thought, if listeners demanded literal corroboration of each signal as I emitted it, refusing to wait until the end before deciding on a response? Finally, it is difficult to see how my utterance could display duality of patterning if listeners demanded literal veracity on the syllable-by-syllable level, obscuring and resisting the possibilities of meaning or patterning on any higher level.

My freedom to speak presupposes that you, the listener, are trusting enough to offer me, at least initially, the benefit of any doubt, demanding and expecting more information before checking out what I have signalled so far. I need you to be willing to internalize literal fictions, evaluating meanings not instantaneously, item by item, but only as I construct larger patterns on a higher, 'combinatorial' level (cf. Studdert-Kennedy, this volume). By primate standards, such collusion with my deceits would appear disastrously maladaptive. Why place reliance on transparent fictions? Under the conditions of ordinary primate 'Machiavellian' politics, the fitness costs of such cognitive surrender would far outweigh any benefits.

Mistrust, then, sets up – simultaneously and on all fronts – selection pressures obstructing the emergence of speech. An intriguing corollary worth exploring is that by the same token, if sufficiently intense ingroup trust could be generated, it would set up reversed selection pressures simultaneously on all fronts, 'unpacking' speech-performance *on the basis of capacities already evolved.*

Such a model would allow us to break with the tradition in which language appears as a bundle of separate components or features, each requiring its own evolutionary explanation. We could instead treat metaphor (Lakoff & Johnson 1980), displaced reference, duality of patterning (both in Hockett (1960)) and syntax (Chomsky 1965) as logically interrelated. Moreover, we could discern a connection with symbolic behaviour more generally, reconceptualizing reliance on speech as a modality of 'faith' – reliance on second-hand information, based on faith in the signalling intentions of others.

We may now begin putting all this together. As modelled in the previous section, imagine a broad, stable coalition of females allied to male kin, targeting deceptive sexual signals at outsiders for the purpose of exploiting their muscle-power. The loud, repetitive signals are patent fictions. Not only do they fail to match reality – they systematically reverse it, point by point. But if all are deploying the same fictions, and if this signalling is *internally* co-operative, then between group members there is no reason to expect resistance. Those colluding in emitting the fictions now have an opportunity to understand one another 'through' them. When deployed internally, moreover, pretend-play routines may be abbreviated and conventionalized. Shorthand portions of pretend-play will now act as referents, not directly to anything in the external world, but to recurrent representations within the domain of pretend-play held in common. 'Displaced' reference – reference to points in a domain of communal imagination – has now come into being. Note that the condition of this was the emergence, thanks to sexual counter-dominance, of a shared domain of reality-defying deception/fantasy in the first place. In what follows, I address some problems in evolutionary linguistics which this approach may help to explain.

7.1 *Conventionalization*

Speech – if this model is accepted – is a special case of 'conspiratorial whispering'. In communicating within an already-established ritual ingroup, there is no need to waste time or energy. There will be minimal resistance to signals, hence no need to repeat, amplify or display. Signallers can abbreviate their pretend-play routines – which, before long, will be so cryptic and conventionalized as to have become, to an outsider, unrecognizable. Convention alone will now link the shorthand gesture to its referent. We need not postulate conscious decision-making to arrive at such 'arbitrary' agreements. Instead, given sufficient ingroup trust, a tendency for all signals to begin as 'song-and-dance' and gradually to become conventionalized will be an inevitable, automatic and continuous process (cf. Heine, Claudi & Hünnemeyer 1991; Klima & Bellugi 1979).

7.2 *Metaphor*

Metaphor – a kind of pretend-play – is central to linguistic creativity and renewal. A metaphor 'is, literally, a false statement' (Davidson 1979). React on a literal level, and the signaller will be rebuffed, denied the freedom to 'lie'. By contrast, where listeners are willing to mindread *through* such fictions, metaphorical usage will flower. Metaphor counters a process of decay intrinsic to conventionalization. As pretend-play sequences get abbreviated and routinized, so listeners become habituated to them, processing them quickly and almost unthinkingly, the whole mind hardly engaged. This does not matter where purely digital, on/off indications of case, tense or other grammatical properties are concerned: all will have standardized, stereotypical 'concepts' on this purely grammatical level, making it immaterial whether communication fully engages the imagination. Conventionalization on this level becomes in fact the secret of speech's astonishing efficiency. Yet genuine, novel human thoughts arise from the whole mind, and, to communicate these, we correspondingly need to engage the imagination of listeners. To this end, speakers counteract conventionalization, exploring the domain of ritual fantasy in search of fresh and dramatic fictions which can be applied in novel contexts. Metaphors are such fictions. Being literally false, they demand full cognitive involvement on the part of listeners if they are not to be mistaken for deceits.

7.3 *Tense/case markers*

Pressures to develop markers indicating tense, case and other such properties will now be felt. Note that primates are under no such pressure. Embedded in the currently perceptible world, their gestures and calls allow listeners to gain all the supplementary information they need simply by checking out the perceptible context of each signal. Metaphorical fictions such as Gods, Unicorns or Eland Bulls have no existence in space or time; listeners wishing to check out the propositional value of any such symbolic usage will therefore need further information. Pressure to connect back to some verifiable position in space/time will drive signallers to find new metaphors capable of specifying such relationships.

7.4 *Grammaticalization*

As the more costly ('ritualized') dimensions of the pretend-play domain become set aside for use against outsiders, the remaining signals – reserved for ingroup use – therefore come under novel selection pressures. Grammatical markers have been shown to be metaphorical expressions which, through a process of long-term linguistic change, have become habitual, abbreviated and formalized. If self-expression through metaphor were blocked – if listeners resisted such fictions instead of exploring the co-operative intentions 'behind' them – grammar could not even begin to evolve. The initial raw material for construction of a linguistic form is recurrently an imaginative and dramatic metaphor, potent in proportion as it is 'displaced' – uprooted from its original setting and reinserted into a novel, unexpected context. All the morphemes comprising a natural language, including even grammatical items such as prefixes or suffixes marking tense or case, were originally just such imaginative fictions. But in being conventionally accepted and circulated, each has become gradually transformed into an increasingly cryptic signal conveying a more and more well-worn, conventional message (Heine *et al.* 1991; Kuryłowicz 1975).

7.5 *Productivity/generativity*

While ritual signals are one-way – targeted repetitively, stereotypically and insistently at the outgroup – ingroup communication is intrinsically two-way, with contradiction, questioning and qualification inevitable. With signallers pressed to reveal the contents of their minds, any single pretend-play routine is likely to be deemed insufficient; listeners will demand one such abbreviated signal followed by another and then another, each narrowing the range of possible interpretations. As conventionalization proceeds, each lower-level fictional representation will now be noted and *rapidly processed* not for its intrinsic value but only as a cue to a higher, combinatorial level of meaning. Signallers are now under pressure to develop skills in assembling uniquely relevant sequences from discrete, recyclable lower-level components (cf. Studdert-Kennedy, this volume). From phonology to syntax, all levels in the emergent hierarchy coevolve.

7.6 *Status-for-relevance*

To the extent that dual loyalties, conflicts and suspicions no longer characterize *ingroup* relations, listeners are now in a position to trust *all insiders* who might potentially offer relevant information, conferring status accordingly (cf. Dessalles, this volume). Note that a *ritually organized* group may far exceed the size of a kin group or personal mutual aid network.

7.7 *Performative force*

Words are cheap, making it difficult to understand why they were ever taken seriously. The solution here suggested is that words evolved not in isolation but as part of a system. Ingroup solidarity at outgroup expense was demonstrated through costly ritual display, targeted against outsiders.

Ritual performance, in conferring authority on participants, then gave weight to those cheap vocal shorthands which members of each ingroup – having paid their admission-costs – could now safely use among themselves.

7.8 *Vocal–auditory reliance*

Within each ritual coalition, 'conspiracy' presupposes not only the trusting, group-wide divulging of relevant information but equally its concealment from outsiders. A 'mimetic' language of dance or gesture, besides being slow and costly, is vulnerable to eavesdropping: it broadcasts information, but is poorly designed for selectively concealing it. Being in conspiratorial contexts a handicap, self-explanatory gesture is therefore rapidly phased out in favour of reliance on cheap, conventionalized vocal signals permitting exclusion of outsiders through frequent switching of codes (cf. Englefield 1977: 123). The primary ingroup communication system is now fully conventional and one-sidedly vocal–auditory.

7.9 *Syntactical competence*

Within each ritual ingroup, vocal mini-routines, in being abbreviated and deprived of their former gestural/mimetic medium, assume novel form. With all former pretend-play linkages removed, linear sequences of conventional vocal signals must now bear the full syntactic load. Note that there is nothing specifically vocal about the neural linkages or skills involved: deaf children of hearing parents, *deprived of a vocal medium within which to embed and link their gestures*, are in a comparable way forced to invent *de novo* a discrete–combinatorial language out of manual signs (Goldin-Meadow 1993). No sudden genetic reorganization of the brain is required to introduce such novel complexity. For the human mind *as already evolved* to switch over to the new system, just one new operational principle may suffice (cf. Berwick, this volume). And now, as signal is placed after signal and fiction set recursively within fiction, 'syntactical complexity' – previously a property of mindreading (Worden, this volume) and communication through mimetic gesture (Armstrong, Stokoe & Wilcox 1994; Donald 1991, this volume) – floods into the vocal–auditory channel. Signallers must now use a linear stream of coded vocal shorthands to recursively embed fictions whose mutual relationships remain represented in the mind as bodily gestures (cf. Johnson 1987). Exapting neurophysiological capacities for handling a system of calls still heavily embedded in gesture, syntactical speech explosively evolves.

8 Conclusion: the 'human revolution'

Bickerton (1990, this volume) posits that speech emerged in an evolutionary quantum-jump. Archaic humans possessed 'protolanguage' – a vocal system with a substantial lexicon but lacking syntax. Vocal signs were strung together like beads on a string, in the absence of any systematic ordering principles. Then, with the emergence of anatomically modern humans, syntax appeared, caused by a genetic mutation which abruptly re-wired the brain.

In this chapter's contrasting scenario, something prefiguring 'syntax' has long been present, but not initially as a way of ordering combinatorial sequences of conventionalized, abbreviated vocal mini-routines. Pre-modern humans in this model are heavily involved in communal pretend-play or 'mimesis' – fantasy-sharing representational activity such as mime, song and dance (cf. Donald 1991); this drives selection pressures for subtle volitional control over emotionally expressive vocalizations and linked gestural representations. At this stage, generativity based on discrete/particulate structure is held back, because signallers must still combine conventional call with emotionally expressive, costly display in each signalling episode, in this respect maintaining continuity with primate 'gesture-call' systems (cf. Burling 1993).

Coalition-members during this evolutionary period have shared interests, allowing them to arrive at cost-cutting shorthands in representing food-items, predators and other things. But there is as yet no polarized binary/digital ingroup/outgroup dynamic structuring relationships across the landscape (cf. Knight 1991: 301–304). Instead, kinship-based coalitions and mutual aid networks cross-cut and overlap, with much dual membership, conflicting loyalties and hence internal flux and instability. In this context, it remains as important to withhold relevant information as to divulge it. Almost any listener is potentially a rival, even when currently an ally, blocking the emergence of a group-wide, trust-based, purely conventional system. Signallers continue to rely on their primate-derived 'hard-to-fake' signals for cajoling, seducing, threatening and so on, such emotionally convincing body-language still retaining primacy over any shared code. An element of 'song-and-dance' therefore remains central to all communication, anchoring and connecting low-cost shorthands or abbreviations in a matrix of more costly gesture – and thereby blocking the emergence of syntax/grammar as an 'autonomous' domain. There is 'syntax', but only in the sense that there is hierarchical, recursive embedding of one pretend-play fiction within another. The hierarchical ordering central to syntax has yet to become mapped onto a *purely conventional* linear sequence of signals. Instead, as with modern children in the pregrammatical stage (Zinober & Martlew 1986), pretend-play based largely on gesture still carries the syntactic load, with any conventionalized vocalizations acting as accompaniments.

The human symbolic revolution (Knight *et al.* 1995) begins to get under way from about 130,000 years ago. At this point, coalitions at last become universalistic, stable and bounded through balanced opposition, each constructing, through communal pretend-play, a shared self-representation – *'the Eland Bull', 'the Rainbow Snake', 'the Totem'*. This morally authoritative enactment – in essence 'wrong sex/species/time' – now functions as the overarching sacred 'Word' (cf. Rappaport 1979), authenticating all lower-order semantic meanings and associated vocal markers. It is in this novel social and ritual context that syntactical speech emerges.

A simple ingroup/outgroup model of this kind has one major advantage. We need no longer suppose that humans evolved to become anomalously honest. Humans are dishonest, exploitative and manipulative – in many respects especially so. But this model allows us to see how a profound coalitionary restructuring could have redistributed honesty and dishonesty, co-operation and competition, such that symbolic culture was the result.

Acknowledgments

I am grateful to Catherine Arthur, Dan Nettle, Camilla Power, Robbins Burling, Adam Kendon, Jim Hurford, Jean-Louis Dessalles and Michael Studdert-Kennedy for critical comments and discussion.

References

Armstrong, D. F., Stokoe, W. C. & Wilcox, S. E. (1994). Signs of the origin of syntax. *Current Anthropology*, 35, 349–368.

Aunger, R. (1995). Are food avoidances maladaptive in the Ituri Fortest, Zaire? *Journal of Anthropological Research*, 50, 277–310.

Austin, J. L. (1978). *How to Do Things with Words*. Oxford: Oxford University Press.

Axelrod, R. & Hamilton, W. D. (1981). The evolution of cooperation. *Science*, 211, 1390–1396.

Barley, N. (1983). *Symbolic Structures. An Exploration of the Culture of the Dowayos*. Cambridge: Cambridge University Press.

Baron-Cohen, S. (1995). *Mindblindness. An Essay on Autism and Theory of Mind*. Cambridge, MA: MIT Press.

Bates, E., Bretherton, I., & Snyder, L. (1988). *From First Words to Grammar. Individual Differences and Dissociable Mechanisms*. Cambridge: Cambridge University Press.

Bickerton, D. (1990). *Language and Species*. Chicago and London: University of Chicago Press.

Bourdieu, P. (1991). *Language and Symbolic Power*. Cambridge: Polity Press.

Bruner, J. S. (1977). Early social interaction and language development. In Schaffer, H. R. (ed.) *Studies in Mother–Child Interaction*. London: Academic Press.

Burling, R. (1986). The selective advantage of complex language. *Ethology and Sociobiology*, 7, 1–16.

(1993). Primate calls, human language, and nonverbal communication. *Current Anthropology*, 34, 25–53.

Byrne, R. & Whiten, A. (1985). Tactical deception of familiar individuals in baboons. *Animal Behaviour*, 33, 669–673.

(eds.) (1988). *Machiavellian Intelligence. Social Expertise and the Evolution of Intellect in Monkeys, Apes, and Humans*. Oxford: Clarendon Press.

Chase, P. G. (1994). On symbols and the palaeolithic. *Current Anthropology*, 35, 627–629.

Cheney, D. L. & Seyfarth, R. M. (1990). *How Monkeys See the World: Inside the Mind of Another Species*. Chicago: University of Chicago Press.

Chomsky, N. (1965). *Aspects of the Theory of Syntax*. Cambridge, MA: MIT Press.

Davidson, R. D. (1979). What metaphors mean. In Sacks, S. (ed.) *On Metaphor*. Chicago: University of Chicago Press: 29–45.

Dawkins, R. (1976). *The Selfish Gene*. Oxford: Oxford University Press.

De Waal, F. B. M. (1982). *Chimpanzee Politics: Power and Sex among Apes*. London: Cape.

Donald, M. (1991). *Origins of Modern Mind: Three Stages in the Evolution of Culture and Cognition*. Cambridge, MA: Harvard University Press.

Dunbar, R. I. M. (1993). Coevolution of neocortical size, group size and language in humans. *Behavioral & Brain Sciences*, 16, 681–735.

Durkheim, E. (1965). *The Elementary Forms of Religious Life*. New York: Free Press.

Englefield, F. R. H. (1977). *Language: Its Origin and its Relation to Thought*. Edited by G. A. Wells & D. R. Oppenheimer. London: Pemberton.

Erdal, D. & Whiten, A. (1994). On human egalitarianism: an evolutionary product of Machiavellian status escalation? *Current Anthropology*, 35(2), 175–183.

Goldin-Meadow, S. (1993). When does gesture become language? A study of gesture used as a primary communication system by deaf children of hearing parents. In Gibson, K. R. & Ingold, T. (eds.) *Tools, Language and Cognition in Human Evolution*. Cambridge: Cambridge University Press: 63–85.

Goodall, J. (1986). *The Chimpanzees of Gombe. Patterns of Behavior*. Cambridge, MA, and London: Belknap Press of Harvard University Press.
Grice, H. P. (1969). Utterer's meanings and intentions. *Philosophical Review*, 78, 147–177.
(1975). Logic and conversation. In Cole, P. & Morgan, J. L. (eds.) *Syntax and Semantics*, vol. III, *Speech Acts*. New York: Academic, pp. 41–58.
Hamilton, W. D. (1964). The genetical evolution of social behaviour. *Journal of Theoretical Biology*, 7, 1–16, 17–52.
Hartung, J. (1995). Love thy neighbour. The evolution of in-group morality. *Skeptic*, 3(4), 86–99.
Hayes, K. J. (1950). Vocalization and speech in chimpanzees. *American Psychologist*, 5, 275–276.
Heine, B., Claudi, U. & Hünnemeyer, F. (1991). *Grammaticalization. A Conceptual Framework*. Chicago and London: University of Chicago Press.
Hockett, C. F. (1960). The origin of speech. *Scientific American*, 203(3), 89–96.
Hurford, J. R. (1989). Biological evolution of the Saussurean sign as a component of the language acquisition device. *Lingua*, 77, 187–222.
(1992). An approach to the phylogeny of the language faculty. In Hawkins, J. A. & Gell-Mann, M. (eds.) *The Evolution of Human Languages*. Reading, MA: Addison-Wesley: 273–303.
Johnson, M. (1987). *The Body in the Mind. The Bodily Basis of Meaning, Imagination, and Reason*. Chicago and London: University of Chicago Press.
Klima, E. S. & Bellugi, U. (1979). *The Signs of Language*. Cambridge, MA: Harvard University Press.
Knapp, M. L. & Comadena, M. E. (1979). Telling it like it isn't: a review of theory and research on deceptive communications. *Human Communication Research*, 5, 270–285.
Knauft, B. (1994). Comment on: On human egalitarianism: an evolutionary product of Machiavellian status escalation? by David Erdal and Andrew Whiten. *Current Anthropology*, 35(2), 181–182.
Knight, C. (1991). *Blood Relations: Menstruation and the Origins of Culture*. London and New Haven: Yale University Press.
(1996). Darwinism and collective representations. In Steele, J. & Shennan, S. (eds.) *The Archaeology of Human Ancestry. Power, Sex and Tradition*. London and New York: Routledge: 331–346.
(1997). The wives of the sun and moon. *Journal of the Royal Anthropological Institute* (n.s.), 3, 133–153.
Power, C. & Watts, I. (1995). The human symbolic revolution: a Darwinian account. *Cambridge Archaeological Journal*, 5(1), 75–114.
Konner, M. (1982). *The Tangled Wing: Biological Constraints on the Human Spirit*. Harmondsworth: Penguin.
Krebs, J. R. & Dawkins, R. (1984). Animal signals: mind-reading and manipulation. In Krebs, J. R. & Davies, N. B. (eds.) *Behavioural Ecology: An Evolutionary Approach*. (2nd edition) Oxford: Blackwell Scientific Publications: 380–402.
Kuryłowicz, J. (1975). The evolution of grammatical categories. In *Esquisses linguistiques II*. Munich: Fink: 38–54.

Lakoff, G. & Johnson, M. (1980). *Metaphors We Live By*. Chicago: University of Chicago Press.

Lattas, A. (1989). Trickery and sacrifice: Tambarans and the appropriation of female reproductive powers in male initiation ceremonies in west New Britain. *Man* (n.s.), 24, 451–469.

Lewis-Williams, J. D. (1981). *Believing and Seeing. Symbolic Meanings in Southern San Rock Paintings*. London: Academic Press.

Maynard Smith, J. & Szathmáry, E. (1995). *The Major Transitions in Evolution*. Oxford: W. H. Freeman.

Pinker, S. & Bloom, P. (1990). Natural language and natural selection. *Behavioral and Brain Sciences*, 13, 707–784.

Power, C. & Aiello, L. (1997). Female proto-symbolic strategies. In Hager, L. D. (ed.) *Women in Human Evolution*. New York and London: Routledge: 153–171.

& Watts, I. (1997). The woman with the zebra's penis. *Journal of the Royal Anthropological Institute*, 3, 1.

Rappaport, R. A. (1979). *Ecology, Meaning, and Religion*. Berkeley, CA: North Atlantic Books.

Rue, L. (1994). *By the Grace of Guile: The Role of Deception in Natural History and Human Affairs*. New York and Oxford: Oxford University Press.

Savage-Rumbaugh, E. S. & McDonald, K. (1988). Deception and social manipulation in symbol-using apes. In Byrne & Whiten (1988): 224–237.

Searle, J. R. (1969). *Speech Acts: An Essay in the Philosophy of Language*. Cambridge: Cambridge University Press.

(1983). *Intentionality*. Cambridge: Cambridge University Press.

Sperber, D. (1975). *Rethinking Symbolism*. Cambridge: Cambridge University Press.

Steele, J. & Shennan, S. (eds.) (1996). *The Archaeology of Human Ancestry: Power, Sex and Tradition*. London: Routledge.

Trevarthen, C. (1979). Communication and co-operation in early infancy: a description of primary intersubjectivity. In Bullowa, M. (ed.) *Before Speech*. Cambridge: Cambridge University Press.

Trivers, R. L. (1971). The evolution of reciprocal altruism. *Quarterly Review of Biology*, 46, 35–57.

(1985). *Social Evolution*. Menlo Park, CA: Benjamin/Cummings.

Whiten, A. & Byrne, R. (1988). The manipulation of attention in primate tactical deception. In Byrne & Whiten (1988).

Zahavi, A. (1987). The theory of signal selection and some of its implications. In Delfino, V. P. (ed.) *International Symposium of Biological Evolution*. Bari: Adriatic Editrice: 305–327.

(1993). The fallacy of conventional signalling. *Philosophical Transactions of the Royal Society of London*, 340, 227–230.

Zinober, B. & Martlew, M. (1986). The development of communicative gestures. In Barrett, M. (ed.) *Children's Single-Word Speech*. Chichester: Wiley: 183–215.

6 Theory of mind and the evolution of language

ROBIN DUNBAR

1 Introduction

While language and its processes have attracted considerable interest from both linguists (with a primary interest in its intrinsic structures) and psychologists (with interests in how languages are learned and how speech is perceived), questions about the function of language and its evolutionary origins have largely been ignored. This has probably been inevitable given the limited information available, but it is ultimately necessary that such questions should be asked. Failure to do so is the equivalent of describing in minute detail the mechanical structures of a motorcar, but refusing to ask either how cars came to be there or what they are used for. If we do not understand why we possess a trait (particularly one that appears to be all but unique to our species), we will never fully understand either its properties or its failures in individual cases.

Biologists have long been used to distinguishing four different kinds of questions that are now widely identified as *Tinbergen's Four 'Whys'* (Tinbergen 1963). These refer to questions about *function* (purpose), *mechanisms* (the machinery), *ontogeny* (development) and *phylogeny* (evolutionary history). These four kinds of questions are logically independent of each other, but all need ultimately to be addressed if we are to claim that we have understood a phenomenon properly. Functional questions are particularly important in this respect, because they lead us to an understanding of just why traits exist. However, functional questions are probably among the most difficult to deal with. Indeed, function is particularly difficult to identify when only a single species possesses the trait, as is the case with language. Nonetheless, considerable in-roads can be made into these kinds of questions without having to resort to 'just-so story-telling'.

In this chapter, I shall try to address some of these issues. One crucial concern will be to identify the functional origins of language in humans. Another will be the relationship between language and the phenomenon now known as 'theory of mind' (one of many elements in the mechanisms category). A third will be the evolutionary history of language: when did language first appear in the hominid lineage? My intention is not to give a full account in each case (these can be found elsewhere: for overviews, see Dunbar (1996, in press)), but rather to draw attention to the kinds of questions that we need to ask and to the kinds of answers that these questions require.

2 The function of language

Conventional wisdom assumes that language is either an epiphenomenon consequent on the evolution of large brains or that it evolved to facilitate information transfer (for more detailed discussion, see Pinker & Bloom (1990), Pinker (1994)). Moreover, if any scenario is offered at all for the latter selective advantage, it is implicitly of either the 'There-are-bison-down-at-the-lake' or the 'How-to-make-a-tool' variety: in other words, language exists to enable humans to exchange factual information about the external world (the unwritten assumption being that this most often had something to do with hunting or toolmaking, and therefore with male activities).

Biologically speaking, the epiphenomenon argument flies in the face of the fact that brains are extraordinarily expensive organs to evolve and maintain (Aiello, this volume; Aiello & Wheeler 1995). The average human brain weighs about 2% of adult body weight, yet consumes something approaching 20% of the body's total energy intake. Such an exceptionally high energy consumption imposes significant costs on the individual in terms of its time budget and its exposure to predation risk while foraging (when it could be resting in a secluded hide). The sheer cost of maintaining brains acts as a steep gradient against which any selection pressure favouring bigger brains has to push. In the absence of any selection pressure, larger brains will not evolve. Yet primates in general (and humans in particular) have unusually large brains, even by mammalian standards (Jerison 1973). Since brains do not come for free, some very powerful selection pressure is required to make it worth a species' while evolving them. Given this, having any space at all dedicated to language (or speech!) must add measurably to the costs incurred by the individual, and would thus be selected against unless countervailing selection pressures made language advantageous.

The main thrust of most of the recent research in this area has favoured the view that the required force was social, not environmental or technological (Barton 1996; Byrne 1995; Byrne & Whiten 1988; Cheney & Seyfarth 1990; Dunbar 1992, in press; Sawaguchi & Kudo 1990). The need to hold large highly structured groups together has been more important than the need to solve ecological problems. (This does not mean that ecology is not, ultimately, the driving force in evolution: the issue is whether ecology influences brain size *directly* or whether it does so *indirectly* via group size. Biologically speaking, these involve two very different mechanisms.) In response to ecological pressures demanding large groups, species were forced to evolve proportionately larger brains in order to allow large groups to remain stable (for the history of this idea, see the early chapters in Byrne & Whiten 1988). This has given rise to the so-called 'social brain' hypothesis (Barton & Dunbar 1997; Brothers 1990) which emphasizes the claim that the primate brain (at least) is largely a social rather than an ecological tool. This view in turn rests on growing evidence that primates (in particular) are significantly more skilled at solving social problems than they are at solving ecological problems (Cheney & Seyfarth 1990) and that a significant component of these social skills involves what has become known as 'Machiavellian Intelligence' (Byrne & Whiten 1988).

The strongest evidence to support this claim is provided by the finding that social group size correlates very closely with relative neocortex size in primates (Barton 1996; Dunbar 1992, in press). More importantly, a number of other analyses have revealed correlations between neocortex size and (a) frequencies of tactical deception (Byrne 1995), (b) alliance clique size (Kudo, Lowen & Dunbar, submitted) and (c) social skills involved in male–male competition (Pawlowski, Dunbar & Lowen, in press). In contrast, neocortex size does not correlate with a number of ecological variables that are associated with foraging demands (e.g. range size; day journey length; degree of frugivory, extractive foraging skills) (Barton & Purvis 1994; Dunbar 1992, in press).

It seems that this relationship between neocortex size and social group size applies even to humans. A group size of 150 is predicted from human neocortex size on the basis of the primate neocortex-to-group-size relationship and groups of this size appear with monotonous frequency in a variety of contexts in both traditional and modern post-industrial societies, particularly those contexts that involve detailed personal knowledge of other group members (Dunbar 1993a, 1996).

The size of these groups creates an interesting problem. Primates bond their social groups by intensive use of social grooming. Exactly how grooming works to bond relationships within groups remains unclear (though we know that at least part of the process involves the fact that grooming acts to release endogenous opiates, and these opiates act as one of the proximate reinforcers for grooming: Keverne, Martinez & Tuite 1989). The important point in this context is that grooming apparently acts to bond primate social groups. This is evident from the fact that there is a linear relationship between group size and the amount of time devoted to grooming (at least among the Old World monkeys and apes (Dunbar 1991, 1993a)) and that, in species like baboons, social groups that devote less than the amount of time predicted by this relationship to social grooming are unstable and highly likely to fragment and/or undergo fission (Dunbar 1993b). The impact of this effect can even be seen clearly at the level of the individual: female baboons attempt to protect their time investment in social grooming against its erosion by the increased demands for feeding time as their babies grow, giving way only once all other sources of alternative feeding time (principally resting time) have been exhausted (Dunbar & Dunbar 1988).

The relationship between group size and grooming time observed in primates can be used to predict the amount of time that humans would have to devote to grooming if they were to bond effectively the groups of 150 predicted by the size of their neocortex. The answer turns out to be something in excess of 40% of total daytime. This is approximately double the highest amount observed in any wild primate group (20% in one population of gelada (Iwamoto & Dunbar 1983)). Clearly, no species that has to live in the real world can afford to devote so high a proportion of its time to social interaction, unless it is prepared to starve.

Ancestral humans thus faced a dilemma: while increased group size was being demanded by ecological pressures, time budget and energy constraints were preventing them from evolving these large groups. A species in this kind of ecological dilemma has two choices: acquiesce quietly (as it were) in the inevitability of extinction or alter its behaviour (and the anatomical mechanisms that underpin this) in such a way as to resolve the problem. I have suggested that our ancestors adopted the second strategy by evolving language to cut through the Gordian Knot of the time budget constraint (Dunbar 1993a, 1996).

Language was an effective solution for several reasons. First, it allows more efficient use of time because an individual can 'groom' up to three individuals at the same time (Dunbar, Duncan & Nettle 1995). In contrast, social grooming is a strictly dyadic activity: you cannot groom more than one individual at a time. Second, language allows the direct exchange of information that can be used to build and service relationships without the need for direct physical contact. Language can be used for advertising oneself, for courting prospective allies or partners, for acquiring information about the behaviour of prospective or existing partners when these are not physically present. The latter seems to be especially advantageous because all other species are totally dependent on direct personal observation to learn about the behaviour of other group members. In contrast, humans can find out very rapidly about the reliability of an ally or about a friend's good or bad behaviour via third parties (Dunbar, Duncan & Marriott, 1997).

One way to test the suggestion that language enables savings of time would be to show that the amount of time devoted to social interaction is no greater in modern humans than the limiting value of approximately 20% of time found in other primates (and certainly lower than the 40% predicted by the primate regression equations). Data are sparse on this topic, and differences in the way activities are categorized make direct comparisons between studies difficult. Nonetheless, there does seem to be general agreement that the amount of time devoted to social interaction in a wide variety of cultures is rarely more than about 20% of the waking day (Table 6.1). This is particularly clear in the two studies that report conversational or social time directly. Emler (1994) found that his Dundee (Scotland) subjects engaged in about 20 conversations a day on average, each typically of about 10 minutes duration. Thus, about 3.3 hours out of a 16-hour active day (approximately 21%) was spent in conversation (the principal mode of interaction among humans). Grossman (1984) provides time budget data on Kapanara (traditional horticulturalists from New Guinea) which suggest that, on average, 20% of the day is spent in social interaction.

The other studies listed in Table 6.1 all concern traditional societies. Unfortunately, they use activity categorizations that do not always coincide precisely with our present interests; nonetheless, estimates of

Table 6.1 Estimates of time spent interacting during a typical day in different cultures

Society	*Ecomony*	*Activity*	*Hrs/day*	*%**	*Source*
Dundee, Scotland	industrial	conversation	3.3	20.6	Emler (1994)
Kapanara (New Guinea)	horticultural	social interaction	3.1	19.4	Grossman (1984)
Maasai (Tanzania)	pastoralist	leisure	2.8	17.5	Biran (1996)
Central African Republic	agricultural	non-work (leisure, dances, visits)	2.7	16.8	Berio (1984)
Nepal	agricultural	leisure/social	5.2	32.3	Berio (1984)
Ivory Coast, Africa	agricultural	social	1.2	7.2	Berio (1984)
Upper Volta, Africa	agricultural	free time (social, religion, errands)	3.3	23.6	McSweeney (1979)

* Assuming a 16-hr waking day (see, for example, Berio 1984)

'non-work' and 'leisure' time in these studies all produce estimates that, with one exception, lie at or below 20%. The mean social time for the seven studies in the sample is 19.6%. Taken together, these data suggest that humans use the same limited social time as primates, but use it in a more efficient way to reach more individuals (see Dunbar *et al.* 1995).

I suggest, then, that the principal function of language was (and still is!) to enable the exchange of social information ('gossip') in order to facilitate bonding in larger, more dispersed social groups. Additional complementary benefits can, of course, be seen in terms of the ability to monitor and control social cheats (Enquist & Leimar 1993) and the spread of malicious propaganda (Machiavellian behaviour (Byrne & Whiten 1988; Kemmerer 1997)). However, it is worth noting that, important as these are in modern human societies, both of them are explicitly a consequence rather than a cause of large social groups. Social cheats only become a problem because they can hide more effectively in large social groups (Enquist & Leimar 1990). Some mechanism is still needed to hold large groups together long enough for freeriding to become a serious nuisance. It is more parsimonious to argue that language must have evolved as a bonding device first, and then later have acquired its more exploitative properties once the opportunities for exploitation became apparent than to argue that the Machiavellian properties were the driving force.

Exploitation is a centrifugal force in social systems because it imposes a cost on the victims. Groups can only persist in time providing the net benefit to *individual* members is positive. Group living always incurs ecological and physiological costs (Dunbar 1988; Van Schaik 1983) and social exploitation merely exacerbates those costs. If the benefits that derive from group living are less than the gross costs, then individuals will prefer to live alone (or in smaller groups). Machiavellian behaviour must be seen as a consequence of group living and the availability of language rather than their cause.

In the light of at least some responses to this argument (e.g. Aitchison 1996), it is probably worth making clear here that the social gossip theory of language evolution is not in conflict with the general principles of the Machiavellian Intelligence hypothesis of Byrne & Whiten (1988) and never has been. Indeed, the original group-size/brain-size relationship on which the gossip theory was built was designed specifically to test the validity of the Machiavellian Intelligence hypothesis (see Dunbar 1992). The substance of the Machiavellian Intelligence theory is really about social skills, with tactical deception (i.e. true Machiavellianism) being a very clear benchmark of advanced social skills.

Logically, then, the most plausible starting point for the evolution of language is as a bonding device based on the exchange of social information concerning relationships within the social network. This does not exclude the potential importance of advertising as a component. Once such a facility has evolved, it is not difficult to see that it must have provided windows of opportunity for exploitation in promoting and controlling more Machiavellian strategies.

This claim is borne out by the evidence that a very high proportion of natural human conversations (i.e. those between familiars that do not involve formal lectures or exhortations of a political or religious nature) are devoted to social information exchange (who-is-doing-what-with-whom, personal experiences, likes and dislikes, etc.). Both our own studies (Dunbar *et al.*, 1997) and those carried out by other researchers (e.g. Emler 1992, 1994) suggest that around 60–70% of all conversation time is devoted to social matters, in these contexts.

There do, however, appear to be important differences between the sexes in this respect. Although female conversations appear to be primarily concerned with social information exchange, male conversations appear to be far more concerned with advertising and exercises in social dominance (Coates 1993; Tannen 1996). Coates (1994, 1996) has shown, for example, that women's conversations tend to be structured in a more collaborative way, with interlocutors commonly finishing off each other's sentences and often speaking simultaneously without losing the thread of the conversation; in contrast, men's conversations tend to be more formal in their structure with fewer overlapping speech acts and less fluidity. Conversations between females thus seem to be concerned much more with 'getting to know', whereas males' conversations are more competitive and appear to be intended either to acquire or reinforce status (when the interlocutor is another male) or to attract a mate (when the interlocutor is female) (Dunbar *et al.*, 1997; see also Dessalles, this volume).

These differences appear to have a very early ontogeny. Although it has been unfashionable to make such claims, there are in fact marked differences between boys and girls, both in the speed of language acquisition and in linguistic fluency. Girls learn to speak and to understand and use grammar significantly earlier than boys (Hirsh-Pasek & Golinkoff 1996); and, as they develop, their conversations are commonly more intimate and social in orientation. Although boys often form larger social groups than girls do, these groups have a very different character: for boys, a relationship consists of kicking a football across a yard, whereas for girls relationships are a far more cliquish and intimate business with conversations often focused around who did what and why and how the participants felt about it (Savin-Williams 1980).

3 Language and the theory of mind

In this section, I want to argue that, important as grammar is in allowing us to exchange information, it is not necessarily the only important feature of the language system. Cognitive mechanisms such as 'theory of mind' play an equally important role. Let me first begin, however, with some comments about the role of grammar in language.

Grammar is often assumed to be the fundamentally important feature of language that gives it its unique character. In one sense, this must, of course, be true. But in another sense, grammar can be seen as a mere outgrowth of a deeper underlying structure. Grammatical form, in which speech is naturally coded into some kind of subject-verb-object form (though not necessarily in that order), bears so close a resemblance to the natural way of thinking about the world that it is difficult to believe that the two are unconnected. The surface form of individual grammars may vary enormously (i.e. from SVO to OVS or SOV, or from simple to complex word structuring), but the fact remains that an ordered relationship between the actor, the action and the recipient forms a basic deep structure that seems to be universal. The origins of this surely lie in that fact that all mammals (at least) seem universally to form hypotheses about the world that are naturally based on causal relationships (Dickinson 1980; Dunbar 1995). This so-called 'mental models' approach to cognition (Johnson-Laird 1983) implies that animals naturally code the events in the world in what amounts to grammatical form.

There is, I think, an obvious reason for this: the world itself is naturally organized in this way. Things (or organisms) do things to other things (or organisms). Parsing the natural processes of the world in this way is simply the most efficient way of both storing knowledge about events and predicting the world's future states (Johnson-Laird 1983). Preference for SVO or OVS forms may indeed be arbitrary (though even this claim can be doubted (Fenk-Oczlon & Fenk 1985, 1996)), but this does not obviate the fact that deep grammatical structure is derivative of natural ways of parsing the world.

But there is another reason why language should conform to this pattern. Language requires more than the mere coding and deciphering of well-formed grammatical statements. Indeed, as has often been pointed out, many everyday conversations are conspicuous by their lack of grammatical structure (Gumperz 1982). However important formal grammar may be in the precision of information transfer, it is surely the intentionality of speech (in the Gricean sense) that is the most demanding feature for both speaker and listener (Worden, this volume). The latter, in particular, has to make judgments about the significance and meaning of the speaker's utterances (Dessalles, this volume). Metaphorical usage is so intrusive in natural language that the listener's task of deciphering what he hears becomes of overwhelming importance. But the speaker's task (as Sperber & Wilson (1986) have pointed out) is just as exacting, for he/she has to monitor the hearer constantly and adjust the delivery and content of further utterances in the light of the evidence that the hearer has understood the intended message.

The latter, of course, is no novel feat. Even primates engage in this kind of careful monitoring and rapid response to signs of 'message-received-and-misunderstood'. Keverne (1982) offers experimental evidence of this from macaques: females who normally rely on olfactory cues to convey information on their sexual receptiveness will rapidly switch to more direct forms of communication (such as presenting) when males' nasal passages are blocked with wax plugs that deny them access to olfactory communication channels. However, such a practice is probably particularly important for human communication using language because of the added complexity and quantity of information involved. The metaphorical content of many speech acts makes this task especially taxing.

The extent to which we take this facet of language for granted is only brought home to us in those rare cases (e.g. autistic individuals) who fail to manage this task and instead take utterances at face value. Happé (1994) provides a classic example: an autistic adult was once asked by his mother to 'pull the door behind him' when he left the house to join her across the road, so he did just that (after wrenching the door from its hinges).

Autistics highlight the importance of understanding speakers' intentions because they lack the crucial capacity commonly referred to as having a 'theory of mind' (Leslie 1987; Premack & Woodruff 1978). More specifically, a theory of mind is the ability to understand another individual's mental state. This trait appears to be unique to humans, though there is evidence to suggest that great apes may also hover on this crucial threshold (O'Connell 1996; Povinelli, Nelson & Boysen 1993). Without theory of mind, there would be no language in the form we know it. To be sure, there would be communication, and there might even be grammatical communication, but what we would hear would be dull factual statements that provided all the human warmth of a conversation with *Star Trek*'s Mr Spock. There would be no poetry and precious little literature. Indeed, the composition of a modern novel is probably dependent on the possession of at least fourth-order intentionality: the writer intends that the reader understand that one character thinks that another character believes something to be the case. By extension, fifth-order intentionality is required whenever the story concerns the eternal triangle of relationships involving three characters.

The crucial deficit exhibited by autistics is the inability to read another individual's mind, to understand an interlocutor's intentions. Monkeys (and some autistics) get by on a form of bootstrapping: they rely on a careful reading of their partner's behaviour, learning what amounts to clever generalizations about superficial behaviour without necessarily coming to any understanding of the mind-states that underpin that behaviour. Cheney & Seyfarth (1990) have characterized the difference rather neatly in observing that monkeys are very good ethologists (they can learn to read behaviour very well), but they are poor psychologists (they cannot learn to read the underlying mind). Humans (and perhaps great apes) are good psychologists as well as being good ethologists.

The crucial issue here is probably the fact that readings of superficial behaviour leave you open to both misinterpretation and deception. Actions are one step removed from intentions, and thus introduce one more point at which errors of transmission and errors of interpretation can occur (thereby making Machiavellian behaviour possible). Being able to get behind the behavioural façade enables you to second-guess the intentions of the speaker more accurately. (This, incidentally, is perhaps the most compelling evidence to support the claim that language evolved to facilitate and/or handle deception. If so, priority must still go to advertising rather than the detection of cheats. However, I would probably still want to insist that the initial impetus for the evolution of ToM would have been the need to integrate groups effectively, even though this might have involved various psychological tactics like coercion, deception and advertising. There may well have been subsequent runaway selection in favour of the evolution of higher orders of intentionality as a result of Machiavellian behaviour, but, once again, this is a consequence rather than a cause of the evolution of language.)

That theory of mind is a costly facility can be illustrated by two observations. Kinderman, Dunbar & Bentall (in press) carried out an experimental study of theory-of-mind abilities in normal adults. In this study, subjects were presented with a set of stories, some of which had to be understood in terms of theory of mind and others that required simple causal analysis and memory for factual events in embedded causal relationships. We found that subjects performed equally well on both types of task up to fourth-order embeddedness: error rates remained constant at about 5–15%. However, while error rates remained at this level on fifth- and sixth-order embeddedness for physical cause tasks, error rates rose significantly on fifth-order theory of mind tasks to around 60%. A fifth-order theory of mind task requires that you remember that '*A* thinks that *B* thinks that *C* thinks that *D* thinks that *E* thinks something is the case' (or alternatively that '*A* thinks that *B* thinks that *A* thinks that *B* thinks that *A* thinks something is the case'). Clearly, subjects found these kinds of tasks exceedingly difficult to do. Fourth-order intentionality probably represents the limit at which people normally operate in real life; most everyday situations probably do not require much more than second-order intentionality.

The second piece of evidence to suggest that this theory-of-mind ability is very costly in cognitive terms is Worden's simulation model (this volume). In effect, Worden has been able to show that the major cost of evolving language is the computational cost of the theory-of-mind module rather than the cost of the grammar module. This is a particularly important demonstration because it has dramatic implications for our understanding of brain evolution in the human lineage. It implies that language (whatever the value of its emergent properties) was not itself the driving force behind the evolution of the superlarge human brain. This would explain why the key language areas (Broca's, Wernicke's and associated areas) are significantly smaller in volume than those areas associated with social skills and theory-of-mind abilities (the prefrontal cortex).

4 Evolutionary history

The last point I want to touch on concerns the timing of language origins. Aiello & Dunbar (1993) exploited the relationships between neocortex size, group size and grooming time in primates to consider how grooming time requirements would have changed over time among hominids had they been trying to bond their groups using the conventional primate mechanism. We can safely assume that during their earliest apelike phase, the ancestral hominids would have been no different to any other primate and groups would have been bonded using social grooming.

By estimating neocortex ratios from cranial capacity (based on regression equations for living primates, including modern humans), we used the primate equations to predict group size and then grooming time requirement for individual fossil hominid crania. This produces a plot of grooming time that rises exponentially (following the brain volume curve) from initial values for the early australopithecines that are well within the range for modern apes. The curve is steeply bowed, and grooming time requirements do not exceed those observed in living primates until well into the *Homo erectus* phase. The crucial issue here is at what point the grooming time requirement would have been so great as to force the evolution of a more efficient bonding mechanism. We suggest that this must have occurred by 250,000 years ago at the latest, but dates as early as 500,000 years ago are not out of the question. In other words, the evolution of language seems to correspond in time to the emergence of our own species, *Homo sapiens*. Late *H. erectus* might have exhibited language in some recognizable form, but this would have been clearly confined to populations close to the *erectus/sapiens* boundary.

These figures are, of course, subject to considerable margins of error (though not of sufficient magnitude to make language origins significantly earlier or later). However, one point does emerge which is, I think, both robust and important. This is the fact that the general trend is smooth rather than catastrophic. Contrary to the views adopted by many linguists (see Bickerton 1990), there was no Rubicon at which language suddenly appeared, fully formed. Rather, language must have evolved piecemeal as more and more complex layers were added onto the existing primate communication system. The view that language evolved suddenly with no precursors seems to be based on a naïve comparison between what humans, on the one hand, and monkeys and apes, on the other, do now, as though neither taxon had an evolutionary history.

Aiello & Dunbar (1993) argued that the data suggest that vocal grooming-at-a-distance gradually supplemented conventional grooming as time budgets became increasingly constrained by the demands of servicing relationships in ever-larger groups. Eventually, these vocalizations would have become sufficiently complex to take on a life of their own, but at this stage they would have been concerned more directly with the business of bonding. Symbolic language (the language of metaphysics and religion, of science and instruction) would have emerged later as a form of software development (it embodies no new structural or cognitive features not already present in social language), probably at the time of the Upper Palaeolithic Revolution some 50,000 years ago when we see the first unequivocal archaeological evidence for symbolism (including a dramatic improvement in the quality and form of tools, the possible use of ochre for decorative purposes, followed in short order by evidence of deliberate burials, art and non-functional jewellery).

I have deliberately said nothing about why the hominid lineage was obliged to increase its group size. The short answer is that, at the moment, we have no idea. Aiello & Dunbar (1993) offered a number of possibilities, but these are at best speculation until we know more about the forces acting on group size evolution in primates as a whole. Two points should, however, be noted.

First, the fact that we cannot offer an explanation for the evolution of large groups in hominids does not weaken the arguments deployed above for the evolution of language. (Nor does it mean that an explanation does not exist!) It is demonstrably the case that group sizes have increased in modern humans, and that is all that is needed to underpin the argument that language evolved as a bonding device. Language is a consequence not a cause of group size evolution. However, the implications of the relationship between group size and neocortex size (and between these and other aspects of behavioural ecology: see Dunbar 1993b; Williamson, Aiello & Dunbar 1996) is that, Bickerton (1996) notwithstanding, we are now increasingly in a position to say a great deal about group size and social structure in fossil species.

Second, it has been suggested that the causal arrow might be reversed: group sizes became large because brain size increased in order to make language possible (perhaps for technological reasons). Plausible as it is at first sight, this argument begs questions that non-biologists commonly overlook about the costs of evolving particular traits. Everything we have learned from the past three decades of research on primate (and more generally animal) behaviour demonstrates that there are costs to living in groups. Animals do not live in groups merely because they can. The same is true of evolving large brains. The only way in which these three variables can be integrated such that the biological equations balance out is in the order I have suggested: the need to evolve large groups drove brain size upwards, and this in turn eventually required the evolution of language as a more effective bonding device.

5 Conclusions

I have tried to spell out the principal steps required of any explanation for the evolution and function of language. In doing so, I have sketched out the particular explanation that I have been led to by the data, as well as the evidence for this. The explanation I have offered runs counter to most conventional thinking on these issues, outside evolutionary psychology. Two important lessons emerge. One is that the past century of work in cognitive psychology and neuroscience has been directed down the wrong channel: all work in this area assumes that cognitive (and hence brain) function is concerned primarily with dealing with perceptual processing skills, but the social brain hypothesis suggests that our skills in these domains are all by-products of the fact that the (primate) brain evolved to handle day-to-day social problems. The second lesson follows on from this: if our brains evolved to handle social problems, then the same is likely to be true of language. Both the functions of language and its *modus operandi* must be sought in the social rather than the physical world.

These are strong challenges to conventional views. Whether they are right or wrong, all such challenges have the merit of forcing loosely conceived conventional assumptions into conflict with alternative hypotheses. Our understanding of processes like language will grow only by being challenged in this way, but it will do so only providing we resort to empirical testing of competing hypotheses. Armchair speculation has been all too characteristic of debate in this area in the past.

One final point is worth making. Bickerton (1996) has asked how it is that individuals who have not served an apprenticeship studying languages can possibly write authoritatively (or otherwise) on language and its evolution. The short answer is that nothing that linguists study is relevant to any of the questions I have discussed. No doubt non-linguists ought to hesitate before commenting on matters relating to the grammatical structures of languages, but these structures of language are not, in themselves, relevant to questions about the functions of language or its evolution. The function of grammar is to enable complex thoughts to be transmitted efficiently, but the function of language (as an activity) is to facilitate the management of social relationships: in other words, *how* language allows us to convey thoughts is not the same question as *why* conveying thoughts is useful. I am happy to leave grammar to the grammarians, if only because there are more than enough questions of interest to go round.

Acknowledgments

I am particularly grateful to Michael Studdert-Kennedy for his comments on this chapter.

References

Aiello, L. C. & Dunbar, R. I. M. (1993). Neocortex size, group size and the evolution of language. *Current Anthropology*, 34, 184–193.

& Wheeler, P. (1995). The expensive tissue hypothesis. *Current Anthropology*, 36, 199–211.

Aitchison, J. (1996). Creating language at a stroke. *The Times* (28 March), p. 38.

Barton, R. (1996). Neocortex size and behavioural ecology in primates. *Proceedings of the Royal Society, London*, ***B***, 263, 173–177.

& Dunbar, R. I. M. (1997). Evolution of the social brain. In Byrne, R. & Whiten, A. (eds.) *Machiavellian Intelligence*, vol. II. Cambridge: Cambridge University Press: 240–263.

& Purvis, A. (1994). Primate brains and ecology: looking below the surface. In Anderson, J., Theirry, B. & Herrenschmidt, N. (eds.) *Current Primatology: Proceedings of XIVth Congress of the International Primatological Society*. Strasbourg: University of Strasbourg Press: 1–11.

Berio, A.-J. (1984). The analysis of time allocation and activity patterns in nutrition and rural development planning. *Food & Nutrition Bulletin*, 6, 53–68.

Bickerton, D. (1990). *Language and Species*. Chicago: Chicago University Press.

(1996). I chat, thereby I groom. *Nature*, 380, 303.

Biran, A. (1996). Time allocation and domestic work among Maasai women: an evolutionary approach. Ph.D. thesis. University of London.

Brothers, L. (1990). The social brain: a project for integrating primate behaviour and neuropsychology in a new domain. *Concepts in Neuroscience*, 1, 27–51.

Byrne, R. (1995). *The Thinking Ape: Evolutionary Origins of Intelligence*. Oxford: Oxford University Press.

Byrne, R. W. & Whiten, A. (eds.) (1988). *Machiavellian Intelligence. Social Expertise and the Evolution of Intellect in Monkeys, Apes, and Humans*. Oxford: Clarendon Press.
Cheney, D. L. & Seyfarth, R. M. (1990). *How Monkeys See the World: Inside the Mind of Another Species*. Chicago: University of Chicago Press.
Coates, J. (1993). *Men, Women and Language*. New York: Longman.
(1994). No gap, lots of overlap: turn-taking patterns in the talk of women friends. In Graddol, D., Maybin, J. & Stierer, B. (eds.) *Researching Language and Literacy in Social Context*. London: Multilingual Matters: 177–192.
(1996). One-at-a-time: the organisation of men's talk. In Johnson, S. & Meinhoff, L. (eds.) *Discourses of Masculinity*. Oxford: Blackwell.
Dickinson, A. (1980). *Contemporary Animal Learning Theory*. Cambridge: Cambridge University Press.
Dunbar, R. I. M. (1988). *Primate Social Systems*. London: Groom Helm.
(1991). Functional significance of social grooming in primates. *Folia Primatologica*, 57, 121–131.
(1992). Neocortex size as a constraint on group size in primates. *Journal of Human Evolution*, 20, 469–493.
(1993a). Coevolution of neocortical size, group size and language in humans. *Behavioral & Brain Sciences*, 16, 681–735.
(1993b). Time: a hidden constraint on the behavioural ecology of baboons. *Behavioural Ecology & Sociobiology*, 31, 35–49.
(1995). *The Trouble with Science*. London: Faber & Faber.
(1996). *Grooming, Gossip and the Evolution of Language*. London: Faber & Faber.
(in press). The social brain hypothesis. *Evolutionary Anthropology*.
& Dunbar, P. (1988). Maternal time budgets of gelada baboons. *Animal Behaviour*, 36, 970–980.
Duncan, N. & Marriot, A. (1997). Human conversational behaviour. *Human Nature*, 8, 231–246.
Duncan, N. D. C. & Nettle, D. (1995). Size and structure of freely forming conversational groups. *Human Nature*, 6, 67–78.
Ekman, P. (1985). Why lies fail. *Bulletin of the British Psychological Society*, 38 (November), A104.
Emler, N. (1992). The truth about gossip. *Social Psychology Newsletter*, 27, 23–37.
(1994). Gossip, reputation and social adaptation. In Goodman, R. F. & Ben-Ze'ev, A. (eds.) *Good Gossip*. Lawrence: University of Kansas Press: 117–138.
Enquist, M. & Leimar, O. (1993). The evolution of cooperation in mobile organisms. *Animal Behaviour*, 45, 747–757.
Fenk-Oczlon, G. & Fenk, A. (1985). The mean length of propositions is seven plus minus two syllables – but the position of languages within this range is not accidental. In D'Ydewalle, G. (ed.) *Cognition, Information Processing and Motivation*. Amsterdam: Elsevier: 355–359.
(1996). Co-evolution of cognitive functions and natural language. Paper given to 13th Conference of the International Society for Human Ethology, Vienna.
Grossman, S. L. (1984). *Peasants, Subsistence, Ecology and Development*. Princeton, NJ: Princeton University Press.

Gumperz, J. J. (1982). *Discourse Strategies*. Cambridge: Cambridge University Press

Happé, F. (1994). *Autism: An Introduction to Psychological Theory*. London: University College London Press.

Hirsh-Pasek, K. & Golinkoff, R. (1996). *The Origins of Grammar: Evidence from Early Language Comprehension*. Cambridge, MA: MIT Press.

Iwamoto, T. & Dunbar, R. I. M. (1983). Thermoregulation, habitat quality and the behavioural ecology of gelada baboons. *Journal of Animal Ecology*, 52, 357–366.

Jerison, H. (1973). *Evolution of the Brain and Intelligence*. New York: Academic Press.

Johnson-Laird, P. N. (1983). *Mental Models*. Cambridge: Cambridge University Press.

Kemmerer, D. (1997). What about the increasing adaptive value of manipulative language use? *Behavioral & Brain Science*, 19, 546–548.

Keverne, E. B. (1982). Olfaction and the reproductive behaviour of nonhuman primates. In Snowdon, C. T., Brown, C. H. & Petersen, M. R. (eds.) *Primate Communication*. Cambridge: Cambridge University Press: 396–412.

Martinez, N. D. & Tuite, B. (1989). Beta-endorphin concentrations in cerebrospinal fluid of monkeys are influenced by grooming relationships. *Psychoneuroendocrinology*, 14, 155–161.

Kinderman, P., Dunbar, R. & Bentall, R. (in press). Theory of mind deficits and causal attributions. *British Journal of Psychology*.

Kudo, H., Lowen, S. & Dunbar, R. (submitted). Neocortex size as a constraint on grooming clique size in primates. *Behaviour*.

Leslie, A. M. (1987). Pretense and representation: the origins of 'theory of mind'. *Psychological Review*, 94, 412–426.

McSweeney, B. G. (1979). Collection and analysis of data on rural women's time use. *Studies in Family Planning*, 10, 379–383.

O'Connell, S. (1996). Theory of mind in chimpanzees. Ph.D. thesis. University of Liverpool.

Pawlowski, B., Dunbar, R. & Lowen, C. (in press). Neocortex size, social skill and mating success in male primates. *Behaviour*.

Pinker, S. (1994). *The Language Instinct*. New York: Morrow; London: Penguin.

& Bloom, P. (1990). Natural language and natural selection. *Behavioral & Brain Sciences*, 13, 707–784.

Povinelli, D., Nelson, K. E. & Boysen, S. T. (1990). Inferences about guessing and knowing by chimpanzees (*Pan troglodytes*). *Journal of Comparative Psychology*, 104, 203–210.

Premack, D. & Woodruff, G. (1978). Does the chimpanzee have a theory of mind? *Behavioral & Brain Sciences*, 4, 515–526.

Savin-Williams, R. (1980). Dominance in a human adolescent group. *Animal Behaviour*, 25, 400–406.

Sawaguchi, T. & Kudo, H. (1990). Neocortical development and social structure in primates. *Primates*, 31, 283–290.

Sperber, D. & Wilson, D. (1986). *Relevance: Communication and Cognition*. Cambridge, MA: MIT Press.

Tannen, D. (1996). *Talking Nine to Five*. London: Virago.

Tinbergen, N. (1963). On the aims and methods of ethology. *Zeitschrift für Tierpsychologie*, 20, 410–433.

Van Schaik, C. P. (1983). Why are diurnal primates living in groups? *Behaviour*, 87, 120–144.

Williamson, D., Aiello, L. C. & Dunbar, R. I. M. (1996). An assessment of the use of chimpanzees as models for early hominid behavioural ecology. Paper presented at Theoretical Archaeology Group meeting, Liverpool.

7 Old wives' tales: the gossip hypothesis and the reliability of cheap signals

CAMILLA POWER

Language has recently been linked to the evolution of social intelligence (Dunbar 1993, 1996; Worden, this volume). These arguments have the advantage of concretely specifying selection pressures, and hence outlining contexts and conditions required to drive the evolution of speech. They can yield hypotheses which are testable not only through observation of modern human behaviour (e.g. Dunbar, Duncan & Nettle 1995; Dunbar & Spoors 1995), but potentially by using data from the palaeontological, archaeological and ethnographic records (Aiello & Dunbar 1993; cf. Knight 1996: 340–341).

Dunbar's 'grooming and gossip' hypothesis of language origins (1993, 1996; Aiello & Dunbar 1993) proposes initial selection for 'vocal communication' in response to increasing pressure on social time budgets as hominid group sizes increased during the Lower to Middle Pleistocene. Dunbar argues that vocal signals were required to supplement and replace physical grooming as a mechanism of social bonding in increasingly complex groups. Compared with manual grooming, vocalization permitted greater efficiency in maintaining social relationships by reducing the time invested in servicing relationships, since multiple relationships could be serviced simultaneously. This chapter addresses some problems raised by Dunbar's 'grooming and gossip' theory for the origins of speech.

1 Co-evolution of neocortex size, group size and language

For primates, group living brings direct and indirect costs (Dunbar 1988: 113ff.) which at worst can lead to reproductive suppression for subordinate individuals, especially females with their high energetic costs of reproduction. In primate social systems, the main buffer against such high costs is to form coalitions as a mutual defence against excessive harassment (pp. 214ff.). As Dunbar describes it, primate groups persist through a process of constant negotiation, achieving 'a state of dynamic equilibrium in which the forces of dispersion are delicately balanced by the forces of collaboration' (1996: 44). Crucial to this process is the ability to monitor relationships and alliances, a capacity apparently limited by relative neocortex size. The best predictor of group size among primates is the ratio of the volume of the neocortex to the volume of the rest of the brain – the neocortex ratio (Dunbar 1992).

Among primates, social grooming is used to service the coalitionary alliances on which the stability of groups depends. Dunbar (1991) demonstrates a linear relationship between group size and the amount of time given to social grooming each day among primates. Estimates of neocortex ratio derived from measurements of cranial capacity of fossil hominids permit inferences of group size in hominid populations (Aiello & Dunbar 1993). This in turn allows estimates of grooming time required by members of those species. Dunbar argues that when social grooming took up more than 25–30% of overall time budgets, a shift toward a more efficient means of social interaction – vocal grooming – occurred. Aiello & Dunbar (1993) associate this shift with the emergence of *Homo erectus*.

In human evolution we see a complex feedback process, driven ultimately by whatever caused the need for larger groups. Increased social complexity leads to a greater requirement for coalitionary alliances (especially for lower-ranked females), in turn leading to selection for larger-brained individuals, which places increased reproductive stress on females, and further drives the need for coalition formation to alleviate that stress. Given the extremely high cost of producing encephalized offspring, the individuals with the severest difficulty in meeting time and energy budgets would be subordinate females. The corollary of the Dunbar model is that because female hominids experienced most acute stress on social time budgets, they would have come under most pressure to develop more efficient means of servicing their alliances (see 1996: 148ff.).

2 Vocal grooming: the commitment problem

How does manual grooming function to build coalitions among monkeys and apes? 'It is a simple statement of commitment:' notes Dunbar, 'I'd rather be sitting here grooming with you than over there grooming with Alphonse' (1996: 44). Investing 10% of your day grooming someone amounts to an 'impressive declaration of interest and, ultimately, loyalty'. Time spent grooming with one animal is time that cannot be spent with another. Therefore, time spent grooming is a currency, placing a quantifiable value on a relationship. The level of commitment is 'hard to fake' thanks to the high price that has to be paid to establish a relationship; this guards against exploitation by 'freeriders', those who accept benefits without paying costs (see Enquist & Leimar 1993). Cheney and Seyfarth demonstrated the way grooming functioned to elicit reciprocal exchange of social support between unrelated vervets (1990: 68–69). They played back recordings of an individual screaming under attack by another group member. The attentiveness of non-kin to these calls was significantly increased if the listener had been grooming with the caller in the previous two hours. Studies of baboons and gelada have also demonstrated a correlation between the amount of time a pair of animals spends grooming and their willingness to support each other in conflict (Dunbar 1988: 253, for references).

These considerations highlight a problem for the vocal grooming hypothesis. If grooming among primates operates as a 'hard to fake' signal of commitment precisely because of its costliness, then the relative 'cheapness' of vocal grooming undermines its value as an index of commitment. Language may enable modern humans to service three times as many relationships for the same amount of social effort as chimps can with manual grooming (Dunbar 1996: 121); but the very fact that you can chatter to three people at once reduces the indication of commitment to each grooming 'partner' to a third. Vocal grooming as an initial preadaptive stage in language evolution can be seen as merely supplementary to manual grooming, involving one-to-one contact calling. As such it would allow some saving in time budgets if foraging activities can continue while social contact is maintained. But to the extent that it is limited to one-to-one contacts, it can only bring marginal savings to social time budgets as group sizes rise. The vocalizations used in contact-calling at a distance would not be evolving in the direction of the low-amplitude, cortically controlled signals of speech.

The type of vocal grooming that formed the basis for the subsequent development of 'gossip' networks surely involved more socially interactive servicing of several 'groomees' at once. But this greater efficiency of vocal grooming necessarily dilutes the signal of commitment provided by one-to-one grooming. We then need to ask, what is the reinforcing mechanism that makes vocal grooming intrinsically pleasurable? For monkeys and apes, being groomed is extremely nice, stimulating production of the body's natural opiates and inducing mild narcotic effects (Dunbar 1996: 36). To the extent that vocal grooming came to replace physical grooming in *erectus* grade populations, what made being groomed worthwhile? It is possible to imagine similar opiate stimulation arising from emotive vocalizations of 'sing-song' or 'motherese' types, perhaps involving collective or synchronized singing that imparted a sense of security and belonging (see Dunbar (1996: 150) on the emotional quality of gelada contact-calling 'choruses'). Given the loss of affect inseparable from conventionalization, it is harder to understand how the purely conventional, highly encoded signals characteristic of syntactical speech could produce similar effects.

3 Gossip: the reliability problem

The above suggests that in the first place vocal grooming among *Homo erectus* would have resembled singing rather than speech in its modern syntactical form. Aiello & Dunbar (1993) argue that the rapid encephalization of the late Middle Pleistocene, associated with archaic grade *Homo sapiens*, evidences further increases in group size. As predicted mean group size in these archaic populations rose above 130 (1993) – more than twice as large as the largest chimpanzee mean group size at 55 – no single individual could gain first-hand social experience with all other members of the group. The pressures on group cohesion in these circumstances led to a new development in vocal communication, whereby spoken language facilitated exchange of information about third parties. This is the 'gossip' hypothesis of language origins.

Vocal grooming needs to be song-like if it is to provide the reinforcing mechanisms of opiate stimulation that make it pleasurable to be groomed. Gossip offers a different kind of benefit – social information. The sounds used in gossip need not be to the same extent intrinsically pleasurable, provided relevant information is conveyed (cf. Dessalles, this volume). This answers the question of why listeners should bother to listen.

Reciprocal exchange of interesting items of gossip could be a viable means of bonding coalitions if one outstanding problem is solved. This is the issue of reliability. How does the listener know that the information is valuable? By definition, she is not gaining any benefit from listening unless she is acquiring information she would not otherwise acquire. This implies that the information comes from a source outside the present context – the feature of human speech which Hockett (1960) termed 'displaced reference'. If the veracity of a signal cannot be corroborated in the immediate context by the listener, the information has to be taken on trust.

As soon as vocalizations take on a 'gossip' function of exchange of social information, reliability of cheap, 'easy to fake' signals becomes crucial. In the light of 'Machiavellian Intelligence' theory (Byrne & Whiten 1988), we must suppose that situations of conflicting interest would give rise to recurrent manipulative and deceptive use of such 'informative' signals. So, again, why should listeners bother to listen?

If the receiver of the information needs to check up with other witnesses every time she receives a possibly interesting piece of information, the costs of receiving social information are driven upwards, undermining the advantages of gossip for maintaining cohesion in large groups. Alternatively, if honest individuals resort to increasingly costly 'hard to fake' signals to prove their reliability (cf. Zahavi 1977, 1987), this would lead gossip to evolve in the opposite direction from the cheap, highly encoded, cortically controlled signals characteristic of speech. Knight (this volume) argues that speech reveals the design hallmarks of 'conspiratorial whispering'. According to Knight, any evolutionary account of language must explain why the volitional signalling of speech is in general assumed by listeners to be intentionally honest – in direct contravention of the expectations of the Machiavellian Intelligence theory of tactical deception. Why are listeners willing to conspire with and vest trust in those who could easily deceive them?

To sum up the problems for the grooming and gossip hypothesis: to the extent that vocal grooming allows more efficient servicing of coalitionary relationships, it also devalues the worth of grooming as a signal of commitment. Admittedly, vocalization of a musical or rhythmic nature could work as a form of grooming in initial stages. But a linguistic system of gossip can only operate to bond coalitions through exchange of social information if the problem of reliability of cheap signals is solved. The gossip hypothesis fails unless we can posit some means of restoring a costly signal of commitment for establishing coalitionary membership, driving up the costs to any individual who breaks 'faith' with the coalition.

Table 7.1 Social reputation/information exchange

Third-party permutations (Female/Male)	*Items of gossip*
1. F about F to F	*sexual behaviour; reproductive value*
2. F about M to F	*warning about philanderer; warning rival off mate*
3. F about F to M	*slagging off rival; sexual behaviour; reproductive value*
4. F about M to M	*yes, he is/no, he isn't a boyfriend*
5. M about F to F	*yes, she is/no, she isn't a girlfriend*
6. M about M to F	*warning about/slagging off rival*
7. M about F to M	*sexual behaviour; reproductive value; warning rival off mate*
8. M about M to M	*checking up on status/alliances*

4 Contexts for gossip: male and female reproductive strategies

Table 7.1 presents a schematic breakdown of permutations for exchange of information about third parties, differentiated by sex (though not by relatedness of parties). Items of information potentially critical to future reproductive success of parties are indicated. At a glance, we can see how little of such information is likely to be offered dispassionately, and how little could be taken on trust. Given the observation of tactical deception among apes (Byrne 1995; De Waal 1982, 1992), the grounds for conflict of interest and for 'Machiavellian' manipulation of gossip among super-intelligent hominids are evident.

Buss (1994; Buss & Schmitt 1993) argues that in the course of human evolution each sex has evolved strategies for mate acquisition which are 'designed' to solve sex-specific adaptive problems. For males, as they became increasingly drawn into investment in offspring, one crucial problem was securing paternity confidence. Buss suggests (1992: 250) that female sexual 'reputation' would provide males with a very important cue in mate selection. Others such as Deacon (quoted in Caird 1994: 96) advance similar scenarios of the benefits of language use in relation to evolving human reproductive strategies. Males who absented themselves from females for lengthy periods would be able to check up on the sexual behaviour of mates on their return by asking a few questions (permutations 3 and 7 on Table 7.1). It is salutory to dub this the 'Iago' hypothesis of language origins. Only in the case of very close relatedness between gossiping parties could such information be trustworthy. Therefore, this scenario of checking up on female behaviour as reinforcement of paternity confidence implies a model of male kin-bonded groups with female dispersal patterns. Even then, when both parties are males, there is liable to be sufficient conflict of sexual interest to undermine reliable exchange of information.

The view of patrilocality as the ancestral human form of social organization on phylogenetic grounds (cf. Foley & Lee 1989; Wrangham 1987) may be fallacious (see, e.g., Dunbar 1996: 148; Hawkes 1996: 289; Knight, Power & Watts 1995: 105). The argument that because our closest relatives, chimpanzees and bonobos, are male philopatric species, therefore so were our hominid ancestors fails to take account of the unique effects of encephalization on female reproductive strategies. The very rapid phase of encephalization, commencing *c.* 400,000 BP and lasting to the transition to anatomically modern humans (*c.* 130,000 BP), not only indicates increasing social complexity. Selection for encephalized offspring leads to severe increases in overall energetic costs for archaic *Homo sapiens* mothers (Foley & Lee 1991), resulting in changes in life-history parameters such as slowing down infant growth rates to enable mothers to spread their energy costs over time. As noted, since female social time budgets would have been compromised first, it is females who would have been motivated to use more efficient means of social interaction. Following Dunbar, we can infer that gossip was taking place especially in contexts of female coalitions. Besides studies of modern societies which demonstrate a tendency for women to maintain closer links with same-sex kin than men (Dunbar & Spoors 1995), evidence supportive of a matrilocal model emerges from molecular genetics. Among small aboriginal human populations such as East African pygmy groups and Khoisan, the distribution of mtDNA comparative to nucleic DNA shows a pattern of variation consistent with female philopatry (Melnick & Hoelzer 1993; Vigilant, Pennington, Harpending, Kocher & Wilson 1989). This pattern differs notably from the genetic structure consistent with female dispersal found in human groups with a long history of property-holding. Any evolutionary account of menopause based on the fitness benefits of 'grandmothering' (mothers improving the reproductive success of children, see Hill & Hurtado (1991), Mayer (1982), Rogers (1993)) also relies on a model of daughters staying near mothers once they reach reproductive age (Hawkes 1996: 298; Peccei 1995: 432). These lines of evidence strongly suggest that female kin-bonding formed the core of late Middle to early Upper Pleistocene societies, prior to the historic development of resource accumulation and land inheritance.

5 Sexual signals and behavioural change

Critical to the reproductive success of females as they came under selection pressure for larger-brained offspring was extracting energy from new sources. The accelerated encephalization rates of the late Middle Pleistocene were necessarily accompanied by major social and sexual behavioural changes (see Foley & Lee 1996: 63–64; Power & Aiello 1997). Above all, those females who secured increased levels of investment provided by males would have enhanced their fitness. It should be stressed that a female need *not* be concerned which particular male provides energy for her offspring. If a male is providing energy on a basis of persistent mating effort, i.e. to improve his prospects of sexual opportunities, then he too is *less* concerned about paternity issues than if he were targeting investment to specific offspring in the form of parental effort. Male investment in this context operates on a basis of probability of paternity rather than certainty. Evolutionary ecologists such as Hawkes (1991, 1993) and Kaplan & Hill (1985) have suggested that mating effort rather than parental effort models characterize male foraging patterns among Hadza and Ache hunter–gatherers. From the viewpoint of female coalitions, key items for gossip therefore concern the reliability of prospective or current sex partners as providers, including any matter affecting this such as possible female rivalry for male resources. So, sexual behaviour and attachments of both sexes come under scrutiny (items 1 and 2 in Table 7.1). Possession of energy-rich food should be of direct concern. Wiessner (1982: 68) reports that 60 per cent of topics of !Kung conversations recorded in a month 'came down to who had what and did or did not give it to whom'.

For females, sexual signals are the primary mechanisms for eliciting behavioural changes in males. It is assumed here that, by the stage of archaic grade *Homo sapiens*, overt signs of ovulation had already been lost and the modern pattern of 'loss of oestrus/continuous receptivity' established. These are effective mechanisms for forcing male attentiveness and promoting longer-term bonds (Alexander & Noonan 1979) which would have assisted early *Homo erectus* females in gaining supplies of energy-rich food and meeting the costs of the earlier phase of brain expansion (*c*. 2mya). The most prominent remaining signal in the modern human female cycle is menstruation (Power & Watts 1996). In a natural fertility population, with most females of reproductive age pregnant or lactating, menstruation occurs relatively rarely and is a good indicator of *imminent* fertility (1996). Pleistocene males who were attentive to recently menstruating females in an effort to improve their mating prospects should therefore enhance their fitness. No male could afford to ignore this signal.

This implies that an archaic female who was menstruating could advertise her signal to males in the vicinity to promote mating effort. Menstrual blood, therefore, would have a material value translatable into energy in the form of male provisioning.

6 Female coalitionary strategies: proto-ritual

For any pregnant/lactating female, a menstrual female is a potential threat capable of diverting male energy and investment away from non-menstruants. In response to this problem, Power & Watts (1996) and Power & Aiello (1997) argue that, as archaic *Homo sapiens* females experienced increasing reproductive stress, a coalitionary strategy of manipulating menstrual signals was adopted. Whenever a coalition member menstruated, the whole coalition joined in advertising this valuable signal as widely as possible to recruit available male energy to the coalition. The female coalition needed to prevent any male from sequestering the imminently fertile female, by surrounding her and restricting sexual access. The strategy succeeded as long as any mating effort generated by the menstruant's signal flowed into the whole coalition, benefiting both non-menstruants and menstruants. Power and Watts (1996) predict that non-menstruant coalition members would confuse matters by borrowing the menstruant's signal or mimicking it with other blood or blood substitutes. This strategy would effectively prevent males from discriminating in favour of cycling females and undermine attempts by would-be dominant males to monopolize imminently fertile females.

Power & Watts (1996) term such a strategy of cosmetic manipulation of menstrual signals 'sham menstruation'. A dynamic of competition between female coalitions would drive an evolutionary arms race of increasingly elaborate sham menstrual advertising as coalitions aimed to recruit available male energy. This would result in ritualistic amplification of displays, involving use of red pigment to spread the menstrual signal further, with multimedia effects of movement, body paint, song and dance.

7 Menstrual ritual as costly signal of commitment

It should be clear that participation in such menstrual ritual is well designed as a costly demonstration of *long-term* commitment to extensive alliances. On the first and each subsequent occasion that a young woman menstruates, she is put on the spot. Is she going to co-operate with members of the coalition in using her menstrual signal to attract the benefits of male provisioning to the whole coalition, or is she going to cheat, and use the signal for her benefit alone? If she shares her signal (and the consequent benefits) each time she menstruates until she gets pregnant, she has proved her reliability and commitment to the coalition in hard-to-fake, material terms. Up to the time she gets pregnant she is 'on probation' and must repeatedly demonstrate her commitment through material sacrifice of her valuable signal whenever she menstruates; once she gets pregnant, and subsequently when she is lactating, her interests are clearly with the rest of the non-menstruants in the coalition. Having proved her commitment to the alliance, she can demand by way of reciprocity her share of the benefits derived from the signals of other menstruating members of the coalition. When she begins menstruating again after weaning, and engages in menstrual ritual, she reaffirms her commitment to the alliance. The beauty of menstrual ritual as proof of commitment is that it is absolutely necessary for the 'probationer' to pay her 'dues' first before she derives subsequent benefits when she is pregnant/lactating.

Knight *et al.* (1995) propose that ritual and speech necessarily co-evolve, ritual acting as the 'hard-to-fake' guarantee of trustworthiness among members of the speech community. It is argued here that sham menstruation, as a precursor or preadaptation to ritual – and specifically puberty ritual – functions as a 'gold standard' to guarantee the veracity of 'gossip' within extensive female alliances. Gossip can work on a basis of trust since the signal of commitment has value in the long term – lasting through the length of at least one inter-birth interval.

8 Predictions from the 'sham menstruation' model: archaeological evidence

The main prediction derived from the 'sham menstruation' model of an evolutionary arms race between female coalitions competing for male energy is that the earliest evidence of ritual traditions in the archaeological record will take the form of a cosmetics industry focused on red pigment. Factors of male sexual selection of cosmetically decorated females should also motor an explosive spread of such traditions (Power 1996).

Power & Watts (1996) argue for a two-tier process of the evolution of ritual, fundamentally determined by degree of reproductive stress on females. During earlier stages of the brain expansion of archaic *Homo sapiens*, they posit *context-dependent* sham menstruation displays, triggered by the incidence of menstruation in local populations. Female coalitions used these, as opportunity arose, to attract and retain male support, securing long-term bonds with mates. This strategy implies less planning depth in obtaining materials for cosmetic usage, with correspondingly greater reliance on biodegradable matter, and only occasional traces of utilized ochre. As late archaic to early anatomically modern females endured acute reproductive stress – roughly the period 160,000–130,000 BP, coincident with the Penultimate Glacial maximum (Jouzel *et al.* 1993) – they posit the emergence of a habitual strategy of cosmetic ritual underpinning the sexual division of labour. Greater regularity, planning and organization of performances would lead us to expect abundant and regular use of ochre.

The archaeological record suggests that archaic grade *Homo sapiens* was the first hominid to use iron oxides. There are fewer than a dozen instances of ochre usage predating the Upper Pleistocene and the majority of these occur in the Late Acheulian and early Middle Stone Age (MSA) in sub-Saharan Africa – within the past 200,000 years (Knight *et al.* 1995). Beginning with the African MSA2a (possibly from as early as 140,000 BP), there is evidence of regular and widespread ochre use, while in MSA2b cave and rockshelter assemblages (from *c.* 110,000 BP) ochre has become ubiquitous, showing an order of magnitude increase across the MSA2a/2b boundary. The scale of ochre use in southern Africa from the MSA2 onwards is unparalleled elsewhere until the Eurasian Upper Palaeolithic. Strong reds occur earliest and massively predominate; black pigments are used very rarely, despite their availability (Power & Watts 1996). Functional uses for ochre (e.g. in treatment of hides) were then, and remain today, subordinate to ritual and symbolic uses (Power & Watts 1996; Watts, 1998). The use of red ochre in Africa contrasts markedly with the picture in Europe before the Upper Palaeolithic. The amount of pigment found in French Middle Palaeolithic sites is considerably less, and black manganese predominates (Couraud 1991). It seems that most Neanderthal pigment use occurred during the late Mousterian (60,000–34,000 BP). Only during the Chatelperronean, when Neanderthals are believed to have been in contact with modern humans, is there a significant increase in amounts of red ochre.

9 Evidence from ethnography: female alliances, puberty ritual and cosmetics

The model of menstrual ritual as costly signal of long-term commitment leads us to expect certain patterns in the ethnographic record of rituals associated with onset of menses in traditional cultures worldwide. Firstly, such rituals should preserve an aspect of 'advertising' or 'displaying' prospective fertility *in coalitionary contexts*. Secondly, menstruant participants themselves should be treated as 'probationers' who must reliably prove commitment (and especially sexual probity) before they are entitled to benefits of membership of a community.

Traditional initiation presents a highly coercive character. Initiates (female or male) frequently have no choice in whether or not they participate. The costs of failure to observe due ceremonies for girls can be extremely high, ranging up to social ostracism and loss of marriageability. Passage through lengthy and painful ritual ordeals is indeed the price of becoming a fully fledged member of the adult women's community.

Cosmetics usage appears virtually ubiquitous in menstrual ritual (see, e.g., Lutkehaus & Roscoe 1995) with red and black predominating colours. Among Khoisan hunter–gatherer groups, application of ochre or haematite, besides vegetable dyes, regularly occurred in ritual contexts and especially menarcheal observances (see Power & Watts 1996, for review). A /Xam female initiate, on emergence from seclusion, would present the women of the band with lumps of haematite for decorating their faces and cloaks (Lloyd 1870–1879: VI-I 3969 rev 3973) and would also adorn the young men in preparation for hunting. In Zu/'hoasi (!Kung) oral narratives, the metaphor for impending ritual action was the sound of women pounding red ochre in camp (Biesele 1993: 163, 196). Haematite, which produces a rich red colour on grinding, was particularly prized – redness and shininess being the qualities especially valued by both the !Kung and the /Xam (Lewis-Williams & Biesele 1978). Fischer (1913, cited in Rudner 1982: 218) notes of Khoisan in Namibia that they painted their faces with red iron oxides at 'the time of menstruation'. In default of the desired haematite, women used other substances such as soot mixed with fat as cosmetics. Wilhelm (1954: 118) writes that !Kung women when menstruating would smear their inner thighs with the fat of a large antelope, and paint soot around their eyes. A menstruating !Kung woman would also cut a tonsure in the hair of her youngest child and paint that with fat and soot – as if advertising her imminent fertility after lactational amenorrhea. During menstrual seclusion, a G/wi or G//ana initiate would have her joints cut and a mixture containing her mother's blood rubbed into the cuts – the blood being drawn from her mother's hips (Valiente-Noailles 1993: 96). For Khoisan initiates generally, seclusion is a time of rigorous taboo. Even visual contact between the girl and men is strictly prohibited, and her conduct is carefully monitored by a group of close kinswomen.

The *liengu* rites of the Cameroon coastal area (Ardener 1975) provide an example of the complex ritual sequences and lengthy periods of seclusion required to prepare a girl for admittance to the women's community. Notable in these rites is the instruction of the girl in a secret *liengu* language (Ardener 1956) which is used prominently at various stages of the rituals. Here we clearly see ritual functioning to admit members to a very extensive coalition, which is bounded by knowledge of a conspiratorial ingroup language (cf. Knight, this volume). The symbolism of *liengu* is intimately bound up with women's fertility – to the extent that a perceived decline in the fertility of women of the community was attributed to modern neglect of *liengu* observances. The candidate's prospective fertility and availability for marriage are certainly advertised by the rituals with use of cosmetics like (red) camwood dye on emergence from seclusion (1975: 9). Severe penalties, including the threat of impotence, apply to men who attempt to interfere with the candidate.

The tripartite initiation rites of the Venda of the Transvaal illustrate how entire age cohorts of girls between puberty and marriage can be drawn into coalitions extending across wide areas (Blacking 1985). The whole initiation cycle can last between one and four years, depending on when a girl joins. Commencing from her first menstruation, a girl would attend the local schools of *vhusha* and *tshikanda* where she was trained in complex dance exercises as a preliminary to the central initiation school of *domba* – held every four to five years in the chief's capital. All girls from the surrounding districts would gradually be drawn into the central school, which culminated after long periods of training in spectacular co-ordinated dance displays by hundreds of young women. The Venda themselves saw the cycle 'as one extended event, as a huge drawing of breath of the whole countryside' (1985: 82). The entire initiation cycle used explicit metaphors of female reproduction and fertility, with dances enacting sex, menstruation, conception and labour – yet any girl who actually became pregnant during the *domba* school would be thrown out in disgrace (1985: 86). Women long afterwards recalled the difficulties of co-ordinating dance movements, the physical contact, closeness and excitement when the dances went well, rather than the spoken instruction in the sophisticated associated symbolism (1985: 86–87). Clearly the physical aspect of the rituals nurtured strong emotional and affective bonds.

Possibly the costliest signal involving manipulation of genital bloodshed is female circumcision, which occurs across wide swathes of Africa and the Middle East. Genital operations are frequently performed as all-women affairs, free of direct male interference, and it is usually women who insist on their practice (see, e.g., Boddy 1982: 687; Parker 1995: 511–513). It is difficult to generalize across such varied cultures as matrilocal Hadza hunter–gatherers and Islamic patrilineal Sudanese villagers. However, it is possible that such operations function *primarily* as high-cost signals to a female ingroup of commitment to 'moral behaviour' (cf. Boddy 1982), only secondarily acting to signal marriageable status to males. In West Africa, rites such as *Bondo* in Sierra Leone (Lamp 1988) clearly function to grant entry to women's secret societies and guilds, which are highly influential in local politics and market affairs, and in protecting the rights and interests of women members (see Ahmadu 1995).

While the above examples are anecdotal and drawn on selectively, they are broadly representative of the dynamics involved in puberty ceremonial, and of the techniques of cosmetic manipulation used by women in contexts of coalitionary alliance.

10 Conclusion: ritual and the gossip hypothesis

I have presented a model of ritual as costly signalling of commitment to extensive coalitions, locating the origins of that mechanism specifically in collective manipulation of menstrual signals. I have argued that such a mechanism was necessary for establishing 'gossip' on a basis of trust within wide-scale social networks. This implies that it is ritual that takes on the 'grooming' function of bonding large-scale coalitions through intense shared physical and emotional experience involving energy-expensive signals like song, dance and cosmetic display (cf. Dunbar 1996: 146). Between coalitions, ritual may function as a form of 'supergrooming', enabling amplified transmission of social information across large groups.

I have not addressed here the question of how gossip works, given that exchanging information about third parties implies displaced reference – that is, reference to a domain of constructs which are not anchored in physical space and time. The only known agency capable of generating such a domain is communal ritual (Durkheim 1912; cf. Gellner 1992: 36–37; see Knight *et al.* 1995). Ritual, in other words, not only serves to signal commitment; it is also the source of the symbolic domain of collective representations (Knight *et al.* 1995; Knight, this volume). On this level also, ritual appears as a prerequisite for gossip to function.

Where most recent contributions to the discussion of the evolution of language (e.g. Bickerton 1990; Lieberman 1991; Pinker 1994) have focused on issues of mechanism, Dunbar's theory specifies selection pressures for the emergence of language. Drawing on behavioural ecological models of primate groups, it relates language precisely to the evolution of social intelligence. I have drawn attention to certain problems that arise in the process of switching grooming from a manual to a vocal modality – problems concerning the signalling of commitment and the reliability of that signalling. I conclude that a necessary condition for the evolution of language as gossip is the coevolution of ritual.

Acknowledgments

Thanks are due to Ian Watts for discussion of his work on the archaeological record of pigment use, and on cosmetics in Khoisan ethnography.

References

Ahmadu, F. (1995). Rites and wrongs. *Pride* (April/May), 43–46.

Aiello, L. C. & Dunbar, R. I. M. (1993). Neocortex size, group size, and the evolution of language. *Current Anthropology*, 34, 184–193.

Alexander, R. D. & Noonan, K. M. (1979). Concealment of ovulation, parental care, and human social evolution. In Chagnon, N. & Irons, W. (eds.) *Evolutionary Biology and Human Social Behavior*. North Scituate, MA: Duxbury Press: 436–453.

Ardener, E. (1956). *Coastal Bantu of the Cameroons*. London: International African Institute.

(1975). Belief and the problem of women. In Ardener, S. (ed.) *Perceiving Women*. London: Dent: 1–17.

Bickerton, D. (1990). *Language and Species*. Chicago and London: University of Chicago Press.

Biesele, M. (1993). *Women Like Meat. The Folklore and Foraging Ideology of the Kalahari Ju/'hoan*. Witwatersrand: University Press.

Blacking, J. (1985). Movement, dance, music, and the Venda girls' initiation cycle. In Spencer, P. (ed.) *Society and the Dance. The Social Anthropology of Process and Performance*. Cambridge: Cambridge University Press: 64–91.

Boddy, J. (1982). Womb as oasis: the symbolic context of pharaonic circumcision in rural northern Sudan. *American Ethnologist*, 9(4), 682–698.

Buss, D. M. (1992). Mate preference mechanisms: consequences for partner choice and intrasexual competition. In Barkow, J. H., Cosmides, L. & Tooby, J. (eds.) *The Adapted Mind. Evolutionary Psychology and the Generation of Culture*. New York and Oxford: Oxford University Press: 249–266.

(1994). *The Evolution of Desire: Strategies of Human Mating*. New York: Basic Books.

& Schmitt, D. P. (1993). Sexual strategies theory: an evolutionary perspective on human mating. *Psychological Review*, 100, 204–232.

Byrne, R. (1995). *The Thinking Ape. Evolutionary Origins of Intelligence*. Oxford and New York: Oxford University Press.

Byrne, R. W. & Whiten, A. (eds.) (1988). *Machiavellian Intelligence. Social Expertise and the Evolution of Intellect in Monkeys, Apes, and Humans*. Oxford: Clarendon Press.

Caird, R. (1994). *Ape Man. The Story of Human Evolution*. London: Boxtree.

Cheney, D. L. & Seyfarth, R. M. (1990). *How Monkeys See the World: Inside the Mind of Another Species*. Chicago: University of Chicago Press.

Couraud, C. (1991). Les pigments des grottes D'Arcy-sur-Cure (Yonne). *Gallia Préhistoire*, 33, 17–52.

De Waal, F. B. M. (1982). *Chimpanzee Politics: Power and Sex among Apes*. London: Cape.

(1992). Intentional deception in primates. *Evolutionary Anthropology*, 1, 86–92.

Dunbar, R. I. M. (1988). *Primate Social Systems*. London and Sydney: Croom Helm.

(1991). Functional significance of social grooming in primates. *Folia Primatologica*, 57, 121–131.

(1992). Neocortex size as a constraint on group size in primates. *Journal of Human Evolution*, 20, 469–493.

(1993). Coevolution of neocortical size, group size and language in humans. *Behavioral and Brain Sciences*, 16, 681–735.

(1996). *Grooming, Gossip and the Evolution of Language*. London and Boston: Faber & Faber.
Duncan, N. D. C. & Nettle, D. (1995). Size and structure of freely forming conversational groups. *Human Nature*, 6, 67–78.
& Spoors, M. (1995). Social networks, support cliques and kinship. *Human Nature*, 6, 273–290.
Durkheim, E. (1912/1965). *The Elementary Forms of the Religious Life*. New York: Free Press.
Enquist, M. & Leimar, O. (1993). The evolution of cooperation in mobile organisms. *Animal Behaviour*, 45, 747–757.
Foley, R. A. & Lee, P. C. (1989). Finite social space, evolutionary pathways and reconstructing hominid behaviour. *Science*, 243, 901–906.
(1991). Ecology and energetics of encephalization in hominid evolution. *Philosophical Transactions of the Royal Society of London*, 334, 223–232.
(1996). Finite social space and the evolution of human social behaviour. In Steele, J. & Shennan, S. (eds.) *The Archaeology of Human Ancestry. Power, Sex and Tradition*. London: Routledge: 47–66.
Gellner, E. (1992). *Reason and Culture*. Oxford: Blackwell.
Hawkes, K. (1991). Showing off. Tests of another hypothesis about men's foraging goals. *Ethology and Sociobiology*, 12, 29–54.
(1993). Why hunter–gatherers work: an ancient version of the problem of public goods. *Current Anthropology*, 34, 341–361.
(1996). Foraging differences between men and women. Behavioural ecology of the sexual division of labour. In Steele, J. & Shennan, S. (eds.) *The Archaeology of Human Ancestry. Power, Sex and Tradition*. London: Routledge: 283–305.
Hill, K. & Hurtado, A. M. (1991). The evolution of premature reproductive senescence and menopause in human females: an evaluation of the 'grandmother hypothesis'. *Human Nature*, 2(4), 313–350.
Hockett, C. F. (1960). The origin of speech. *Scientific American*, 203(3), 89–96.
Jouzel, J., Barkov, N. I., Barnola, J. I., Bender, M., Chappellaz, J., Genthon, C., Kollyakov, V. M., Lipenkov, V., Lorius, C., Petit, J. R., Raynaud, D., Raisbeck, G., Ritz, C., Sowers, T., Stievenard, M., Yiou, F. & Yiou, P. (1993). Extending the Vostok ice-core record of palaeoclimate to the penultimate glacial period. *Nature*, 364, 407–412.
Kaplan, H. & Hill, K. (1985). Hunting ability and reproductive success among male Ache foragers. *Current Anthropology*, 26, 131–133.
Knight, C. D. (1996). Darwinism and collective representations. In Steele, J. & Shennan, S. (eds.) *The Archaeology of Human Ancestry: Power, Sex and Tradition*. London: Routledge: 331–346.
Power, C. & Watts, I. (1995). The human symbolic revolution: a Darwinian account. *Cambridge Archaeological Journal*, 5(1), 75–114.
Lamp, F. (1988). Heavenly bodies: menses, moon, and rituals of license among the Temne of Sierra Leone. In Buckley, T. & Gottlieb, A. (eds.) *Blood Magic. The*

Anthropology of Menstruation. Berkeley: University of California Press: 210–231.

Lewis-Williams, J. D. & Biesele, M. (1978). Eland hunting rituals among northern and southern San groups: striking similarities. *Africa*, 48(2), 117–134.

Lieberman, P. (1991). *Uniquely Human. The Evolution of Speech, Thought and Selfless Behavior*. Cambridge, MA: Harvard University Press.

Lloyd, L. C. (1870–1879). Unpublished notebooks. Jagger Library, University of Cape Town.

Lutkehaus, N. C. & Roscoe, P. B. (1995). *Gender Rituals. Female Initiation in Melanesia*. London and New York: Routledge.

Mayer, P. J. (1982). Evolutionary advantage of the menopause. *Human Ecology*, 10(4), 477–494.

Melnick, D. & Hoelzer, G. (1993). What is mtDNA good for in the study of primate evolution? *Evolutionary Anthropology*, 2, 2–10.

Parker, M. (1995). Rethinking female circumcision. *Africa*, 65(4), 506–523.

Peccei, J. S. (1995). The origin and evolution of menopause: the altriciality-lifespan hypothesis. *Ethology and Sociobiology*, 16(5), 425–449.

Pinker, S. (1994). *The Language Instinct*. New York: Morrow; London: Penguin.

Power, C. (1996). A sexual selection model for the origins of art. Paper delivered at the Human Behavior and Evolution Society Conference, Northwestern University, Evanston, 1996.

& Aiello, L. C. (1997). Female proto-symbolic strategies. In Hager, L. D. (ed.) *Women in Human Evolution*. New York and London: Routledge: 153–171.

& Watts, I. (1996). Female strategies and collective behaviour. The archaeology of earliest *Homo sapiens sapiens*. In Steele, J. & Shennan, S. (eds.) *The Archaeology of Human Ancestry. Power, Sex and Tradition*. London: Routledge: 306–330.

Rogers, A. R. (1993). Why menopause? *Evolutionary Ecology*, 7, 406–420.

Rudner, I. (1982). Khoisan pigments and paints and their relationship to rock paintings. *Annals of the South African Museum*, 87, 1–280.

Valiente-Noailles, C. (1993). *The Kua. Life and Soul of the Central Kalahari Bushman*. Rotterdam and Brookfield: Balkema.

Vigilant, L., Pennington, R., Harpending, H., Kocher, T. D. & Wilson, A. C. (1989). Mitochondrial DNA sequences in single hairs from a southern African population. *Proceedings of the National Academy of Sciences (USA)*, 86, 9350–9354.

Watts, I. (1998). The origins of symbolic culture: the southern African Middle Stone Age and Khoisan ethnography. Ph.D. thesis, University of London.

Wiessner, P. (1982). Risk, reciprocity and social influences on !Kung San economics. In Leacock, E. & Lee, R. (eds.) *Politics and History in Band Societies*. Cambridge: Cambridge University Press: 61–84.

Wilhelm, J. H. (1954). Die !Kung-Buschleute. *Jahrbuch des Museums für Völkerkunde zu Leipzig*, 12, 91–188.

Wrangham, R. W. (1987). The significance of African apes for reconstructing human social evolution. In Kinzey, W. G. (ed.) *The Evolution of Human Behavior: Primate Models*. Albany: State University of New York Press: 51–71.

Zahavi, A. (1977). The cost of honesty (further remarks on the handicap principle). *Journal of Theoretical Biology*, 67, 603–605.

(1987). The theory of signal selection and some of its implications. In Delfino, V. P. (ed.) *International Symposium of Biological Evolution*. Bari: Adriatic Editrice: 305–327.

8 Altruism, status and the origin of relevance

JEAN-LOUIS DESSALLES

1 Introduction: relevance as a basic property of language

In his 430-page book *The Language Instinct*, S. Pinker (1994) devotes only five pages to issues related to pragmatics and relevance. The minor role played by pragmatics in this natural history of language is quite surprising. Perhaps we are so accustomed to relevance that, like fish unaware of water, we fail to notice how strong a constraint it is. Relevance is indeed not limited to language. In front of a judge, you may be asked to give relevant justifications for your actions. If you see somebody in danger and begin to look for four-leaf clovers, your behaviour will probably be perceived as irrelevant: relevant behaviour would be some direct or indirect attempt to ward off danger. If relevance applies to human behaviour in general, it is of special importance when we deal with language: as we shall see, the structure of conversation is a consequence of the requirement that utterances be relevant. Even if you see casual conversation as a behaviour of secondary importance, the specific form which utterances have to meet in order to appear relevant has still to be explained. If you see conversation as the most basic and most natural use of language, as I do, then understanding why conversation is organized to meet the relevance requirement may be of crucial importance to understanding why language, in its argumentative form, emerged.

I shall first present a formal criterion for relevance in conversation. From this, it will follow that relevant information is valuable information, and thus that any relevant utterance is potentially altruistic. This will bring us to a first paradox: if it is altruistic, the communicative behaviour of human beings should not exist, unless we are able to show that some cheating detection device is systematically employed by talking people. The quest for such a device will lead us to a second paradox:

relevant information, however valuable it may be, has a 'negative value'. People involved in a conversation often have a hard time being heard and having an opportunity to make their point. We will attempt to resolve these paradoxes by proposing that language is an advertising device, and that relevance is the price paid to get some status in return.

2 Linguistic relevance

Like many other systems, human language can be described as a system of rules. There are well-known phonetic, syntactic and semantic rules; there are also explicit social rules, like politeness, and in-between we find pragmatic rules. If, in the middle of a conversation, you say '31 times 3 is 93', participants will find that your utterance is inappropriate and will quite probably answer with something like 'So what?' Nothing is wrong at the phonetic or at the syntactic level. The meaning of this utterance can be easily understood, so the trouble is not at the semantic level. The problem is not disconnected from language, however: we could hardly say that the confusion comes from an inappropriate social act, from an explicit social rule that has been violated. The trouble actually comes from disregard of a pragmatic rule: in most contexts, an utterance like '31 times 3 is 93' is not *relevant*.

Relevance is a requirement of language, which we only notice when some utterance does not comply with it. We may wonder why language, as we use it during many hours each day, conforms to such a constraint. This question proves to be of crucial importance for the problem of language origin. Relevance is indeed more than an interesting feature of linguistic usage. The content of most utterances is partly motivated by the fact that utterances should be relevant. Hence we may almost invert roles, and see language as an efficient way of being relevant. From such a perspective, the study of relevance should shed light on the question of the *function* of language. In order to deal with such issues, we first have to give a precise description of the constraint of relevance.

It is now generally considered that one of the main purposes of pragmatics is to account for the relevance phenomenon. This has not always been so. The concept of relevance did not appear in the Speech Acts theory developed by Austin and Searle (Searle 1969). The so-called *felicity conditions* specify when an utterance, understood as a social act, is correctly achieved. A definition of relevance through felicity conditions would not be very interesting for our discussion. It would change with the social context. Relevance in bridge (e.g., announcing 'three hearts' when appropriate) would thus be quite different from relevance in a poker game. What we are seeking is a general, formal definition of relevance. Grice's well-known maxim 'Be relevant' (Grice 1975) gives us no such formal criterion. It is only one among several maxims that are supposed to guarantee the pragmatic quality of utterances. Recent developments of the Speech Acts theory based on plan recognition (see Airenti, Bara & Colombetti 1993) are more promising: any utterance that is not related to a plan is considered irrelevant. Such a definition is however too restrictive for our present purpose.

The honour for having recognized the significance of relevance goes to Sperber & Wilson (1986). In their Relevance Theory, they show that relevance is an automatic feature of any intended communication: the emitter is expected to be relevant as soon as he shows his intention to communicate. Actual relevance is achieved if the hearer is able to draw inferences from what he heard. The more inferences, the greater the relevance. For instance, the statement 'Mary bought a new car' is relevant insofar as I am able to draw conclusions, such as 'She will be able to come back every week-end.' This criterion is interesting because it draws attention to the fact that relevance requires cognitive computation. However, while drawing inferences is sometimes a necessary condition to perceive relevance, it proves to be insufficient. Relevance in casual conversation is indeed much more restrictive than the Sperber & Wilson criterion leads us to expect. Consider our previous example '31 times 3 is 93'. The fact that we can easily draw inferences from this statement, such as '3 times 31 is also 93', '93 divided by 3 is 31', '93 is not prime' and so on, does not *in any way* affect its lack of relevance when it is uttered in the middle of a conversation.

The reader may have the feeling that an utterance like '31 times 3 is 93' is irrelevant simply because, as common sense suggests, it does not bring any new information. As Pinker (1994) remarks, 'Dog bites man' is not worth a front-page title, but 'Man bites dog' could be. Before accepting the amount of information as the ultimate criterion for relevance, remember how often you have felt obliged to say 'Sorry, I'm late' when arriving obviously late at an important meeting. Your statement hardly brought any new factual information to other participants, but was nevertheless relevant.

The study of many hours of conversation has led us to another definition of relevance (Dessalles 1985, 1993), or more accurately to three definitions of relevance. We would have preferred a single characterization, but data cannot be bent to one's desires. Maybe our present discussion of the origin of relevance will afford a unified view of the phenomenon. As illustrated by many conversations, a first way to be relevant is to bring information, in the Shannon sense. If the event you report is perceived *a priori* as *improbable*, then it will be considered as relevant. This is why 'Man bites dog' is newsworthy, while 'Dog bites man' is not. A second way to be relevant is to point to an *undesirable* state of affairs, or conversely to a *desirable* state of affairs. When you are able to show that there is something at stake, you are relevant. This explains why you may be relevant when, arriving at your meeting, you declare 'I'm late.' A third way to be relevant is to describe an amazing situation, a situation that looks *inconsistent*. If you are visiting the Monet exhibition in Chicago and you see a blind man listening to explanations given by the guide, you feel obliged to draw your friend's attention to him, wondering how he can enjoy the visit in any way. These three properties – improbability, (un)desirability and inconsistency – exhaust the possibilities for a first utterance to be relevant. The model correctly predicts that '31 times 3 is 93' will not be perceived as relevant in most contexts. Let us sum up these three properties by saying that a first utterance must be about a *problematic* event. If we analyse further utterances, we come upon a slightly broader definition of relevance: *an utterance must either refer to a problematic situation, or attempt to reduce the problematicity of a situation.*[1] This definition can be formalized by using probabilities, first-order logic, and by extending the Shannon definition of information to integrate the desirability dimension (Dessalles 1993).

Checking the validity of this criterion is quite easy. When quietly talking with friends, try to mention a neutral, obvious fact like 'This table is made of wood' or 'There's water here.' Unless your friends imagine that you need water, you will get replies like 'So what?' or 'What does that mean?', or sarcastic remarks, but no elaboration. Conversely, if one

1 At this point, readers may try to find an explanation for the blind man story. Maybe the blind man was formerly a painter, lost his sight accidentally, but is still interested in comments about Monet's paintings. Finding such an explanation is an attempt to cancel the inconsistency. It is one of the few means by which one can reduce problematicity.

asks subjects to give contexts in which a statement, like 'There's water here', may have been uttered, the answers one gets are fully predicted by the criterion. Here are a few examples:

Context produced	***modality***	***comment given***
You are in a desert	*desirable*	(you will not suffer from thirst)
It's leaking	*undesirable*	(things get wet, you must fix the problem)
Glass over candle	*inconsistent*	(water appears on the inner surface of the glass, the child is puzzled)
Old well	*improbable*	(one did not expect to find water in such an old well)

Interested readers are invited to perform such experiments for themselves. If they are not fully convinced of the generality of the criterion, they may read the remainder of this chapter, substitute their own criteria and see if the conclusions still hold. Notice that this criterion is extremely constraining. For instance, when an inconsistent situation is pointed out, you can either echo the speaker's surprise, or try to provide an explanation that has the logical effect of invalidating the inconsistency. There is no other option. Your liberty in such situations is thus much more limited than one might have anticipated. Conversation is guided by the relevance requirement to such an extent that it is sometimes possible to predict accurately what interlocutors will say, as shown by computer simulations (Dessalles 1990).

3 Relevance is altruistic

At this point, there are several questions to be addressed. First, why do people feel obliged to be relevant? Second, why is linguistic relevance specifically attached to problematic issues? Third, if this behaviour has a biological basis, how could it evolve from a situation where this specific form of relevance did not exist? In order to approach these questions, let us observe first that relevance seems very natural to us, but that it should appear very peculiar to a hypothetical non-human observer. Computers, for instance, are seldom relevant. When I turn my computer on, it indicates the amount of memory, the current date, then names of hardware and software manufacturers and gives many indications I have no time to read before the screen changes. Humans do not interact this way: 'Good morning John. My body temperature is 36.9°C, my heart rate is 66. I have been trained at the University of Paris.' Non-relevant human communication can be found in some university lectures: 'Chapter one: Generalities. Point 1: Definitions. Let us call signature an application from a finite set F into N.' In these examples, the listener can hardly find anything improbable, (un)desirable or inconsistent. Such utterances are impossible in spontaneous communication.

If relevance is peculiar, why does it have this specific form? We must explain why people feel obliged to use language this way:

(a) they draw attention to a problematic situation, or
(b) they acknowledge the fact that a (present or evoked) situation is problematic, or
(c) they reduce the problematicity of a (present or evoked) situation.

Admittedly, language is used for many other purposes. By saying 'I am late', you apologize for being late. You are thus performing a social act, but the point is that your utterance, whatever its conscious purpose, *must* be relevant. 'I am late' may be meant as an excuse, but it also acknowledges an undesirable state of affairs, which is one of the few possibilities required by the relevance criterion. The question is then: why are we bound to this relevance constraint?

To understand the biological origin of this aspect of our linguistic behaviour, we have to make clear what is at stake in a linguistic exchange, at the pragmatic level. As we shall verify, by talking together informally, interlocutors give important information to each other. Sharing information, like sharing food, is altruistic and thus, from a Darwinian perspective, requires an explanation. Let us first stress this altruistic aspect of language use.

Let us suppose that an utterance makes you aware of a problematic situation (case (a) above):

(i) The utterance mentions an improbable event. This may be a good occasion for the listener to detect hidden correlations and reassess some probabilities he assigns to events. We should remember that every time we go outside, take our car or walk over a bridge, we trust these probabilities that help us avoid real danger. A correct assessment of probabilities is vital.
(ii) The utterance mentions an inconsistent situation. The listener, who is able to perceive the paradox, knows that his beliefs are, at least momentarily, logically

inconsistent. Since this may prevent him from correctly predicting events or acts, becoming aware of an inconsistency is very important.

(iii) The utterance mentions something desirable or undesirable. The listener's attention may be drawn to a situation that is to be avoided, or conversely to be pursued, in the future.

While the cases (i) and (ii) are straightforward, the reader may question whether mentioning an undesirable event (case (iii)) always brings valuable information. For instance, when someone complains about his health, it may seem like a request for help. But even in such cases, problems encountered by others may be an occasion for the listener to acquire knowledge that can be useful for its own sake.

The point here is not that relevant utterances are systematically biologically significant and useful. It is rather that they are much more likely to be significant and useful than irrelevant ones. Important data can be given in a non-problematic context: a general lecture about game migration, botany or toolmaking could be very helpful in a hunter–gatherer life. Unfortunately, there are no formal lectures in hunter–gatherer tribes. Useful knowledge, as far as we can judge from the observation of everyday life, is always presented *in context*, and such contexts are problematic. Irrelevant statements will most probably be mere noise and should not be remembered.

Not only problematic issues, but also tentative solutions (case (c) above) are helpful. Typical attempts to get out of a problematic state of affairs involve: explanations, for cancelling an inconsistency; mention of similar cases, to diminish improbability; balancing pros and cons, to diminish (un)desirability. All these contributions are likely to be profitable to the listener. By contrast, situation (b), in which a speaker acknowledges the problematic status of the situation, generally does not bring any new factual information, but simply acknowledges the fact that the interlocutor has made a relevant point.

The previous discussion suggests that spontaneous language is altruistic because its *content* is relevant. This altruistic aspect can also be indirectly inferred from the attitude of speakers toward each other. According to Grice (1975), conversation is basically co-operative, since speakers take care to give necessary, sufficient and reliable information to listeners so that the latter can reconstruct the intended meaning. Since any altruistic behaviour needs an explanation to make it compatible with Darwinian principles, the remainder of this chapter is devoted to this issue.

4 Altruistic communication: possible accounts

Altruism is problematic from a Darwinian perspective. When useful information is given by an individual *A* to another individual *B*, it will be at *A*'s expense, either directly or indirectly. For instance, after signalling an improbable source of food, *A* may be obliged to share it. Even if there is no such direct negative consequence on *A*, there are likely indirect negative effects because quite often *A* and *B* are genetic competitors. Any possibility offered to *B* to be more successful will increase *B*'s relative reproductive expectancy. Since the contribution to further generations has to be shared, a consequence of *B*'s increased success is a lower expected reproductive success for *A*, all things being equal. As a consequence, we should expect a strict avoidance of altruistic acts. The observation that altruistic behaviour is in contradiction with Darwinian evolution, except under a few specific conditions, was made by Hamilton (1964). Possible exceptions are altruistic behaviour directed toward children or relatives (1964) and reciprocal co-operation, in which helpful actions are rewarded in the future by similar positive acts performed by the initial recipient (Trivers 1971). Which of these two scenarios is the correct model for language?

It is easy to rule out the first alternative. Admittedly, one can find some peculiarity in the language between mother and child or between twins, but no qualitative bias is to be found in adult speech that indicates a different pragmatic behaviour according to kinship. The only possibility left seems thus to be reciprocity. Conversation is indeed quite symmetrical: participants speak in turn, bringing each other relevant information. The company of silent people who merely listen or utter trivialities is not actively sought. From this we get a picture of language as a reciprocal game: I give you relevant, useful information, and I get useful information in return. This way of considering human dialogue is widely accepted and seems to solve the problem of altruism in language use (Ulbaek, this volume). However, as we shall see, if we accept that language is an instance of symmetrical co-operation, we might expect some behavioural features that are not, in fact, observed.

Co-operation can only exist when deception is controlled; otherwise optimistic co-operators will be rapidly exploited by parasites. If language relies on social co-operation, the main prediction, for our concern, is that it must be protected against social 'cheaters' who take relevant information and give nothing in return. Since relevant information is valuable, speakers will first consider to whom they are speaking in order to decide if the addressee will be co-operative. Axelrod (1984) studied some strategies that were efficient in the presence of parasites. It has been argued that humans have specific cognitive devices for handling social exchanges (Cosmides 1989). However, as we will see in the next section, evidence suggests a different picture for language. Cheating detection is seldom performed by the person who gives the information. It is rather achieved by the listener! This is in contradiction with the co-operation scenario.

Communication, if it was co-operative, should also be characterized by a specific form of signal. Krebs & Dawkins (1984) showed that signalling evolves among living beings from the joint action of manipulation and mindreading. Krebs & Dawkins distinguish two cases, depending on the co-operative character of the interaction: 'Co-operative communication, in which manipulator and mind-reader roles share a common interest, should lead to cost-minimising, muted signals, while non-cooperative signalling should give rise to conspicuous, repetitive signals' (1984: 40). Human language can be both highly repetitive and remarkable, as in commercial advertisement, and highly discreet as in whispering. However, none of these features is characteristic of casual conversation. Conversations, as we saw, convey potentially valuable information. If they were based on mutual co-operation and reciprocity, care would be taken to avoid non-participants spying on them. However, such precaution is far from being systematic. In certain cultures, even private conversations have to be so loud that everybody nearby can hear them (Hall 1966).

At this point, we are left with a difficulty: conversation conveys altruistic messages, but it seems to be based neither on kinship nor on reciprocal co-operation. Normally, natural selection should have favoured non-cooperative speakers who listen but return no relevant information. How can we explain the fact that virtually all normal people, in presumably any culture, display a spontaneous conversational behaviour characterized by relevance? Perhaps we should consider conversation at the level of the speaking group, and not at the level of a single speaker. If the role of language is to contribute to group efficiency, then it may be altruistic simply because speakers get an advantage from being members of a better-functioning group. As Pinker puts it, 'There is a fantastic payoff in trading hard-won knowledge with kin and friends, and language is obviously a major means of doing so' (Pinker 1994: 367). Other accounts present the main purpose of language as located not in objective information exchange, but rather in sociality. For Donald (1993), 'the natural collective product of language was narrative thought (essentially, storytelling), which evolved for specific social purposes'. Such accounts of language function are not by themselves sufficient, because any behaviour that is beneficial at the collective level must also be beneficial at the individual or genetic level (Williams 1966; Dawkins 1994).[2] Dunbar (1996) suggests that language may have played among proto-humans the role played by grooming among primates, allowing groups of larger size to emerge. However, even if social bonding is among the language functions, it cannot be the only determinant that shaped our language ability. After all, mere synchronized growls could do as well. Why should language show all the particular complex features that can be observed, especially the relevance requirement? A further hypothesis, suggested by Dunbar, is that language allows the acquisition of information about social relationships. According to Dunbar, we spend a significant part of our time gossiping. From this observation, we may be tempted to see in language a device devoted to the preservation of social co-operation: non-cooperative individuals are denounced during conversation. Gossiping, however, is as problematic as relevance: if we consider that social knowledge is critical for survival and reproductive success in intricate social contexts, any information concerning a third party's unwillingness to co-operate is highly valuable, and thus gossiping is altruistic. As such, and insofar as gossiping can be shown to be a systematic feature of language use, it requires exactly the kind of explanation we are seeking for relevance.

If none of the usual accounts for altruistic behaviour hold, then we are left with the necessity of finding another justification for the existence of the language faculty. For this, we may get some insight from an analogy.

5 The negative value of relevant information

The emergence of language as an altruistic behaviour is not the only puzzle to be solved. Since relevant information is valuable, it should be

2 Any behaviour which is beneficial at the group level (i.e., members benefit collectively from the action of a few of them) without being beneficial at the individual level is genetically neutral. Mutants lacking this behaviour will take the benefits as well, and they will have on average the same success as their contributing fellows. In the long run, such a behaviour will disappear as do the eyes of species living in the dark.

highly appreciated and much sought after. What we observe in casual conversation, however, is the reverse. Participants do not wait for questions, but rather take advantage of the first opportunity to make an original, relevant point in the flow of conversation. When such attempts to attract others' attention fail, most people, in most conversational situations, become frustrated. In the 'valuable information' scenario, this is unexpected, since people should be happy not to give away relevant information. It looks as if relevant information has in fact a negative value. To understand this second paradox, we may consider an audacious analogy.

We may compare casual conversation with a process that readers may know well, the scientific publication system. We can observe that scientists make great efforts to give their best ideas to their most direct competitors (in this case competition is not genetic!). What do they get in return? Before answering, let us consider the validity of the analogy. Information given in scientific papers is often valuable. Most information used by scientists is obtained from other scientists' publications. The parallel holds with everyday life: a good part of the knowledge you need to behave in your physical and social environment was given to you through conversation. In both cases, people are prone to give this valuable information to others. In the case of the scientist, communicating knowledge to others is, as is often acknowledged, more time-consuming than research itself. In both situations, the information given is not only valuable, it is relevant. The relevance of a scientific paper is formally assessed by reviewers who check whether the paper addresses an important problem and brings admissible solutions. Scientific and technical problems are most often presented as paradoxes or undesirable states of affairs, and admissible theoretical or technical solutions have to cancel such problematic situations. This is, as we suggest, what also happens in casual conversation. As we can see, the parallel between scientific communication and conversation is quite close, as far as information exchange is concerned. Why not bring the analogy further, by considering actual effects of communication in both cases?

An obvious answer to our previous question about scientific communication is that scientists get *status* by publishing useful results. The effect of publishing good papers, even if it is not consciously pursued, is that the author is accepted and recognized as a good scientist and gets a higher status in the scientific community. The hypothesis suggested here is that the same is true for conversation: by making relevant points during conversation, you are likely to get a bit of social status. If we temporarily accept that the analogy holds, then it is no wonder that people make every effort to make relevant points. If the communication of information is part of a kind of unconscious trade in which status is the payment, then one can understand why information is willingly given and still has a positive value.

6 Language as an advertising device

The hypothesis of an exchange between information and status is attractive because it solves our two paradoxes: relevant information is not given for altruistic purposes, and it has a positive value. This idea is also a first step toward an answer to the question of the origin of relevance in communication. It is widely accepted that status hierarchies exist in hunter–gatherer societies and that high status is correlated with a higher reproductive success (Eibl-Eibesfeldt 1967; Mellen 1981).[3] The ability to engage in relevant discourse would have been retained by natural selection because it indirectly provided a higher reproductive expectancy. As Pinker (1994: 369) puts it, 'anthropologists have noted that tribal chiefs are often both gifted orators and highly polygynous'.

An immediate question arises in this scenario: why is there a correlation between status and communicative ability? Status could be connected with physical strength, eye colour or ear shape. A possible answer could be that the status–relevance correlation was initially fortuitous. Then, through a process similar to the evolution of the peacock tail (Dawkins 1982), a positive feedback produced our complex linguistic ability. Another conjecture would compare communication of information with food sharing, perhaps a necessary condition for the hunter to have access to females (Knight 1991). A more specific hypothesis, to justify the assignment of status according to the ability to be relevant,

3 In such scenarios, status is correlated with reproductive success for both sexes. Our ancestors, both females and males, were those who had a high status in their society and who mated partly for this reason, as is generally suggested. Male ancestors attracted many females and left many descendants. High-status females attracted high-status males and, as far as predisposition to obtain status has a genetic basis, their sons also left many descendants. Status and alliance are also crucial for child protection among primates, and this holds for both sexes (De Waal 1982; Hrdy 1988).

suggests that the human status system evolved from coalition formation among higher primates. The main difference between a coalition and the whole group is that roles must be distributed among members for the coalition to function (De Waal 1982). As a consequence, even if competition among members still exists, status is willingly attributed by each individual to others. By contrast, in the whole group, status is extorted through coercion. Within chimpanzee coalitions, status seems also to be granted according to physical strength, but this is done voluntarily and subordinate members in the coalition benefit from being protected by their champion (Goodall 1971; De Waal 1982). A possible assumption is that, among hominids, status was accorded to a member of the coalition depending on the utility of the information he or she was able to bring.

The purpose of the previous discussion was not to determine the right scenario through which relevant communication appeared in the human lineage, but rather to make this emergence less implausible. Scenarios that claim to explain the evolutionary origin of some behaviour or organ have sometimes been called 'just-so stories', as if they were easy to coin. In fact, consistent 'stories' are quite hard to design. In the next section, we shall examine some evidence that supports this relevance–status association.

The model of status–relevance coupling proposed here is close to Zahavi's model of co-operation among birds: 'Individuals invest in their collaboration in order to increase their social prestige. They do so by advertising their qualities and their motivation to collaborate. The benefit to the group is a consequence of, rather than the factor that selects for, the investment' (Zahavi 1995). If relevance is a way to obtain status from others, we expect that individuals will compete with each other in eloquence to draw attention to themselves and to obtain status from the audience. If we see in language a tool for bringing out information and highlighting its relevance, then language may be considered in this context as an advertising device, in Zahavi's sense. Linguistic complexity and refinement, the combinatorial power of phonetics and syntax, the ability to formulate sound analogies, clear proofs, and so on, would thus be motivated by the necessity of enhancing the perceived relevance of a speaker's utterances. This explains the fact, well pointed out by Sperber & Wilson (1986), that the burden of making communication possible and easy lies with the speaker, not with the listener, contrary to what would be expected if communication was altruistic.

7 Evidence for the status–relevance association

Evidence to support the close association between relevance and status may come from disciplines like ethnology, psychology and sociology. It has been observed that, in a group, individuals most often prefer to speak to the 'leader' and make every effort to obtain his/her approbation. This accords well with the idea that status given by a high-ranking individual is of greater value than status given by a person who is not highly regarded. Similarly, information is more influential when it comes from a high-status source (Doise, Deschamps & Mugny 1978). In what follows, we will restrict ourselves to evidence from conversational pragmatics.

A banal fact, like a dispute between husband and wife, cannot constitute a relevant story, except of course if the two are your best friends or if they are king and queen. People feel especially concerned by anything connected with individuals they regard as high-ranking. This makes the coupling between status and relevance symmetrical: by being relevant, one gets status in return, and conversely one is more likely to be relevant if one has high status or is talking about high-ranking people. The analogy with the scientific communication system still holds: famous authors are more likely to be read, and quoting them sometimes helps the writer to put up a good performance.

A prediction of the status–relevance association model is that the value of the information will be checked and negotiated by listeners. In the following excerpt, an improbable fact, a whole family speaking very loud, is thought to be relevant by *A*. The reaction in *B2* shows however that this event does not look so improbable to *B*.

A1- Speaking of which they had the Loud Family. Remember the Loud Family? On Saturday Night Live? (*TV program*)
B1- What was the Loud Family?
A2- Dju hear about that? THEY TALK LIKE THIS.
B2- I know lots of people in New York who talk like that.

(from Tannen (1984: 101))

This reaction, which consists in belittling the actual amount of information given, is quite typical of conversations about improbable events. On the other hand, when an event is rightfully improbable, the first one who brings the news becomes an important personage at least for a few seconds, unless others already hold the information, as illustrated by the following excerpt.

C1- Did you see? There are hot air balloons again this morning!
D1- Yes, I know.
C2- Shut up, I'm not talking to you, I'm talking to the others. (*Turning towards E, the father*) Did you see that there are hot air balloons this morning?
(conversation between two boys, 8 and 10, translated from French)

The effect of reactions like *B2* or *D1* recalls the attitude of a customer appraising the quality of merchandise. This behaviour of addressees who evaluate utterances is not predicted by mutual co-operation models of conversation. However, it is fully compatible with a model in which making a relevant point deserves approbation, since it is a way of publicly bringing out the true relevance of what others say to its true value.

Whenever utterances are rightfully relevant, addressees may acknowledge the fact by echoing the problematic modality or by agreeing on a solution. Notice also that when an observation is considered genuinely relevant, its authorship is generally well acknowledged by listeners retelling it. This is consistent in the context of a trade: second-hand information should not be too much rewarded, and forgetting to mention the source would be interpreted as usurpation. Mention of the source is not predicted by a model of conversation based on altruism.

Conversation provides us with another phenomenon of great importance in the present context: individuals are always ready to point out logical inconsistencies. Consider the following excerpt:

F1- I remember, I was relatively old, about 10. (. . .) A nice guy came to our house with a tape recorder. I'd never seen one before.
G1- A tape recorder? Didn't your mother even have one?
(translated from French)

G finds it surprising that *F*'s mother, who was a language teacher, did not have any tape recorder at that time. Interlocutors make use of their knowledge to call what is said to them into question. We can observe the same behaviour in scientific lectures, where most interventions from the audience aim at confronting elements of the talk with background knowledge and at checking logical consistency. The role of this ability to assess the validity of information fits well with the scenario of status–relevance exchange. The scenario is indeed non-altruistic, but may nevertheless be corrupted by deception. If status can be obtained just by telling improbable stories or by pointing out undesirable contingencies, why not recount false events? A possible conjecture is that our ability to check logical consistency evolved from the necessity to protect oneself against lies. An altruistic model of conversation, based on reciprocity, would predict that cheating detection is the task of the speaker, who verifies that the addressee is trustworthy and will reciprocate. In the status–relevance association model, it is the listener who checks the speaker's reliability. Reactions like *G1* support the latter model.

Interpreting spontaneous communication as a trade allows us to solve another problem. As Knight, Power & Watts (1995) point out, typical human conversation consists neither of high-cost, repetitive signals, nor of 'conspiratorial whispering', contrary to what Krebs & Dawkins (1984) lead us to expect. Let us borrow an analogy from economics. When supply is greater than demand, we may expect conspicuous signals like commercial advertising. When demand is greater than supply, we may observe confidential signals and repeated requests. None of these descriptions is appropriate for describing spontaneous language use. Conversation lies in-between, involving well-designed signals and attentive listeners. In our analogy, conversation is like a balanced exchange in which supply matches demand. This type of balanced communication seems to be characteristic of our species.

The consequence of the behaviour of the listener who repeatedly evaluates information is the emergence of conversation. The rules of the conversational game, from the perspective adopted in this chapter, may be formulated this way:

Give information that is directly valuable, by pointing at improbable, desirable or undesirable states of affairs.
Try to lower the informational value of previous utterances.
Point out any logical inconsistency in the state of affairs described or observed.
Attribute status to speakers who are successful in the above.

This description of the mechanism of conversation is well supported by observation (Dessalles 1993). The last point about status is hypothetical and has been added to put the description in a phylogenetic perspective.

8 Conclusion

If we fail to notice that information given in conversation is valuable, then the existence of the language faculty, with its complex structure, remains highly mysterious, as would the existence of a complex organ with no apparent function. The phenomenon of relevance makes us realize that utterances are profitable to the listener. Language thus seems to be an altruistic behaviour. In this chapter, I have tried to show that the predictions of an altruistic model are not verified: conversational information is indeed valuable, but instead of being requested by listeners, as expected, it is generally put forward by speakers. To resolve this paradox, I proposed that linguistic behaviour is not altruistic, but rather is a form of trade: relevant information is given in exchange for status. I have tried to make this status–relevance association plausible from a phylogenetic point of view, by showing that it is consistent with what we know of the pragmatics of conversation.

The hypotheses presented here can be checked in several ways. We are currently working at computer simulations aiming to show that a communication system can evolve and reach stability, when coupled with a system of status allowance. Also, while status has been studied from psychological and sociological perspectives, it has not been sufficiently studied in connection with relevance. Further studies may reveal how each aspect of relevance is related to status change within the group. Highly regarded people around us are not only those who have performed heroic acts or who have been appointed to official positions. A person who merely makes sound remarks, expresses articulate thoughts and can hold the interest of an audience is likely to deserve esteem. The main point of this chapter is that our instinctive respect for eloquent people may partly explain the origin of relevance.

References

Airenti, G., Bara, B. G. & Colombetti, M. (1993). Conversation and behavior games in the pragmatics of dialogue. *Cognitive Science*, 17, 197–256.

Axelrod, R. (1984). *The Evolution of Cooperation*. New York: Basic Books.

Cosmides, L. (1989). The logic of social exchange: has natural selection shaped how humans reason? Studies with the Wason selection task. *Cognition*, 31, 187–276.

Dawkins, R. (1982). *The Extended Phenotype – The Gene as the Unit of Selection*. Oxford: W. H. Freeman and Company.

(1994). Burying the vehicle. *Behavioral and Brain Sciences*, 17, 617.

De Waal, F. B. M. (1982). *Chimpanzee Politics: Power and Sex among Apes*. Baltimore: The Johns Hopkins University Press.

Dessalles, J.-L. (1985). Stratégies naturelles d'acquisition des concepts et applications EAO. In *COGNITIVA 85*. Paris: CESTA: 713–719.

(1990). The simulation of conversations. In Kohonen, T. & Fogelman-Soulié, F. (eds.) *COGNITIVA 90 – Proceedings of the Third Cognitiva Symposium (Madrid)*. Amsterdam: North Holland: 483–492.

(1993). Modèle cognitif de la communication spontanée, appliqué à l'apprentissage des concepts. Ph.D. thesis. Paris: ENST-93E022.

Doise, W., Deschamps, J.-C. & Mugny, G. (1978). *Psychologie sociale expérimentale*. Paris: Armand Colin.

Donald, M. (1993). Précis of *Origins of the Modern Mind*. *Behavioral and Brain Sciences*, 16(4), 737–791.

Dunbar, R. I. M. (1996). *Grooming, Gossip, and the Evolution of Language*. London: Faber & Faber.

Eibl-Eibesfeldt, I. (1967). *Ethologie – biologie du comportement*. Paris: Naturalia et Biologia ed. scientifiques.

Goodall, J. (1971). *In the Shadow of Man*. Boston: Houghton Mifflin Company.

Grice, H. P. (1975). Logic and conversation. In Cole, P. & Morgan, J. L. (eds.) *Syntax and Semantics*, vol. III, *Speech Acts*. New York: Academic: 41–58.

Hall, E. T. (1966). *La dimension cachée*. Paris: Seuil. Originally in English as *The Hidden Dimension* (1966). Garden City, NY: Doubleday.

Hamilton, W. D. (1964). The genetical evolution of social behavior. *Journal of Theoretical Biology*, 7, 1–52.

Hrdy, S. B. (1988). Raising Darwin's consciousness: females and evolutionary theory. In Bellig, R. & Stevens, G. (eds.) *The Evolution of Sex*. San Francisco: Harper & Row.

Knight, C. (1991). *Blood Relations: Menstruation and the Origins of Culture*. London and New Haven: Yale University Press.

Power, C. & Watts, I. (1995). The human symbolic revolution: a Darwinian account. *Cambridge Archeological Journal*, 5(1), 75–114.

Krebs, J. R. & Dawkins, R. (1984). Animal signals: mind-reading and manipulation. In Krebs, J. R. & Davies, N. B. (eds.) *Behavioural Ecology: An Evolutionary Approach*. (2nd edition) Oxford: Blackwell Scientific Publications: 380–402.

Mellen, S. L. W. (1981). *The Evolution of Love*. Oxford: W. H. Freeman and Company.

Pinker, S. (1994). *The Language Instinct*. New York: Morrow; London: Penguin.

Searle, J. R. (1969). *Les actes de langage – essai de philosophie du langage*. Paris: Hermann. Originally in English as *Speech Acts: An Essay in the Philosophy of Language* (1969). Cambridge: Cambridge University Press.

Sperber, D. & Wilson, D. (1986). *La pertinence*. Paris: Les Editions de Minuit. Originally in English as *Relevance: Communication and Cognition* (1986). Cambridge, MA: MIT Press.

Tannen, D. (1984). *Conversational Style – Analyzing Talk Among Friends*. Norwood: Ablex Publishing Corporation.

Trivers, R. L. (1971). The evolution of reciprocal altruism. *Quarterly Review of Biology*, 46.

Williams, G. C. (1966). *Adaptation and Natural Selection: A Critique of some Current Evolutionary Thought*. Princeton: Princeton University Press.

Zahavi, A. (1995). Altruism as a handicap – the limitations of kin selection and reciprocity. *Journal of Avian Biology*, 26(1), 1–3.

9 The evolution of language from social intelligence

ROBERT WORDEN

1 Introduction and summary

A theory of language evolution can be assessed by four criteria:

(a) **Evolution**. It should be consistent with the constraints of the theory of evolution, given the fossil evidence of human evolution and the selection pressures on our ancestors.
(b) **Language use**. It should agree with what we know about the uses of language – including the range of meanings language can express, the speed and robustness with which we use it, and the facts of language learning, structure and diversity.
(c) **Neurophysiology and anatomy**. It should agree with what we know from PET scans, lesion data and other sources about the locations of language processing in the brain.
(d) **Computation**. It should give a working account of how language computations are done in the brain – how we represent language meanings, how we convert word sounds into those meanings when understanding language, how we convert in the reverse direction to generate language, and how we learn a language.

These requirements get harder in ascending order. The constraints of the theory of evolution are quite loose; but very few theories of language evolution give any good account of how the computations in the brain – which support the rich syntax and semantics of language – evolved or are done today.

This chapter presents a theory of language and its evolution which, I believe, agrees well with all the constraints (a)–(d). The theory proposes that language is an outgrowth of primate social intelligence, which is a distinct faculty of the primate mind, not found in other land mammals.

A lot is now known about primate social intelligence, from recent observations such as those by Cheney & Seyfarth (1990), and we can build a computational model of how it works (Worden 1996). In this model, social situations are represented internally as scripts, similar to those introduced by Schank & Abelson (1977). If the model of social

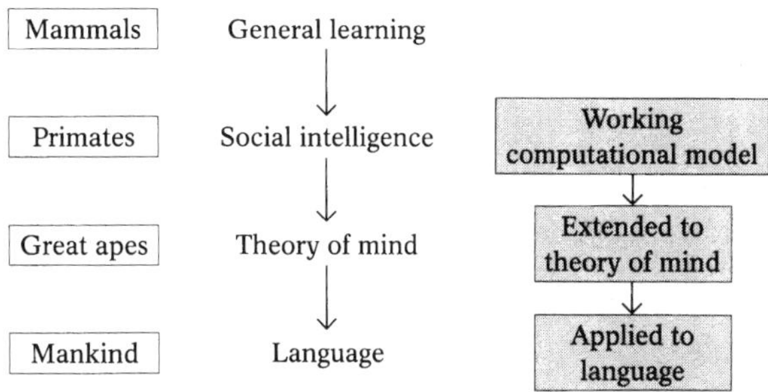

Figure 9.1 How social intelligence extended to give a theory of mind, and the same computational elements were then applied to give language.

intelligence is then extended to describe a theory of mind, this requires the use of script functions to transform from what we might know (and infer) to what others might know.

It is not known whether any other primates, such as chimps, have a theory of mind (Carruthers & Smith 1996); some field observations suggest that they do, while laboratory evidence suggests that they do not. However, it is clear that people have a theory of mind which evolved at some stage in our primate or hominid ancestors, and that (as we use the theory of mind for social purposes) it is a facet of social intelligence.

Scripts and script functions, as required for social intelligence with a theory of mind, are also the computational basis of language. I have built a working computational model of language using the same ingredients. In this model, each word in a language is a reversible script function; we apply these functions in one direction to generate sentences, in the other direction to understand them. This model gives a working account not only of how we use language, but also of how we learn it, learning the script function for each word.

Social intelligence and a theory of mind are vital pre-requisites for language. I propose that language is not just a new mental faculty which uses these two, but is a direct application of them. There is one working computational model of social intelligence, which extends to the theory of mind, which can then be applied to give language – both learning and performance. This progression is illustrated in Figure 9.1.

This model fits well with the usage and properties of language, and resolves an evolutionary puzzle – how did language evolve so fast (probably in less than 2 million years)? It evolved fast because new computational abilities were not needed. It is an application of a pre-existing cognitive faculty – social intelligence with a theory of mind.

2 An evolutionary speed limit

A theory of language evolution should be consistent with the neo-Darwinian theory of evolution. In this framework, there is a proven limit on the speed of evolution (Worden 1995), which places powerful constraints on the evolution of language. This is a limit on the rate at which new design information in the brain can be created by natural selection. The proof of this speed limit is rather abstract, but its intuitive rationale is clear; in evolution, as in other games of chance, there is no quick way to beat the bank.

How fast can evolution design brains? If the complexity of appropriate design is measured in bits, the human brain cannot improve at a rate of, say, 10 bits per generation. How could your children be 10 bits better designed than you? Natural selection can only make a 10-bit design improvement (i.e. choose the best design out of 2^{10} = 1,024 designs) by trying out 1,024 different brain designs, and rejecting all but the best – which can only happen in one generation if you have 1,024 children. So the total rate of improvement in human design can at best be about 1 bit per generation, and this must be split between brain improvements, disease resistance, physical design and so on – leaving an estimated 1/10 bit per generation for improvements in brain design. Brains evolve that slowly.

In the 350,000 generations since our divergence from chimps, this amounts to only about 5,000 bytes of information (equivalent to one typed page). That is all the new brain design which separates us from chimps (our increase in brain size and power is not necessarily a big change in design); in particular, it is all the new brain design allowed for language.

To those who have built computational models of language, it seems highly unlikely that the whole human language faculty – with its capacity for unbounded meaning structures, complex syntax, robust production, understanding and learning, links to the auditory channel and to other meaning structures in the brain – could be specified in a mere 5,000 bytes of design information. Therefore we should look for theories in which language did not arise *de novo* in the human brain, but is based in pre-existing animal cognitive faculties. The theory of this chapter is such a theory.

Language probably did not emerge before *Homo erectus* 2 million years ago, as several important concomitants of language (enlarged brain size, larger group size, changes in vocal capability) are linked to the emergence of terrestrialism and bipedalism at this time. Furthermore it is likely (given the stability of the Acheulian tool culture and brain size over the preceding 1.5 million years) that complex language has only arrived within the timeframe of *Homo sapiens*, during the last 250,000 years.

In these timescales, the speed limit implies an even tighter bound. If language depends on new cognitive faculties evolved during the time of *Homo sapiens* (of the order of 250,000 years, or 12,000 generations) then the maximum amount of new design information in the brain over that period is of the order of 150 bytes, or less than the information in this paragraph. Or if (as proposed by Bickerton, this volume) language arose through an extraordinary genetic change in one generation, the maximum amount of useful design information which can arise in one generation is of the order of 40 bits, or 5 bytes (any more productive mutation only has a probability of order 2^{-40} of occurring).

If the key events in the origin of language occurred in these shorter timeframes, then it is even more important (for a credible theory) that they are built on pre-existing design information in the brain. This pre-existing cognitive faculty, I propose, is social intelligence.

Other theories presented at this conference (Bickerton, Newmeyer, in this volume) propose that large parts of the cognitive faculties needed for language pre-dated its emergence, needing only minor extensions (e.g. the linking of different representations in the brain) for language to mature. In this respect, those theories are quite consistent with the speed limit constraint. This theory goes further, proposing that essentially no new cognitive faculties or links were needed for the emergence of language.

3 Primate social intelligence

We know from many observations that most primates have an acute social intelligence, not found in other land mammals (see e.g. Cheney & Seyfarth 1990; De Waal 1982; Tomasello & Call 1994; Worden 1996).

They recognize one another as individuals, know all about each others' kin and alliance relations, and can rapidly learn simple rules about who will do what in what circumstances. Little of this has been observed in other land mammals.

Primate social intelligence is illustrated by an observation of vervet monkeys in Ambolesi National Park by Cheney & Seyfarth (1990). By replaying recorded calls of selected individuals over hidden loudspeakers, Cheney & Seyfarth showed that mothers recognized their own infant's alarm calls and would go to their help. More interesting, however, was the reaction of other females present. They looked at the mother of the calling infant, often before she herself had reacted – showing that they knew the mother and infant as individuals, knew their kin relations and knew how mothers typically react. This is typical of the complex social knowledge primates can acquire by observation, and use to their own advantage.

To have this social intelligence, monkeys and other primates need to do three things:

(a) To represent in their minds information about social situations, past and present – facts such as 'Profumo is Shelley's mother' or 'Shelley just screamed';
(b) To learn, and represent internally, the causal regularities whereby one social situation leads to another; regularities such as 'if X screams and Y is X's mother, then Y will react';
(c) To combine knowledge of the present social situation with knowledge of causal regularities to predict what may happen next; in this case to know that 'Profumo will react'.

With these three abilities, primates are able to predict social events, and to choose actions which further their own ends of stronger alliances and increased rank. For the moment we just concentrate on (a) – the ability to represent social situations.

To be effective, internal representations in the brain should match the properties of the things they represent (Johnson-Laird 1983; Marr 1982). For instance, the representation of the visual field in the V1 visual cortex matches the two-dimensional character of the visual field itself. So the social representation in the primate brain should match the properties of social situations, which are:

(a) **Structured**. A social situation consists of a number of individuals with attributes (identity, sex, rank, mood . . .) and relationships or interactions (mother-of, grooming, threatening . . .). The structural way in which these are combined is important; it matters who is grooming whom.

(b) **Complex and open-ended**. There may be several individuals in one incident, in a variety of relationships; and several incidents together may constitute a particular situation; the set of possible social situations is a very large set.
(c) **Discrete-valued**. Many of the important variables which characterize social situations are discrete-valued (e.g. identity, sex, rank, kin and alliance relations).
(d) **Extended in space and time**. The incidents which make up a social situation may take place over several days or more, at different places.
(e) **Dependent on sense data of all modalities**. Important information about the social situation may come from vision, hearing, smell, movement or bodily feelings; the social representation must be connected in the brain to all these sense data.

The representation of social situations in the primate brain should ideally have all the properties (a)–(e). This list bears a remarkable resemblance to the properties of language meanings. The meanings we can express in a sentence are structured, complex and open-ended, discrete-valued, extended in space and time, and involve sense data of any modality.

This leads to a key hypothesis: *the internal representation of language meaning in the brain derives from the primate representation of social situations*. No other candidate meaning structure has such a good fit to language meanings.

4 The uses of language and the theory of mind

While some use of language is internal, for thought processes, its main use is a social one involving other people; this suggests strongly that it is an outgrowth of social intelligence. Specifically, we use language to influence what other people know and intend to do. Thus if we did not have any idea about 'what other people know' we could hardly use language effectively (Dennett 1983; Grice 1968). This is demonstrated in every sentence we speak; we constantly build a detailed knowledge of 'what the hearer now knows', using this knowledge to guide what we say, and what we can miss out (e.g. what can be referred to by a pronoun, because the hearer knows what it is).

A knowledge of what other people know, from moment to moment, is a key pre-requisite for language. This mental faculty of knowing what others know is referred to as our 'theory of mind' and it has been intensively studied in recent years – to understand its development through childhood, its possible role in autism (as a theory-of-mind deficit) and its development in other primates (Carruthers & Smith 1996; Whiten

1991). The study of the theory of mind is, at the moment, quite unsettled, with divergent views on two key questions:

How does the human theory of mind work? There are two main theoretical proposals: the 'theory theory' that our knowledge of other minds is embodied in an explicit symbolic theory along the lines of a folk psychology, with axioms and rules of inference, from which we may deduce what others know and want (e.g. Gopnik & Wellman 1992); and the 'simulation theory' that we mentally simulate others' thought processes and feelings, using our own mental resources as a model of theirs (e.g. Gordon 1986). Within these two camps are several variants, and a hybrid picture with some ingredients of both is now becoming popular (e.g. Perner 1996).

Do other primates have a theory of mind? While it seems clear that monkeys and most primates have no theory of mind, the picture in great apes (particularly chimps) is far from clear. Some evidence from field studies suggests that they do (Byrne & Whiten 1992), while recent evidence from laboratory studies is more negative (Povinelli 1996), suggesting that young chimps do not even understand some basic aspects of visual attention, which are pre-requisites for knowing what others know. However, the interpretation of both lines of evidence is controversial; at present we simply do not know whether chimps have a working theory of mind (Povinelli & Preuss 1995).

In the face of this uncertainty, what can we say about the relation of the theory of mind to language? It seems likely that the adult human theory of mind is a complex, multi-faceted thing; we may well use a mix of folk-psychology rules, mental simulation and verbal introspection to figure out what others might be thinking. It is not surprising that several different theoretical models have been proposed. However, the earliest theory of mind in our ancestors could not have been so complex. Whatever its form, we can be fairly sure that the earliest primate theory of mind was an outgrowth of social intelligence – since a theory of mind is used for entirely social purposes. There is usually no point in working out the contents of another's mind if you are not going to interact with him or her socially.

I propose, therefore, that primate social intelligence was incrementally extended to include a working theory of mind (initially much simpler than today's adult human version). This theory of mind was an essential pre-requisite for language use, and the computational ingredients of the theory of mind were co-opted for language (see section 6). By proposing that language evolved from a pre-existing theory of mind, we minimize the amount of new cognitive design required for language – as required by the evolutionary speed limit.

Some authors (e.g. Smith 1996) propose that language is necessary for the adult human theory of mind – that we cannot fully work out what others are thinking unless they can tell us about it. If so, this is still consistent with a picture in which the adult, multi-faceted theory of mind requires language, but its primitive precursor did not.

5 Neurophysiological evidence

If language evolved from social intelligence, and uses the theory of mind within social intelligence, then we would expect an overlap in the brain between the language centres and the location of social intelligence. Several lines of evidence (Passingham 1993) suggest that social intelligence is located in the ventral pre-frontal cortex (VPC):

VPC receives sense data of all modalities, mainly via the temporal cortex (e.g. visual, auditory, somatosensory, olfactory), as required to construct social representations from multi-modal sense data.

VPC is strongly linked to the amygdala and hypothalamus. They are directly involved in many social/emotional responses (such as increasing blood pressure, pupil dilatation, altered breathing rate, etc.) which often follow from appraisals of the social situation.

VPC is involved in cross-modal learning, in learning with time delays (as is required for many social causal regularities) and in so-called 'voluntary' actions made in the absence of immediate external stimulus; all these are relevant to social action.

There is evidence that the size of VPC has increased, as a proportion of total brain volume, over primate evolution through apes to mankind (Deacon 1992) – as one would expect with an increase of social intelligence through this timeframe.

PET activation of the neighbouring orbital prefrontal cortex has been demonstrated in humans performing a theory-of-mind task (Baron-Cohen, Ring, Moriarty, Schmitz, Costa & Ell 1994).

Lesions to the prefrontal cortex in humans produce deficits in social and emotional behaviour (Damasio 1994).

These together imply that VPC is the main location of social intelligence in the primate brain. For language, Broca's area overlaps with VPC, although it is located a little behind it. Evidence from PET scans shows that the 'higher' semantic/syntactic aspects of language (as opposed to motor and auditory aspects) are located most forward in the Broca area, most overlapping with VPC. For instance, measurements of PET activity associated specifically with verbs shows strong overlap with VPC (Fiez, Raichle, Balota, Tallal & Petersen 1996).

Therefore the hypothesis that language evolved from social intelligence is quite consistent with neuroanatomical data; both language and social intelligence are strongly linked to ventral prefrontal cortex.

6 A computational model of social intelligence and the theory of mind

The hardest problem to confront for a theory of language evolution is the rich structure of language and the complex mental computations which it requires. What computations in the brain enable us to understand complex sentences, to generate them from complex meanings, and to learn a language? How did those computations evolve? Many accounts of language evolution cannot yet provide satisfactory answers to these questions.

The strength of the 'social intelligence' theory of language is that it makes just this link. We can build a working computational model of primate social intelligence (as in vervet monkeys), extend it to provide a working theory of mind, and then show that the same computations support a powerful working model of complex language. One working computational model describes social intelligence, the theory of mind, and language.

This model does not shirk the harder features of language such as complex verbs, nested meanings, ambiguity and anaphora; and it handles generation, understanding and learning in the same framework. I have built this computational model in Prolog to handle a significant fragment of English. There is not space here to give full details of the progression from social intelligence through the theory of mind to language, but I shall describe some key points of the model. Details of the Prolog program (and source code) are available from the author, and more information is available at the web site http://dspace.dial.pipex.com/jcollie/.

For a model of social intelligence, we first model the internal representations of social situations in the primate mind, using information structures with the properties (a)–(e) of section 3 – which match the properties of the primate social world. For this we use **scripts**, which are simple tree-like discrete information structures denoting the essence of a social situation. A typical script, denoting the fact that 'I bit Portia and then Portia bit me' is shown in Figure 9.2.

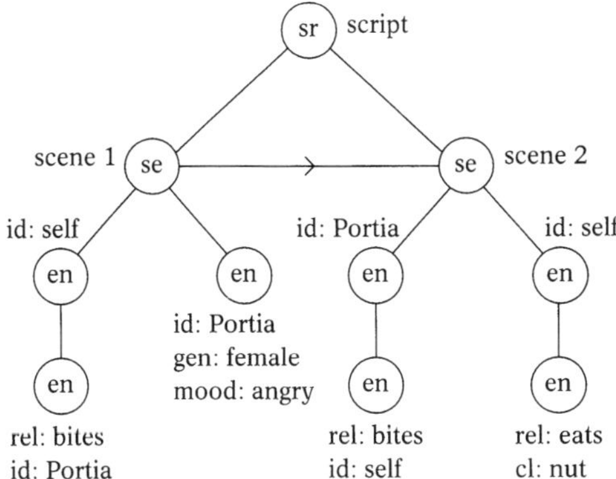

Figure 9.2 A simple primate script.

Each half of this diagram is itself a script, each denoting one scene. The first scene denotes 'I bit Portia' and the second scene denotes 'she bit me'; the arrow between them denotes the time-ordering of the two scenes.

These script structures are well matched to the primate social domain, and also have the properties we require for language meanings; in fact they strongly resemble the tree-like meaning representations used in many computational linguistic implementations. By allowing suitable types of nodes and attributes on the nodes, and allowing trees of greater depth, we can represent the meanings of the most complex sentences. But for vervet monkeys, it seems that script trees only need to have a depth of about four nodes.

Scripts have a tree-like structure, like language meanings and syntax; scripts evolved first for social intelligence, and were later used for language. This argument is *not* circular; the tree-like structure of scripts evolved because social situations have composite structure, and the meanings of scripts are defined by their links to other representations in the brain; for instance, in a monkey's mind the slot 'id: Portia' may be a link to a mental image of Portia. Monkey scripts have no dependence on language. Language evolved to use scripts because they already had meaning.

If monkeys simply recorded the social events of their lives in a script form, this in itself would not help them to compete socially. To be practically useful, primate social intelligence must be able to represent

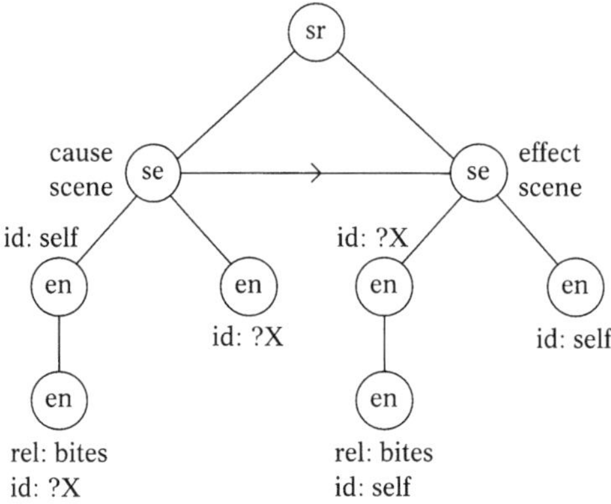

Figure 9.3 A rule script which decribes a causal regularity of monkey social life.

causal regularities of the social milieu; to infer these regularities from experience; and to apply the regularities to predict outcomes and choose actions.

Inferring regularities from experience is done by a process of rule induction. Suppose the same monkey (as in the example above) goes around biting several other monkeys, and in each case gets bitten back. In each case she will record a script similar in form to that of Figure 9.2, but with different individuals involved and different 'irrelevant' details. There is a computational operation of *script intersection* which combines these different scripts to project out their common structure. Intersection is a simple computation, matching the nodes of different scripts together and projecting out common information; the result of this is shown in Figure 9.3.

This script is similar in structure to the examples (such as that in Figure 9.2) from which it was induced; but instead of the identity of specific individuals, it has a variable (shown as id: ?X) which denotes 'any individual'. So this script in effect says 'If I bite any other individual ?X, then ?X will later bite me' – an important causal regularity of monkey life.

The rule induction process is very efficient and robust, using a Bayesian test of statistical significance. It can induce a rule correctly from just a few examples, and will do so in the presence of a lot of extraneous information, irrelevant to the rule; the script intersection mechanism efficently prunes out the irrelevant detail. There is evidence that primates can learn social regularities from just a few examples; the selection pressure of intense social competition has given them just such an efficient learning mechanism.

Once having learnt such a causal regularity, our monkey needs to apply it to avoid future retaliations. Suppose she is considering biting yet another monkey, and so forms the script in her mind describing this forthcoming event. That script looks much like the left-hand side of Figure 9.2, but with a different individual as victim. By an operation of *script unification*, her plan script can be combined with the rule script of Figure 9.3 to deduce the consequence – that the victim will then bite her back. By this means, she can anticipate the consequences of her social actions, and perhaps alter her plans appropriately.

Script unification is a simple computation, similar to the unification in unification-based grammar approaches to language (e.g. Kaplan & Bresnan 1982; Kay 1984), and again involves matching scripts together node by node. Script intersection and unification together form a simple algebraic structure, the *script algebra*, which underpins the self-consistency of this model of social intelligence.

In this example, there is a 'cause' script such as 'I bite Nero' and an 'effect' script such as 'Nero bites me back.' The effect script depends on the cause script, through the identity (Nero); so the effect script is a function of the cause script. In this respect, the rule script of Figure 9.3 acts as a *script function*, which may be written as Cause $\leftrightarrow$ Effect, in this case (I bite X) $\leftrightarrow$ (X bites me). The double-ended arrow reflects the fact that the function is reversible, and can be applied in either direction – forward (to predict consequences) or backwards (to plan to achieve goals). If a monkey wanted to get bitten, he could plan to do so.

This functional view of primate rule scripts will link closely with functional approaches to language syntax, such as categorial grammars and situation semantics. However, in the example above, the effect script depends on the cause script only through the identity of an individual, which can have only a finite number of different values; so there can only be a bounded number of possible result scripts. The rules we need for general primate social intelligence are *bounded script functions*, and are not yet powerful enough for language. Much more powerful functions are used, for instance, in categorial grammars (Oerhle, Bach & Wheeler 1988), Montague semantics (Dowty, Wall & Peters 1981) and situation semantics (Barwise & Perry 1983).

This script-based model of social intelligence can account for most observations of monkey intelligence, such as those of Cheney & Seyfarth (1990). To enable it to describe a theory of mind (i.e. social reasoning about others' mental states, rather than just about their behaviour) two extensions are necessary:

(a) deeper script trees (which can, for instance, represent 'X knows Y', where Y is a subtree describing any social knowledge);
(b) more powerful script functions, which can convert, for instance, from a script representing 'Y is happening' to deduce that 'X knows that Y is happening.' This requires transplanting the subtree 'Y is happening' from one part of a script tree to another.

The rules and generalizations required for a theory of mind can be expressed in the more powerful script functions. Typical rules can be written in a semi-formal, functional notation as:

(Z is present and S occurs) ↔ (Z knows that S)
(Rule R holds) ↔ (Z knows that rule R)

These rules contain variables (S and R) which denote not just 'any individual' but 'any script'. These variables can have an unbounded set of (script) values, so the result of the function has an unbounded set of possible values. They are *unbounded script functions*. The two-headed arrows denote that the functions can be applied either left-to-right or right-to-left; they are *reversible* functions.

Reversible, unbounded script functions are an essential part of the theory of mind, and are the key ingredient of the computational model of language. Language needs the unbounded functions to build up an unbounded set of possible meaning scripts (e.g. trees of arbitrary depth for nested meanings), and it needs reversible functions to support the reversible processes of language generation and understanding. How this works is outlined in the next section.

7 The computational model of language

The computational model of language is based on two key hypotheses:

(a) **Language meanings are scripts**: the meaning of every sentence is a script, with suitable nodes, attributes and values to represent the full range of language meanings, and using scripts of greater depth to represent nested clauses and phrases. A script meaning-structure is not a mental image, but may be used as an intermediate stage in constructing one from heard language.

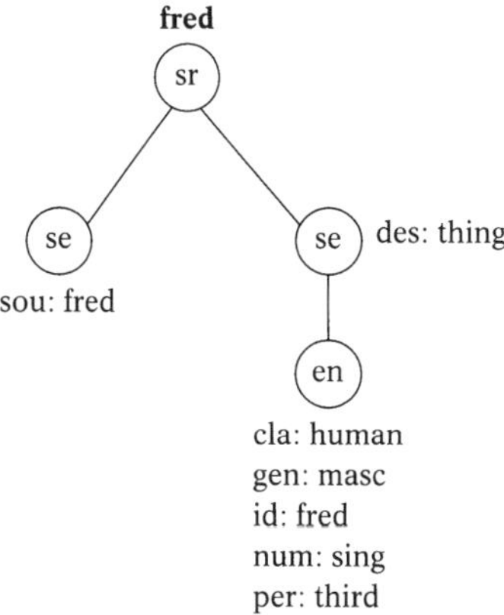

Figure 9.4 A word script function for a proper noun.

(b) **Every word is a script function**: words are reversible, unbounded script functions, and so can be applied in one direction for generation, the opposite direction for understanding; and they can build up an unbounded set of meanings by repeated function application.

The use of scripts as a meaning-structure has many precedents in computational linguistics, going back to the scripts introduced by Schank & Abelson (1977), and having many parallels with the conceptual structures analysed by Jackendoff (1991), Pinker (1989) and others.

To illustrate how words act as script functions, I shall use two typical English words. Figure 9.4 shows the script function for a proper noun, the word 'Fred'.

Word script functions are always shown as trees with one top script 'sr' node, below which there are several scene 'se' nodes. These form left and right branches which are the argument and the result of the function; if the branches are written as S_1 and S_2, the reversible function can be written as $S_1 \leftrightarrow S_2$, or $f(S_1) = S_2$ with the inverse function $f^{-1}(S_2) = S_1$.

The script function of Figure 9.4 can be written as 'Fred' $\leftrightarrow$ X, where the left-hand subtree 'Fred' is a script with one scene (the 'se' node) denoting just the sound 'Fred', and the right-hand subtree X has one scene with one entity (the 'en' node), denoting the individual, Fred; this is the internal mental representation of that person. So this function simply converts (reversibly) between the sound 'Fred' and the script representation of that individual.

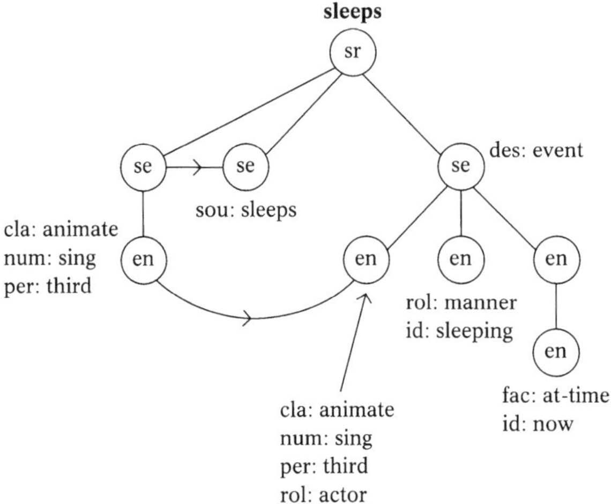

Figure 9.5 Script function for the verb 'sleeps'.

Nouns are the simplest script functions of a language. A script function for a typical verb 'sleeps' is shown in Figure 9.5.

This is a function which converts its left branch (a scene describing an animate entity, followed by a scene denoting the sound 'sleeps') into its right branch (a scene denoting the same animate entity sleeping); or it can convert in the other direction. It can be written as (X 'sleeps') $\leftrightarrow$ Y, where Y is the scene which denotes X sleeping. The curved arrow is a 'trump link', by which the function can transplant any complex subtree (describing a composite entity) from the left branch to the right – thus embedding any entity in a sleeping scene. It is the trump links which allow words to be unbounded script functions.

The one structure of Figure 9.5 embodies the full syntactic and semantic constraints of the word 'sleeps':

It denotes an act of sleeping (the meaning of the right-hand subtree);
The act takes place in the present (rightmost branch of RH subtree);
It selects for a single, animate entity (leftmost entity node);
The words denoting 'X sleeps' must appear in that time order (time-order arrow between scenes in the left subtree).

Hearing the sentence 'Fred sleeps', we start with just the sound scenes 'Fred' and 'sleeps'. We then apply the function of Figure 9.4, to convert 'Fred' to the scene X denoting Fred; then we apply the function of

Figure 9.5, to convert (X 'sleeps') to the script Y which describes Fred sleeping. To generate a sentence from the meaning script Y, we would apply the same functions in the reverse direction – giving the words 'Fred sleeps.'

This script function approach will work not just for a toy subset of language, but for a wide range of mature languages. Two lines of evidence confirm this.

(a) I have built a Prolog implementation of the model which works for a 400-word subset of English, including many of the complexities of adult language – including all parts of speech, complex verbs, tense, aspect, mood, passives, anaphora, gaps, ambiguity and so on. It can work in either the generation or understanding direction, handling complex sentences.

(b) Script functions are applied by unification, as in unification-based grammars. The formalism can be placed in close correspondence with unification-based grammar models, such as LFG (Kaplan & Bresnan 1981), HPSG (Pollard & Sag 1987), categorial grammars (Oerhle *et al.* 1988) or the Core Language Engine (Alshawi 1992) These have been applied to many languages, and can handle essentially all language features; the script function model can handle the same features, in similar ways.

However, the most distinctive feature of the model is its account of language learning. The basic operation of structure intersection, which all primates use to learn rule scripts like that in Figure 9.3 from experience, can also be used in learning the script functions which are words. If a child hears several sentences involving some unknown word, and in each case can deduce the intended meaning script, she can form a script structure which includes both the syntactic environment of the word (the left branch of the script function) and its meaning (the right branch). By intersecting these example scripts together, she can form the m-script for the new word, and thus learn it. Doing this for many words, the child acquires her native language (including its syntax, which is embodied in the word m-scripts).

The Prolog implementation of the language theory can learn any word m-script from a few examples by this intersection mechanism. In this way it has 'bootstrap'-learnt a fifty-word subset of English from zero linguistic knowledge, and could go much further. More details are given in Worden (in draft).

In summary, the computational model of language which follows from primate social intelligence can handle the complexities of adult language in both understanding and generation, and gives a general working model of language acquisition.

8 Conclusions

I have described a theory of how language evolved from primate social intelligence. This theory does well by the four criteria mentioned in the introduction:

(a) **Evolutionary constraints**. Because of an evolutionary speed limit, the amount of new information in the design of the human brain since our divergence from chimps cannot be more than 5 Kbytes. Therefore the computational faculties underlying language need to be based on some pre-existing mental capacities; in this theory, language is based on primate social intelligence – a suitable basis for the complexity and subtlety of language.

(b) **Language use**. Language is used for social purposes, to alter what other people believe or intend. We expect language to be tightly linked to social intelligence, particularly to that part of social intelligence – the theory of mind – which is about other people's knowledge and goals.

(c) **Neuroanatomy**. Both language and primate social intelligence are closely linked with the ventral prefrontal cortex – supporting the idea that they have a common evolutionary origin.

(d) **Language computations**. The meaning representations required for social intelligence – being structured, open-ended, multi-sensory, extended in space and time, and discrete-valued – are well suited to serve as the basis for language meanings. Social intelligence requires a robust learning mechanism, which, extended for learning a theory of mind, provides just the operations needed for language learning. The reversible, unbounded script functions which primates need for complex social planning and anticipation are the same operations we use for reversible language generation and understanding. This computational model of language works.

This theory explains how language arose, by reuse of pre-existing structures and operations in the brain for social intelligence and the theory of mind. It does not explain why language arose, or (in detail) when it arose; but many accounts of the 'why' and the 'when' (Dunbar, this volume; Knight, this volume; Miller 1992; Power, this volume) seem perfectly compatible with this account of the 'how'.

References

Alshawi, H. (ed.) (1992). *The Core Language Engine*. Cambridge, MA: MIT Press.

Baron-Cohen, S., Ring, H., Moriarty, J., Schmitz, B., Costa, D. & Ell, P. (1994). Recognition of mental state terms – clinical findings in children with autism and a functional neuroimaging study of normal adults. *British Journal of Psychiatry*, 165, 640–649.

Barwise, J. & Perry, J. (1983). *Situations and Attitudes*. Cambridge, MA: MIT Press

Byrne, R. W. & Whiten, A. (1992). Cognitive evolution in primates: evidence from tactical deception. *Man*, 27, 609–627.

Carruthers, P. & Smith, P. K. (eds.) (1996). *Theories of Theories of Mind*. Cambridge: Cambridge University Press.

Cheney, D. L. & Seyfarth, R. M. (1990). *How Monkeys See the World: Inside the Mind of Another Species*. Chicago: University of Chicago Press.

Damasio, A. (1994). *Descartes' Error: Emotion, Reason and the Human Brain*. New York: Grosset/Putnam.

Deacon, T. W. (1992). Brain–language coevolution. In Hawkins, J. A. & Gell-Mann, M. (eds.) *The Evolution of Human Languages*. Reading, MA: Addison-Wesley: 49–83.

Dennett, D. C. (1983). The intentional stance. *Behavioral and Brain Sciences*, 3, 343–350.

De Waal, F. B. M. (1982). *Chimpanzee Politics: Power and Sex among Apes*. London: Cape.

Dowty, D. R., Wall, R. E. & Peters, S. (1981). *Introduction to Montague Semantics*. Dordrecht: Reidel.

Fiez, J. A., Raichle, M. E., Balota, D. A., Tallal, P. & Petersen, S. E. (1996). PET activation of posterior temporal regions during auditory word presentation and verb generations. *Cerebral Cortex*, 6, 1–10.

Gopnik, A. & Wellman, H. (1992). Why the child's theory of mind really is a theory. *Mind and Language*, 7, 1–2, 145–71.

Gordon, R. M. (1986). Folk psychology as simulation. *Mind and Language*, 1, 158–171.

Grice, H. P. (1968). Utterer's meaning, sentence-meaning and word meaning. *Foundations of Language*, 4, 225–242.

Jackendoff, R. (1991). *Semantic Structures*. Cambridge, MA: MIT Press.

Johnson-Laird, P. N. (1983). *Mental Models*. Cambridge: Cambridge University Press

Kaplan, R. M. & Bresnan, J. (1982). Lexical Functional Grammar: A Formal System for Grammatical Representation. In Bresnan, Joan (ed.) *The Mental Representation of Grammatical Relations*. Cambridge, MA: MIT Press.

Kay, M. (1984). Functional Unification Grammar. In *Proc. COLING-84*.

Marr, D. H. (1982). *Vision*. Oxford: W. H. Freeman.

Miller, G. F. (1992). Sexual selection for Protean expressiveness: a new model of hominid encephalisation. Paper delivered to the 4th Annual Meeting of the Human Behaviour & Evolution Society, Albuquerque, New Mexico.

Oehrle, R. T., Bach, E. & Wheeler, D. (eds.) (1988). *Categorial Grammars and Natural Language Structures*. Dordrecht: Reidel.

Passingham, R. (1993). *The Frontal Lobes and Voluntary Action*. Oxford: Oxford University Press.

Perner, J. (1996). Simulation as explication of predication-implicit knowledge about the mind: arguments for a simulation–theory mix. In Carruthers, P. & Smith, P. K. (eds.) *Theories of Theories of Mind*. Cambridge: Cambridge University Press.

Pinker, S. (1989). *Learnability and Cognition: The Acquisition of Argument Structure*, Cambridge, MA: MIT Press.

Pollard, C. & Sag, I. (1987). *Head-driven Phrase Structure Grammar*. Chicago: University of Chicago Press.

Povinelli, D. (1996). Chimpanzee theory of mind? The long road to strong inference. In Carruthers, P. & Smith, P. K. (eds.) *Theories of Theories of Mind*. Cambridge: Cambridge University Press.

Povinelli, D. J. & Preuss, T. M. (1995). Theory of mind: evolutionary history of a cognitive specialisation. *Trends in Neurosciences*, 18(9), 418–424.

Schank, R. C. & Abelson, R. P. (1977). *Scripts, Plans, Goals and Understanding: An Inquiry into Human Knowledge Structures*. Hillside, NJ: Lawrence Erlbaum Associates.

Smith, P. K. (1996). Language and the evolution of mind-reading. In Carruthers, P. & Smith, P. K. (eds.) *Theories of Theories of Mind*. Cambridge: Cambridge University Press.

Tomasello, M. & Call, J. (1996). Social cognition in monkeys and apes. *Yearbook of Physical Anthropology*, 37, 273–305.

Whiten, A. (ed.) (1991). *Natural Theories of Mind: Evolution, Development and Simulation of Everyday Mindreading*. Oxford: Basil Blackwell.

Worden, R. P. (1995). A speed limit for evolution. *Journal of Theoretical Biology*, 176, 137–152.

(1996). Primate social intelligence. *Cognitive Science*, 20, 579–616.

(in draft). A theory of language learning. Paper in draft, available at http://dspace.dial.pipex.com/jcollie/.

Part II The emergence of phonology

10 Introduction: the emergence of phonology

MICHAEL STUDDERT-KENNEDY

The infinite semantic scope of language derives from its two hierarchically related levels of structure. At the lower level, that of phonology or sound pattern, a dozen, or a few dozen, meaningless units (consonants and vowels) are combined in regular, language-specific patterns to form words. At the upper level, that of syntax, words are combined in regular, language-specific structures to assert or question relations among persons, objects, events or concepts. Both levels achieve an unbounded set of structures – words, sentences – by sampling, permuting and combining a bounded set of discrete elements.

How did this novel combinatorial system arise? What drove the switch from continuously variable, analog primate call to categorically discrete, digital speech? What role, if any, did manual gesture play? Were changes in the primate vocal tract a cause or a consequence of the evolution of speech? Why do the consonants and vowels of every language form a balanced system of binary oppositions, of acoustic, articulatory and perceptual contrasts? These are among the questions that the following chapters address.

Before we sketch some of the lines of answer, we should draw attention to a fact that may surprise readers unfamiliar with modern speech research. The basic elements of language, its consonants and vowels, are not objective, physical units, but rather psychologically defined entities that can be reliably identified only by a human listener. Speech is not a simple left-to-right sequence of discrete and invariant alphabetic segments such as we see on a printed page. The reason for this is that we do not speak phoneme by phoneme, or even syllable by syllable. Typical rates of speech – 10 to 15 phonemes/second – are possible because we coproduce, or coarticulate, the units. At each instant, our articulators are executing overlapping patterns of movement that may correspond to several neighbouring phonemes, including phonemes in neighbouring syllables. The result of this shingled pattern of movement is, of course, a shingled pattern of sound, in which the acoustic structure of a given consonant or vowel varies from one context to another. Thus, the units of the acoustic signal do not correspond, one for one, with the units of perception.

Here we have the classic 'invariance issue' that has defeated, and still defeats, attempts at automatic speech recognition. This is not to say that engineers may not eventually devise machine algorithms to solve the problem, but it is to say that the final and necessary arbiter of machine performance is a native speaker. That is why the goal of many linguists and psycholinguists since the 1950s has been to specify what every human must know, or learn, in order to learn and know a language (Chomsky, e.g. 1972, 1986). That is also among the reasons why standard ethological procedures for studying vocal communication in other animals – namely, analysing acoustic records and correlating acoustic patterns with situational context – are useless for the study of speech and language.

Indeed, even for the study of primate calls, these methods are not without their difficulties, as Ujhelyi's chapter shows. Searching for precursors of human combinatorial processes in the calls of apes and monkeys, Ujhelyi reviews evidence for systematic variations in the order of perhaps meaningful elements across long, or extended, calls ('lexical syntax'), or in the perhaps meaningless acoustic properties of brief, integral calls ('phonological syntax'). She reports indications of the former in the calls with which gibbons, gorillas and chimpanzees claim or 'label' territory, and of the latter in the close contact calls of animals with 'sophisticated social relations', such as macaques and chimpanzees. Within-call variation may have arisen in these species as a side effect of the communicative use of facial gesture (particularly lip movements). As Ujhelyi herself remarks, however, 'syntax' implies clear differences of meaning between call variants or different call combinations, and these no one has yet demonstrated. Of course, if primate calls were generally independent of context, with the capacity for displaced reference of human speech, reliable differences of meaning might prove impossible to establish. On the other hand, if primate calls are not independent of context, their semantic scope may be too modest to require even a minimal 'phonological syntax'.

Implicit in this last observation is the assumption, common to most chapters in this section, that the function of phonology is to afford a large lexicon. None of these chapters has anything to say about the complex social conditions that must have prevailed among hominids before pressures toward extended referential communication could have taken effect. But all authors (except Carstairs-McCarthy) assume, either implicitly or explicitly, that phonological differentiation was a response to lexical pressure.

At first glance, Locke might also seem to be an exception, since he adopts a view of early hominid 'sound-making' close to that of Dunbar (this volume). Locke distinguishes 'speaking', an activity intended to convey information, from 'talking', an activity intended to facilitate social cohesion. Talking, the earliest mode of sound-making in children and, by hypothesis, in hominids, is rhythmic, repetitive and pregrammatical; it has 'little to do with thoughts', and can indeed be dissociated from language in a variety of disorders. Moreover, vocal volubility in infancy predicts amount of talking in childhood, and talking predicts the rate of vocabulary growth. But, in the end, for Locke too, it was 'independent advances in representational capacity' of hominids that encouraged naming, and so the emergence of phonology – very much along the lines laid out in the chapters that follow.

Why then did phonology take the form that it did? Where do its units come from, and why do they form a balanced system of perceptuomotor contrasts in every language? These are among the questions taken up by Studdert-Kennedy, MacNeilage, Lindblom and Kohler in chapters for which the guiding principle would seem to be: 'Derive language from non-language!' These four chapters, taken together, present what we believe to be the first systematic attempt to account for the evolutionary origins of language generativity. Their goal is to show that we do not have to postulate phonemes and features as the innate axioms of structuralist tradition. We may see them rather as emerging from prior constraints on perception, articulation and learning, according to general biological principles of self-organization.

Studdert-Kennedy sets the origin of the language hierarchy in the physical world of which language is a part. Following Abler (1989, 1997), he sees this hierarchy as a special case of 'the particulate principle of self-diversifying systems' (Abler 1989: 1), common to other natural systems, including physics, chemistry, genetics and number. The unlimited diversity of these systems would not be possible if their basic elements (e.g. atoms, genes, integers) blended. Infinite diversity emerges because units at a given level retain their integrity, yet combine to yield structures higher in a hierarchy with broader and qualitatively different ranges of function in comparison to their components. The particulate principle is a property of the physical universe to which any system that 'makes infinite use of finite means' necessarily conforms. Critical to biological exploitation of the principle for communication is a particulated motor machinery, such as the vocal tract or hand, that can be adapted for rapid distribution of coherent action over more or less independent parts. The first question then concerns the nature of the units that the machinery affords.

Two mutually supportive approaches to this question have been taken. First is the purely descriptive approach of both Studdert-Kennedy and MacNeilage, who turn to children and other primates for an answer. Here they assume that because ontogeny epitomizes (although it does not recapitulate) phylogeny, we can model the evolution of speech on its development in the child. Second is the mathematically grounded deductive approach of Lindblom.

MacNeilage begins with the neurobiology of motor control: how did we evolve the capacity to organize speech in the time domain into syllable-sized packages of consonants and vowels? He proposes that the mandibular cycle, the rhythmic oscillation of the jaw for ingestive purposes in mammals, already engaged with the respiratory and phonatory systems for vocalization in other primates, came under control of cortical areas specialized for 'intrinsic' or self-generated motor action, to yield the basic motor 'frame' of all speech, the syllable. Consonants and vowels, the 'content' of the frame, emerged by differentiation of the syllable into its closed and open phases, a process still followed by every normal child over the first year or so of life. For MacNeilage, as for Studdert-Kennedy and Lindblom, the one novel capacity, crucially distinguishing humans from other primates, is for vocal imitation, the basis of lexical acquisition.

A challenge to the priority of the syllable as the basic unit of action from which all language evolved might come from a language of manual gesture. A gestural origin for language attracts proponents because the evident iconicity of gesture seems to offer the thin end of a wedge into symbolic capacity. The early appearance of tools in the archaeological record, often with a right-handed bias, combined with the statistical association between handedness and language representation in the brain in modern populations, has added force to the argument. Yet further encouragement has come in recent years from one of the most remarkable discoveries of modern linguistics, namely, that sign languages of the deaf are full languages, independent of the surrounding spoken language, with a dual hierarchical structure of sign formation ('phonology') and syntax, analogous to that of spoken languages.

Yet each of the contributors to this section, either implicitly or explicitly, rejects the hypothesis of gestural origins. MacNeilage himself makes the fullest case, with a novel account of the association between manual and linguistic lateral biases. We will not rehearse his argument here beyond remarking that the gestural case has been weakened in recent years by evidence for right-hand biases in non-human primate populations, and for specialization of the left hemisphere for vocal communication in monkeys, mice, hamsters, birds and frogs. We may add that the striking structural correspondence between spoken and signed language may lose some force as an argument for homologous neural underpinnings in light of the necessary formal convergence imposed by the particulate principle.

The second approach to the origin of units is Lindblom's deductive account, developed in a series of papers since the 1980s, and here elaborated to include the effects of learning. Lindblom sees no more reason to reject the formalisms of linguistic description than an evolutionary biologist sees to reject the morphological descriptions of zoological taxonomy. On the contrary, the task is not to reject formalisms, but to explain them.

Lindblom therefore undertakes to derive phonological systems from universal constraints on speaking, listening and learning. Taking a cue perhaps from Darwin's reference to the 'struggle for existence' and 'natural selection' among words (Darwin 1871: 466), Lindblom sets the locus of a language system squarely in the individual rather than in the group, and proposes a model for the evolution of phonological forms within a language. The main dimension of phonetic variation from which phonological forms are selected is the continuum from a hyperarticulated, listener-oriented mode to the reduced, hypoarticulated mode of casual speech: '[T]he variability of speech is systematically structured by the continual tug-of-war between production and perception demands', that is, between ease of articulation and perceptual distinctiveness. The value of each item in the system, relative to every other item, is estimated by an articulatory to perceptual cost–benefit ratio, and the system is optimized to a least squares criterion. The effect of learning is to reduce the articulatory cost of the learned item, making articulatory ease language-specific, to some degree, and dependent on the size of a speaker-listener's lexicon. The key point for the present brief discussion is that lexical items are initially stored by a learner as unanalysed wholes. Units then emerge by a process of 'self-segmentation' to facilitate lexical storage and access, as items sharing movements (syllables, gestures) are grouped together. The theoretical interest of this elegant, and eminently testable, model is that it offers a principled mechanism by which the discrete units, essential to language generativity, may have emerged evolutionarily, and may still emerge ontogenetically, from continuously variable non-linguistic capacities.

Finally, Kohler files a friendly criticism of 'the seminal work by Lindblom and coauthors'. His point of departure is a paper by Lindblom & Maddieson (1988) in which they tested an ordinal scale of articulatory difficulty (Basic, Elaborated, Complex) with a set of eleven obstruent and seven sonorant consonants observed in a large sample of the world's languages. Kohler suggests that their 'data-oriented' argument here came close to circularity. He therefore proposes an alternative approach to the vexed concept of articulatory ease, more rigorously grounded in extralinguistic facts and assumptions. He adopts MacNeilage's concepts of 'frame' and 'content' as 'the principal step in the evolution of human language'. Then, working from a set of ten assumptions and their corollaries, Kohler motivates the concept of 'sound simplicity', with appeals to both articulatory and perceptual constraints, proceeding from the elementary vocalizations observed in other primates through articulations that exploit short movements, aided by gravity, to the complex articulatory reductions of rapid speech. In conclusion, he emphasizes the need to supplement paradigmatic studies of language systems with work on the syntagmatic aspects of spontaneous speech.

As earlier remarked, the four chapters just reviewed constitute what we believe to be the first attempt to account for the evolution of language generativity. It is true that they have nothing to say about recursion, a property of both syntax and the number system (Abler 1997), often taken to be essential for language generativity. They do, however, offer a principled account of the first step from analog primate call to discrete combinatorial hierarchy, without which linguistic recursion would not be possible.

The final chapter by Carstairs-McCarthy links aspects of grammar, lexicon, syntax and phonology that seem, on the face of it, quite unrelated. We will not summarize his ingenious and entertaining discussion of such topics as synonymy avoidance (the Principle of Contrast that, turning Lindblom's lexical hierarchy on its head, favours new words over old) and the perhaps superfluous distinction between sentences and noun phrases. For phonology, Carstairs-McCarthy's novel proposal is that lexical elaboration was a consequence, not a cause, of vocal tract reconfiguration. In fact, there is both evidence and argument for the hypothesis that, whatever later changes in the neuroanatomy of the vocal machinery may have been necessary for full speech, the initial impetus for lowering the larynx came from a shift in the relation between the skull base and the respiratory tract, consequent upon the evolution of bipedal locomotion (Du Brul 1977; Laitman & Reidenberg 1988). With the lowered larynx came syllables – more syllables, in fact, than hominids had meanings for. Aided by the Principle of Contrast, 'sound differences . . . [became] . . . the driving force in the creation of "meanings" '. Yet, no less important than lexical elaboration was the structure of the syllable itself, with its characteristic contrast between sonority peak and margins; for this, according to Carstairs-McCarthy, became the model for the distinction between noun phrase and sentence. Neural control mechanisms that had evolved to govern syllable structure were then co-opted for syntax. As a result, this provocative chapter concludes, 'certain fundamental aspects of language, not only syntactic but semantic, may be mere byproducts of a change in vocal tract anatomy'. Since these words might very well be true, even if none of Carstairs-McCarthy's other arguments were to go through, they form a fitting conclusion to the chapters on the emergence of phonology, and a neat transition to the chapters on syntax.

References

Abler, W. (1989). On the particulate principle of self-diversifying systems. *Journal of Social and Biological Structures*, 12, 1–13.

(1997). Gene, language, number: the particulate principle in nature. *Evolutionary Theory*, 11, 237–248.

Chomsky, N. (1972). *Language and Mind*. New York: Harper & Row.

(1986). *Knowledge of Language: Its Nature, Origin, and Use*. New York: Praeger.

Darwin, C. (1871). *The Descent of Man*. London: John Murray.

Du Brul, E. L. (1977). Origins of the speech apparatus and its reconstruction in fossils. *Brain and Language*, 4, 365–381.

Laitman, J. T. & Reidenberg, J. S. (1989). Advances in understanding the relationship between the skull base and larynx with comments on the origins of speech *Human Evolution*, 3, 99–109.

Lindblom, B. & Maddieson, I. (1988). Phonetic universals in consonant systems. In Hyman, L. M. & Li, C. N. (eds.) *Language, Speech and Mind*. London & New York: Routledge: 62–78.

11 Long-call structure in apes as a possible precursor for language

MÁRIA UJHELYI

1 Introduction

Human language is a tool for communication. The origin and evolution of human language can therefore be appropriately treated within the framework of the evolution of communication systems.

However, some authors have reservations concerning this view. Bickerton (1990), for example, claims that the differences between animal communication and human language are so large in every respect that the gap between them is unbridgeable. Undoubtedly, there are many qualitative differences between animal communication and human language. Nevertheless, animal communications are not uniform systems, they – like other behaviours – may represent different evolutionary stages.

Primate communication is prominent in this respect among animal communication systems. In the course of the evolution of the primate order several structural features of vocal communication have been established, which appear to show some elementary characteristics of human language. Unlike human language, which is built from meaningless elements (speech sounds) forming meaningful units (words), and from these units combining to make more complex utterances, animal vocal signals typically can neither be broken into more elementary sounds, nor combined into more complex vocal structures. However, several primate species (as well as birds) seem to possess capacities to produce either the one or the other mode of the above-mentioned operations. Based on the reports of natural vocalizations, both modes seem to occur in chimpanzees' and bonobos' long-distance calls, as well as in human language. That is, in the vocalization of our nearest relatives (and presumably already in that of our common ancestor) important structural linguistic characteristics appear. Furthermore, social transmission of acoustic variants of given call types also seems to exist in them.

Consequently, the evolutionary stage represented by great apes' communication may be considered as an intermediate one between lower-level animal communication and human language, and, as such, as a precursor of human language. One may conclude that possibilities or preconditions for a language-like evolution could arise within the scope of primate communication.

2 Mechanisms for producing call variants

Human language has a capacity to generate an infinite number of utterances, by variable use of a limited number of hierarchically ordered linguistic units, which are in human speech of two types: meaningless units (sounds) and meaningful units (sound combinations, or words).

We can use these terms to make a comparison between animal vocal signals and language. Some years ago Peter Marler (1977) suggested that we should distinguish between phonological and lexical syntax when describing animal communicative signals. Syntax here means arrangement of elements. As he defined them, lexical syntax varies meaningful elements, while phonological syntax varies meaningless elements. We can naturally talk about syntax only if discrete elements (units) are available for differential arrangement at all.

Typical animal vocalizations can produce only a limited (species-specific) set of meaningful signs, because of the absence of mechanisms for producing variants.

However, it has been known for some years that several monkey species produce long calls built from smaller, stable, clearly distinguishable units, for example titi monkeys (Robinson 1984) and tamarins (Cleveland & Snowdon 1982). Such species also occur in prosimii, for example the indri (Thalmann, Geismann, Simona & Mutschler 1993), and in apes: the gibbons (e.g. Marshall & Marshall 1976; Raemaekers, Raemaekers & Haimoff 1984).

The units of these long calls are 'traditional' communicative signals functioning, for example, as alarm call or contact call, etc. That is, they are meaningful elements, which are combined in different arrangements in different compound calls.

The number of elementary units in long calls differs across species. Tamarins use only two types of unit (Snowdon 1993), while Robinson observed six unit types in titi monkeys (Robinson 1984). According to Mitani & Marler's analysis, thirteen basic note types can be distinguished in the gibbon song (Mitani & Marler 1989).

Not only the number of units, but also the complexity of their combination differs. The calls of tamarin and titi monkeys seem to be relatively simple vocalizations repeating the same elements many times over, whereas the songs of gibbons are highly elaborated. Acoustically different songs can be created by changing number, type and position of elements (notes).

Chimpanzees and bonobos also emit long, compound calls – named 'pant hoot' and 'high hoot', respectively – which can be divided into acoustically distinct segments (Clark & Wrangham 1993; Hohmann & Fruth 1994; Mitani, Hasegawa, Gros-Louis & Marler 1992). Although chimpanzees do not change the order of the four fundamental units of the long call, they insert individually selected vocal elements (for example barks) into different positions of the call (Arcadi 1996).

Other monkey species, for example vervets (Owren 1990) and macaques (Hauser, Evans & Marler 1993), can produce acoustic variants within a call type. In this case, while the fundamental identity of a given call is maintained, articulatory differences arise at some points in the sound sequence. The acoustic variants are produced through facial gestures modified by mandibular positions or lip configurations.

Bauer found a similar situation in chimpanzees as well. Analysing a series of screams by a male chimpanzee, he pointed out that fundamental frequency in the sequence changed in association with modified lip configuration (Bauer 1987).

This type of call variant production may represent phonological syntax, since the altered parts of the call do not possess their own meaning independently of the call.

In the case of lexical syntax, the originally available, typical animal calls are composed to form a more complex vocal structure. In phonological syntax, the originally unitary sound sequences are compartmentalized through series of oppositions of articulatory call variants. We must add that the process of compartmentalization is just at the beginning at subhuman level.

3 Function and social background of forming variations

Except for common chimpanzees and bonobos, species with lexical syntax share a common feature in their social behaviour, namely monogamous territoriality. This is in spite of the fact that they represent very different taxonomic groups: the indris belong to the prosimii, the titi and the tamarin are New World monkeys, the gibbon is an ape.

Monogamous territoriality as a social organization is in sharp contrast with that of the majority of primate species. Most primate species live in groups and possess group territory. In these cases boundaries between territories are not very strict. In contrast, indris, gibbons and the above-mentioned New World species possess individual territory, which is marked and defended. The marking – unlike that of other territorial mammals, but like that of birds – is realized by acoustic signals. This method of marking is perhaps – at least partly – due to primates' lower olfactory sensitivity.

I suggest that it is just this territorial behaviour which establishes lexical syntactic capacity. Labelling one's own territory requires individually different signs. If the labelling channel is an acoustic one, and the primary sounds are limited and genetically fixed, then differences in signs can only be achieved by compositions of the invariant elementary sounds and by varying their arrangements.

By contrast, species capable of producing within-call acoustic variants live in large groups with complex social interactions.

For monkeys living in groups the face plays a very important role, becoming the most important individual identifying feature during evolution (Grüsser 1984). At the same time, the most important (primate-specific) tool for expressing emotions is the facial gesture (Van Hooff 1972). A number of experiments demonstrate clearly that facial expressions convey information, which can guide the behaviour of others (e.g. Miller, Banks & Ogawa 1963). That is, producing modifiable facial gestures has an immediate communicative function. Probably this was the driving force in the evolution of facial gestures. But as a secondary result, acoustic variations arise if an animal changes its facial gesture during vocalizing.

Primates have mobile, nonattached upper lips, which enable them to produce different facial expressions. Different facial expressions include different lip configurations forming different barriers to the passage of air. Thus they may result in different acoustic outcomes. Although a human-like vocal tract is yet absent, the face will be the main tool for producing articulatory variants (Hauser *et al.* 1993).

In this way facial gestures, especially lip postures, became associated with some types of sounds. The strength and evolutionary significance of this association are shown by the fact that in humans it is inborn: Kuhl & Meltzoff (1982) demonstrated with an elegant experiment that human neonates can recognize a face belonging to a vowel being spoken without learning.

However, a problem seems to come about with this association. A number of experiments have reported evidence that both macaques (Hauser 1993) and chimpanzees (Morris & Hopkins 1993), like humans, have right hemisphere advantages for face processing, while phonological analysis in humans and recognition of species-specific calls in macaques are lateralized to the left hemisphere. Nevertheless, recent experiments demonstrate that lipreading can be dissociated from other aspects of face processing. It seems that effective lipreading requires access to a left hemisphere phonetic processing site. Patients with left inferior temporal damage are unable to identify sound from lips, but their ability to recognize individual faces or understand emotions remains intact (Campbell 1992). In agreement with these findings, Ojemann (1983) has shown that electrical stimulation of the same cortical sites disrupts both the production of oral facial movements and the ability to discriminate phonemes.

In sum, phonological syntax is established in monkeys with sophisticated social relations by production and perception of different facial gestures. Naturally, both chimpanzee species displaying very complex social behaviour are also capable of producing such articulatory variations.

But what is the root of their having lexical syntax as well, even though they do not hold individual territories? This contradiction can be resolved by an evolutionary explanation. It seems that we must posit territorial monogamy as an antecedent to their present-day group system.

4 Rationale for the ancestry of territorial behaviour in chimpanzees

Territorial monogamy as a closed social unit seems to be a very ancient and simple form of social organization in the primate order. Primitive prosimii, mostly nocturnal and arboreal animals, have no stable social units; they have a solitary way of living. Some of the prosimian species became monogamous, e.g. the indri and the spectral tarsier (Itani 1985). It seems that the only way for nocturnal, arboreal animals to form social bonds is monogamy. Only the transition from a nocturnal to a diurnal life style provided an opportunity for aggregation and the formation of larger groups. This grouping pattern is characteristic of Cercopithecoidea. But some New World monkey species and all species of lesser apes seem to preserve monogamy. Based on species distribution and foraging strategies, it has been suggested that, in New World primates, monogamous pairing might be an ancient form from which the other forms of social structures evolved (Eisenberg 1981; Robinson, Wright & Kinsey 1987).

In the case of chimpanzees and bonobos the evolutionary descent of their social systems from monogamy is demonstrable with more difficulty. One of the possible arguments for their monogamous ancestry comes from their unique migratory trend. In monogamous species, subadults of both sexes leave their natal group, and establish a new family with new territory; but nobody is allowed to enter the already existing groups. In large multimale–multifemale communities, individuals leave their natal groups as they become adolescent, and others enter from outside, but only one of the sexes migrates. In common monkeys it is always the males which leave their natal group and enter another one, while females stay at home, so they are all kin. By contrast, the social structure of apes – chimpanzees, bonobos, and essentially also gorillas (Maryanski 1987) – is based upon male-kin bonding. That is, females migrate, but males never leave their natal group. Transformation to this special pattern appears to be more likely from an ancestral monogamous structure than from a stabilized female-based grouping.

Based upon the kin-system, co-operative actions in monkeys are established mainly between females. In common chimpanzees, in turn, co-operation – which is of a wider range – occurs essentially between males. In monogamous species, prosocial interactions and co-operation hardly occur outside the pair. However, fathers and subadult sons do sometimes co-operate: fathers may help their sons to compete against males from neighbouring groups in order to establish a new territory (Smuts 1987). The tendency for co-operation between adult kin males might be the key to understanding processes that led to the special reorganization of social structure in the course of great apes' evolution. Further arguments come from the vocalization itself.

Gorillas also have a long call named 'hoot', which is connected with the moving of the group. As Mori (1983) pointed out, the basic pattern of the gorilla's and chimpanzee's hoot is similar, although they differ in acoustic nature and in function. 'Both species begin with slow vocalization in repetition, the repeated sounds gradually become quicker, and higher in note.' We must add that gibbon song is characterized by a similar sequence (personal observation). The hoot of the gorilla is of the nature of a territorial call, since it is emitted only when encountering another group (Fossey 1972; Mori 1983). Gorillas have also another call type, named 'wrah', with the function of cohesive calling. A similar sound sometimes appears in the final part of the chimpanzee 'pant-hoot'.

Mori speculates about the existence of a compound call of the common ancestor of gorilla and both chimpanzee species, the function of which was territorial. As the species diverged, the call divided into pieces that acquired different functions in the separated lines.

Another important argument may be the mode of presentation of long calls, strongly reminiscent of territorial song. Territorial songs are generally presented in duet form, in which the members of a pair perform a mutually co-operative and co-ordinated display. Reviewing the duet songs of primate species, Haimoff (1986) concludes that 'there have been no observations of any stable monogamous and territorial primate species in which duetting does not occur, or any polygynous primate species in which duetting does occur'.

Despite the strong correlation between duet performance and monogamy, co-ordinated call display does exist in great apes. As De Waal observed (1988), bonobos show a high degree of gibbon-like synchronization between vocalizations of different individuals. In common chimpanzees, males often call together (Mitani & Brandt 1994), while in bonobos a male–female pair duet occurs (Hohmann & Fruth 1994). (This difference is in agreement with the different structure of their inter-individual and sexual relations.) The ability to perform co-ordinated calls seems to be a remnant of an ancestral territorial song display.

5 Changes in call functions

Should the long call have a territorial antecedent, its survival is nevertheless closely connected with the special way of life of both chimpanzee and bonobo.

Territorial song marks the territory of a family, and serves to maintain spacing between members of neighbouring families. On the other hand, in chimpanzee species long calls serve to maintain connections between group members. In contrast, for example, to the macaques, where the members of the whole group spend their time permanently together, chimpanzees associate in temporary parties that vary in size and composition. The group members and even the favoured partners are often spatially separated (Mitani 1994). However, they have a strong need to be assured of the permanent possibility of meeting and co-operating. Long-call vocalization is an effective means of maintaining relations in such circumstances.

In connection with the changed function, the circumstances of producing long calls also change. In gibbons (and in the other non-hominoid monogamous species, too), duet songs are performed at given times of the day. Moreover, in indris, duets are produced only at a given period of the year, since a breeding season still exists in them. In both chimpanzee species, duetting or chorusing can be heard all day in relation to different activities, as they try to assemble community members for various purposes.

There also appears to be some shift in the meaning of long call. Marler defined lexical syntax in this respect as 'the use of compound signals which derive their meaning from the multiplexing of the meaning of the components as used separately or in other combination' (Marler 1977). We can see that the building units of long calls or songs frequently occur independently of the songs with the meaning as usual. But have the compound calls a different meaning from the units?

Robinson tried to match the use of simple and compound calls in capuchin monkey vocalization with different situations in a contact-seeking – contact-avoiding scale. Although he found that in different circumstances there was a slight difference in the use of simple and compound calls, he could not detect a strict trend of differential use (1984).

A more striking difference appears if callers rather than situations are considered. In most mammals marking of territory is carried out by physical or chemical signals, leaving more or less permanent traces. Such signals can be placed directly on the territory, and even in the absence of the owner they inform other animals. The acoustic nature of the primate signal makes it impossible to mark the territory directly. Instead, the presence and location of the territory owner are broadcast. Since the different applications of the available elements result in inter-individual differences in call production, a special construction may be characteristic to the identity of the caller. In tamarins, for example, the different number of elements used distinguishes male and female calls (Masataka 1987). In gibbons, however, the significantly larger song repertoire makes finer differentiation possible. Singing displays convey information about the territory owner's presence and location, and also indicate sex, rank and marital condition (Cowlishaw 1992). For example, the songs of males and females are very different, and Raemaekers observed that mated and unmated males sing in different ways (Raemaekers *et al.* 1984). Furthermore, interindividual differences arise not only according to social status. Mitani & Marler emphasize that gibbon males compose different note orders and even use different sets of the available note types. A gibbon male uses a given number (seven, eight or ten etc.) of the thirteen available notes. Note preference and song structure seem to be characteristic of a given male (Mitani & Marler 1989). Song variants mark individual identity.

Consequently, the units in themselves mean something quite different from the composite forms. The latter even include some representational meaning, since – in my opinion – the marking of individual identity is already a representational function.

The precise function of the within-class articulatory variants produced by macaques is not yet known. However, Hauser suggests that they reflect the status of the caller (Hauser 1991). Clark & Wrangham's conclusion is similar for the chimpanzee pant-hoot variants (Clark & Wrangham 1993).

We can say that in primate communication an elementary form of representation comes into existence, at least in social contexts. However, field studies report a peculiar manner of presentation of the pant-hoot in chimpanzees, which may be in contrast with this suggested function. Chimpanzee males often give the long call together, during which they attempt to match the acoustic characteristics of each other's vocalizations. Moreover, single males alter the acoustic structure of their calls when chorusing with different partners (Mitani & Brandt 1994; Arcadi 1996). This matching tendency is obviously in contrast to the exclusive use of given call variants functioning as individual markers, and it raises at least an abstract possibility of extrapolating representation toward more complex contexts.

Anyhow, the matching tendency unquestionably shows that call variants can be learned. There are some instances in which song transfer may occur in gibbons – for example, when a female becomes widowed, she may adopt and perform the male song and so produce a pseudoduet

(Geismann 1983). However, the exclusivity of songs, due to individual identity marking, hinders their transmission, even if the possibility of learning is accepted. Similarly, in large groups of macaques call variants are not transmitted, since the need and the mechanisms for transmission are absent. In vervet monkeys the acoustic realization of different alarm calls is genetically determined and invariant, only their proper use is learned.

In chimpanzees and bonobos, chorusing or duetting is an effective mechanism for spreading call variants. This mechanism results in standardization of the call variants. As a consequence, a 'call pool' containing a large number of call variants arises, which is not exclusive for a given animal, but available for and usable by other group members. This tendency toward standardization also results in – at least slight – differences between the call structures of different chimpanzee groups (Arcadi 1996; Mitani *et al.* 1992). The possibility of 'cultural' transmission is a fundamental requirement for any communication system to function in a language-like manner.

6 Conclusion

For primate species, vocalization plays an important role within their communicative actions. In addition to the ordinary function of animal vocal communication, primate vocalization acquired another function. For primates with evolved social systems, recognition of individual group members and distinction between them became more and more important. A main tool for this function is individually distinguishable voices. This function can be performed by creating signal variances. Consequently, there has been strong selective pressure toward sophistication of mechanisms creating variations.

This also means that vocal communication evolved as a part of social systems. We have seen that each mode of forming variations in vocal signals is rooted in different social systems. It seems that both preconditions are necessary, since neither monogamous species nor group-living species without monogamous traditions could achieve the level that can be found in great apes. Integrating the two types of operations which produce call variants (lexical and phonological syntax), chimpanzee and bonobo communication establishes a structurally and functionally distinct level in comparison to lower-animal communication. In sum, in the course of primate evolution, essential language characteristics emerged in vocalization (see MacNeilage, this volume).

However, this level still lacks many essential linguistic functions. Although, in so-called phonological syntax, sound modifications occur at certain points in the sound sequence, this is only a first step toward the emergence of human-like speech sounds. Here the sound variants are not yet independently produceable and freely combinable, but the existence of articulatory variants is a precondition for the evolution of a separate faculty of producing more elementary, standard sounds. Perhaps integration of the two mechanisms of producing variants (articulation and combination), as they exist in present-day chimpanzees, might contribute to the evolution of freely combinable sounds of human type, since in lexical syntax a free combination of elements already functions. If freely combinable, stable sound phenomena are already present, the sound system may evolve by further differentiation on the one hand, and by forming new sounds on the other hand. These processes were presumably long, and have only been completed with the appearance of modern *Homo*, as evidenced by the evolution of the vocal tract.

Rules, semantic and grammatical limitations on arranging and combining linguistic elements, are also absent (or nearly absent) at the subhuman level. Evolution of finer phonological processing, the exact representation of the articulated object-world, and true grammar represent further stages in language evolution, establishing essential structural changes in the system.

Acknowledgments

I am very grateful to John Maynard Smith, Kathleen Gibson, Jim Hurford, Michael Studdert-Kennedy, Chris Knight, Paul Buk and Eva Pap-Davies for helpful comments on the previous versions of this chapter.

References

Arcadi, A. C. (1996). Phrase structure of wild chimpanzee pant hoots: patterns of production and interpopulation variability. *American Journal of Primatology*, 39, 159–178.

Bauer, H. (1987). Frequency code: orofacial correlates of fundamental frequency. *Phonetica*, 44, 173–191.

Bickerton, D. (1990). *Language and Species*. Chicago & London: University of Chicago Press.

Campbell, R. (1992). The neuropsychology of lipreading. *Philosophical Transactions of Royal Society London B*, 335, 39–45.

Clark, A. P. & Wrangham, R. W. (1993). Acoustic analysis of wild chimpanzee pant hoots: do Kibale Forest chimpanzees have an acoustically distinct food arrival pant hoot? *American Journal of Primatology*, 31, 99–109.

Cowlishaw, G. (1992). Song function in gibbons. *Behavior*, 121, 131–153.

De Waal, F. B. M. (1988). The communicative repertoire of captive bonobos (Pan paniscus) compared to that of chimpanzees. *Behavior*, 106, 183–251.

Eisenberg, J. F. (1981). The mammalian radiations. Chicago: University of Chicago Press.

Fossey, D. (1972). Vocalizations of the mountain gorilla (Gorilla gorilla beringei). *Animal Behavior*, 20, 36–53.

Geismann, T. (1983). Female capped gibbon sings male song. *Journal of Human Evolution*, 12, 667–671.

Grüsser, O. J. (1984). Face recognition within the reach of neurobiology and beyond it. *Human Neurobiology*, 3, 183–190.

Haimoff, E. H. (1986). Convergence in the duetting of monogamous old world Primates. *Journal of Human Evolution*, 15, 51–59.

Hauser, M. D. (1991). Sources of acoustic variation in rhesus macaque vocalization. *Ethology*, 89, 29–46.

(1993). Right hemisphere dominance for the production of facial expression in monkeys. *Science*, 261, 475–477.

Evans, C. S. & Marler, P. (1993). The role of articulation in the production of rhesus monkey, Macaca mulatta, vocalization. *Animal Behavior*, 45, 423–433.

Hohmann, G. & Fruth, B. (1994). Structure and use of distance calls in wild bonobos (Pan paniscus). *International Journal of Primatology*, 15, 767–782.

Itani, J. (1985). The evolution of primate social structures. *Man*, 20, 593–611.

Kuhl, P. K. & Meltzoff, A. N. (1982). The bimodal perception of speech in infancy. *Science*, 218, 1138–1144.

Marler, P. (1977). The structure of animal communication sounds. In Bullock, T. H. (ed.) *Recognition of Complex Acoustic Signals* (*Report of the Dahlem Workshop*). Berlin: Dahlem Konferencen: 17–35.

Marshall, J. T., Jr, & Marshall, E. R. (1976). Gibbons and their territorial songs. *Science*, 193, 235–237.

Maryanski, A. R. (1987). African ape social structure: is there strength in weak ties? *Social Networks*, 9, 191–215.

Masataka, N. (1987). The perception of sex-specificity in long calls of the tamarin (Saguinnes labiatus labiatus). *Ethology*, 76, 56–64.

Miller, R. E., Banks, J. H. & Ogawa, N. (1963). Role of facial expression in 'co-operative-avoidance conditioning' in monkeys. *Journal of Abnormal and Social Psychology*, 67, 24–30.

Mitani, J. C. (1994). Ethological studies of chimpanzee vocal behavior. In Wrangham, R. W., McGrew, W. C., De Waal, F. B. M. & Heltne, P. G. (eds.) *Chimpanzee Cultures*. Cambridge, MA & London: Harvard University Press.

& Brandt, K. L. (1994). Social factors influence the acoustic variability in the long-distance calls of male chimpanzees. *Ethology*, 96, 233–252.

Hasegawa, T., Gros-Louis, J. & Marler, P. (1992). Dialects in wild chimpanzees? *American Journal of Primatology*, 27, 233–243.

& Marler, P. (1989). A phonological analysis of male gibbon singing behavior. *Behavior*, 106, 20–45.

Mori, A. (1983). Comparison of the communicative vocalizations and behaviors of group ranging in Eastern gorillas, chimpanzees and pygmy chimpanzees. *Primates*, 24, 486–500.

Morris, R. D. & Hopkins, W. D. (1993). Perception of human chimeric faces by chimpanzees: evidence for right hemisphere advantage. *Brain & Cognition*, 21, 111–122.

Ojemann, G. A. (1983). Brain organization for language from the perspective of electrical stimulation mapping. *Behavior and Brain Sciences*, 6, 189–230.

Owren, M. J. (1990). Acoustic classification of alarm calls by vervet monkeys (Cercopithecus aethiops) and humans: I Natural calls. *Journal of Comparative Psychology*, 104, 20–28.

Raemaekers, J. J., Raemaekers, P. M. & Haimoff, E. H. (1984). Loud calls of the gibbons (Hylobates lar): repertoire, organization and context. *Behavior*, 91, 146–189.

Robinson, J. G. (1979). An analysis of the organization of vocal communication in the titi monkey, Callicebus moloch. *Zeitschrift für Tierpsychologie*, 49, 381–405.

(1984). Syntactic structures in the vocalizations of wedge-capped capuchin monkeys, Cebus olivaceus. *Behavior*, 90, 46–79.

Wright, P. C. & Kinzey, W. G. (1987). Monogamous cebids and their relatives: intergroup calls and spacing. In Smuts, B. B., Cheney, D. L., Seyfarth, R. M., Wrangham, R. W. & Struhsaker, T. T. (eds.) *Primate Societies*. Chicago & London: University of Chicago Press: 44–53.

Smuts, B. (1987). Sexual competition and mate choice. In Smuts, B. B., Cheney, D. L., Seyfarth, R. M., Wrangham, R. W. & Struhsaker, T. T. (eds.) *Primate Societies*. Chicago & London: University of Chicago Press: 370–384.

Snowdon, Charles, T. (1993). Linguistic phenomena in the natural communication of animals. In Roitblatt, H. L., Herman, L. M. & Nachtigall, P. E. (eds.) *Language and Communication: Comparative Perspectives*. Hillsdale, NJ: Lawrence Erlbaum Associates: 175–194.

Thalmann, U., Geismann, T., Simona, A. & Mutschler, T. (1993). The indris of Anjanaharibe-Sud, northeastern Madagascar. *International Journal of Primatology*, 14, 357–381.

Van Hoof, J. A. R. A. M. (1972). A comparative approach to the phylogeny of laughter and smiling. In Hinde, R. A. (ed.) *Non-Verbal Communication*. Cambridge: Cambridge University Press: 209–241.

12 Social sound-making as a precursor to spoken language

JOHN L. LOCKE

The organs of talking are at least two normally associated human beings.
[John Rupert Firth, 1937]

Over eighty years ago, a young social anthropologist named Bronislaw Malinowski began a period of fieldwork on the Trobriand Islands of New Guinea. After some years of living among and observing the highly homogeneous tribe that inhabited the Trobriands, Malinowski commented that 'We use language exactly as savages do . . . Our talk . . . serves to establish bonds of personal union between people brought together by the mere need of companionship . . . It is only in certain very special uses among a civilized community and only in its highest uses that language is employed to frame and express thoughts' (Malinowski 1923). These observations nicely set the tone for what I will have to say here.

I wish to begin my own comments about language by calling attention to an anomaly that is embedded in recent writings on the evolution of linguistic capacity in our species. In one of the more impressive of these efforts, it was argued that the ability of our prelinguistic ancestors to work and co-operate would have been, and in the evolutionary fact of the matter was, enhanced by language (Pinker & Bloom 1990). This, according to the claim, contributed to the evolution of grammar by natural selection, generation by generation. Strangely missing from the theory was an attempt to explain a fundamental characteristic of all 6,000–8,000 normal human languages in the world – they are spoken; not 21 per cent, not 63 per cent, *all* of them!

Theoretical silence on this issue is no minor omission, to be waved away with an insubstantial remark. Moreover, little has been said about the actual steps taken by our evolutionary ancestors that took our species from having no linguistic capacity to the richly complex level that we enjoy today. If language came into full flower gradually, as has been argued, what were the intermediate behaviours? Bickerton (1996) has suggested that a capability for protolanguage, which is characterized by short, crudely formed utterances, preceded full grammatical capacity. However, he too has said little or nothing about the social antecedents to, or functions of, prelinguistic utterances.

What did the early behaviours look like? To some theorists, 'look like' is precisely the right term, for they assume that language began as a gestural system, and then was 'simply' switched over to the oral mode. However, the reasons for the shift of modalities have not been clarified or even treated as a fact that needs to be addressed (Corballis 1991). Of course it has long been said that speech works better than gestural systems. It can be used in the dark and around corners, and leaves the hands free for work. But these perfectly correct statements suggest that our hominid ancestors, having thoughts to convey, rationally looked around for the ideal communication system. It is far more plausible that our ancestors had the means to express their feelings vocally and then discovered, over many generations, that this same modality could be manipulated to convey thought and co-ordinate action.

Before proceeding further, I will define three vocal behaviours that are relevant to spoken language: sound-making, speaking and talking (see Locke 1998, for more detailed discussion).

1 Vocal behaviours

From a physical standpoint, *sound-making* involves the production of syllabic vocal material in a repetitive and rhythmic fashion. This is done by raising and lowering the mandible in particular ways while phonating. Coincidentally, the lips and tongue may be actively or passively positioned to produce various points of constriction. The functions of sound-making vary.

Speaking is sound-making that is directed to one or more listeners and expresses unshared information that has been encoded in spoken language. People speak in order to convey information. In the typical case, the articulatory co-ordination required by speaking is handled primarily by mechanisms that are situated in the left cerebral hemisphere of the brain. The rhythmic and melodic aspects draw more heavily on mechanisms in the right hemisphere.

In *talking*, the individual engages in sound-making in order to achieve and maintain cohesion with others. Cohesion is achieved through a range of social behaviours that promote meshing and synchronization, and are manifested in co-ordinated vocal turns, gaze patterns and bodily movements; and a host of vocal, lexical and gestural accommodations. Since one of the rules of verbal engagement is that there must be a topic, propositional speaking frequently occurs during talking, but in many circumstances this is optional, and is waived by tacit consent of both parties.

The material of talk is vocal and facial, and is supported by manual gesticulation and gesture. The eyes play a major role in the expression of emotion. As a vehicle for the expression of feeling, talking relies heavily on mechanisms in the right cerebral hemisphere that regulate emotional and social behaviour. Where speaking terminates with message transmission, talking occurs in episodes – chats, bull sessions, conversations – that serve as minimal units of social interaction. Talking is a socially oriented process that has little to do with thoughts, and it taps no more than the most superficial levels of language. Talking tends to be repetitive and rhythmic. How things are said, and the relationship between the manner of talking and the identity of the talker, is almost as important as what is said.

Dissociations between talking and language suggest that there are mechanisms that are specialized for sound-making and talking. But we need not turn to exotic Oliver Sacks-like syndromes and patterns of brain damage to see these dissociations. In typical language development, infants engage in sound-making and talking long before they know that others have mental lives that differ from their own, and presumably are unaware that the talkers to whom they are exposed are exchanging information with arbitrary symbols (Locke 1996). My personal attraction to talking as a precursor to language in the species began with the observation that normally developing infants take vocal turns, use word-like sounds and sentence-like prosodies, and in some cultures talk on toy telephones long before they produce words and do anything grammatical (Locke 1993).

Of course there are also some unusual disorders, such as elective mutism or stuttering, that affect talking while leaving speech and language alone, and patterns of brain damage, such as jargon aphasia, that impair language and speech but not talking. Jargon-aphasic patients understand little or no language but display fluent sound-making, usually with normal conversational emotion, intonation and facial expression, yielding the floor when interrupted, reassuming the floor when appropriate. For all intents and purposes, they have no language whatsoever, but their ability to produce talk-like behaviours is undiminished (Brown 1981).

It thus appears that humans have a mechanism in the brain that controls sound-making, possibly operating in some isolation from other mechanisms that are needed for vocabulary acquisition or grammar. If one were to look for this mechanism, neurosurgical and neuropathological findings suggest that a good place to start would be the Supplementary Motor Area (SMA), a structure that is located in the frontal lobes, along the mesial surface of the superior frontal gyrus. When the SMA is electrically stimulated, the patient tends to produce syllables involuntarily in a repetitive manner (Penfield & Welch 1951). When lesions invade or compromise the area, repetitive vocalic or syllabic utterances are a frequent result (see reviews in Jonas 1987; MacNeilage, this volume).

2 Ontogeny

In the development of language, it is becoming clear that vocal volubility in infancy is correlated with talking in childhood. Children who are just noticeably delayed in the acquisition of vocabulary are already less voluble than typically developing children. Lexically delayed children as young as eighteen to twenty-four months produce significantly fewer utterances than their peers, independent of measures of utterance quality (Paul & Jennings 1992; Rescorla & Ratner 1996; Thal, Oroz & McCaw 1995).

While it seems that vocalizing leads to talking, it also appears that talking leads to grammar. Except for unusual syndromes and brain diseases, nearly every child who begins to talk on time proceeds the rest of the way into language. Many of those who are delayed in the onset of talking, and remain delayed for the next four years, develop life-long specifically grammatical difficulties (Locke 1997). In ontogeny, there is a correlation between the number of words used or known and the age of onset of grammatical operations (see below).

Let us take a look at why this might be. The child's first words and formulaic phrases appear to be stored in a prosodic type of memory (Echols 1993). As a system that presupposes no discrete, combinable units like the phoneme, prosodic memory is assumed to have a limited storage capacity (Lindblom 1989). If lexical items continue to accumulate in prosodic form, the system will overload. The issue may be forced by the so-called 'lexical spurt', a sharp increase in the rate at which new utterances are added to the infant's receptive and expressive vocabulary (Benedict 1979; Reznick 1990).

When children have a 'critical mass' of words in their expressive lexicon they begin to apply the rules of linguistic morphology (Bates, Dale & Thal 1994; Marchman & Bates 1994; Plunkett & Marchman 1993). In English, this produces overregularized irregular verbs and noun plurals (e.g. 'goed' for 'went' and 'foots' for 'feet'; Marcus (1995); Marcus, Pinker, Ullman, Hollander, Rosen & Xu (1992)). This is the first solid evidence of a grammar at the level of morphology and phonology. Talking thus seems to play a role in the activation of grammatical mechanisms. Indeed, it is extremely rare for a neurologically normal child to vocalize and talk freely over the first several years of life and then begin to slow down when approaching the developmental phase in which grammatical operations normally start up (Locke 1997).

In light of the fact that all normal human languages are spoken, it makes sense to consider the possibility that social sound-making and talking preceded the development of grammar, and that linguistic grammars represent a functional adaptation that enhanced the efficiency, utility or flexibility of vocal communication. Let us take a look at how this adaptation might have arisen.

3 Nonhuman primates

It is obvious that free-ranging nonhuman primates engage in social sound-making, but most of the work has addressed alarm calls. By concentrating on this class of vocal behaviours – far and away the easiest to elicit, record and interpret – ethologists have passed up opportunities to learn about the more likely phylogenetic precursors to human sound-making; for alarm calls are unlikely to be learned, to vary much from one group to another, or to reveal a flexibility of use as in, say, deception or paraphrase. The more interesting class of vocalizations would be produced by contented animals, vocalizing quietly among themselves in a family or small group situation, and very difficult to get on tape (Harcourt, Stewart & Hauser 1993). These vocalizations would not *mean* anything, in the sense that audio playback could be expected to elicit specific actions unambiguously.

One type of vocalization that is not screamed but *uttered* by various species of monkeys is the girney (Marc Hauser, personal communication). Girneys are most frequently produced by mothers who are interacting with other mothers, or with juvenile females. Because girneys seem to be produced behind closed lips, they tend to sound nasal, and resemble the sound of an individual who is talking with food in his mouth. Girneys may be issued interchangeably with lip-smacking, which evidently has an affiliative function, and are common among animals in small, intimate groups (Redican 1975). They thus resemble talking from a social standpoint. From a physical standpoint, girneys lack the rhythmicity of lip- or tongue-smacking but, unlike these activities, are typically phonated.

It is unknown how hominids developed vocal-motor control. Through ritualization, sound-making movements may have been physiologically emancipated and made available for intentional deployment. If the phonatory aspect of girneys were combined with the pulsatile character of lip- and tongue-smacking, a human-like type of sound-making could have been achieved. Why this would have happened is unclear.

3.1 *Proximity favours variegation*

Moynihan's (1970) analysis of a number of different mammals, birds and fish indicates that most species have a numerically restricted range of displays, generally between fifteen and thirty-five. He speculated that there might be a 'saturation point' – an absolute limit on the number of displays a species exhibits. Moynihan asked why the number of displays should be so few, in relation to the almost limitless number of unritualized behaviours that animals are able to interpret and generate. One possibility, among others, is that processing efficiency declines as displays exceed some manageable number.

Early sound-making would have been accompanied by at least those vocal–facial displays that arise within particular 'pragmatic' contexts in nonhuman primates today (see Green 1975). It only remained for the source of variation to expand from the strictly prosodic domain – where variation alters vocal pitch, loudness, duration and quality – into the articulatory domain, and subsequently, when certain oral gestures were used recurrently, for our ancestors to discover the fact that these sound-making movements could be combined in various ways to produce a range of distinctive phonetic forms: words. But how did the movements of talking come to variegate at the articulatory level? One possibility, arising from outside the general motor domain, is that independent advances in representational capacity encouraged differential 'labelling' practices.

W. John Smith's extensive review suggests that 'in species in which individuals are continuously and closely together, displays are often more variable in form and more likely to intergrade than they are in species in which individuals have much less intimate and frequent access to each other' (Smith 1979: 60). Talking would have constituted a social and physical frame capable of accommodating constituent gestures and units of meaning.

The abundance of characteristically different sound patterns known by our ancestors was not, in and of itself, a purely linguistic matter. Rather, it was needed for individual and group identification. A large-capacity system for scanning and recognizing vocal patterns, including words, thus existed and became available when needed for talking.

3.2 *Grooming talk*

Hominid talk was probably just one step beyond grooming. Robin Dunbar (1996, this volume) has argued that social grooming was, in fact, an evolutionary precursor to speech in our species. His thesis is that primates were increasingly pressured to make use of vocal grooming as group size increased and, with it, intra-group competition and the time needed to service alliances.

Anticipating Dunbar, Desmond Morris invented the term 'grooming talking' in the 1960s. He had in mind

> the meaningless, polite chatter of social occasions, the 'nice weather we are having' or 'have you read any good books lately' form of talking. It is not concerned with the exchange of important ideas or information, nor does it reveal the true mood of the speaker, nor is it aesthetically pleasing. Its function is to reinforce the greeting smile and to maintain the social togetherness. It is our substitute for social grooming. By providing us with a non-aggressive social preoccupation, it enables us to expose ourselves communally to one another over comparatively long periods, in this way enabling valuable group bonds and friendships to grow and become strengthened. [Morris 1967: 204]

4 Hominids

How did hominids progress from their own version of grooming talk to modern linguistic capacity? Like other cognitive specializations, we may assume that the capacity for linguistic grammars arose as an adaptation to a need. To assume otherwise makes no sense. Even Malinowski, who had his hands full just describing the many facets of life in New Guinea, ventured a remark on this issue: 'It is nothing short of absurd', he said, 'to assume . . . that grammar has grown up as a sort of wild weed of human faculties for no purpose whatever except its own existence' (Malinowski 1923: 327).

In emergently talk-oriented societies, increasing specificity of reference would have created a need for more elaborate statements and, with them, increasingly complex organizational schemas. That is, as words proliferated and utterances became increasingly variable and unpredictable, speakers and listeners would have needed a means of organizing the material that is manipulated in talking. We may thus assume that hominids made vocal sounds and talked before they achieved grammatical capability. Talk would thus have arisen socially, but pregrammatically.

The central tenet of evolutionary psychology is that highly specialized cognitive systems are available to us modern humans because they solved problems that were experienced by our evolutionary ancestors (see Cosmides & Tooby 1994). Our ancestors needed to tell one individual from another, and so we have cognitive (and neural) mechanisms that activate to the appearance of faces and the sound of voices. Lacking a reason to suppose that the evolution of grammatical capacity was somehow exempted from this general principle, one assumes that it, too, arose as an adaptation. It is unlikely that a dedicated and specialized utterance-analytic and -computation system would have developed prior to its first obvious need, and its first social applications, in talking.

I assume, then, that social sound-making, talking and language evolved to serve the needs of individuals who were alike and knew each other. The pressure to speak elaborately would have come from an overriding imperative – the need to monitor and share with others, and jointly puzzle out, the perceived intentions and actions of fellow members of the tribe (Locke 1998).

The phonological principle presumes the prior discovery of the phoneme. While an utterance reproduction capability would have allowed prephonological individuals to talk, it would not have enabled them to achieve a large lexicon. The reason is that every utterance they knew would have been an idiom, an irreducible and unalterable 'figure of speech'. There are presumed to be absolute storage limitations for this kind of emblematic material (Lindblom 1989).

Prosodically organized vocal patterns are not, by definition, particulated at levels corresponding to the units that are so freely recombined in linguistic phonologies (see Abler 1989; Studdert-Kennedy, this volume). Lacking analysis at the level of the segment, there would have been no way for our prephonological ancestors to store or manipulate anything like the number of utterance units that characterize modern levels of language. Thus I assume that the solution to the first problem gave rise to a second problem: as the capacity for reference expanded, stereotyped utterances would have proliferated to an unmanageable level without some implicit recognition of phonetic regularities – the basis by which their burgeoning store of vocal utterances were, and thus could be, organized.

4.1 *From recurrent gestures to segments*

I submit that our evolutionary ancestors evolved a capability for utterance analysis – a critical component of grammar – in response to a rapidly increasing need to store and manipulate vocal forms that, until that point, had been poorly analysed at the level of the phonological segment. When this need arose, it is less than daring to suppose that our hominid ancestors, like modern primates, already enjoyed some ability to identify patterns and detect the organization in hierarchically organized material (see Greenfield 1991). Since humans are adaptive, it is reasonable to suppose that hominids had some level of a domain-general ability to organize their own behaviour (see Thelen 1991; Thelen & Fogel 1989).

But how was this general ability to detect patterns and perceive organization applied to the speech domain? How would our evolutionary ancestors have discovered, and hence created, a segmental organization for their stereotyped vocalizations? I think the answer is linked to the process of social sound-making. To achieve surface discriminability for more than several dozen vocal patterns, hominids would have needed to modify phonated signals with movements of the tongue, lips and other movable parts of the vocal tract. But our species can only chop up the sound stream in so many ways, as archives of phonological and sound-making behaviour reveal (see Locke 1983). Thus, hominid talkers would have quickly discovered, from feedback in several channels, the regular recurrence of particular gestures. Since utterances in need of formal organization would already have enjoyed some intrinsic organization at the level of the gesture (Browman & Goldstein 1989), implicit recognition of this level of utterance organization would have created the basis for an elementary phonetic and, later, phonological system.

I assume that those who discovered the segment and its recombinability were able to store, retrieve, execute and compute vocal–verbal forms with unusual ease. By itself, this would not have delivered our evolutionary ancestors deeply into grammar, which undoubtedly rests on many different developments. What I have suggested here is that discovery of commutable segments, through social sound-making and talking, was among them. Social sound-making supplied the frame that promoted proximity, and proximity was among the factors that encouraged variegation of the vocal stream into recombinable gestures. This gave our ancestors languages that were spoken, and an enduring biological commitment to phonetic communication that survives, tens of millennia later, in modern humans.

References

Abler, W. L. (1989). On the particulate principle of self-diversifying systems. *Journal of Social and Biological Structures*, 12, 1–13.

Bates, E., Dale, P. S. & Thal, D. (1994). Individual differences and their implications for theories of language development. In Fletcher, P. & MacWhinney, B. (eds.) *Handbook of Child Language*. Oxford: Basil Blackwell.

Benedict, H. (1979). Early lexical development: comprehension and production. *Journal of Child Language*, 6, 183–200.

Bickerton, D. (1996). *Language and Human Behaviour*. London: UCL Press.

Browman, C. P. & Goldstein, L. (1989). Articulatory gestures as phonological units. *Phonology*, 6, 201–251.

Brown, J. W. (ed.) (1981). *Jargonaphasia*. New York: Academic Press.

Corballis, M. C. (1991). *The Lopsided Ape: Evolution of the Generative Mind*. Oxford: Oxford University Press.

Cosmides, L. & Tooby, J. (1994). Origins of domain specificity: the evolution of functional organization. In Hirschfeld, L. A. & Gelman, S. A. (eds.) *Mapping the Mind: Domain Specificity in Cognition and Culture*. Cambridge: Cambridge University Press.

Dunbar, R. (1996). *Grooming, Gossip and the Evolution of Language*. London: Faber & Faber.

Echols, C. H. (1993). A perceptually-based model of children's earliest productions. *Cognition*, 46, 245–296.

Firth, J. R. (1937). *The Tongues of Men*. London: Watts & Co. Reprinted as *The Tongues of Men and Speech*. Westport, CT: Greenwood Press, 1986.

Green, S. (1975). Variation of vocal pattern with social situation in the Japanese monkey (*Macaca fascata*): a field study. In Rosenblum, L. A. (ed.) *Primate*

Behavior: Developments in Field and Laboratory Research. New York: Academic Press.

Greenfield, P. M. (1991). Language, tools and brain: the ontogeny and phylogeny of hierarchically organized sequential behavior. *Behavioral & Brain Sciences*, 14, 531–595.

Harcourt, A. H., Stewart, K. & Hauser, M. D. (1993). The social use of vocalizations by gorillas: I. Social behaviour and vocal repertoire. *Behavior*, 124, 89–122.

Jonas, S. (1987). The supplementary motor region and speech. In Perecman, E. (ed.) *The Frontal Lobes Revisited*. Hillsdale, NJ: Lawrence Erlbaum.

Lindblom, B. (1989). Some remarks on the origin of the phonetic code. In Von Euler, C., Lundberg, I. & Lennerstrand, G. (eds.) *Brain and Reading: Structural and Functional Anomalies in Developmental Dyslexia with Special Reference to Hemispheric Interactions, Memory Functions, Linguistic Processes and Visual Analysis in Reading*. New York: Stockton Press.

Locke, J. L. (1983). *Phonological Acquisition and Change*. New York: Academic Press.

(1993). *The Child's Path to Spoken Language*. Cambridge, MA: Harvard University Press.

(1996). Why do infants begin to talk? Language as an unintended consequence. *Journal of Child Language*, 23, 251–268.

(1997). A theory of neurolinguistic development. *Brain and Language*, 58, 265–326.

(1998). *The Devoicing of Society: Why People Don't Talk to Each Other Anymore*. New York: Simon & Schuster.

Malinowski, B. (1923). The problem of meaning in primitive languages. In Ogden, C. K. & Richards, I. A. (eds.) *The Meaning of Meaning*. London: Routledge and Kegan Paul.

Marchman, V. A. & Bates, E. (1994). Continuity in lexical and morphological development: a test of the critical mass hypothesis. *Journal of Child Language*, 21, 339–366.

Marcus, G. F. (1995). Children's overregularization of English plurals: a quantitative analysis. *Journal of Child Language*, 22, 447–459.

Pinker, S., Ullman, M., Hollander, M., Rosen, T. J. & Xu, F. (1992). Overregularization in language acquisition. *Monograph of the Society for Research in Child Development* 57 (serial no. 228).

Morris, D. (1967). *The Naked Ape: A Zoologist's Study of the Human Animal*. New York: McGraw-Hill.

Moynihan, M. (1970). The control, suppression, decay, disappearance and replacement of displays. *Journal of Theoretical Biology*, 29, 85–112.

Paul, R. & Jennings, P. (1992). Phonological behavior in toddlers with slow expressive language development. *Journal of Speech and Hearing Research*, 35, 99–107.

Penfield, W. & Welch, K. (1951). The supplementary motor area of the cerebral cortex. *AMA Archives of Neurology and Psychiatry*, 66, 289–317.

Pinker, S. & Bloom, P. (1990). Natural language and natural selection. *Behavioral and Brain Sciences*, 13, 707–784.

Plunkett, K. & Marchman, V. (1993). From rote learning to system building: acquiring verb morphology in children and connectionist nets. *Cognition*, 48, 21–69.

Redican, W. K. (1975). Facial expressions in nonhuman primates. In Rosenblum, L. A. (ed.) *Primate Behavior: Developments in Field and Laboratory Research*. New York: Academic Press.

Rescorla, L. & Ratner, N. B. (1996). Phonetic profiles of toddlers with specific expressive language impairment (SLI-E). *Journal of Speech and Hearing Research*, 39, 153–165.

Reznick, J. S. (1990). Visual preference as a test of infant word comprehension. *Applied Psycholinguistics*, 11, 145–166.

Smith, W. J. (1977). *The Behavior of Communicating: An Ethological Approach*. Cambridge, MA: Harvard University Press.

Thal, D. J., Marchman, V., Stiles, J., Aram, D., Trauner, D., Nass, R. & Bates, E. (1991). Early lexical development in children with focal brain injury. *Brain and Language*, 40, 491–527.

Oroz, M. & McCaw, V. (1995). Phonological and lexical development in normal and late talking toddlers. *Applied Psycholinguistics*, 16, 407–424.

Thelen, E. (1991). Motor aspects of emergent speech: a dynamic approach. In Krasnegor, N., Rumbaugh, D., Studdert-Kennedy, M. & Schiefelbusch, R. (eds.) *Biological Foundations of Language Development*. Hillsdale, NJ: Lawrence Erlbaum.

& Fogel, A. (1989). Toward an action-based theory of infant development. In Lockman, J. & Hazen, N. (eds.) *Action in a Social Context: Perspectives on Early Development*. New York: Plenum.

13 The particulate origins of language generativity: from syllable to gesture

MICHAEL STUDDERT-KENNEDY

1 Introduction

Generativity here refers to two 'creative' aspects of normal language use: unbounded scope of reference and freedom from control by identifiable stimuli (Chomsky 1966: *passim*). These two aspects, though obviously independent, are closely related in their origin (as will be argued below) and in their effects. Together they distinguish language from all other forms of animal communication. So far as we know, the vocal repertoires of other species, including our closest primate relatives, are limited to a few dozen calls, associated with present needs, such as food, sex, predators and various social contingencies. Humans, by contrast, can talk about whatever they choose: past, present, or future, concrete, abstract, or even imaginary objects and events.

Not surprisingly, Maynard Smith & Szathmáry (1995) regard the shift from primate call to human speech as 'the decisive step in the origin of specifically human society' (p. 12). They view the step as the latest of eight major evolutionary transitions in the way information is transmitted between generations. Human speech introduced a new code, a new physical medium of transmission, and a shift from largely genetic to largely cultural inheritance. Drawing the familiar parallel between language and the genetic code, Szathmáry & Maynard Smith (1995) observe: 'Grammar enables a speaker with a finite vocabulary to convey an indefinitely large number of meanings, just as the genetic code enables DNA to specify an indefinitely large number of proteins' (p. 231). But they do not ask how or why the two systems have such extraordinary power.

In fact, until recently, the principle that links them was no better understood than a quarter of a century ago, when Roman Jakobson (1970) wrote: 'One could venture the legitimate question whether the isomorphism exhibited by these two different codes, genetic and verbal, results from a mere convergence induced by similar needs, or whether, perhaps, the foundations of the overt linguistic patterns superimposed upon molecular communication have been modeled directly on its structural principles' (p. 440). Here, Jakobson framed the issue as a question, but was evidently inclined to reject functional, evolutionary convergence in favour of structural homology. The answer to the question came, however, from William Abler (1989) who recognized that at least three natural systems – chemical compounding, biological inheritance and human language – share a hierarchical structure, based on particulate units.

2 The particulate principle

Abler (1989) dubbed chemistry, biological inheritance and language 'Humboldt systems', because they all conform to Von Humboldt's characterization of language: they draw on combinatorial mechanisms to make 'infinite use of finite means' (Von Humboldt 1836/1972: 70) by 'a synthetic process . . . [that] creates something . . . not present *per se* in any of the associated constituents' (p. 67). Humboldt systems exploit what Abler called 'the particulate principle of self-diversifying systems'. According to this principle, elements drawn from a finite set (e.g., in spoken language: phonemes, words) are repeatedly permuted and combined to yield larger units (words, sentences) higher in a hierarchy, and more diverse in structure and function than their constituents. The particulate units in chemical compounding include atoms and molecules, in biological inheritance genes and proteins.

Abler's (1989) central insight was that Fisher's (1930) arguments concerning the mechanism of biological inheritance could be extended to chemistry and language. Fisher reasoned that, if the characteristics of parents blended, they would be lost in the average of their offspring, and the characteristics of the offspring would lie between, not outside, those of their parents; variation, critical to the process of natural selection, would then diminish from generation to generation. What we see instead is that variation is conserved, or even increased, across generations, and that characteristics of parents are not lost, but (as Darwin knew and Mendel showed) may reappear in later generations due to crossing. Conserved variation across generations and reappearance of parental characteristics in later generations demonstrate that biological inheritance rests on a particulate mechanism. The essentially unlimited variation that results from that mechanism provides the stuff on which natural selection works. Hence, the diversity of species.

Similarly, the properties of chemical compounds lie outside, not between, those of the elements from which they are formed: hydrogen burns, oxygen sustains burning, but their combination extinguishes fire. Yet the elements themselves can be recovered from the compound by appropriate analysis. Thus, chemical compounds arose by a particulate mechanism, and the resulting diversity of inorganic and organic compounds was then subject to selection under the chemical conditions of the prebiotic earth (Maynard Smith & Szathmáry 1995). Hence, the diversity of terrestrial non-living matter.

Similarly again, if words were formed by blending portions of the acoustic spectrum, or if sentences were formed by blending words, we would rapidly exhaust the communicative potential of speech. The particulate principle, by contrast, affords a vast range of typological variation: unbounded sets of potential phonetic segments, lexical items and lexical combinations, that are then subject to competing perceptual, motoric and memorial pressures selecting among them for cognitive utility, ease of production and ease of comprehension. Hence, the diversity of languages.

The power of the particulate principle does not stem simply from combinatorics – the world is more than a collection of chemical and genetic anagrams – but from the fact that structures at each higher level of the hierarchy have a broader and entirely different range of function in comparison to those below. We cannot derive the properties of common salt from those of sodium and chlorine, nor of a protein from the gene that controls its formation; in language, we cannot derive the meaning of a word from the phonetic elements that compose it, nor the meaning of a proposition from the lexical meanings of its words without regard to their syntactic grouping.

Finally, although the systems form a chronological sequence from the formation of elements to planetary chemistry to biological inheritance to language, they are not (so far as we can tell) homologs: they do not all descend from a single common ancestral system, nor do the later systems seem to stem from the earlier. Rather, Abler (1989) concludes, the particulate principle is an axiomatic property of the physical world to which any self-diversifying system necessarily conforms. The answer to Jakobson's 'legitimate question', then, is that the genetic and verbal codes converged on the only mechanism by which a natural system can 'make infinite use of finite means' '[through] a synthetic process . . . [that] creates something . . . not present *per se* in any of the associated constituents'. Genes and the elements of speech are therefore functional analogs, not structural homologs.

3 The logic of the particulate principle in language

In his discussion of particulate inheritance, Fisher (1930) notes the 'remarkable fact that had any thinker in the middle of the nineteenth century undertaken, as a piece of abstract and theoretical analysis, the task of constructing a particulate theory of inheritance, he would have been led, on the basis of a few very simple assumptions, to produce a system identical with the modern scheme of Mendelian or factorial inheritance' (p. 7). Much the same might be said, *mutatis mutandis*, of a twentieth-century thinker undertaking to construct a particulate theory of language.

Let us assume that the goal is to devise a system for symbolically representing an unbounded set of objects, events and their relations as specified in simple propositions, by means of a finite set of discrete signals. Our imaginary theorist would no doubt immediately see that if he assigned each signal to a different object or event, he would soon exhaust the signal set. It would not then be long before he hit on the idea of repeatedly sampling, permuting and combining the signals, and so took the first step into language: the number of different possible meanings would now be limited only by the number of possible permutations and combinations (and by our theorist's tolerance for homonymy). Notice, however, that the enterprise could only go forward in this fashion if the component signals were bleached, as it were, of meaning. For if the same basic elements are to be repeatedly permuted to construct different minimal units of meaning ('words'), the elements themselves must be meaningless. The resulting loss of direct signal-to-meaning correspondence would be without precedent in animal communication, giving rise to a unique characteristic of human language, namely, a level of structure between signal and message, or, for spoken language, phonology.

Once our theorist had hit upon the combinatorial principle to build an indefinitely large lexicon from a few dozen signal units, he might be tempted to consider his task done, because language users could now continue indefinitely assigning signals to objects, events and propositions concerning their relations. He would soon see, however, that the system placed a prohibitive tax on creative phonetic invention and memory by obliging its users to construct a new word for every new proposition. Under his charge to achieve unbounded representational scope, our theorist would then surely take the second step into language when he saw, for example, that the six distinct signals for 'X', 'X verbs', 'X verbs Y', 'Y', 'Y verbs', and 'Y verbs X' could be reduced to three by breaking holistic signals with complex referents into new basic components of meaning, and marking each for its thematic role in a proposition by means of sequential order, or some other arbitrary device. Thus, our theorist would arrive at a simple subject–predicate syntax by having recourse to the combinatorial principle a second time, introducing a second level of structure between signal and message.

According to the particulate principle, then, the properties that distinguish language from all other modes of communication are the formal structures interposed between signal and meaning. Animal signals, as best we can judge, directly express a sender's needs or emotions and directly elicit a receiver's response. Language, mediated by phonology and syntax, puts computational distance between signal and message, introducing a cognitive buffer impervious to the immediate environmental demands of stimulus or response. Evidently, a system of communication with the unbounded scope of reference afforded by the particulate principle necessarily dissociates signal from meaning, and thereby sets up a cognitive preadaptation, perhaps, for its evolution into a system free from stimulus control. Thus, the two properties that assure language its unique power, though conceptually independent, have a common origin in the particulate principle.

Here, I should emphasize again an aspect of Abler's thesis that can easily be missed. The particulate principle is a property of the physical universe to which any system that 'makes infinite use of finite means' – any system with the scope and freedom of language, and so of human thought – necessarily conforms (Abler 1989, 1997). Once a system of referential communication began to evolve, its evolutionary terminus, in a hierarchical particulate structure, was as mathematically inevitable as, say, the hexagonal form of a honeycomb cell or the logarithmic spiral of a snail-shell (Thompson 1961). The task for a theory of language evolution is not therefore to derive its hierarchical structure. Rather the tasks are, first, to understand the selection pressures which forced that structure into existence by demanding a referential lexicon of increasing scope, and, second, to specify the physical and psychological conditions that have shaped properties of phonology, morphology and syntax common to all languages.

The latter task comes into focus if we compare spoken and signed languages. That these two forms of language share the same overall hierarchical structure is, according to the particulate principle, physically and mathematically inevitable. What we have to understand is how differences between the modalities, between hand and mouth, eye and ear, forced language into different surface manifestations (Bellugi & Studdert-Kennedy 1980).

4 Some preliminaries to an account of language evolution

I will not speculate on the complex social and cognitive infrastructure that must have been in place before pressures toward referential vocal communication could arise and take effect. I merely draw attention to Bickerton's (1990, 1995) and Donald's (1991) excellent discussions of these matters. Here I address, rather, two perhaps more answerable questions: what are the basic particles of speech, and how did they evolve? In what follows, I shall argue: (a) that the basic particles of speech are not, as generally assumed, phonetic segments (consonants and vowels) or their descriptive features, but the gestures that form them; (b) that gestures arose evolutionarily by differentiation of holistic, syllable-like vocalizations, and so of the hominid vocal tract and its component articulators, in response to pressure toward an increased vocabulary (see Lindblom, this volume). I will support the argument with data from early child speech. But, first, some preliminaries.

4.1 The lexicon, precursor of syntax

The two steps sketched above, first into naming (phonology), then into discursive statement (syntax), correspond exactly to Bickerton's (1990, 1995) two stages of protolanguage and full language. I am not concerned here with dating these stages, with their relation to hominid brain/body ratio, or with their role in advancing hominid culture, but merely with their logical sequence in the evolution of language according to the particulate principle. Bickerton (1995) recognizes that 'syntax could not have come into existence until there was a sizable vocabulary whose units could be organized into complex structures' (p. 51). But, curiously, he does not recognize that a sizable vocabulary could not have come into existence until holistic hominid vocalizations had been differentiated into phonetic units that could be organized into words. The present thesis therefore supplements and complements Bickerton's by arguing that precisely because a sizable lexicon is a precondition of syntax, the hominid breakthrough into naming by means of a particulate phonetics was the first step into language.

4.2 *Particulation of the vocal machinery*

I take a single phonated cycle in the closed–open oscillation of the primate mandible to be the first unit of referential meaning, a protosyllable (see MacNeilage, in press). The problem for the early hominid, under pressure for an increasing vocabulary, was then to produce a sufficient number of articulatorily and perceptually distinct protosyllables. The critical step into particulation, and so into the vast lexicons of human languages, was evidently accomplished by internal modulation of the spectral properties of the protosyllable.

Some evidence for modulation of rhesus calls by jaw and lip action comes from recent studies by Hauser and his colleagues (Hauser 1996: 182ff.), but the full range of human vocalization rests on evolutionary changes in the hominid supralaryngeal airway (Lieberman 1984) and in the neuro-musculature of larynx, tongue, velum and lips (Lenneberg 1967). These changes transformed the primate vocal tract from a straight, largely inflexible tube to a bent tube with several more-or-less independently movable parts; particularly important was differentiation of the tongue, affording partially independent action of root, body and blade. The resulting articulatory flexibility permitted the vocal tract to become a variable musical instrument, as it were, the equivalent of as many different instruments with their characteristic resonant properties as there are distinct configurations of the vocal tract, each excited by as many different pitches or patterns of airflow as there are distinct settings of the vocal cords. Here, then, is the particulation of the vocal machinery and its neural controls on which the hierarchy of language was raised.

This assertion challenges the familiar observation that: 'It is not the mere power of articulation that distinguishes man from other animals, for as everyone knows, parrots can talk' (Darwin 1871: 54). Although their vocal mechanism is not, so far as I know, fully understood, parrots evidently imitate speech in a continuous, non-particulate fashion, much as they imitate fire sirens and lawnmowers. Certainly, a parrot trained to speak German phrases does not then speak novel English phrases with a German accent (Fernando Nottebohm, personal communication). Nor do we have reports of psittacine spoonerisms.

Also well beyond the reach of talking parrots are rates typical of conversational speech (in English, as many as 120–180 words/minute, or roughly 10–15 phonemes/second). Distribution of the communicative load over independently movable parts was, in fact, critical to the execution of movements fast enough to evade the limits of short-term memory (Lieberman 1984; Studdert-Kennedy & Liberman 1963). Such a rate can be achieved

> only if separate parts of the articulatory machinery – muscles of the lips, tongue, velum, etc., – can be separately controlled, and if . . . a change of state for any one of these articulatory entities, taken together with the current state of others, is a change to another phoneme . . . It is this kind of parallel processing that makes it possible to get high-speed performance with low-speed machinery. [Liberman, Cooper, Shankweiler & Studdert-Kennedy 1967: 446]

Similarly, hand configurations in American sign language or in finger-spelling (where rates of 5 letters/second are standard (Wilcox 1992)) depend on rapid movements distributed across wrist and fingers.

4.3 *Segments, features and gestures*

The functional status of phoneme-sized phonetic segments (consonants and vowels) is attested by the alphabet: the speech of any language can be transcribed in alphabetic symbols by a competent listener/writer, and recovered from the script by a competent reader/speaker. Indeed, without the notational system of the alphabet and our intuitive grasp of its principles, study of language would scarcely be possible at all. Nonetheless segments cannot be the basic particles of speech for at least two reasons. First, consonants and vowels have no status outside language; they are linguistic entities, defined by their phonetic function in the formation of a syllable, and are therefore part of what an evolutionary account, undertaking to derive language from its non-linguistic precursors, must explain. Second, consonants and vowels are not primitive units, but compounds, analogs of the molecule, not the atom; according to the standard structuralist formulation, they are 'bundles' of features (Bloomfield 1933: 79; Jakobson & Halle 1956: 8).

Note, however, that the features themselves have no substance. As is evident from the adjectival terminology of all feature theories (nasal, coronal, continuant, etc.), features are not independent entities (like atoms), but properties or attributes of the segments they describe (Fowler, Rubin, Remez & Turvey 1980). In fact, Jakobson and Halle (1956) write, referring to features: 'Phonemic analysis is a study of *properties*, invariant under certain transformations' (p. 13, my emphasis). On the standard account, then, a segment is defined as the sum of its featural properties. On the account adopted here and elaborated somewhat below, a segment is a recurrent constellation of articulatory gestures and their acoustic consequences, of which features may then serve as classificatory descriptors. We thus move toward a substance-based, explanatory account rather than a purely formal account of the origins of speech, and so of language (Lindblom 1980, 1986; Lindblom, MacNeilage & Studdert-Kennedy 1984).

4.4 *Coevolution of speaking and listening*

Language belongs to a large class of complex, interlocking social behaviours in which two or more members of a species differ, but are mutually adapted. Sex is another obvious example. A third is the distribution of functions – provisioning, building, protecting, reproducing – over individuals in an insect colony. Such adaptively complex social patterns presumably reflect the interlocking action of many genes and are therefore incompatible with a saltationist account of their evolution. If a single mutation had granted some hominid the power of speech, it would have had no one to talk to.

Language differs from the other examples because the complementary behaviours (speaking and listening) are lodged in a single individual, and from other primate vocal communication, because the behaviours are learned. Vocal learning is largely confined to a few species of birds and to humans (Hauser 1996). Evolution of the capacity evidently entailed gradually aligning perception and production to achieve 'parity' between sender and receiver (Liberman 1996: 31; Liberman & Mattingly 1989), so that the sounds of one came to specify for the other the motor components deployed in their production, and vice versa (Studdert-Kennedy 1983). Implicit here is the notion that the underlying units of speech production and speech perception are abstract, formally identical, neural control structures (or processes), and this will be my assumption in what follows.

4.5 *Ontogeny epitomizes phylogeny*

For Darwin the facts of embryology were 'second in importance to none in natural history' (1859/1964, p. 450) for the light they could throw on a species' ancestry: 'the embryonic state of each species . . . partially shows us the structure of . . . less modified ancient progenitors' (p. 449). Today, of course, we know that ontogeny does not recapitulate phylogeny in the fashion posited by Haeckel's 'biogenetic law'. That 'law', with its Lamarckian assumptions, was evidently accepted by Darwin himself (Richards 1992), but fell with the rise of Mendelian genetics (Gould 1977). Since all genes are present from the start of development, evolutionary changes do not have to be tacked on at the end of development (as Haeckel's 'law' required), but can be inserted into the sequence at any point.

Consider here the phenomenon of babbling and the early onset of syllable differentiation, documented by MacNeilage & Davis (1990; Davis & MacNeilage 1995). If the assumption that differentiation of the hominid protosyllable evolved in response to pressure for increased vocabulary is correct, the onset of differentiation before the first words in modern children must be a relatively late evolutionary novelty, selected and inserted into the developmental sequence for whatever facilitatory effect it may have on later processes of differentiation.

Nonetheless, parallels between development and evolution do exist for at least two reasons. First, both evolution and development proceed by successive cycles of differentiation. However diverse the developmental paths of individual organisms, the sequence is necessarily from simple to complex. Second, every evolutionary change is a change in development, preserved and passed on to later generations. Even if the exact evolutionary sequence is lost, development is a summary record of those changes (Gould 1977). The next section draws on this fact to sketch the evolution of particulate speech as epitomized in early development.

5 Learning to (p)articulate

We now have to see how development of the particulate principle in the child (and so, by inference, its evolution in the species) arises from and depends on a particulate vocal machinery. We begin with an account of the gesture as currently defined in the developing theory of articulatory phonology.

5.1 *Articulatory phonology*

The term 'gesture' is often used intuitively to refer to intentional movements of the speech articulators, but recently has been given a precise (if preliminary) definition in the articulatory phonology of Browman, Goldstein and their colleagues at Haskins Laboratories (e.g. Browman and Goldstein 1992). They have incorporated the gesture as the basic phonetic and phonological unit of articulatory action into the only explicit model of speech production currently available. What follows is a brief sketch of that model.

If we watch, or listen to, someone speaking, we see, or hear, the speaker's mouth repeatedly closing and opening, forming and releasing constrictions. In the framework of articulatory phonology, each such event, each formation and release of a constriction, is an instance of a gesture (cf. Bell 1911: 38–39). Constrictions can be formed within the oral, velic or laryngeal articulatory subsystems; within the oral subsystem, they can be formed by the lips, the tongue tip or the tongue body. The function of each gesture, or act of constriction, is to set a value on one or more vocal tract variables that contribute to the shaping of a vocal tract configuration, by which (in conjunction with pulmonic action) the flow of air through the tract is controlled, so as to produce a characteristic pattern of sound.

Figure 13.1 displays the tract variables and the effective articulators of a computational model for the production of speech, at its current stage of development (Browman & Goldstein 1992). The inputs to the model are the parameters of sets of equations of motion for gestures; thus, within the model, a gesture is an abstract description of an articulator movement, or of a coordinated set of articulator movements, that unfolds over time to form and release a certain degree of constriction at a certain location in the tract. Settings of the parameters permit constriction degree to vary across five discrete values, corresponding to stop closure, fricative approximation and three degrees of vowel height; constriction location for oral gestures varies across nine discrete places of articulation, from lips to pharynx.

Note that a gestural description is not simply a change in terminology. Gestures do not correspond one-to-one with either segments or features, and a gesture is not, as is sometimes supposed, the functional form of a feature. For example, if we take glottal approximation for

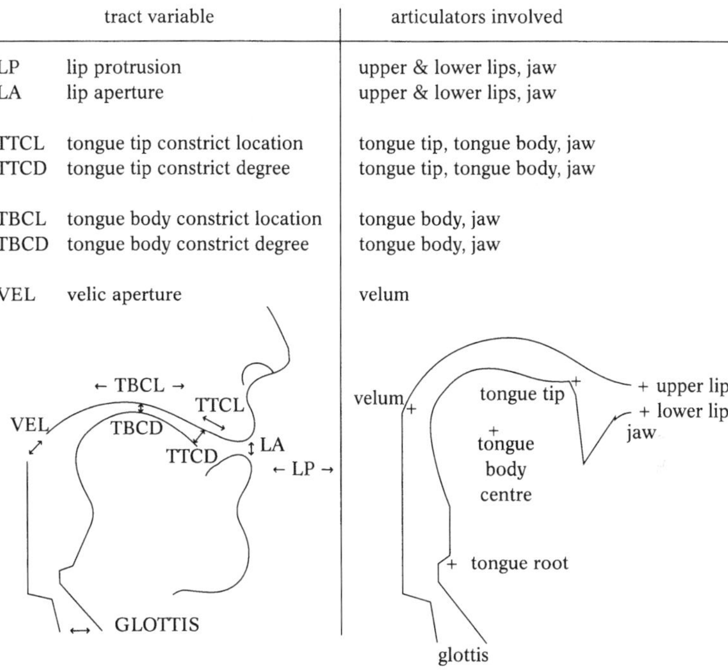

	tract variable	articulators involved
LP	lip protrusion	upper & lower lips, jaw
LA	lip aperture	upper & lower lips, jaw
TTCL	tongue tip constrict location	tongue tip, tongue body, jaw
TTCD	tongue tip constrict degree	tongue tip, tongue body, jaw
TBCL	tongue body constrict location	tongue body, jaw
TBCD	tongue body constrict degree	tongue body, jaw
VEL	velic aperture	velum

Figure 13.1 Tract variables and articulators in a model of speech production.

voicing to be the unmarked state of the glottis, the initial segment of the word *dip* corresponds to one gesture (alveolar closure), while its nasal counterpart in *nip* corresponds to two (alveolar closure and velic lowering). Of these two gestures, the first corresponds to three features [+consonantal], [+anterior], [+coronal], the second to one, [+nasal].

The gestures for a given utterance are organized into a larger co-ordinated structure, represented by a gestural score. The score specifies the values of the dynamic parameters for each gesture, and the period over which the gesture is active. Figure 13.2 (centre) schematizes a stripped-down score for the word *nut* ([nʌt]), as a sequence of partially overlapping gestural activation intervals. Each gesture has an intrinsic duration that varies with rate and stress. Correct execution of an utterance then requires accurate timing of the gesture itself, and accurate phasing of gestures with respect to one another, both sources of 'error' in early child speech.

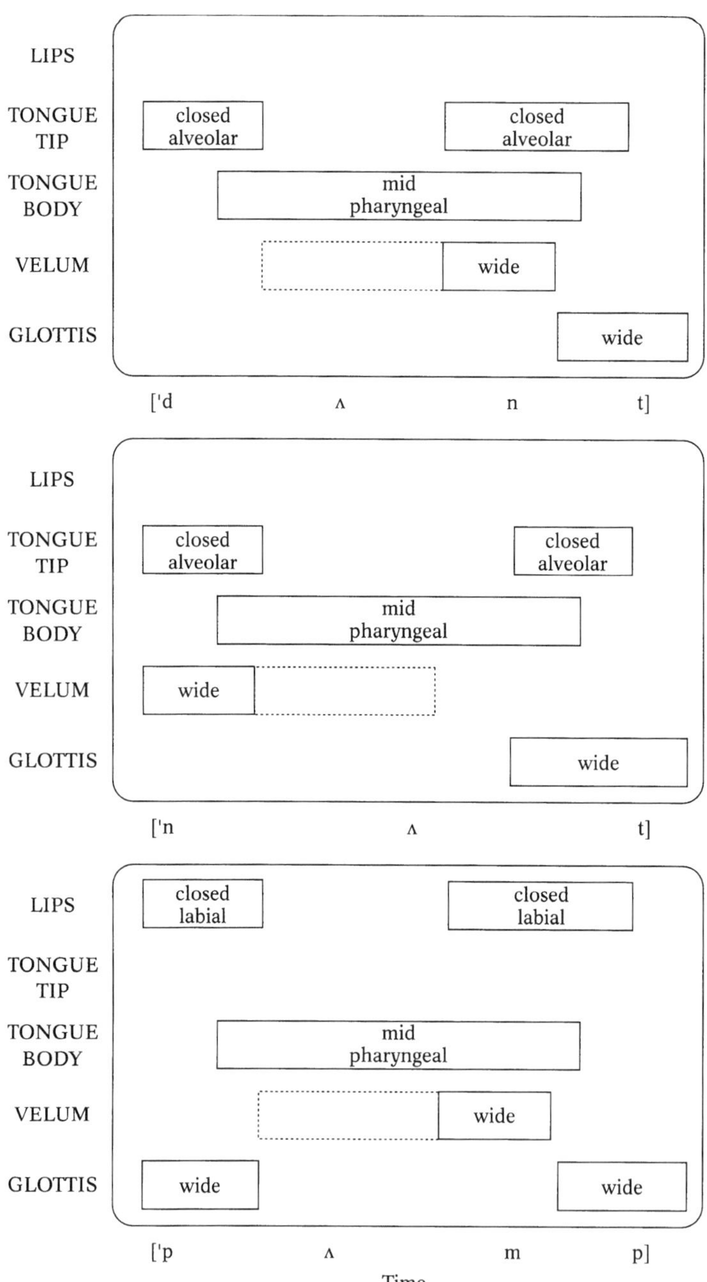

Figure 13.2 Gestural scores for ['dʌnt], ['nʌt] and ['pʌmp].

5.2 *Differentiation of the syllable*

The syllable is the central integrative unit of spoken language, the smallest utterance in which segmental phonology, prosody, syntax and meaning can come together. The syllable is also the apparent homolog of certain primate vocalizations (MacNeilage & Davis 1990), and the first unit recognizable as speech in the infant's vocal development. With emergence of the syllable in canonical babble around the seventh month of life, listeners begin to transcribe infant utterances with a fair degree of reliability. We should not infer from this, however, that the babbling infant has independent control over the segmental components of the syllable; the segments are in the ear of the listener, not in the mouth of the speaker.

Indeed, MacNeilage & Davis (1990) have presented evidence and argument that the syllable trains of reduplicative babbling (e.g. [bæbæbæ], [nɛ̃nɛ̃nɛ̃]) reflect rhythmic up–down movements of the jaw with no internal modulation of the syllable by the tongue or velum. The different closant (consonant-like) values across utterances (e.g. [b] vs [n] above) reflect differences in the resting positions of tongue and velum at syllable onset, maintained throughout the string; the different vocant (vowel-like) values (e.g. [æ] vs [ɛ̃] above) reflect different amplitudes of jaw lowering. The importance of this interpretation is that it warrants a basic unit of articulatory action, presumably homologous with the hominid protosyllable, from which the gesture can emerge by differentiation, as the child gains independent control over its articulators.

The first move toward such control comes with the beginning of 'variegated babble' (Oller 1986) in which syllable onsets and/or nuclei vary from one syllable to the next (e.g. ['we:'da'wi:'da'me:'na'mu:'ni]. Yet here the data are ambiguous. Because babbled syllable trains are typically voiced throughout, we usually cannot tell whether the child is executing a variegated string of segments, as MacNeilage & Davis (1990) suppose, or a variegated string of gestures, as the present account supposes. And because the child has no evident adult model, or target, for its babbling, we have no way of inferring the units from its 'errors'. In fact, not until the child's first words can we plausibly infer units of motor control below the level of the syllable.

5.3 *Differentiation of the word*

No doubt the vocal play of babble facilitates motor development, but it is communicative intent, or meaning, that starts a child talking. The earliest vocal unit of meaning is probably the prosodic contour; the earliest segmental unit of meaning (or of segmental sound contrast) is the word (Ferguson & Farwell 1975; Menn 1983; Waterson 1971), and it is by differentiation of the syllables of a word that the gesture first emerges as a phonological unit (Lindblom 1992; Studdert-Kennedy 1987). Evidence for this process comes from the varying phonetic forms with which a child, on the cusp between babble and words, attempts a word slightly beyond its phonetic reach.

At least two facts about these variants argue for the gesture as the basic unit of articulatory action and for the word as the domain over which gestures are organized: (a) variants are often composed of many, or all, of the gestures, but few, or none, of the segments in the target word; (b) erroneous segments in the variants can often be seen to arise from incorrect phasing of correct gestures.

My first example comes from Ferguson & Farwell (1975) who report ten radically different attempts by a fifteen-month-old child to say *pen* [pɛn] within one half-hour session: [mãə], [ˇʌ̃], [dɛ^{dṇ}], [hɪn], [mbõ], [p^{h}ɪn], [t^{h}ṇt^{h}ṇt^{h}ṇ], [ba^{h}], [d̥^{h}au^{N}], [buã] (cf. Studdert-Kennedy 1987). On the surface, these variants seem absurdly diverse from one another and from their target. Yet every token includes between two and five of the five gestures in the target (labial closure, glottal opening, tongue tip raising, alveolar closure, velic lowering), although incorrectly phased with respect to one another. For example, lip closure for initial [p^{h}], correctly executed with open glottis and raised velum, will yield [^{m}b], as in [^{m}bõ], if velic lowering for [n] is momentarily activated and if glottal closure for [ɛn] is initiated at the same time as lip closure, tens of milliseconds earlier than in the correct utterance. Note that, out of some thirty-seven gestures transcribed in these ten attempts, only ten (27 per cent – those for the vowels [ʌ] [ɪ], [a], [o] and [u]) do not occur in the target; on the other hand, out of the twenty-seven full segments transcribed, twenty-one (78 per cent) do not occur in the target.

My second example, drawn from Studdert-Kennedy & Goodell (1995), describes the attempts of a two-year-old child to say the same syllable, [nʌt], in the disyllabic words *doughnut* and *peanut*. This syllable elicited quite different patterns in the two contexts and in the same context on different occasions. The pattern of errors demonstrates unequivocally that, while the syllable retains its role as an organizing motor template, or 'frame' (MacNeilage, in press, this volume; MacNeilage & Davis 1990) within the word, the word itself is the domain over which gestures are organized.

Table 13.1 Variability within and between words spoken by a two-year-old child: the same target syllable executed differently in different phonetic contexts and on different occasions. The utterances are listed chronologically, but the columns for *doughnut* and *peanut* are not synchronized.

Nut as in doughnut and peanut			
***doughnut* ['do:nʌt] ---►**	***nut***	***nut***	**◄--- *peanut* ['pi:nʌt]**
['do:'di:dʌt]	dʌt	də	['pe:'də]
['du:'dʌtʃ]	dʌtʃ	tə	['pe:n'tə]
['du:'dʌts]	dʌts	de:	['pe:'de:]
['du:'də]	də	pʌmp	['pe:m'pʌmp]
['du:n'dʌnt]	dʌnt	pʌp	['pi:'pʌp]
['do:'nʌt]	nʌt	nʌt	['pi:'nʌt]

Table 13.1 lists in chronological order some of the variations on *nut* in *doughnut* and *peanut*. Among the child's first attempts at *doughnut* were ['du:'dʌtʃ] and ['du:'dʌts]. Word-final alveolar constrictions added apparent fricative segments not present in the model. They were not attempts at the plural, because the child was given only part of a doughnut to eat, only heard the word in the singular, and did not yet command the plural morpheme. Rather, they seem to have resulted from a relatively slow release of [t], making the fricative portion of the release more salient. Subsequent attempts at this word varied over forms as diverse as ['du:də] and ['du:n'dʌnt]. The consonantal pattern of the latter seems to result from prolongation of the alveolar closure for medial [n] after velic release, giving an unwanted [d], combined with prolongation of the alveolar closure for final [t] and a shift in (or harmonious repetition of) the medial velic gesture, giving the unwanted final cluster. Figure 13.2 (top) displays a schematic gestural score illustrating the errors in alveolar closure duration and in phasing of velic action required to make the shift from ['nʌt] to ['dʌnt].

For *peanut* the child first tried ['pe:'də], omitting velic action, and a few days later, ['pe:n'tə], where prolongation of the medial alveolar closure, combined with a shift in the phasing of the final glottal opening, relative to velic closure and the tongue body gesture, gives rise to an apparent shift in the ordering of the target consonant-vowel-consonant sequence. Later, she offered ['pi:'pʌp], omitting the velic gesture and succumbing to labial harmony, and ['peːm'pʌmp]. The latter, formally analogous to ['duːn'dʌnt] for *doughnut*, with its velic harmony, mistimed velic action and resulting unwanted segments, is further complicated by the substitution of harmonized labial closures for the alveolar closures called for by the target. Figure 13.2 (bottom) illustrates the errors of gestural location and duration and of the phasing of velic action required to make the shift from ['nʌt] to ['pʌmp]. My point in these examples is that a featural or segmental account may well describe the form of the errors, but can give no account of the process by which the errors came to be made. By contrast, a gestural account offers a simple description of both the process and the outcome.

6 Summary and conclusion

The generativity, or openness, of language rests on 'the particulate principle of self-diversifying systems', a physical principle, common also to chemistry and genetics, by which discrete particles or elements, drawn from a finite set (in spoken language: phonemes, words), are repeatedly permuted and combined to yield larger units (words, sentences), higher in a hierarchy and more diverse in structure and function than their constituents. Evolution of such a system in primate communication had the unprecedented effect of inserting computational processes between signal and message, a necessary preadaptation for the emergence of language as a system of thought and self-expression, free from identifiable stimulus control. The complex social and cognitive conditions in hominid communities that selected for referential vocal communication are a matter for speculation, but the eventual effect of those pressures was differentiation of the hominid vocal tract to form a particulate vocal machinery, adapted for rapid execution of gestures, the elements of the emerging hierarchy. Because ontogeny is a summary record of phylogeny, and because complex structures necessarily emerge from simpler structures by successive steps of differentiation, we can trace a possible course of hominid evolution by tracking the developing child from the undifferentiated mandibular oscillation of early babble through the imprecise and poorly timed gestural patterns of early words to the rapid articulatory routines of mature speech.

By establishing the gesture as the irreducible element of phonetic perception and action, and by demonstrating that gestures emerge from syllables as a child strives to negotiate its first words, we not only offer a model for the origin of the particulate principle in the evolution of speech, and so in language, but also take a step toward grounding language and thought in human anatomy and physiology.

Acknowledgments

My thanks to William Abler for his papers and stimulating correspondence, and to Cathi Best, Noam Chomsky, Louis Goldstein, Marc Hauser, Alvin Liberman and Ignatius Mattingly, for instructive comments on an earlier version. Preparation of this chapter was supported in part by Haskins Laboratories.

References

Abler, W. (1989). On the particulate principle of self-diversifying systems. *Journal of Social and Biological Structures*, 12, 1–13.

(1997). Gene, language, number: the particulate principle in nature. *Evolutionary Theory*, 11, 237–248.

Bell, A. G. (1911). *The Mechanism of Speech*. New York: Funk & Wagnalls.

Bellugi, U. & Studdert-Kennedy, M. (eds.) (1980). *Signed and Spoken Language: Biological Constraints on Linguistic Form*. Deerfield Beach, FL: Verlag Chemie.

Bickerton, D. (1990). *Language and Species*. Chicago and London: University of Chicago Press.

(1995). *Language and Human Behaviour*. Seattle: University of Washington Press.

Bloomfield, L. (1933). *Language*. New York: Holt, Rinehart & Winston.

Browman, C. P. & Goldstein, L. (1992). Articulatory phonology: an overview. *Phonetica*, 49, 155–180.

Chomsky, N. (1966). *Cartesian Linguistics*. New York: Harper & Row.

Darwin, C. (1859/1964). *On the Origin of Species*. (Facsimile edition.) Cambridge, MA: Harvard University Press.

(1871). *The Descent of Man, and Selection in Relation to Sex*. London: John Murray.

Davis, B. L. & MacNeilage, P. F. (1995). The articulatory basis of babbling. *Journal of Speech & Hearing Research*, 38, 1199–1211.

Donald, M. (1991). *Origins of the Modern Mind: Three Stages in the Evolution of Culture and Cognition*. Cambridge, MA: Harvard University Press.

Ferguson, C. A. & Farwell, C. B. (1975). Words and sounds in early language acquisition. *Language*, 51, 419–439.

Fisher, R. A. (1930). *The Genetical Theory of Natural Selection*. Oxford: Clarendon Press.

Fowler, C. A., Rubin, P., Remez, R. E. & Turvey, M. T. (1980). Implications for speech production of a general theory of action. In Butterworth, B. (ed.) *Language Production*, vol. I. London: Academic Press.

Gould, S. J. (1977). *Ontogeny and Phylogeny*. Cambridge, MA: Belknap Press of Harvard University Press.

Hauser, M. (1996). *The Evolution of Communication*. Cambridge, MA: MIT Press.

Jakobson, R. (1970). *Main Trends of Research in the Social and Human Sciences*. Paris/The Hague: UNESCO/Mouton: 437–440.

& Halle, M. (1956). *Fundamentals of Language*. The Hague: Mouton.

Lenneberg, E. H. (1967). *Biological Foundations of Language*. New York: Wiley.

Liberman, A. M. (1996). *Speech: A Special Code*. Cambridge, MA: MIT Press.

Cooper, F. S., Shankweiler, D. P. & Studdert-Kennedy, M. (1967). Perception of the speech code. *Psychological Review*, 74, 431–461.

& Mattingly, I. G. (1989). A specialization for speech perception. *Science*, 243, 489–494.

Lieberman, P. (1984). *The Biology and Evolution of Language*. Cambridge, MA: Harvard University Press.

Lindblom, B. (1980). The goal of phonetics, its unification and application. In *Proceedings of the Ninth International Congress of Phonetic Sciences*, vol. III. Copenhagen: Institute of Phonetics: 3–18.

(1986). Phonetic universals in vowel systems. In Ohala, J. J. & Jaeger, J. J. (eds.) *Experimental Phonology*. Orlando, FL: Academic Press: 13–44.

(1992). Phonological units as adaptive emergents of lexical development. In Ferguson, C. A., Menn, L. & Stoel-Gammon, C. (eds.) *Phonological Development: Models, Research, Implications*. Timonium, MD: York Press: 131–163.

MacNeilage, P. & Studdert-Kennedy, M. (1984). Self-organizing processes and the explanation of phonological universals. In Butterworth, B., Comrie, B. & Dahl, O. (eds.) *Explanations for Language Universals*. New York: Mouton: 181–203.

MacNeilage, P. F. (in press). The frame/content theory of evolution of speech production. *Behavioral & Brain Sciences*.

& Davis, B. L. (1990). Acquisition of speech production: the achievement of segmental independence. In Hardcastle, W. J. & Marchal, A. (eds.) *Speech Production and Speech Modelling*. Dordrecht: Kluwer: 55–68.

Maynard Smith, J. & Szathmáry, E. (1995). *The Major Transitions in Evolution*. Oxford: W. H. Freeman.

Menn, L. (1983). Development of articulatory, phonetic and phonological capabilities. In Butterworth, B. (ed.) *Language Production*, vol. II. London: Academic Press: 3–50.

Oller, D. K. (1986). Metaphonology and infant vocalizations. In Lindblom, B. & Zetterstrom, R. (eds.) *Precursors of Early Speech*. New York: Stockton Press: 21–35.

Richards, R. J. (1992). *The Meaning of Evolution*. Chicago: University of Chicago Press.

Studdert-Kennedy, M. (1983). On learning to speak. *Human Neurobiology*, 2, 191–195.

(1987). The phoneme as a perceptuo-motor structure. In Allport, A., MacKay, D G., Prinz, W. & Scheerer, E. (eds.) *Language Perception and Production*. London: Academic Press: 67–84.

& Goodell, E. W. (1995). Gestures, features and segments in early child speech. In De Gelder, B. & Morais, J. (eds.) *Speech and Reading*. Hove: Erlbaum (UK), Taylor & Francis: 65–88.

& Liberman, A. M. (1963). Psychological considerations in the design of auditory displays for reading machines. *Proceedings of the International Congress on Technology and Blindness*, vol. I. New York: American Foundation for the Blind: 289–304.

Szathmáry, E. & Maynard Smith, J. (1995). The major evolutionary transitions. *Nature*, 374, 227–232.

Thompson, D. W. (1961). *On Growth and Form*. (Abridged edition edited by J. T. Bonner.) Cambridge: Cambridge University Press.

Von Humboldt, W. (1836/1972). *Linguistic Variability and Intellectual Development*. Translated by G. C. Buck & F. A. Raven. Philadelphia: University of Pennsylvania Press.

Waterson, N. (1971). Child phonology: a prosodic view. *Journal of Linguistics*, 7, 179–211.

Wilcox, S. (1992). *The Phonetics of Fingerspelling*. Philadelphia, PA: John Benjamins.

14 Evolution of the mechanism of language output: comparative neurobiology of vocal and manual communication

PETER F. MACNEILAGE

1 Introduction

The topic of my chapter is one that has received remarkably little attention among the myriad topics subsumed under the heading of language evolution. It is: what is the nature of the capacity for organization of language *output* and how did this capacity evolve? At a first pass, my topic is that of motor skill for language. *Modern* humans produce consonants and vowels at the rate of 15 per second – one every 70 milliseconds – often 15 *different* phonemes per second. The product of the number of preprogrammed movements available and the rate at which they can be deployed probably exceeds that in any other species-typical behaviour of life forms. The first question I want to raise is: how did we evolve this particular skill by descent with modification?

Of course, many people believe that sign language and not spoken language developed first. I will next consider this possibility in the context of the evolution of the left cerebral hemisphere for language, as its common control of speech and the right hand in modern humans is a central datum in attempts to understand which language modality evolved first. There are two main schools of thought regarding the role of manual function in language evolution, both anthropocentric in character. According to one, the evolution of right-handedness for tool use/construction in *Homo habilis* facilitated the evolution of an initial manual language (e.g. Kimura 1993). The other is that some abstract mental consequence of this tool-related capacity, such as sequencing capacity, analyticity or generativity, was then utilized for language (e.g. Corballis 1983). I will review evidence that both vocal and manual specializations of the left hemisphere probably predated hominid evolution, which makes both of these anthropocentric scenarios unlikely. In addition, evidence that hemispheric specialization for language is more closely related to a whole-body postural specialization than to handedness for fine skilled tasks makes the hypothesis regarding a transfer of abstract manual capacities a less likely one.

Additional problems for the hypothesis of a manual origin of language are the problems of why and how a subsequent transfer of language to a vocal modality occurred. The hypothesis that there is a left hemispheric specialization for language independent of the modality gives the impression that intertranslatability between modalities would have been easy to accomplish. I review the evidence for this claim adduced by Poizner, Klima and Bellugi (1987) from sign language aphasiology, and evidence for the same claim by Petitto (1993) from sign language acquisition, and conclude that in neither case is the claim justified. My conclusion will be that there was no initial sign language and no significant manual impetus toward vocal language: the vocal medium was always the predominant medium for language transmission.

2 The evolution of speech production

In this section I will present a summary of the frame/content theory of evolution of speech production (for details, see MacNeilage, in press, a). According to this theory, the crucial step in speech evolution was the adoption of the open–close alternation of the mandible, previously used for ingestive cyclicities (e.g. chewing) and visuofacial communicative cyclicities (e.g. lipsmacks) as the 'frame' for syllables. Subsequently, there was an expansion stage involving the generation of internal segmental 'content' of frames – separately controllable consonants and vowels – which allowed the transmission of the extremely large message sets demanded by language. (See Studdert-Kennedy, this volume, for a discussion of this possibility.)

Modern speech is the result of the action of three subsystems – respiratory, phonatory and articulatory. In all mammals, the first two of these subsystems operate as modulated cyclicities (MacNeilage, in press, a). The expiratory phase of the respiratory system is modulated to produce a power source for phonation. At the phonatory level, the vocal fold vibration cycle is modulated to produce variations in fundamental frequency, heard as pitch variations. The species-specific organization property of speech is to be found primarily in the articulatory system. It consists of a continual mouth open–close alternation primarily controlled by the mandible. The two phases are subject to continual modulation by means of the other three articulators, the lips, the tongue and the soft palate. The open phases are associated with vowels, and the closed phases with consonants. The complete open–close cycle is coextensive with the syllable. To me the main question about the evolution of speech production is how did this *third level of modulated cyclicity* evolve? The answer requires a solution to the central problem posed by Lashley (1951) – the problem of serial order in behavior. The form of the problem for speech is: how did we evolve the universal capacity to organize speech in the time domain into syllable-sized packages of consonants and vowels? (See MacNeilage, in press, b, for a discussion of Lashley's views.)

A clue as to how this might have happened comes from the form of serial order errors in speech, as Lashley had suspected. The main unit participating in serial ordering errors at the sound level of speech production is the segment – the individual consonant or vowel. It is beyond dispute that errant segments obey a syllable-structure constraint (Levelt 1992). Segments are misplaced into the same position in the syllable that they apparently came out of. Syllable-initial consonants are misplaced into the beginnings of syllables, vowels are misplaced into the middles of syllables, from whence they came, and syllable-final consonants are placed into the ends of syllables. Most importantly, vowels and consonants never occupy each others' positions in syllable structure.

How did the mutually exclusive roles of consonants and vowels in on-line syllable organization arise? Surely they must be derived from a prior open–close alternation originating at the *motor* level. Rather than putting together the components of this alternation from separately existing open mouth vocalizations and closed mouth vocalizations, the alternation must have come into communicative use as a whole. How would this have occurred? However different it is from other primate vocalizations, the syllable is unlikely to have evolved *de novo*. As Jacob (1977) points out, evolution is not an engineer building new devices from scratch. It is a tinkerer, taking already-existing structures and functions and modifying them for new purposes. A source of raw material for the syllabic alternation is not difficult to imagine. The earliest mammals (circa 220 million years ago) presumably tinkered mandibular oscillation into place for various ingestive purposes – chewing, sucking and licking. However, the consistent use of mandibular oscillation for communicative purposes probably did not evolve until primates evolved. The widespread use of repetitive lipsmacks, tonguesmacks and teeth-chatters in living primates (Redican 1975) suggests that this capacity was present in primates ancestral to hominids. Some living primates even have the basic combination of phonation with smacks (see Andrew 1976). Score another one for Lashley (1951), who recognized the importance of 'rhythm generators' in serially organized behaviours.

3 Comparative neurobiology of the frame/content mode

If the mandibular cycle was the initial articulatory building block for speech, this would help us understand why Broca's area became important for the control of speech production. The lateral frontal cortical region most commonly acknowledged to be part of Broca's area, namely Brodmann's area 44 and the immediately posterior area 6, and their homologs in cats and monkeys at least, are the main cortical loci for the control of ingestive processes in mammals (Woolsey 1958). Electrical stimulation of area 6 in humans evokes chewing movements (Foerster 1936).

What apparently occurred was that, once the mandibular cycle became useful for communicative purposes, it came under control of a region of medial premotor cortex, the region most responsible for cortical control of vocalization in other primates. The anterior cingulate cortex is important for vocal control in monkeys and humans (see Jurgens (1987) – monkeys; Paus, Petrides, Evans & Meyer (1993) – humans). In addition, a region adjacent to cingulate cortex and derived from it (Sanides 1969), namely the Supplementary Motor Area (SMA), is always active during speech production (Roland 1993). Two additional findings suggest that the SMA has a primary role in frame generation in human speech. A number of studies have found that both electrical stimulation of the SMA (e.g. Dinner & Luders 1995) and irritative lesions of the SMA (see Jonas (1981) for a summary) often have the effect of inducing the production of rhythmic syllable sequences (e.g. dadadada).

It is now well accepted that the two frontal cortical regions described here are parts of two fundamentally different motor subsystems for bodily motor control in general, in monkeys as well as humans. Anterior cingulate cortex and the SMA, together with the basal ganglia, are associated primarily with 'intrinsic' or self-generated activity, while areas of lateral premotor and paramotor cortex, together with the cerebellum, are part of a system associated primarily with 'extrinsic' actions (Goldberg 1992). Consistent with these different roles, the medial region receives relatively little sensory input, primarily from deep somatic afferents, while the lateral region receives relatively heavy multimodal sensory input – somesthetic, visual and auditory – the latter from superior temporal cortex including Wernicke's area (Pandya 1987). Patients with medial damage are often initially mute and akinetic, and subsequently have difficulty initiating speech and other voluntary actions, though their ability to repeat what is said to them remains intact (Rubens 1975). One symptom pattern related to the extrinsic role of lateral cortex is the repetition difficulty typical of conduction aphasics who tend to have damage in the region of the parietotemporal junction (Green & Howes 1977).

Typical bodily actions are visually guided. Evidence suggests that, while medial frontal cortex may help provide a basic action skeleton (e.g. Penfield & Welch 1951), the action itself is normally accomplished with the aid of target-related visual information provided by the lateral system. Spontaneous speech episodes are not sensorily guided to any significant degree. However, humans have a remarkable ability to repeat what is said to them at extremely short latencies (Porter & Castellanos 1980). The utility of this capacity and the probable reason for its origin become clearer when one notes that, while humans learn whichever one of the 6,000 or so languages they grow up with, monkeys have negligible learning capacity (Jurgens 1995). The human repetition capacity is presumably associated with the 'phonological loop' of working memory which involves subvocalization as an aid in temporary storage of speech material (Baddeley 1995). Baddeley has recently speculated that this capability probably evolved in order for language to be learned. Thus, while in adults the primary role of the lateral system in spontaneous speech is probably transmission of previously learned and now-stored information relevant to pronunciation from Wernicke's to Broca's area, the primary role of the lateral system in evolution and in infants is that it allows speech to be learned. However, as in its use of two motor systems, speech is not unique, in that the learning capacity of the lateral system also presumably applies to action in general. It presumably mediates an important general-purpose evolutionary development – a 'mimetic' capacity of modern hominids reflected in a wide variety of behaviours such as tribal ritual, dance, games, singing and music in general (Donald 1991).

4 Acquisition of speech production: problems of the innatist perspective

The evidence that the most fundamental evolutionary change for speech, relative to other primate vocalization, is an ability to learn it makes the actual process of learning to speak in modern hominids of more interest. Another reason for considering this area is that it has been adopted as the main proving ground for the formalist view of language (e.g. Chomsky 1986; Pinker 1994), according to which language results from our possession of an innate universal grammar. The main basis for this claim is the argument from 'the poverty of the stimulus' for language acquisition. In essence, the argument is that there is insufficient information in the world to make language learning possible, and so language must be genetically specified.

In early work it had been claimed that the course of speech acquisition was consistent with this innatist view. Lenneberg (1967) had asserted that deaf infants began to babble at the same time as normal infants, suggesting that maturation of an innate capacity was sufficient for the purpose. Jakobson (1968) had proposed that infants acquired the sound patterns of their first words in an innate universal sequence of appearance of the basic context-independent units of formal phonology, the distinctive features. Learning played no significant role in these scenarios. However, subsequent work has shown that, whereas normal infants begin to babble by seven months of age, hearing-impaired infants do not typically begin until several months later and the patterns they produce are distinctly abnormal (e.g. Eilers & Oller 1994). In addition, studies of infants who were unable to vocalize during the babbling and early speech periods, because they had been tracheostomized for medical reasons, show that these children took several months to acquire normal speech following removal of the tracheostomy, in spite of their normal auditory histories (Locke & Pearson 1990). Thus it appears that both normal hearing and normal access to vocal imitative attempts are necessary in the early stages of speech acquisition, as might be surmised from the important role that the extrinsic motor system appears to have played in the evolution of speech.

Another error made by Jakobson (1968) was his claim that, whereas infants babble all the sounds of the world's languages without favour, the sounds of the first words are entirely unrelated to the unimportant earlier display of 'external phonetics' (p. 27). There is now a consensus that the sounds and sound patterns of babbling are very limited, and they are basically identical to the sounds of the first words. Babbling is defined in terms of a rhythmic alternation between an open and a closed mouth (e.g. *bababa*, *mamama*), a pattern similar to that proposed here as underlying the form of the first language. Consonantal sounds are mostly confined to stops, nasals and glides, and vowels to the lower left quadrant of the vowel space.

Davis and I have described the overall pattern of babbling (Davis & MacNeilage 1995) and early words (MacNeilage, Davis & Matyear, 1997) as one of 'Frame Dominance'. Most of the variance in both stages is due to the frame produced by mandibular oscillation, with a limited ability of other articulators (tongue, lips, soft palate) to make active intrasyllabic or intersyllabic changes. Consequently – apart from the open–closed alternation pattern – adjacent consonants and vowels within syllables, and even successive syllables, tend to share vocal tract configurations.

Finally, it should be noted that, although normal experience including auditory experience seems to be necessary for normal babbling to occur, babbling does not simply mirror the sound preferences of the ambient language. Though fricatives, liquids and high and back vowels are common in languages they are not common in babbling. It would seem therefore that, in addition to auditory experience and imitative experience, which might jointly be sufficient to induce the basic oscillatory pattern in infants, given a very old propensity to produce this pattern, motor constraints might severely limit the range of manifestations of this basic form (see MacNeilage & Davis 1993). One might guess that in earlier hominids some imitative capacity, together with a propensity to produce frame cycles limited in their variety by motor constraints, might have been the determinants of the sound patterns of the first words. (See MacNeilage (1994) for a detailed exploration of this theme.)

This picture is in marked contrast to what would be expected if speech acquisition was driven by the phonological component of universal grammar. The concept of frame dominance entails a lack of context-independence of any putative consonantal or vocalic distinctive features. Moreover this lack of discrete units of output during the entire first year of speechlike behaviour occurs in an environment in which there is no poverty of the stimulus. Infants hear the words they cannot say, over and over again. It appears that future scenarios based on the supposed power of innate universal grammar in language acquisition may need to omit the phonological component of grammar, which would result in a curiously heterogeneous view of the basic nature of language.

5 The evolution of left hemisphere specialization for speech production

Up until now, our attention has been devoted to the evolution of *spoken* language. We now need to consider the possibility that the first language may have been a sign language, and that at a later stage language changed from a signed to a spoken language. In order to consider this possibility from the perspective of brain–behaviour relationships we must obviously come to grips with the fact that, for most people, language production and right-handedness are both the responsibility of the left cerebral hemisphere. This basic fact has spawned theories which give manual function priority in language evolution by providing the initial impetus for a left hemisphere speech specialization. How did the co-existence of manual and vocal specializations in one hemisphere come about? A step toward the answer may have been made in a 'postural origins' theory considered in more detail elsewhere (MacNeilage 1991, 1997) and summarized here.

The most common explanation for the left hemisphere locus for language is that a left hemisphere manual specialization arose with right-handedness in *Homo habilis*, and then this manual specialization led to a language specialization either for signed language or for spoken language. This anthropocentric conclusion is becoming increasingly problematical. There is mounting evidence that both the manual and the vocal specialization of the left hemisphere predated hominids. There are now over fifty studies showing hand preferences in other primates. The general outlines of the findings are as follows. Over a dozen studies, most by Jeanette Ward and her colleagues, have shown a *left* hand preference in prosimians, the suborder most closely related to the earliest primates (Ward, Milliken & Stafford 1993). The fact that one of the most momentous adaptations of the earliest prosimians – the first primates – was for unimanual predation, which is necessarily an asymmetrical act, has led me to suggest that the origin of this left-handedness was in a visuospatiomotor specialization of the left-hand/right-hemisphere system, an adaptation which may have been a forerunner of the present human right hemisphere spatial specialization (MacNeilage 1991, 1997). A complementary right-side/left-hemisphere postural control specialization may also have arisen at this time because of the postural demands of unimanual predation from the vertical clinging posture typical of early prosimians.

In higher primates there are a large number of studies showing right hand preferences (MacNeilage 1997). Findings include right hand preferences for throwing and in bimanual co-ordination, neonatal right-handed thumb sucking and a rightward supine postural bias, and right-handed stone tool use. Two common conditions across subsets of these studies are a demand for manipulation, and the presence of upright posture. I have interpreted this trend toward favouring the right side in higher primates in the following way: with the abandonment of vertical clinging, more omnivory and more invasive foraging and manual food processing in higher primates, the right side of the body, with its greater physical strength and its postural heritage of on-line control, may have become the operative side (MacNeilage 1991, 1997).

The possibility that right-handed manipulation in other primates could be a precursor to right-handedness is an obvious one. What of posture, by which I mean the disposition of the body parts during both movement and stasis? Upright posture is noted as having the effect of setting the hands free for alternate uses following the origin of bipedalism in hominids. From an anthropocentric perspective, many would concede that it might have contributed to the right-handedness of *Homo habilis*. But upright posture is not uncommon in other primates, and it introduces new rather stringent postural control demands, relative to quadrupedal posture. It seems likely that one systematic response to these demands would be a division of labour between a unimanual action and a contralateral postural support capability. With this development, the postural control role of the left hemisphere may have been extended to mediate the postural support operations of the left side of the body for right-handed acts.

Together with the findings of right hand preferences, there are also further instances of left hand preferences in higher primates in tasks which are visuospatially demanding, such as catching goldfish, for squirrel monkeys (King & Landau 1993), and adjusting the positions of clear plexiglass screens, for monkeys and gorillas (Vauclair & Fagot 1993). In one case, a left hand preference for unimanual prehension co-existed with a right hand preference for manipulation in a group of ten stumptail macaques (Beck & Barton 1972). A finding of Lee (1980), that standing right-handed humans make faster reaction-time movements with their left hands, suggests that a residue of this specialization even remains present in humans, though it no longer has an adaptive basis.

6 Manual–vocal relations in language evolution

All this evidence suggesting that right-handedness may have evolved before hominids makes the linkage between hominid tool use and right-handedness – as divined from flint knapping patterns (Toth 1985) – a much less momentous one. There is also evidence for a left hemisphere vocal communication specialization in monkeys, birds, mice, hamsters and frogs, which calls into question the hand-to-mouth part of the typical anthropocentric scenario for left hemisphere language evolution (MacNeilage 1997). Thus it seems that neither right-handedness nor a left hemisphere communication specialization first evolved in hominids. An extremely large body of work by Bianki (1988) and other Russian investigators suggests that both the manual and the vocal specialization may have had an origin in a basic left hemisphere motor control specialization in vertebrates (MacNeilage 1997).

What are the implications of this discussion of the evolution of left hemisphere specializations for the role of manual capabilities in language evolution? Note again that there are two versions of the hand-to-mouth scenario for language evolution, both with an anthropocentric focus. According to one view which I will call the 'Sign First' (SF) view, the gains made in manual capability, from the evolution in hominids of right-handedness for tool construction and use, made the right hand able to take the lead in the evolution of the first language. According to the other view which I will call the 'Borrowed Manual Talent' (BMT) view, some general-purpose or metafunctional capacity of the left hemisphere accruing from the manual developments, such as a sequencing ability or an analytic ability, was co-opted from the manual modality for use in the vocal auditory modality.

The first point to make is that, given the apparently deep-seated nature of the left hemisphere specialization for vocal communication in vertebrates, the hand-to-mouth scenario is not necessary to account for the left hemisphere locus of spoken language. Second, the fact that most left-handers seem to have left hemisphere language while the most important contribution to hand control in left-handers is apparently most often crossed (Kimura 1993) is a problem for the hand-to-mouth view, though admittedly in a small proportion of the population. However, the repeated finding that, in subjects with mixed limb preferences, whether left- or right-handed, the locus of the hemispheric specialization for language is more closely related to foot preference than to hand preference is distinctly problematical for the hand-to-mouth view (e.g. Day & MacNeilage 1996). It suggests, in particular, that none of the most highly prized capabilities associated with handedness, such as a sequencing specialization or an analytic specialization or a skill specialization, constitute a basis for the language specialization in these cases.

Of the two hand-to-mouth theories, the SF theory would seem, *a priori*, to be more plausible than the BMT theory. It is difficult to imagine the nature of the selection pressures that could transfer some *abstract* capability of one motor system, such as a sequencing capability independent of what is being sequenced, from one set of brain loci to another. It seems to me that the borrowing of an actual movement pattern already in the oral apparatus – the mandibular cycle – is a more likely possibility. In contrast to the implausibility of the BMT scenario from the standpoint of the selection mechanism itself, the possibility that sign language may have gained an impetus from pantomiming acts that the hands themselves actually performed does not seem so outrageous. The possibility of an iconic origin is always attractive to many people in my classes because it is a possible solution to a problem that has bothered many people in the history of thought – the problem of how particular signs get attached to particular concepts (Hewes 1973). But although the SF theory might be more plausible than the BMT theory, they both have a problem with the fact that the present-day language specialization is more closely related to foot preference than to hand preference.

Another problem with the SF theory – and I personally see this problem as insuperable – is the problem of explaining the disappearance of sign language from normal life if indeed it was the first form of language. There are two parts to this problem. First, I believe that the reasons usually given for sign eventually being superseded by language – its lack of omnidirectionality, the fact that it pre-empts the hands, and its lack of utility in the dark – are also reasons why it would not have gained pre-eminence in the first place. At the least, these problems do not seem important enough for sign language to have been *entirely* eliminated as a code with rules shared by sender and receiver. Second, and more important in my mind, is the translation problem. What is the precise means whereby a particular sign became the corresponding spoken word? For one who takes these two action systems seriously, the problem of selection of correspondence rules between the main parameters of sign language – say hand-shape, hand orientation, location and movement – and the main parameters of spoken language – say place, manner and voicing of consonants, and tongue position and lip configuration for vowels – does not have a plausible solution. Certainly there is at present no straightforward relation between spoken and signed language that would encourage the thought that the two languages are easily translatable at the phonological level. In addition, there is no sizeable body of entities in the world which would allow a natural linkage between iconic gestures in the two modalities (such as an animal roar with a pounce).

There is one additional view of the status of language modalities which has implications for the evolution of the output mechanism for language. It is the view shared by Poizner, Klima & Bellugi (1987 – henceforth PKB) and some others that humans possess an 'innate' left hemisphere specialization for language, independent of the modality. This view, in my opinion, has the effect of trivializing the role of modality in language evolution. It implies that a transfer from one modality to another could have readily occurred in the history of language. It has the consequence of making a totally abstract universal grammar key to the human language capability, independent of the history and neurology of the output mechanism. However, language could not have *evolved* independent of the modality any more than an animal's food preferences could have evolved independent of their ingestive capabilities, and any clues as to what the original modality was can only enlighten us about language evolution in general.

One problem with the view of PKB that the left hemisphere specialization is modality-independent is that it is unable to account for the fact that the only truly natural language existing today is the vocal–auditory one. If language structure had no obligatory linkage with one particular modality, why did we end up with only one modality, except in special conditions? But another problem of more immediate concern is that PKB did not succeed in their attempt to show that the neural mechanisms of language are, in fact, modality-independent. Their approach to this question took the form of an analysis of brain–behaviour relations in a group of sign language users with brain damage. Part of the problem of this work is that it was based on an inappropriate underlying assumption. They assumed explicitly that, as language tends normally to be in the left hemisphere and a visuospatial specialization in the right, the relative importance of modality and what they called 'central' language can be revealed by the relative role of the left and right hemispheres in sign language. Their conclusion was quite unequivocal: 'the left cerebral hemisphere in humans may have an innate predisposition for the central components of language independent of language modality' (p. 212). It is an extremely curious fact that a monograph entitled *What the Hands Reveal about the Brain* did not consider the obvious alternative possibility that sign language control is predominantly in the left hemisphere because all the subjects studied were right-handed, and this right-handedness is usually part of the manual–gestural *modality*. In addition, as the authors themselves note, the *left* hemisphere also has visuospatial abilities.

There were a number of individual results which were inconsistent with the claim of modality independence, some of which were acknowledged by the authors themselves. First, two of the patients with right hemisphere damage showed problems in the comprehension of spatialized syntax (e.g. accompanying pronouns by pointing to an arbitrary position in space previously assigned to the proper noun) which were not satisfactorily accounted for in terms of nonlinguistic effects of right hemisphere lesions. Second, two of the *left* hemisphere patients with parietal lobe damage also had problems in spatialized syntax, suggesting an important role of left hemisphere spatial function, which is inconsistent with the authors' overall rationale (right is for space, left is for language). The left parietal lobe is not ordinarily implicated in syntactic comprehension in normals, so this seems to be a modality-specific effect. Third, the patient G. D., who was similar to a classic Broca's aphasic in many aspects of symptomatology and in lesion site, did not show the typical syntactic comprehension problems of Broca's aphasics. The authors attributed this lack of deficit to the role of left parietal cortex, but if this was so, it is another instance of a modality-specific effect.

A fourth problem involved PKB's assertion of a dissociation between linguistic deficits and nonlinguistic normality in control of the hands in the three right-handed patients. This distinction was important to the authors because the linguistic deficits were considered to involve 'central' aspects of language, while the nonlinguistic acts were not. Kimura (1988) has pointed out that an inappropriately lenient criterion of normalcy may have been used in the nonlinguistic test, and that one patient had had repeated practice on the test over a number of years. In addition, in an intensive study of the patient G. D., Whittemore (1987) found that the relative frequencies of the various categories of sublexical sign production errors were proportional to the motor difficulty of the items. For example, large numbers of errors were made on difficult hand-shapes and on the movement parameter.

A final problem, not so much with PKB's work but with the interpretation of it by others, is the claim that the relation between aphasic syndrome (Broca's, Conduction, Wernicke's) and lesion site was similar in the three left hemisphere sign aphasics to those typical of spoken language aphasics. For example, in the introduction to the PKB monograph Marshall states that 'these findings do indicate broadly congruent cortical and subcortical areas committed to different aspects of modality neutral language processing'. This is not the case. While the lesion site of G. D. was a classical one for Broca's aphasics (even though not all aspects of her symptom pattern were), the lesion sites for K. L. and P. D., which were both mostly subcortical, were far from typical for Conduction and Wernicke's aphasia respectively. Even if the sites *were* typical, one could not necessarily conclude that there was modality-neutral language processing, because the typical posterior sites for Conduction and Wernicke's aphasics also have visual connectivities and the anterior site for Broca's Aphasia has manual connectivities (Pandya 1987).

I conclude from this work not only that there is no modality independence in left hemisphere processing, but also that there is an elaborate pattern of modality dependence. In addition, although there is no space to elaborate on it here, I would argue that the pattern of modality dependence may turn out to be exactly what we might have expected from our knowledge of the neural bases of manual and visuospatial function in humans. I would also argue that the failure of the attempt to demonstrate modality independence is evidence for my claim that a translation from one modality to another in language evolution would have been far from a trivial matter, and therefore probably did not occur.

7 The relation between acquisition of sign and speech

The claim that there is an innate language capacity independent of the modality has also been made by Petitto who believes that this independence can be shown in early acquisition. In a well-known paper based on only 182 signs from 2 deaf infants, Petitto & Marentette (1991; see also Petitto 1993) claim sign language babbling begins at the same time as spoken babbling, that there is an exact parallel in syllable structure between spoken and signed language, and that, while deaf infants show sign babbling, hearing infants do not.

The claim of an identical onset time for spoken and signed babbling was based on unpublished evidence from 2 subjects. Apart from the problem of attempting to prove the null hypothesis, a considerably larger sample than 2 is necessary for a comparison of spoken and signed babbling onsets. The standard deviation of babbling onset times in a study of 56 infants by Koopmans-van Beinum and Van der Stelt (1986) was 2 weeks. If the babbling onset times of two-thirds of a group of normal subjects are scattered across a 4-week period and others are more widely scattered, as this standard deviation indicates, how likely is it that the sign babbling onsets of 2 subjects would give us an accurate indication of the typical time of sign babbling onset? Secondly there is little agreement in the literature on a sign analog of the spoken syllable, let alone on a homolog (reflecting a putative common consequence of a central language capacity) which Petitto requires (see Coulter 1993).

Petitto & Marentette claimed that, while their deaf infants produced signs, the hearing infants did not. However, their description of their classification procedures was too brief to indicate exactly how they made a sign–nonsign distinction. In a much more comprehensive study of 5 deaf infants and 4 hearing infants, which included a sizeable method section, Meier & Willerman (1995) failed to replicate Petitto & Marentette's findings. The only difference that they found between deaf and hearing infants was a strong tendency for the deaf infants to make longer series of rhythmic repetitive movements.

Evaluation of the differences between the manual behaviour of the deaf and hearing infants requires some background. Earlier, I characterized spoken babbling as primarily due to a single basic frame produced by rhythmic mandibular oscillation. Lack of normal input from others delays babbling onset considerably and makes it distinctly abnormal in quality. One major difference between the Meier & Willerman results on sign babbling and the work on speech babbling is that, while deaf infants show drastic effects of loss of access to speech in both vocal babbling onset and babbling patterns, neither of these effects of lack of input from adult signers were shown in the manual patterns of hearing infants without access to sign. There was no indication that sign onset was delayed in the infants without access to sign, which one might have expected by analogy from hearing-impaired infants, if signing is innate. Apart from a lower frequency of repetitive movements, there was no indication that the sign babbling patterns of the infants without access to sign were different. This suggests a fundamental difference between the acquisition of vocal and of manual babbling which casts doubt on the claim that they have a common amodal base.

Perhaps it is the one difference between the manual behaviours of the deaf and hearing infants studied by Meier & Willerman that is most significant. The deaf signers but not their normal counterparts were similar to normal infants acquiring *vocal* language in favouring rhythmic repetitive sequences. I argued earlier that in its vocal form this behaviour reflects in part a propensity to simulate spoken language input. I would suggest that the manual sequences reflect the same type of propensity, one that would be perhaps expected from Donald's view of the evolution of a general-purpose mimetic capacity in hominids (Donald 1991). But while the vocal propensity for repetitive frame production results in a behaviour that forms a specific motor basis for the entire subsequent course of speech acquisition, the manual sequences do not provide such a basis for sign acquisition. Unlike speech, sign language does not have a single specific motor oscillation analogous to mandibular oscillation continually running through it. Thus whatever type of manual movement is repeatedly made during the sign babbling stage, it cannot form an actual motor basis for a sequence of signs.

The *sine qua non* of evolution is complex design for adaptive use (Pinker & Bloom 1990). I have just claimed that spoken babbling provides a better basis for subsequent adaptive use of speech than the behaviour which presently seems most characteristic of sign babbling. To me, this suggests that the vocal–auditory mechanism of *spoken* language has a better claim to be the main output mechanism for language evolution than the manual–visual one.

To conclude this section and this chapter, I believe that Petitto has not adequately justified her claim that acquisition data in the vocal and manual modalities show that the process of acquisition is modality-independent. Instead I take the current evidence regarding sign acquisition as further evidence for my contention that the vocal–

auditory modality of spoken language was the first and only output mechanism for language.

Acknowledgements

Preparation of this chapter was supported in part by Grant HD-27733 from the National Institutes of Health.

References

Andrew, R. J. (1976). Use of formants in the grunts of baboons and other nonhuman primates. *Annals of the New York Academy of Sciences*, 280, 673–693.

Baddeley, A. D. (1995). Working memory. In Gazzaniga, M. S. (ed.) *The Cognitive Neurosciences*. Cambridge, MA: MIT Press.

Beck, C. H. M. & Barton, R. L. (1972). Deviation and laterality of hand preference in monkeys. *Cortex*, 8, 339–363.

Bianki, V. L. (1988). *The Right and Left Hemispheres of the Human Brain: Cerebral Lateralization of Function*. New York: Gordon and Breach.

Chomsky, N. (1986). *Knowledge of Language: Its Nature, Origin, and Use*. New York: Praeger.

Corballis, M. C. (1983). *Human Laterality*. New York: Academic Press.

Coulter, G. R. (ed.) (1993). *Phonetics and Phonology*, vol. III: *Current Issues in ASL Phonology*. San Diego: Academic Press.

Davis, B. L. & MacNeilage, P. F. (1995). The articulatory basis of babbling. *Journal of Speech & Hearing Research*, 38, 1199–1211.

Day, L. B. & MacNeilage, P. F. (1996). Postural asymmetries and language lateralization in humans (*Homo sapiens*). *Journal of Comparative Psychology*, 110, 88–96.

Dinner, D. S. & Luders, H. O. (1995). Human supplementary sensorimotor area: electrical stimulation and movement-related potential studies. In Jasper, H. H., Riggio, S. & Goldman-Rakic, P. S. (eds.) *Epilepsy and the Functional Anatomy of the Frontal Lobe*. New York: Raven Press.

Donald, M. (1991). *Origins of the Modern Mind: Three Stages in the Evolution of Culture and Cognition*. Cambridge, MA: Harvard University Press.

Eilers, R. E. & Oller, D. K. (1994). Infant vocalizations and the early diagnosis of severe hearing impairment. *Journal of Pediatrics*, 124, 199–203.

Foerster, O. (1936). The motor cortex in man in the light of Hughlings Jackson's doctrines. *Brain*, 59, 135–159.

Goldberg, G. (1992). Premotor systems: attention to action and behavioral choice. In Kein, J., McCrohan, C. R. & Winlow, W. (eds.) *Neurobiology of Motor Program Selection*. New York: Pergamon Press.

Green, E. & Howes, D. H. (1977). The nature of conduction aphasia: a study of anatomic and clinical features and of underlying mechanisms. In Whitaker, H. & Whitaker, H. A. (eds.) *Studies in Neurolinguistics*, vol. III. New York: Academic Press.

Hewes, G. W. (1973). Primate communication and the gestural origin of language. *Current Anthropology*, 14, 5–24.

Jacob, F. (1977). Evolution and tinkering. *Science*, 196, 1161–1166.

Jakobson, R. (1968). *Child Language, Aphasia, and Phonological Universals*. The Hague: Mouton.

Jonas, S. (1981). The supplementary motor region and speech emission. *Journal of Communication Disorders*, 14, 349–373.

Jurgens, U. (1987). Primate communication: signalling, vocalization. In Adelman, G. (ed.) *Encyclopedia of Neuroscience*. Boston: Birkhauser.

Kimura, D. (1988). Review of *What the Hands Reveal about the Brain* by H. Poizner, E. Klima & U. Bellugi. *Language and Speech*, 31, 375–378.

(1993). *Neuromotor Mechanisms in Human Communication*. Oxford: Oxford University Press.

King, J. E. & Landau, V. I. (1993). Manual preferences in varieties of reaching in squirrel monkeys. In Ward, J. P. & Hopkins, W. D. (eds.) *Primate Laterality: Current Evidence of Primate Asymmetries*. New York: Springer-Verlag.

Koopmans-van Beinum, F. J. & Van der Stelt, J. M. (1986). Early stages in the development of speech movements. In Lindblom, B. & Zetterstrom, R. (eds.) *Precursors of Early Speech*. New York: Stockton Press.

Lashley, K. S. (1951). The problem of serial order in behaviour. In Jeffress, L. A. (ed.) *Cerebral Mechanisms in Behaviour: The Hixon Symposium*. New York: Wiley.

Lee, W. A. (1980). Anticipatory control of postural and task muscles during rapid arm flexion. *Journal of Motor Behaviour*, 12, 185–196.

Lenneberg, E. H. (1967). *Biological Foundations of Language*. New York: Wiley.

Levelt, W. J. M. (1992). Accessing words in speech production: stages, processes and representations. *Cognition*, 42, 1–22.

Locke, J. L. & Pearson, D. M. (1990). Linguistic significance of babbling: evidence from a tracheostomized infant. *Journal of Child Language*, 17, 1–16.

MacNeilage, P. F. (1991). The postural origins theory of neurobiological asymmetries in primates. In Krasnegor, N., Rumbaugh, D., Studdert-Kennedy, M. G. & Schiefelbusch, R. (eds.) *The Biological Foundations of Language Development*. Hillsdale, NJ: Erlbaum.

(1994). Prolegomena to a theory of the sound pattern of the first language. *Phonetica*, 51, 184–194.

(1997). Towards a unified view of the evolution of cerebral hemispheric specializations in vertebrates. In Milner, A. D. (ed.) *Comparative Neuropsychology*. Oxford: Oxford University Press, pp. 167–183.

(in press, a). The frame/content theory of evolution of speech production. *Behavioral and Brain Sciences*, 21(4).

(in press, b). Whatever happened to articulate speech? In Corballis, M. C. & Lea, S. (eds.) *Evolution of the Hominid Mind*. Oxford: Oxford University Press.

& Davis, B. L. (1993). Motor explanations of babbling and early speech patterns. In De Boysson Bardies, B., De Schonen, S., Jusczyk, P., MacNeilage, P. & Morton, J. (eds.) *Developmental Neurocognition: Speech and Face Processing in the First Year of Life*. Dordrecht: Kluwer.

Davis, B. L. & Matyear, C. L. (1997). Babbling and first words: Phonetic similarities and differences. *Speech Communication*, 22, 269–277.

Meier, R. & Willerman, R. (1995). Prelinguistic gesture in deaf and hearing infants. In Emmorey, K. & Reilly, J. S. (eds.) *Language, Gesture and Space*. Hillsdale, NJ: Erlbaum.

Pandya, D. (1987). Association cortex. In Adelman, G. (ed.) *The Encyclopedia of neuroscience*. Boston: Birkhauser.

Paus, T., Petrides, M., Evans, A. C. & Meyer, E. (1993). The role of the human anterior cingulate cortex in the control of oculomotor, manual, and speech responses: a position emission tomography study. *Journal of Neuropsychology*, 20, 453–469.

Penfield, W. & Welch, K. (1951). The Supplementary Motor Area of the cerebral cortex: a clinical and experimental study. *American Medical Association Archives of Neurology and Psychiatry*, 66, 289–317.

Petitto, L. (1993). On the ontogenetic requirements for early language acquisition. In De Boysson-Bardies, B., De Schonen, S., Jusczyk, P., MacNeilage, P. & Morton, J. (eds.) *Developmental Neurocognition: Speech and Face Processing in the First Year of Life*. Dordrecht: Kluwer.

& Marentette, P. (1991). Babbling in the manual mode: evidence for the ontogeny of language. *Science*, 251, 1493–1496.

Pinker, S. (1994) *The Language Instinct*. New York: Morrow.

& Bloom, P. (1990). Natural language and natural selection. *Behavioral and Brain Sciences*, 13, 707–784.

Poizner, H., Klima, E. & Bellugi, U. (1987). *What the Hands Reveal about the Brain*. Cambridge, MA: MIT Press.

Porter, R. J. & Castellanos (1980). Speech production measures of speech perception: rapid shadowing of VCV syllables. *Journal of the Acoustical Society of America*, 67, 1349–1356.

Redican, W. K. (1975). Facial expressions in nonhuman primates. In Rosenblum, L. A. (ed.) *Primate Behaviour: Developments in Field and Laboratory Research*, vol. IV. New York: Academic Press.

Roland, P. (1993). *Brain Activation*. New York: Wiley.

Rubens, A. B. (1975). Aphasia with infarction of the territory of the anterior cerebral artery. *Cortex*, II, 239–250.

Sanides, F. (1969). Comparative architectonics of the neocortex of mammals and their evolutionary implications. *Annals of the New York Academy of Sciences*, 167, 404–423.

Toth, N. (1985). Archeological evidence for preferential right handedness in the Lower and Middle Pleistocene, and its possible implications. *Journal of Human Evolution*, 14, 607–614.

Vauclair, J. & Fagot, J. (1993). Manual specialization in baboons and gorillas. In Ward, J. P. & Hopkins, W. D. (eds.) *Primate Laterality: Current Behavioral Evidence of Primate Asymmetries*. New York: Springer-Verlag.

Ward, J. P., Milliken, G. & Stafford, D. K. (1993). Patterns of lateralized behaviour in prosimians. In Ward, J. P. & Hopkins, W. D. (eds.) *Primate Laterality: Current Evidence of Primate Asymmetries*. New York: Springer-Verlag.

Whittemore, G. L. (1987). The production of ASL signs. Unpublished Ph.D. dissertation, University of Texas at Austin.

Woolsey, C. N. (1958). Organization of somatic sensory and motor areas of the cerebral cortex. In Harlow, H. F. & Woolsey, C. N. (eds.) *Biological and Biochemical Bases of Behaviour*. Madison: University of Wisconsin Press.

15 Systemic constraints and adaptive change in the formation of sound structure

BJÖRN LINDBLOM

1 The adaptive patterns of speech

A walking or running animal makes movements that depend on its goals and are harmoniously styled in response to the surrounding terrain. Conditions are never exactly the same, necessitating flexible performance. To deal with unforeseen problems, motor systems have evolved to be adaptive. Numerous studies show that speech shares this property with other motor behaviours.

In an experiment on 'compensatory articulation', speakers were asked to produce normal-sounding vowels with an atypically large jaw opening maintained by a 'bite-block' (Lindblom, Lubker & Gay 1979). Although the subjects had no previous experience of the task and were not allowed to practise beforehand, their output nonetheless closely matched normal vowels.

Such output-oriented control is also evident in different speaking styles. For instance, in 'clear speech', talkers shape phonetic patterns for perceptual processing by articulating more forcefully which makes phonetic segments longer and more audible and reduces ambiguities due to coarticulation (Moon & Lindblom 1994).

These and other findings indicate that speech is adaptively organized. Significantly, they also suggest that movements are simplified when external conditions permit. The default articulation of an [i] does not consist in lowering the jaw drastically and simultaneously making an extreme compensatory tongue movement (as for a bite-block [i], Gay, Lindblom & Lubker 1981). Rather, it involves a synergistic, and energetically more efficient, elevation of both tongue and jaw. Similarly, in the absence of social and communicative demands, the speaker defaults to an effortless casual style rather than to clear speech. Two characteristics stand out in this behaviour: *plasticity* and *economy*.

Viewing speech in this manner suggests a solution to the classical 'invariance issue', which arises from looking at spoken utterances in two different ways: psychologically, as a sequence of discrete and invariant entities, and physically, as a quasi-continuous flow of variable and context-dependent signal information. One approach to this paradox sees phonetic variability as systematic rather than accidental: 'intra-speaker phonetic variations need not be seen as invariants embedded in linguistically irrelevant variability. Rather they represent genuine behavioral adaptations that may jeopardize or demolish signal invariance but that transform speech patterns in essentially principled ways' (Lindblom, Brownlee, Davis & Moon 1992: 357).

2 An approach to the evolution of sound structure

Compared with the motor and perceptual systems now used by speech, spoken language is the evolutionary newcomer. When our ancestors took the first steps toward language, mechanisms were in place for hearing as well as for breathing, chewing, swallowing and other motor functions. Hence, when language appeared, the principles of plasticity and economy had already been around for a considerable period of time.

Such considerations suggest the following approach to the evolution of sound structure:

(1) *If phonological systems were seen as evolutionary adaptations to universal constraints on speaking, listening and learning to speak, what would they be like?*

In addressing this formulation, we shall look for general mechanisms not specific to speech and try to assess their role in shaping the world's sound patterns. A theme running through the chapter is the hidden, but powerful, reach of the 'system'. That will become evident as we consider the topics of sound change, phonetic inventories and lexical development.

3 Sound change: from phonetics to phonology

Ohala (1981, 1993) has proposed that sound changes originate as listener misperceptions. Contextual modifications play a major role in triggering errors. Normally listeners cope with context effects because they expect them and are able to correct for them by applying, in Ohala's terms, 'reconstructive' rules.

The process is illustrated with a hypothetical speaker who aims at producing the syllable /ut/ (Ohala 1981: 181). Because of coarticulation, the /u/ is fronted by the following /t/ and the result is phonetically more like [yt]. In the normal case, listeners would identify the [t] as the 'cause' of the vowel change and derive the intended /ut/ syllable by factoring out the coarticulation. However, when some disturbance makes it impossible to take context into account, the rules have nothing to work on, and no 'reconstruction' takes place. Incorrectly, the vowel is identified as [y].

The initiation of sound change occurs when the misperceiving listener turns speaker and substitutes the new target /yt/ for the old form /ut/. Ohala proposes this as the phonetic mechanism that underlies most of sound change. The process begins with a 'copying error' involving only a single speaker–hearer. Eventually, this person is copied by other speakers, and the mini-sound-change becomes a regular sound change as it spreads by borrowing, imitation, etc., and finally becomes established in the speech community (Ohala 1981: 184).

Restating Ohala's analysis, we can say that speech percepts have a bimodal distribution: when context is taken into account, focus is placed on *what* is being said; speech perception is content-oriented. In the absence of context, processing is signal-oriented and focus is on *how* things are said. This how-mode serves as a breeding-ground for new pronunciations and is the source of phonological innovations.

The perceptual dissociation of signal- and content-oriented modes is easily demonstrated experimentally, for instance in tasks where subjects judge a set of stimuli either as speech or non-speech (e.g. Williams 1986). It is also the basis of the skill involved in making auditory judgments of phonetic quality and narrow transcriptions.

Two aspects require comment. First, there may be several ways in which the perceptual system could record unnormalized how-representations. Access to the surface value of a particular pronunciation does not necessarily presuppose making a perceptual error. Any transform of speech could in fact be a potential source of a new pronunciation provided that: (a) there is a significant contextual change in the phonetic pattern; (b) that change calls for perceptual normalization; and (c) there is a possibility for that normalization not to be applied.

However, Ohala's central idea remains: it is from the pool of decontextualized phonetic percepts that new pronunciations and sound changes are drawn.

Second, it may be unnecessary to limit the phonetic contribution to sound change to the initiation stage. In Ohala's model, the speech community's acceptance of an innovation occurs solely 'by social means'. However, phonetics could play a role also during spreading, for, once an innovation is being 'tried out' by other speakers, a tacit evaluation process is under way. The new form gets tested implicitly on a number of dimensions: 'articulatory ease', 'perceptual adequacy', 'social value' and 'systemic compatibility'. If the change facilitates articulation and perception, carries social prestige and conforms with lexical and phonological structure, its probability of acceptance goes up. If the change violates the criteria, it is likely to be rejected.

We now combine the revised sound change model with the account of 'on-line' speech. If, as suggested, the variability of speech is systematically structured by the continual tug-of-war between production and perception demands, phonetic forms should statistically occur along a hyper–hypo continuum. Ranging from listener-oriented to more reduced pronunciations, this is one of the main dimensions from which phonological forms are selected. The step from phonetics to phonology is taken by a single speaker and is followed by an implicit evaluation by other speakers. Since hyper–hypo forces must be assumed to work both in innovating and in evaluating a change, statistically there ought to be a hyper–hypo pattern also at a phonological level.

Typological data on sound change bear this out (Kiparsky 1988), grouping into 'strengthening' processes (e.g. vowel shifts and consonant fortitions) and 'weakenings' (e.g. assimilations, vowel reductions, consonant deletions and lenitions). This taxonomy is compatible with the 'hyper' and 'hypo' distinction, although the latter distinction refers to phonetic and the former to phonological facts.

4 Role of systemic constraints: distinctiveness

Vowel systems show the effect of auditory processes on phonological structure. To investigate this claim, a computational model was constructed (Lindblom 1986) with number of vowels per system as input, and formant frequencies F1, F2 and F3 as output. Two questions had to be answered to simulate vowel systems on this model: (a) what is a possible vowel? (b) what phonetic constraints govern the selection of optimal vowel systems?

The first was obtained from a numerical model of the vocal tract whose input parameters provide independent control of the lips, tongue, jaw and larynx as they vary over physiologically motivated ranges. Combining parametric values systematically yields a set of vowel articulations with associated formant patterns. The total set of articulations and formant patterns of the model constitutes its *phonetic space*.

Vowels can also be described in auditory dimensions. This specification takes the form of an 'auditory spectrum' which is derived from a spectral analysis with 'critical-band' filter characteristics.

These steps define 'possible vowel' as a point located in the phonetic space specified in articulatory, acoustic or auditory dimensions. In the present experiments, the vowel space was represented by a set of 19 sample points.

The second question was answered by using a definition of 'perceptual contrast' applicable to both speech and non-speech sounds (Bladon & Lindblom 1981). It estimates the perceptual distance between two spectra by integrating their differences in critical-band excitation levels across frequency. This measure, D_{ij}, was incorporated into an algorithm that finds, for a given system size, a set of vowels that are perceptually maximally dispersed from each other. 'Optimal system' is given by:

$$\text{(2)} \quad \sum_{i=2}^{k} \sum_{j=1}^{i-1} 1/(D_{ij})^2 \Rightarrow \textbf{minimized}$$

where **k** represents inventory size which ranged from 3 to 11. A program was written that examined all the ways in which **k** vowels could be chosen from the 19 'cardinal' vowels. For each combination of **k** vowels, the formula was computed and the configuration that best satisfied the criterion was retained. The results of Lindblom (1986) compare favourably with observed systems (Crothers 1978). In particular, when evaluations are made in terms of the number of contrasts along the high–low and the front–back dimensions, there is perfect agreement across all system sizes.

These results support the idea that vowel systems are adaptations to mechanisms of auditory analysis common to both speech and non-speech sounds. Note that Eq (2) does not pick vowels on the basis of individual absolute properties such as 'stability'. Distinctiveness is relational and hence a systemic attribute presumably originating in the task of the speech signal: to discriminate among competing candidates in the lexical system.

5 Contrasts easy to make

If vowel systems had evolved in response to a demand for 'maximum perceptual contrast' we might expect to find, say, /i ẽ a̤ o̰ uˤ/ to be universally favoured, rather than /i e a o u/, since the former enhance perceptual distances by secondary processes. This is not the case as is shown by the patterning of consonants.

Inventory size seems to be a good predictor of a system's phonetic contents. Sorting the consonants of UPSID[1] (Maddieson 1984) into three categories: Basic, Elaborated and Complex articulations, Lindblom & Maddieson (1988) plotted the total number of Basic, Elaborated and Complex segments used by any given UPSID language as a function of the total number of consonants of each language. Basic, Elaborated and Complex segments increased linearly as a function of inventory size. In small systems, only Basic consonants were invoked. Medium systems used Basic and Elaborated segments. Large inventories recruited all three types. The implication is that segments more 'difficult' to pronounce are absent from small systems, but grow more numerous in proportion to inventory size (the 'Size Principle').

A recent study of pronouns throws additional light on this result (Willerman 1994). It shows that pronouns of a given language tend to form a significantly biased subset of the total set of consonants used and that this bias is manifested as a strong tendency to favour motorically 'elementary' consonants.

Since the patterning of pronouns and small UPSID inventories is similar, I give Willerman's results and the 'Size Principle' a common interpretation. In a small system, the average information carried by each consonant is smaller than in a large system. Hence, smaller paradigms entail less competition among units and make them, in relative terms, more predictable. Greater predictability implies reduced

1 UPSID = the UCLA Phonetic Segment Inventory Database which contains typological consonant and vowel data on 317 languages.

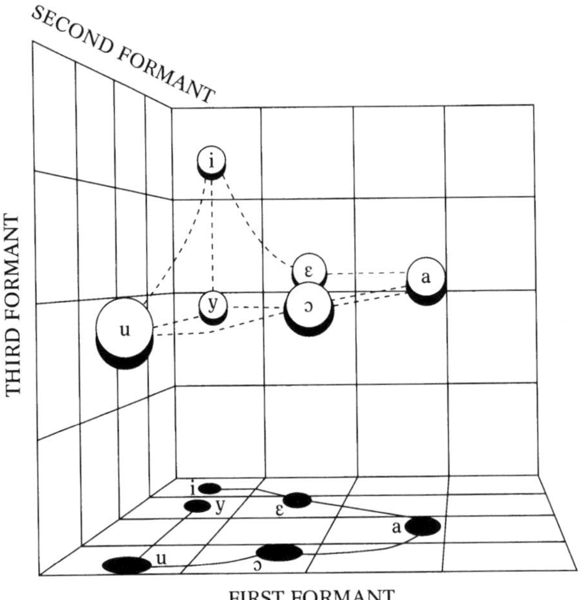

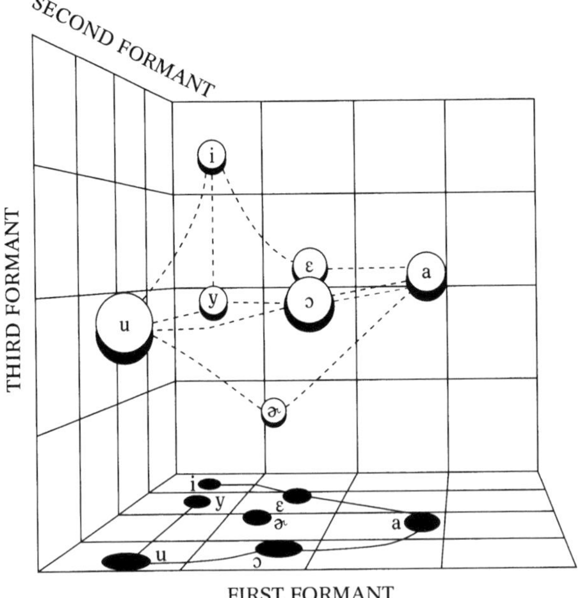

Figure 15.1
Top row: acoustic space for 'plain' vowels.
Below: retroflex articulations included.

demands on perceptual distinctiveness. Such demands could, in principle, be met by random selection of phonetic values from a universal set, but, instead, language prefers to exhaust its choices among the 'less complex' segments before it recruits 'more complex' possibilities for additional distinctions.

These observations suggest an extension of (2) for predicting phonetic systems:

$$\textbf{(3)}\quad \sum_{i=2}^{k}\sum_{j=1}^{i-1}(A_{ij}/D_{ij})^2 \Rightarrow \textbf{minimized}$$

where $\mathbf{A}_{ij}$ represents the articulatory cost of selecting the $\boldsymbol{ij^{th}}$ pair of contrasting units. Eq (3) selects a system of contrasts that are simultaneously 'easy to hear' and 'easy to say'. The effect of (3) is illustrated in Figure 15.1.

Two versions of the acoustic vowel space are shown three-dimensionally. Above is the space of 'plain' vowels used in the vowel system simulations. The space below includes 'plain' and 'retroflex' vowels as evident from the extreme low F3 values. Predicting systems from this space would incorrectly make [ɚ] as favoured as [i], [u] and [a] (Lindblom 1986).

Eq (3) explains why the data do not show that pattern. In minimal comparisons of plain and retroflex vowels, plain vowels show lower $\boldsymbol{A}$ scores. Although retroflexion enhances a vowel's distinctiveness, its $\boldsymbol{D_{ij}}$ value in a given contrast would be attenuated by its corresponding $\boldsymbol{A_{ij}}$ score. For small systems, plain vowels satisfy the $\boldsymbol{A_{ij}/D_{ij}}$ criterion better than retroflex vowels. However, as the number of plain vowels increases, the space gets more crowded and the average $\boldsymbol{D_{ij}}$ score decreases. To preserve distinctiveness in a larger system, new dimensions must be added. Significantly, those dimensions are not invoked in small systems, suggesting that there is a penalty attached to their use. That penalty 'delays' the selection of more complex segments (such as retroflex vowels). That delay is captured by the $\boldsymbol{A}$ term in Eq (3) and is what generates the size-principle effect.

6 Recalibration and the development of a lexical system

The goal of this section is to propose a refinement of Eq (3). This formula adequately summarizes the role of the 'system' and appropriately reflects the balance between articulatory and perceptual constraints in structuring phonetic inventories. However, it does not satisfactorily model what Ohala (1980) called 'maximum use of available distinctive features' (MUAF). As inventory size increases, Eq (3) postpones marked segments, but, once they appear, it offers no guarantee that the derivation will obey MUAF – that is will make *consistent use* of one secondary mechanism before moving on to the next. In fact, for large systems, Eq (3) predicts a collection of 'assorted bonbons', a mixture of Elaborated and Complex segments rather than subsets of *consistently* nasalized, or *consistently* retroflex, elements. It offers only one half of the explanation why five-vowel systems such as /i ẽ a̤ o̰ uˤ/ are absent. For the other half we must invoke developmental constraints.

To motivate the revision, which will be stated in Eq (6), we sketch a numerical model of lexical development. On the road to this formulation, we present definitions, conventions and data for an algorithmic implementation. Once Eq (6) is reached, the main theme will return: sound structure as an adaptive response to behavioural and systemic constraints.

6.1 *Phonetic boot-strapping*

Extrapolating from the preceding typological analyses, I hypothesize that phonological learning involves a search through phonetic space that begins with low-cost articulations and gradually progresses to energetically more demanding tasks. It proceeds from 'Basic' to 'Complex'.

This point takes us back to *articulatory ease* whose relevance has long been recognized (Passy 1890), but which is difficult to define. Recent developments indicate that this situation is about to change.

In building physiologically realistic models (Laboissière, Ostry & Perrier 1995; Wilhelms-Tricarico & Perkell 1995), investigators typically find that their frameworks offer an infinite number of solutions for predicting articulatory movements. Technically, this is known as the too-many-degrees-of-freedom problem (Saltzman & Munhall 1989). Evidence is now accumulating that the nervous system solves this problem by minimizing energy consumption (read: 'articulatory effort'). Various criteria have been evaluated, most of them defined in terms of the input forces to the articulators (Nelson 1983; Kabugari & Honda 1996).

An intuitive appreciation of this research can be obtained from a few examples. First, consider a swing set in motion. Left alone it will move back-and-forth like a pendulum at its own preferred rate ('natural frequency'). Second, imagine an object placed on a horizontal surface, attached to a wall by a spring, moved away from the wall and then released. If 'weakly damped', this system will oscillate much like the swing until reaching its rest position. But if the mass, the friction of the surface and the elasticity of the spring are chosen so as to make it 'strongly damped', it will behave more sluggishly and approach the rest position without oscillating around it. In principle, it would be possible to have the damped system produce a perfect imitation of the undamped movement, but that would involve activating it in a more elaborate way than simply displacing and releasing it. Significantly, it would require that more energy be expended. Highlighted here is the fact that mechanical systems have a preferred response, determined by their physical properties and manifest when they are in free vibration. Forcing a departure from their natural default behaviour inevitably means an increased energy cost.

Speech articulators exemplify the 'strongly damped' case. An articulator's 'preferred behaviour' is a function of its speech-independent physical characteristics which can be estimated empirically and described in terms of an 'impulse response' (Boubana 1995). A description anchored in biomechanics offers the advantage of uniquely connecting input force, impulse response and output movement. Knowing the impulse response and the input force, we can derive the resulting movement. And, given the input force and a cost function, articulatory 'effort' can be estimated (see, e.g., Kabugari & Honda 1996).

A number of qualitative predictions follow from this analysis. For instance, if initially children do indeed favour low- over high-cost movements, their early vocal activity would be expected to depart minimally from intrinsic articulatory propensities. Two examples illustrate that this is clearly the case.

First, 'canonical babbling' has been analysed as an open–closed alternation of the mandible involving minimum activity in other articulators (MacNeilage & Davis 1993). Approaching the preferred rate of jaw movement (Boubana 1995), this oscillation represents a low-cost form of behaviour. Second, in early phonetic forms, there is a strong tendency toward 'co-occurrence patterns'. Front 'consonants' go with front 'vowels', posterior closures with back 'vowels', showing that children favour assimilatory sequences. This is another instance of low-cost behaviour, since assimilations make articulations more similar, thus decreasing both articulatory displacements and rates – which, in biomechanical terms, translates into less effort.

6.2 *Articulatory naturalness*

A production model with a cost function provides a metric for assigning a 'pronounceability score' to any movement pattern. On the basis of such a criterion, the pattern in question can be ordered in relation to all other patterns. In the present discussion, that rank order, an important role part of the model, will be called the articulatory naturalness hierarchy (ANH).

For a given model, an infinite number of movement patterns is possible. However, it is convenient to quantize the articulatory space into a finite number of discrete points (cf. work on vowel space). ANH refers to the rank order defined on those points.

'Lexical development' proceeds by incrementing N, vocabulary size. The phonetic shapes in a lexicon of N items are generated by outputting the first N patterns from the ANH-based ranking list.

According to the present scenario, phonetic learning is a recalibration of the language-independent ANH. The probability that a given phonetic form will be used, or learned, depends on three interacting factors: (*a*) its articulatory naturalness; (*b*) its salience in the input; and (*c*) how it compares with other forms already in the lexicon.

6.3 *Ambient recalibration*

Ambient recalibration takes a form's input status into account. It associates a heard phonetic pattern with its articulatory representation. Every time this link is made, a modification of the item's naturalness score occurs. The strength of the ambient influence is related to frequency (perceptual salience). Ambient exposure thus changes the ANH-score. In due course, recalibration will revise the rank order. (This revised order is denoted LH, the *learnability hierarchy*.) Read-outs from LH produce articulations reflecting both articulatory naturalness and ambient exposure.

It may be objected that the proposed routine is no more than a copying procedure trivially guaranteed eventually to produce the language-specific effects. That is true but not trivial. The copying interacts with pronounceability constraints which leads to the testable prediction that easier (harder) pronunciations take shorter (longer) to copy.

6.4 *Lexical storage*

One possibility is that phonetic information is stored lexically in terms of 'motor scores' (Browman & Goldstein 1992). For reasons of parsimony, we assume that this pattern represents an unanalysed whole whose parts have yet to be discovered. The whole point of the present approach is that we must not prematurely attribute 'units' to the learner. Nor should we assume that, at the onset, individual articulatory parameters of the score could be independently accessed. However, it does seem possible to envision a process by which the discovery of units might occur in a completely unsupervised way. A fragment of an algorithm that does precisely that will be presented next. Interestingly, its derived entities correspond to 'phonetic gestures' (Studdert-Kennedy, this volume).

6.5 *Self-segmentation*

The algorithm performs a distributional analysis not unlike selecting, from a stack of cards, items with the same holes punched (Studdert-Kennedy 1987; Lindblom 1992). In relying on minimal pairs it also resembles classical phonemic analysis. However, it differs from that procedure in using analog phonetic information rather than discrete and prespecified segments. Figure 15.2 illustrates the process.

Table 15.1 compares the motor scores of two hypothetical vocabularies: set I contains [ba], [da], [bi] and [di]. Set II contains [bɑ], [ɖɯ], [ɟə] and [ɢü]. The lip movement in [ba] and [bi] goes from closure to neutral. The tongue moves from neutral to constricted and the jaw from close to more open. The 'minimal pairs' of (I) show more sharing of movements than (II) (hence more pluses). Synthesizing (I), we would minimally need to combine two control functions for the initial (lip and

Table 15.1

	[ba]	[da]	[bi]	[di]
[ba]	.	+	+	–
[da]	+	.	–	+
[bi]	+	–	.	+
[di]	–	+	+	.

	[bɑ]	[ɖɯ]	[ɟə]	[ɢü]
[bɑ]	.	–	–	–
[ɖɯ]	–	.	–	–
[ɟə]	–	–	.	–
[ɢü]	–	–	–	.

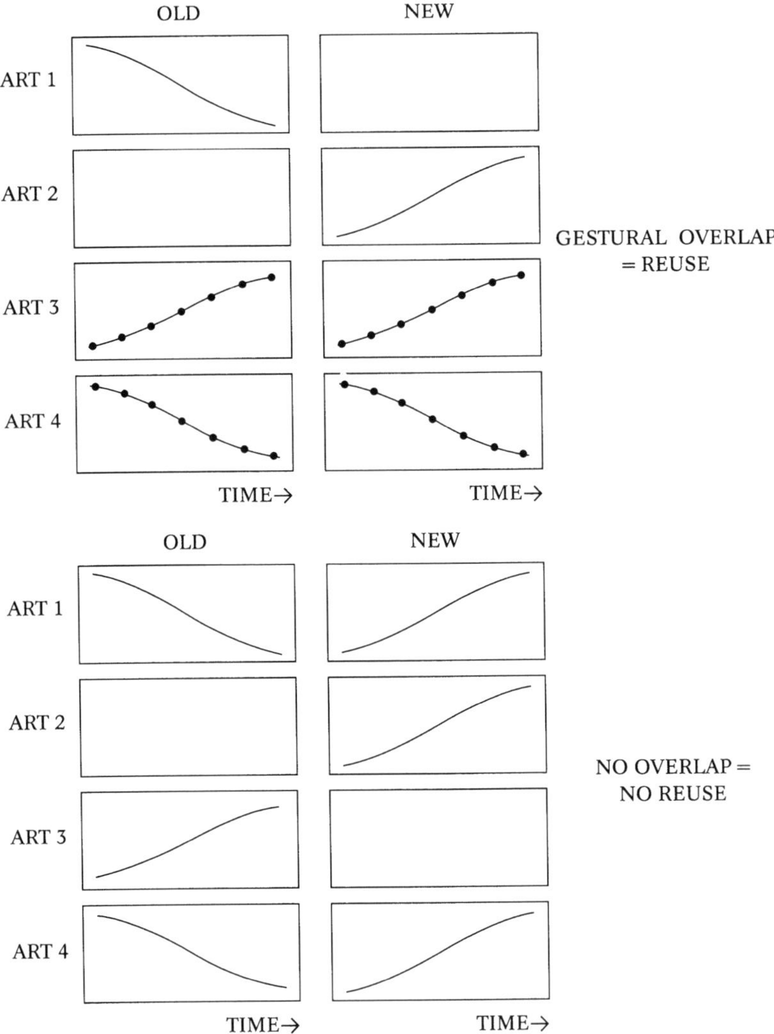

Figure 15.2
Top row: comparison of two hypothetical motor scores for an old and a new form that share movements (dotted curves).
Below: old and new form show no movement overlap.

tip) closures with two jaw-tongue-lip patterns for the following open configurations. The lack of movement overlap in (II) necessitates eight control patterns, four closures and four opening gestures. Thus the 'unmarked' set recruits fewer commands than (II) (Carré 1996).

6.6 *'Syllables' and 'gestures' as lexical emergents*

Shared movement is the key to self-segmentation. If two items make use of the identical movement, a question arises concerning their storage. Does the brain repeat the memory trace of the shared movement in two different locations? Or does it store that information only once? That trace must minimally record two things: the identity of the articulator and data for deriving the particular movement. Neurophysiological observations (cf. sensory and motor 'homunculi' (Kandel, Schwartz & Jessell 1991)) make it seem plausible that the identity of the articulator is handled somatotopically. Thus, tongue activity is stored in brain tissue connected with tongue movement. Analogously, activity in other articulators gets stored in tissue dedicated to those articulators. The answer to the question is provided by somatotopic organization: if the movement is indeed shared, although used by two or more motor scores, it gets stored only once in a single place.

Note that, when this process takes place, a break-down of the holistic motor score has in fact been initiated. Gradually, as more forms are acquired, new loci of movement overlap will automatically be identified and old ones will be reinforced.

Self-segmentation could apply at several levels. 'Disyllables' would do as well as 'diphones' as a starting point. In [baba], [bibi], [babi], [dada], etc., the movement overlap identifies chunks similar to both 'syllabic' structures ([ba, ab, bab, bi, ib, bib, da, ad, dad]) and 'phonemes' /b, a, i, d/. Since the element derived in the diphone comparisons is a time-varying articulatory movement, it is more accurate to say that the process identifies a 'phonetic gesture'.

Two results are worth noting: (a) the derivation of gestures and syllables is *systemic* (presupposes the lexicon) and (b) phonological units are *emergents* of the developing lexical system rather than prespecified entities (Lindblom 1992).

For self-segmentation to occur, a large portion of the acquired forms must show a 'minimal-pair' relationship. The lexicons of human languages make extensive use of that relationship, as evident from the universal principle of phonemic contrast. How do children 'discover' that principle? How do they learn to (p)articulate (Studdert-Kennedy, this volume)? According to the present account, phonemic coding is an automatic consequence of the accumulation of a large lexicon (absent in other species), and the fact that word and morpheme memories are built from gestural overlap. If correct, the key question becomes: where does phonemic coding come from in the first place?

As a step toward suggesting an answer I first draw attention to an interesting property of the proposed scenario. If somatotopic storage does indeed put identical movements in single memory locations, the ease with which new forms are acquired may be affected not only by how pronounceable and perceptually strong they are. The extent to which they share movements with old forms could also matter. Everything else (articulatory cost and perceptual salience) being equal, learning a new form that overlaps with old patterns should involve storing less information in memory than acquiring one with nothing in common with old items, since part of the new motor score is already in storage. Gestural overlap reduces the number of bits to be memorized. Is that true also for phonetic learning? A brief look at relevant literature throws some light on this question.

6.7 *Supporting data and interpretations*

The following remarks are from reviews of work on phonological development. They come close to the present argument:

> Reliance on subroutines . . . also maximizes utilization of skills already acquired, for the child adding a new word to his/her lexicon can simplify that task if he/she can assimilate the word to existing subroutines. [Menn 1978: 165]

> [P]hysiological causes are only one factor in determining 'ease of articulation' for the individual child. The other factor, and I propose that it is the major factor, is the state of the child's knowledge at a given time . . . [l] is 'easier' than [j] only because this child happens to have found out how to make an [l] first. [Menn 1983: 21]

Studying children with severe articulation problems, McReynolds & Bennett (1972) investigated the extent to which a distinctive feature, once learned, would generalize to unlearned items. They found that training decreased feature errors and that a feature generalized across several phonemes, although training in only one phoneme was administered.

In an experiment on lexical learning, Schwartz & Leonard (1982) presented sixteen invented lexical concepts, each represented by nonsense words, to twelve children with vocabularies of no more than five words. Half of these items had phonetic characteristics previously seen in the children's production, half of them were phonetically novel. The children imitated, and spontaneously used, words earlier and in greater numbers when the items were phonetically compatible with existing patterns.

In an imitation task involving novel, specially designed test words, Beckman & Edwards (in press) found that preschool children produced familiar sequences more accurately than new sequences. The experiment controlled for novelty of the phonemes tested and for the compatibility of the stimuli with familiar phonotactic patterns. The investigators conclude that: 'the frequency of the sequence in extant lexical forms influences the phonological representation of the sublexical units relevant for their production'.

Six phonologically disordered children tested in parallel performed more poorly than their age peers overall. They showed an even larger effect of familiarity on imitation accuracy.

Finally some observations from a study of UPSID segments marked as 'loan phonemes': Maddieson (1986) investigated whether 'added segments must be capable of being "generated" by combinations of familiar features already in the recipient language' (p. 3), and concluded that the evidence is indeed heavily in favour of this view and that 'languages have a strong tendency to reject as loan segments those segments that are remote from their existing phonetic resources, or to modify them in such a way that they are no longer remote' (p. 13).

A similar observation concerns 'gestural economy' as a universal property of sound systems (Maddieson 1995). This principle is illustrated with data from Ewe: 'doubly-articulated labial-velar stops appear to be made in the simplest way possible – by combining the well-rehearsed movements that are used in simple labial and velar stops . . . We hypothesize that languages take maximal advantage of such opportunities for limiting the number of distinct gestures employed, as part of a general preference of gestural economy' (Maddieson 1995: 576).

6.8 *Learnability*

It is tempting to put the above observations under one umbrella, proposing that their common background is the preference for *reuse* of lexically established movements. There may be several causal factors.

Imitating a new form involves linking its perceptual representation to its motor score. Conceivably, the imitative search could proceed by modifying old motor scores: the smaller the change, the easier the task.

Moreover, as argued before, gestural overlap between new and old patterns should reduce the amount of information to be stored. We know from animal experimentation that memory formation changes the brain physically, with neural structures undergoing biochemical, morphological and physiological alterations (Rose 1993). It is not known whether there is a physical cost, analogous to biomechanical cost, associated with forming a long-term phonetic memory. Nevertheless, a memory-based reuse of (hidden) parts of old motor scores would produce some interesting consequences. Let it be stipulated that the learnability of a given form (the probability that it will be committed to memory, and/or used) is influenced by the degree to which it invokes articulatory movements that are part of already-mastered forms.

6.9 *Lexical recalibration*

Movement sharing is the basis of lexical recalibration. I propose that its interaction with naturalness and salience be numerically developed as follows.

In quantifying *articulatory cost*, I follow Nelson (1983) in choosing the time integral of the force magnitude as the cost of activating the ith articulator. The cost of a motor score m (with activation of several articulators) is defined by summing the individual force-time integrals:

$$(4)\quad A(m) = i\int_{1}^{n}\sum_{0}^{\tau} f_i(m,t)\,dt$$

Ambient recalibration of the mth item in the ANH is introduced as $e^{-x(m)}$ which represents the current strength of the form in the input. If $x(m)$, the exponent, gets incremented every time m is observed in the input, then $e^{-x(m)}=1$ for no occurrences and 0 for a high-frequency item.

Lexical recalibration is implemented by α, a binary parameter controlling the presence or absence of the ith parameter in the cost computation. If that parameter is shared with old forms, it is free of charge. Accordingly, $\alpha_i(m)$ is set to zero, and the ith contribution vanishes from the calculations reducing the net score. If there is no sharing, $\alpha_i(m)$ equals unity, and no lexical recalibration takes place. (Articulatory cost is A. The post-lexical score is denoted A^*.)

$$(5)\quad A^*(m) = i\sum_{1}^{n}\alpha_i(m)\int_{0}^{\tau} f_i(m,t)\,dt$$

From these definitions we obtain **Eq (6)** which specifies the 'developmental' score of the mth form. Its value depends on the item's articulatory naturalness, its perceptual salience and its lexical compatibility. The smaller it is, the higher its LH-rank and the greater the probability that it will be used and learned.

(6) $A^*(m)e^{-x(m)}$

The refinement of **Eq** (3) can now be made by inserting A_{ij} as

(7) $A_{ij} = A^*_i + A^*_j$

To translate this formalism into words, let us consider the acquisition of ejectives. In terms of the criteria proposed here, producing a syllable with an ejective is a relatively demanding task presupposing a precisely timed co-ordination of several activities: supraglottal articulation, glottal closure and larynx elevation (Ladefoged 1993). We would therefore expect ejectives not to be frequent in children's early vocalizations. However, at some point, Amharic or Tigrinyan children will for the first time begin to use an ejective consistently, perhaps in the form [k'a]. When that happens, it suggests that [k'a] has improved its learnability score, by ambient recalibration. It has obtained a better rank than many more pronounceable, competing patterns implicitly available in the children's ANH. Furthermore, the presence of [k'a] in the lexicon implies that [t'a], [k'u], and all other potential utterances with ejectives would share the glottal and laryngeal gestures needed for ejectives, whereas many articulations of comparable articulatory cost would not. Across the board, ejectives improve their learnability.

Lexical recalibration is a form of 'phonetic nepotism'. It will improve the learnability of all forms having the same movement components as a lexical motor score, irrespective of their original ANH-scores. We also note that, as suggested by Menn, it is responsible for making 'articulatory ease' language-specific.

7 Sound systems for speakers, listeners and learners

Different meanings must sound different and, at the same time, be signalled with minimal motor extravagance. We saw that these goals are balanced by speakers in their on-line efforts to produce intelligible and socially adequate speech. The tension between those goals is an

Table 15.2

(a)	p	.	.	t	.	.	k	.	.
	b	.	.	d	.	.	g	.	.
	m	.	.	n	.	.	ŋ	.	.
(b)	.	.	.	.	t	.	.	q	ʔ
	b	.	d̪	.	.	.	g	.	.
	.	ɱ	.	n	.	ɲ	.	.	.

important source of the phonetic variation from which speech community members select innovations of the phonological system. Selections are made blindly and without awareness of the functional consequences of the new speech patterns. This, we propose, is the mechanism by which sound systems become adapted for use by speakers and listeners.

Their structure may also facilitate lexical development. For instance, if speech development is characterized by a process similar to lexical recalibration, we would expect children to have difficulty learning the (b) inventory of table 15.2, but to find (a) easy.

I note that the effect of lexical recalibration is to bias development in the direction of (a) rather than (b).

MUAF patterns like that in (a) may seem like a typical instance of an 'arbitrary, formal idiosyncracy' often mentioned in work on syntax and Universal Grammar. Should it be attributed to our 'genetic endowment' for language? A strong case can be made for arguing instead that MUAF patterns are adaptations to phonological development. Learning languages having them is easier, because of an intrinsic bias toward gestural economy in both imitating and remembering phonetic patterns.

8 Origins of digital and combinatorial coding

How did human phonologies go digital? The preceding remarks have touched on several preconditions.

The formation of sound structure is semantically driven. A large number of meanings creates a large conceptual pressure (whose origins have not been addressed here). The forms that accumulate represent the 'system'. As their phonetic shapes are selected, entities interact within that system, both in development and phylogenetically. The system interaction means that the selection of an element's phonetic value, e.g. its distinctiveness, is never in terms of that element in isolation. It always occurs in relation to all other values of the paradigm. Phonologies are systems *où tout se tient.*

We also saw systemic forces at work in the derivation of the 'phonetic gesture' and its combinatorial patterning. What was the basis of that result? Both derive from the *reuse* of articulatory movements which is caused by two circumstances. First, the cost of a component movement is incurred only when it is first learned. On reappearing in new forms, it is not penalized. Second, there would not be a 'component movement' unless motor scores were made up of parts. In other words, self-segmentation depends on the fortuitous fact that the speech production system uses multiple channels (Studdert-Kennedy, this volume). It is anatomically segmented. The 'lexicon' modelled here contains a set of analog scores which intersect (share movements). Such sharing is possible only because speech is 'big band', it is produced with an 'orchestra' with many 'instruments'. Speech shares that feature with sign which also exhibits submorphemic structure (Bellugi & Studdert-Kennedy 1980), but not with systems for pitch control (cf. human prosody and bird song).

These considerations offer a preliminary in-principle solution to the problem of 'Where does the phonemic principle come from?' What discontinuities were we forced to postulate in developing the account? Very few.

My claim is that it is possible to construct an algorithm that simulates a lexicon combinatorially coded in terms of a small set of discrete units. The lexical patterns are shaped by conditions not specific to speech: the multi-channel structure of the vocal tract, properties of the auditory system determining distinctiveness, vocal imitation, economy of motor memory and performance. When those factors are put into play by a large number of lexical meanings, discrete entities (read: 'perceptually tuned gestures') emerge in combinatorial patterns.

Acknowledgments

This research was supported by a grant (*Emergent Phonology*) from the Swedish Council for Research in the Humanities and the Social Sciences.

References

Beckman, M. E. & Edwards, J. (in press). Lexical frequency effects on young children's imitative productions. In Pierrehumbert, J. & Broe, M. (eds.)

Papers on Laboratory Phonology V. Cambridge: Cambridge University Press.

Bellugi, U. & Studdert-Kennedy, M. (1980). *Signed and Spoken Language: Biological Constraints on Linguistic Form*. Deerfield Beach, FL: Verlag Chemie.

Bladon, R. A. W. & Lindblom, B. (1981). Modeling the judgment of vowel quality differences. *Journal of the Acoustic Society of America*, 69, 1414–1422.

Boubana, S. (1995). Modeling of tongue movement using multi-pulse LPC coding. Doctoral thesis, Département Signal, ENST, Paris.

Browman, C. P. & Goldstein, L. (1992). Articulatory phonology: an overview. *Phonetica*, 49, 155–180.

Carré, R. (1996). Prediction of vowel systems using a deductive approach. *Proceedings of the ICSLP-96* (Philadelphia), pp. 434–437.

Crothers, J. (1978). Typology and universals of vowel systems. In Greenberg, J. H., Ferguson, C. A. & Moravcsik, E. A. (eds.) *Universals of Human Language*, vol. II. Stanford, CA: Stanford University Press.

Gay, T., Lindblom, B. & Lubker, J. (1981). Production of bite-block vowels: acoustic equivalence by selective compensation. *Journal of the Acoustic Society of America*, 69, 802–810.

Kabugari, T. & Honda, M. (1996). A model of articulator trajectory formation based on the motor tasks of vocal tract shapes. *Journal of the Acoustic Society of America*, 99(5), 3154–3170.

Kandel, E., Schwartz, J. & Jessel, T. (1991). *Principles of Neural Science*. (3rd edition) New York: Elsevier.

Kiparsky, P. (1988). Phonological change. In Newmeyer, F. J. (ed.) *Linguistics: The Cambridge Survey*, vol. I: *Linguistic Theory: Foundations*. Cambridge: Cambridge University Press, pp. 363–415.

Laboissière, R., Ostry, D. & Perrier, P. (1995). A model of human jaw and hyoid motion and its implications for speech production. In Elenius, K. & Branderud, P. (eds.) *Proceedings of the 13th International Congress of Phonetic Sciences Stockholm*, vol. II, pp. 60–67.

Ladefoged, P. (1993). *A Course in Phonetics*. (3rd edition) New York: Harcourt, Brace & Jovanovich.

Lindblom, B. (1986). Phonetic universals in vowel systems. In Ohala, J. J. & Jaeger, J. J. (eds.) *Experimental Phonology*. Orlando, FL: Academic Press, pp. 13–44.

(1992). Phonological units as adaptive emergents of lexical development. In Ferguson, C. A., Menn, L. & Stoel-Gammon, C. (eds.) *Phonological Development: Models, Research, Implications*. Timonium, MD: York Press, pp. 131–163.

Brownlee, S., Davis, B. & Moon, S.-J. (1992). Speech transforms. *Speech Communication*, 11, 357–368.

Lubker, J. & Gay, T. (1979). Formant frequencies of some fixed-mandible vowels and a model of speech programming by predictive simulation. *Journal of Phonetics*, 7, 147–162.

& Maddieson, I. (1988). Phonetic universals in consonant systems. In Hyman, L. M. & Li, C. N. (eds.) *Language, Speech and Mind*. London & New York: Routledge, pp. 62–78.

MacNeilage, P. F. & Davis, B. L. (1993). Motor explanations of babbling and early speech patterns. In Boysson-Bardies, B. *et al.* (eds.) *Changes in Speech and Face Processing in the First Year of Life*. Dordrecht: Kluwer.

Maddieson, I. (1984). *Patterns of Sounds*. Cambridge: Cambridge University Press.

(1986). Borrowed sounds. In Fishman, J. A. *et al.* (eds.) *The Fergusonian Impact*. The Hague: Mouton, pp. 1–16.

(1995). Gestural economy. In Elenius, K. & Branderud, P. (eds.) *Proceedings of the 13th International Congress of Phonetic Sciences Stockholm*, vol. IV, pp. 574–577.

McReynolds, L. V. & Bennett, S. (1972). Distinctive feature generalization in articulatory training. *Journal of Speech and Hearing Disorders*, 37(4), 462–470.

Menn, L. (1978). Phonological units in beginning speech. In Bell, A. & Hooper, J. B. (eds.) *Syllables and Segments*. Amsterdam: North Holland, pp. 157–171.

(1983). Development of articulatory, phonetic and phonological capabilities. In Butterworth, B. (ed.) *Language Production*, vol. II. London: Academic Press.

Moon, S.-J. & Lindblom, B. (1994). Interaction between duration, context and speaking style in English stressed vowels. *Journal of the Acoustic Society of America*, 96(1), 40–55.

Nelson, W. L. (1983). Physical principles for economies of skilled movements. *Biological Cybernetics*, 46, 135–147.

Ohala, J. J. (1980). Chairman's introduction to the Symposium on Phonetic Universals in Phonological Systems and their Explanation. In Fischer-Jorgensen, E., Rischel, J. & Thorsen, N. (eds.) *Proceedings of the Ninth International Congress of Phonetic Sciences 1979*. Copenhagen: Institute of Phonetics, University of Copenhagen, pp. 184–185.

(1981). The listener as a source of sound change. In Masek, C., Hendrick, R. A. & Miller, M. F. (eds.) *Papers from the Parasession on Language and Behaviour*. Chicago: Chicago Linguistic Society, pp. 178–203.

(1993). The phonetics of sound change. In Jones, C. (ed.) *Historical Linguistics: Problems and Perspectives*. London: Longman, pp. 237–278.

Passy, P. (1890). *Etudes sur les changements phonétiques et leurs caractères généraux*. Paris: Firmin-Didot.

Rose, S. (1993). *The Making of Memory*. New York: Bantam Books.

Saltzman, E. L. & Munhall, K. G. (1989). A dynamical approach to gestural patterning in speech production. *Ecol Psychol*, 1, 91–163.

Schwartz, R. G. & Leonard, L. B. (1981). Do children pick and choose? An examination of phonological selection and avoidance in early lexical acquisition. *Journal of Child Language*, 9, 319–336.

Studdert-Kennedy, M. (1987). The phoneme as a perceptuo-motor structure. In Allport, A., MacKay, D. G., Prinz, W. & Scheerer, E. (eds.). *Language Perception and Production*. London: Academic Press, pp. 67–84.

Wilhelms-Tricarico, R. & Perkell, J. S. J. (1995). Towards a physiological model of speech production. In Elenius, K. & Branderud, P. (eds.) *Proceedings of the 13th International Congress of Phonetic Sciences Stockholm*, vol. II, pp. 68–75.
Willerman, R. (1994). Phonetics of pronouns: The articulatory bases of markedness. Ph.D. dissertation, University of Texas at Austin.
Williams, D. (1986). Role of dynamic information in the perception of coarticulated vowels. Ph.D. dissertation, University of Connecticut.

16 The development of sound systems in human language

KLAUS J. KOHLER

1 Introduction

This chapter presents a few ideas on the question of the nature of a speech sound, and it takes as its point of departure the seminal work by Lindblom and co-authors, especially Liljencrants & Lindblom (1972), Lindblom (1975, 1984, 1986, 1990a, b), and Lindblom & Maddieson (1988). So the aim is a contribution to the explanation of fundamental general phonetic categories in human speech and of descriptive language facts from the perspectives of universals in phylogenetic evolution, ontogenetic acquisition, communicative function and historical change. The following theoretical premises of Lindblom are essential for this discussion.

(a) The approach is deductive and hypothesis-driven, i.e. it is grounded in facts and assumptions that lie outside the field to be explained, in particular in the biology of the sound producing, receiving and understanding systems of *Homo loquens*. (This does not negate the additional importance of sociological factors, but they will be excluded from consideration here.)

(b) Sound systems in human languages are the way they are as the result of balancing sufficient acoustic/auditory contrast for a listener and articulatory economy for a speaker under varying conditions of speech communication: they both tend to be maximized in the pursuit of communicative goals (H&H theory).[1]

(c) Basic and Elaborated or Complex sound types have to be distinguished: [a] and [t] are intuitively simpler than [ĩ] and [ɗ]; the task is to provide externally motivated reasons for this intuition.

I shall attempt to apply principle (a) more rigorously in connection with (c), where, I think, under the influence of Maddieson's data-oriented approach, Lindblom & Maddieson (1988) come close to circularity because the postulation of their basic consonant set of eleven

1 The hypo-hyper theory of articulatory reduction and elaboration, cf. Lindblom 1990a.

obstruents and seven sonorants is primarily governed by the observed systems in the languages of the world; what we want is independent articulatory and perceptual justification for the notion of simplicity in elementary sound types. I shall also argue in favour of a more clearly two-stage evolution model – sound-space delimitation followed by selection. The first step – of delimiting the human speech sound space and of constraining vowel or consonant systems – is considered to be grounded in articulation, i.e. in the neuromuscular and biomechanical constraints imposed by the anatomy and physiology of the apparatus available to humans for noise generation and in the general tendency to minimize articulatory effort. An acoustic/auditory selection principle then shapes speech as an instrument of communication between a speaker and a listener in a second step. This means that I wish to put a stronger emphasis on the articulatory basis of sound systems than Lindblom has done, due, no doubt, to his work on vowels having originated in the field of perception, although he also clearly recognized the importance of an articulation component in the shaping of vowel systems (Lindblom 1986).

I shall put forth a set of ten assumptions and discuss the corollaries of each one, proceeding from articulatory considerations to perceptual constraints.

2 Assumption 1: the vegetative function origin

We can start from two sets of facts:

(a) Vocal language developed to address the ear as a more distal system of communication than the gestures of sign language, which have to rely on eye contact in face-to-face interactions under favourable lighting conditions. This development at the same time freed the hands and arms for other activities, an important factor in the struggle for survival. Seen from this perspective, we can expect that sounds produced with the help of hands and fingers to shape the vocal tract do not form part of human vocal language at its original evolutionary stage. This rules out a large proportion of Fred Newman's 'mouthsounds' (Newman 1980) as possible speech sounds. The development of the whistled language of La Gomera (Classe 1957) is no contradiction, because here the finger-assisted labial whistle is quite clearly superimposed on articulatory tongue movements of the primary vocal language, which was thus subsequently adapted for special long-distance communication.

(b) All sound-producing structures used in human language have primary vegetative functions that guarantee survival: the chest/lungs, larynx, velum, tongue, teeth, lips, mandible for breathing, protection of the breathing system, stabilization of the rib cage, swallowing, sucking, chewing. Speech is thus an adaptation of the pre-existent anatomy and physiology of the vegetative system to the new function of speech communication to increase the chances of survival. From this fact we may conclude that only those noise productions enter into the formation of speech sounds that are related to the basic mechanisms already used for these non-speech functions. This excludes more of Newman's 'mouthsounds' and all of Pike's minor air-stream mechanisms (Pike 1943), i.e. all sound productions that employ generators which are not part of the vegetative basis. It leaves us with pulmonic, glottalic and oral air-stream mechanisms, with the exclusion of the egressive oral one.

Viewed from this angle, clicks, although very rare in the world's languages (Maddieson 1984), must be regarded as being among the basic archetypal phonemic elements of sound systems, rather than in Lindblom & Maddieson's Elaborated set. This point is strengthened by the fact that outside the area of click languages there is, in Africa, a wide geographical distribution of labio-velars, which can be derived from (bilabial) clicks by eliminating the sucking motion and thus integrating the production into an overall pulmonic air-stream, while still preserving the tongue–lip configuration of clicks. Oral air-streams offer the additional advantage of not interfering with vegetative breathing, which may be very important in strenuous outdoor activity. Furthermore, they can have a high degree of perceptual salience, e.g. the palatoalveolar click. But these advantages are completely outweighed by the extreme limitation of paradigmatic differentiation as well as syntagmatic concatenation in oral air-stream productions. They have a restricted place continuum and very limited possibilities for manner categories (stop and affricate types, compared with the distinction of plosives, fricatives, affricates, nasals, approximants, trills, taps and flaps in the pulmonic mechanism); they thus lack the generation of vowel types, which are essential as carriers of syllable units (see Assumption 2). Moreover, the glottal and nasal modifications of clicks, which may be very elaborate in some languages (see !Xũ in Maddieson 1984), are pulmonic by definition. The pulmonic mechanism is therefore by far superior, and selection has led to its dominance, relegating clicks to a peripheral position structurally and geographically, mostly in a paralinguistic function, rather than as linguistic speech sounds.

The modification of the pulmonic air-stream from vegetative breathing to sound production also shows the results of the adaptation and selection principles. The egressive air-stream becomes highly controlled and thus allows speech generation over long periods of time without the need for breathing in. On the other hand, the ingressive air-stream cannot be so regulated for physiological reasons, and is consequently only used paralinguistically, not for concatenative elements of phonological sound systems.

The vegetative origin of speech is also suggested by the way humans produce hesitation 'particles' in the speech stream, largely irrespective of the particular language they speak: when they forget what to say and search for words, they use a non-word vocalization instead. The vehicle for this is an unrestricted oral or nasal air-stream, or a combination of the two, either simultaneously or in sequence, e.g. [ɛː], [mː], [ɛ̃ː], [ɛːm], [ɛ̃ːm]. In this the mouth opening (degree and rounding) is of secondary importance, and may vary a great deal from speaker to speaker, but it is interesting and significant to note that only more open-type vowel qualities, approximately representable in IPA symbolization as [ɛː], [æː], [ɜː], [ɐː], [œː], not [iː], [yː] or [uː], occur, and that the labial nasal is preferred. Moreover, the vowel qualities of these hesitations do not coincide with those of the phonemes in lexical items of the particular language (Pätzold & Simpson 1995); they just act as non-closed vocal tract carriers and thus still retain many characteristics of the egressive phase of vegetative breathing. This leads us to Assumption 2.

3 Assumption 2: articulation vs vocalization – the emergence of syllables, vowels and consonants

The simplest sound productions on the basis of the air-stream mechanisms, especially the pulmonic one, set out under Assumption 1, are elementary vocalizations, as they are found in other species, particularly in primates, as well. But human language entails more: it is articulated speech, i.e. short-term local gestures are interspersed into more long-term global movements, articulation rides on vocalization. The precursor to this is the well-known lipsmack, which is a widespread communicative gesture in higher primates, consisting of mandibular opening–closing movements on an oral or a pulmonic mechanism, combined with phonation in ‘girney’. It constitutes a direct link back to vegetative suction and forward to language clicks and labio-velars.

In hominids this basic pattern has been expanded in the syntagmatic as well as in the paradigmatic plane:

by the sequencing of slow mandibular, linguodorsal and labial movement complexes
by varying these long-term motion units
- in the vertical dimension: different degrees of mandibular and linguodorsal elevation
- in the horizontal dimension: front to back linguodorsal and labial movements

by varying the short-term action inside the global dynamics
- through extreme strictures on the three air-streams: closure (complete, or central with lateral opening), turbulence narrowing (central/lateral)
- through velic raising/lowering.

This elaboration of an elementary mandibular opening–closing has resulted in the emergence of concatenative syllables, i.e. motion units of long time constants with short-time-constant articulatory separators, and vowels/consonants inside these units, representing the slow and the faster gestures, respectively. In this connection, MacNeilage talks about segmental ‘content’ in syllable ‘frames’ (MacNeilage & Davis 1990). The basic consonant types emerging from this expansion of the fundamental dynamic articulation unit are stops, fricatives, nasals and liquids.
The ideal syllable contains a complete articulatory contrast: extreme mandibular opening as well as linguodorsal lowering for the slow setting, and complete supraglottal closure, combined with velic raising, for the faster gesture, resulting in an interruption of the air-stream. This interruption can also be brought about more quickly and efficiently by a glottal closure, which is the most elementary means of cutting off the pulmonic air-stream, being also rooted in vegetative function.

In this connection I must also mention the use of assertion and negation ‘particles’ instead of the words for ‘yes’ and ‘no’, found in many languages. Some of these versions can be transcribed in IPA notation as [a'ha], [a'ɦa], [m'm̥m], [m'm̤m], [ã'hã], [ã'ɦã] (for assertion), ['aʔa], ['mʔm], ['ãʔã] (for negation). They follow the same principle of elementary sound production as the hesitation ‘particles’ discussed under Assumption 1: an oral or a nasal air-stream or a superposition of both is the carrier for non-lexical vocalizations with situational meaning, and again the degree and shape of mouth opening are not crucial, as long as there is a central or open vowel quality, which once more does not coincide with the vowel phonemes of the particular language.

What is, however, different in these 'particles' from the shaping of hesitations is the introduction of a syllable structure, which represents a further step in the evolution of human language – from vocalization to articulation: these sound productions are thus more speech-like. In both cases the chunking of the air flow into syllabic units is accomplished by glottal activity. The *gradual division*, achieved by a change from modal to breathy voice or to voicelessness and back to modal voice, is linked with the meaning *'yes'*; the *abrupt division* by a glottal stop, with the meaning *'no'*. In German the assertion is additionally associated with a medial pitch peak or a pitch valley on the second syllable, the negation with an early pitch peak on the first (Kohler 1991). These different links make a high or a low pitch on these 'particles' perceptually salient. According to an ethological perspective (Ohala 1983, 1984), high/low pitches have become associated in the course of evolution across species with small/large body size of the vocalizers and secondarily with their submissive/threatening behaviour. A 'frequency code' has thus developed for the signalling of the attitudes of submission and dominance by high and low pitch, respectively. The elementary syllabification of a pulmonic air-stream by basic glottal mechanisms can thus be supplemented by an equally fundamental use of pitch to strengthen the meanings of acceptance and refusal in these non-lexical, but articulated, speech interactions.

4 Assumption 3: coronals – typical consonants

Tongue tip/blade articulations (coronals: apicals/(sub)laminals) are ideal riders on syllable frames because they can be executed faster than tongue dorsum and lip movements. Their production is governed by the short and fast intrinsic tongue muscles as well as the small movable mass, as against the extrinsic tongue or the lip muscles responsible for moving the greater mass of the tongue body or lips. Coronals thus have a shorter time constant than labials or dorsals, and can therefore function as optimal syllable separators because their interaction with the slow global dorsal and lip gestures can be kept minimal, and the articulatory contrast between the two movement types can thus be maximized. Consequently consonants may be assumed to be primarily coronal, vowels non-coronal (dorsal). This is indeed supported by the general occurrence of coronal consonants in the languages of the world, especially in the fricative, nasal and liquid categories, where a unique class element is always coronal. It is further supported by the scarcity of coronal (apical, laminal or sublaminal/retroflex) vowels.

The frequently observed occurrence of [t] instead of [k] in the speech development of children may also have an articulatory, vegetative base, in addition to its possible origin in a reduced acoustic/auditory contrast between the two sounds. [t] and [k] may be looked upon as phylogenetic and ontogenetic developments from the [t͜k] double articulation needed in sucking, which is an established reflex right from birth. This would account for the interchangeability of the coronal and dorsal stop articulations in speech sound development. The preference for the coronal element could in turn find an explanation in the greater afferent control of the tongue tip area as against the tongue body, because of the richer supply of kinesthetic and tactile sensors.

5 Assumption 4: constraints on phonation – obstruents and sonorants

In stop and turbulent fricative strictures, vocal fold vibration can only be maintained if the subglottal–supraglottal pressure differential is actively controlled through, for example, cavity expansion (e.g. larynx lowering). In the case of voiced fricatives, this is particularly costly because maintaining friction simultaneously with glottal pulsing requires the generation of a strong air-stream, which in turn presupposes glottal abduction and raises the supraglottal pressure, both processes being opposed to voicing. From the point of view of production economy, stops and fricatives are therefore naturally unvoiced; they become articulatorily more elaborated if they are voiced. In historical sound change, on the other hand, voiced stops tend to be simplified in terms of this concept of articulatory ease, i.e. they become unvoiced. Voiced fricatives may be simplified in two ways: they either lose their voicing, or their friction, becoming approximants. Both processes are widespread in the languages of the world.

In the case of non-stop and non-fricative consonants, voicing is not impeded, and they are generally voiced, thus producing a maximal articulatory contrast with the other consonant class. In the case of nasals, lack of vocal fold vibration also minimizes the perceptual distinctiveness, and voiceless nasals are, therefore, not basic consonant types.

This difference in the control of phonation in different consonant productions, due to biomechanical constraints, leads to the emergence of the consonant classes of obstruents and sonorants.

6 Assumption 5: a force contrast in obstruents – fortis/lenis

A force contrast is associated with the formation and release of pulmonic obstruents. In the case of plosive articulations it manifests itself as a fast/slow occlusion, a long/short hold and a strong/weak release. In fricatives the movement into the turbulence stricture is again fast/slow, and the turbulence itself is characterized by high/low air-stream energy. This leads to the fortis and lenis categories. In stops, either the one or the other may be intensified by subsidiary phonation components to generate more elaborated consonant productions:

the fortis class may be
- aspirated, or
- glottalized, or
- produced with a glottalic air-stream mechanism, intensifying the stop category still further by heightening glottalization through an upward larynx movement;

contrariwise, the lenis class may be
- fully voiced, or
- breathy voiced, or
- fully voiced combined with an ingressive glottalic air-stream.

These articulatory intensifications at the same time increase perceptual distinctivity.

7 Assumption 6: degrees of opening vs front–back in vowels

Degrees of mandible and linguodorsal raising/lowering dominate over the front–back dimension, because along the latter the tongue does not have the synergy of the mandible, and the gesture is therefore more costly with regard to biomechanics and neuromuscular control. So from the viewpoint of articulatory economy, vowel differentiation is to be expected to be greater in the vertical than in the horizontal parameter, which is supported by the empirical data from the world's languages. The principle of sufficient perceptual contrast then operates on the basis of these production constraints. This two-stage evolution model, in which articulatory factors determine the sound space for auditory selection, will generate vowel systems in greater conformity with empirical findings than will Lindblom's more exclusive focus on perceptual determinants.

8 Assumption 7: the labial and lingual parameters in consonants

Assumption 3 has underlined the basic status of coronals in consonant systems. However, cutting off the air-stream is an elementary gesture of any one of the active articulators, i.e. the lips, the tongue tip/blade and the tongue body (over and above the glottis, see Assumption 2), or of both lips and tongue body. The latter, double articulation provides a link with clicks (see Assumption 1). The same considerations apply to the formation of an oral closure combined with velic opening, i.e. to nasals, at these articulators.

In the case of plosives the perceptual salience is relatively weak, if not supported by additional phonatory features, and it does not seem to differ much between any two of them, as is evidenced by confusions in noise (Miller & Nicely 1955). In the case of nasals the auditory differentiation between the three places is much weaker, and in particular the labial and dorsal articulations are poorly contrasted. The empirical data of the world's languages show the preponderance of three-term plosive and of two-term nasal systems, including [ptk]/[bdg] and [mn], respectively, thus supporting the general assumptions about articulatory and perceptual constraints.

In fricatives one would expect the same distribution across the articulators lips, tongue tip, tongue body (and glottis), because, apart from the weighting of coronals, there does not seem to be any further *a priori* reason rooted in production for preferring certain turbulence strictures. But here the perceptual salience associated with each one varies very unevenly from weakest for [f] to strongest for [s] and [ʃ]; i.e. the coronals, which are already given articulatory weight in consonant production (see Assumption 3), are also, at least partly, singled out on an auditory basis. This can explain the general occurrence of [s] in the fricative systems of the world's languages, either as the only element or besides others, especially [f] and [ʃ], with dorsal fricatives being quite rare.

Just as [ʔ] constitutes a very basic stoppage of the pulmonic air-stream, [h] provides a similarly elementary turbulence stricture at the glottis. Its occurrence in the majority of languages testifies to this. However, its by no means rare absence from consonant systems requires a separate explanation. [h], in contradistinction from [ʔ], is not an optimal syllable separator because, due to the lack of localized supraglottal articulation on an uninterrupted air-stream, it is integrated into the slow syllable dynamics. Since its differentiation from the context is by glottal abduction only, this parameter may become adjusted as well, resulting in breathy voice, which is perceptually weak and may thus disappear. This is a case of articulatory reduction of short time-constant consonants and their submergence in long time-constant syllable frames (see Assumption 10).

As regards laterals, their labial production generates sound that is not substantially different from a central fricative or approximant. Auditory selection thus eliminates it. This only leaves coronal and dorsal types. As argued in Assumption 3, the coronal articulation is rated higher, and according to Assumption 9 the dorsal one is to be treated as an elaboration, partly originating from coarticulation in syllable frames.

Finally, trills can be generated most efficiently by the tongue tip: the lips have greater mass and the uvula less muscular control for quick movement. This explains the almost universal occurrence of coronal productions.

9 Assumption 8: the basic vowel and consonant systems

As a conclusion from the foregoing discussion we can postulate the following:

Basic speech sound systems				
Vowels				
high vowels	i		u	
low vowels		a		
Consonants				
clicks	ʘ	ǂ		
plosives	p	t	k	ʔ
	b	d	g	
fricatives	s	h		
nasals	m	n		
laterals	l			
trills	r			

This gives a frequency of roughly 70 per cent to 30 per cent for obstruents vs sonorants. As Lindblom & Maddieson (1988) have pointed out, the elaboration of these two basic consonant system parts occurs proportionally so that the basic relation stays the same across all the systems found in the world's languages.

10 Assumption 9: elaboration of the basic systems

The basic vowel system is elaborated in the vertical dimension in the first instance, leading successively to five- and seven-term vowel systems, the former being the most common in languages; in the second instance there are also elaborations along the horizontal parameter. In both cases the initial articulatory weighting of the vertical dimension is further controlled by the principle of sufficient auditory contrast.

The basic consonant system is elaborated in two ways.

(a) There is further differentiation in the horizontal plane:
separating bilabial from labiodental and dental from (post)alveolar/retroflex articulations
adding the labial and dorsal tongue gestures in fricatives.

(b) More elaborations originate from coarticulation, i.e. from integration of 'content' into 'frame':
palatal fricatives, nasals, laterals for dorsals in front vowel contexts
uvular fricatives for dorsals in low back vowel contexts
secondary articulations of labialization, palatalization, velarization and pharyngealization in the appropriate vowel contexts
creaky voice phonation (glottalization) in consonants in the context of plosive-related glottal stops.

The coarticulatory origin within the syllable also applies to vowels:

nasal vowels always develop in nasal consonant contexts
retroflex vowels originate in the neighbourhood of retroflex consonants
creaky vowels occur in glottal stop onsets
breathy vowels occur in breathy consonant contexts.

11 Assumption 10: articulatory reduction

The initial separation of 'content' from 'frame' is counteracted by articulatory reduction, integrating the former into the latter for economy of effort:

intervocalic lenis stop syllable separators become approximants
glottal stops are reduced to low-frequency irregular glottal pulsing superimposed on vowels and sonorants
for nasal consonants the oral occlusion is no longer effected, resulting in nasal vowels
coronal stops and nasals are assimilated to the labial or the dorsal articulator, thus removing the consonantal specificity and adjusting to the always ongoing lip and tongue movements
intervocalic lenis fricatives become approximants
trills are reduced to taps and further to approximants, which may then be integrated into the vowels.

This is just a small selection of possible processes, which may be multiplied and abound in spontaneous speech. But in all these cases the extent of integration of short-term into long-term movements is checked through the demands for perceptual contrast imposed by the listener in the communicative situation. These synchronic reduction processes may then lead to petrified patterns in historical sound change, when the perceptual check by listeners is relaxed.

The integration of 'content' into 'frame' may also result in new content elements, such as palatals, nasal vowels and glottalized sonorants. So what we find in languages at any particular point in time is the result not only of long-term phylogenetic evolution of human sound systems, but also of much more short-term historical changes due to the striking of a new balance between articulatory ease and perceptual distinctivity under specific cultural settings for communication.

12 Conclusion

The original emergence of 'frame' and 'content', separating two time constants in articulatory units, was the principal step in the evolution of human language. But the boundary between the two categories can become blurred in listener-tolerated reduction of articulatory effort. This may in turn lead to the emergence of new 'content' elements, and the cyclic change from 'content' to 'frame' to 'content' may continually repeat itself in historical time, under changes in the complementary control of articulatory effort and perceptual contrast.

This means that consonant and vowel system surveys, like Maddieson (1984), of the world's languages can only be a rough guide for questions of human language evolution and of language universals, because the data represent different historical stages in the 'content' –'frame' cycles, which are bound to cover up general evolutionary trends of human language, if taken at face value, clicks and glottalized consonants being cases in point.

For example, if German were an unwritten language a field-worker, coming across the word pair 'können' [kœnn] and 'könnten' [kœn̰n] (Kohler 1994a, 1995), would conclude that German has a consonant opposition between clear and creaky-voice nasals, which comes under the subsidiary, more elaborated features of human sound systems and is relegated to a more peripheral occurrence. But what we are really dealing with here is the most elementary cutting off of the pulmonic airstream by glottal closure, which may in turn be weakened to irregular pulsing, i.e. creaky voice, thus creating a secondary contrast between two types of phonation. What is important from the evolutionary point of view is the basic glottal action, not the 'elaborated' sound contrast.

Considering the procedure adopted for collecting the UPSID data base, examples like this one from German may be expected to be quite numerous, and therefore valid divisions into evolutionary Basic, Elaborated and Complex sets cannot be made on the strength of this corpus. Moreover, the data focus entirely on the paradigmatic aspect of sound systems, ignoring the syntagmatic domain completely, thus missing the essential distinction between 'frame' and 'content'. Finally, the approach is exclusively linear, segmental and phonemic and thus also excludes componential aspects of sound systems, which are associated with the 'frame'.

So future research into language evolution, universals and typology will have to put greater emphasis on syntagmatic aspects of speech production. In particular, paradigmatic systems need supplementing by sound patterns of connected, especially spontaneous, speech. This expanded range of phenomena also needs more adequate phonological tools that will give equal importance to componential elements beside segmental ones in a 'complementary phonology' (Kohler 1994b).

References

Classe, A. (1957). Phonetics of the silbo Gomero. *Archivum Linguisticum*, 9, 44–61.

Kohler, K. J. (1991). Prosody in speech synthesis: the interplay between basic research and TTS application. *Journal of Phonetics*, 19, 121–138.

(1994a). Glottal stops and glottalization in German. Data and theory of connected speech processes. *Phonetica*, 51, 38–51.

(1994b). Complementary phonology: a theoretical frame for labelling an acoustic data base of dialogues. In Kitawaki, N. (ed.) *Proceedings of the International Conference on Spoken Language Processing 94*, vol. I. Yokohama: The Acoustical Society of Japan, pp. 427–430.

(1995). The realization of plosives in nasal/lateral environments in spontaneous speech in German. In Elenius, K. & Branderud, P. (eds.) *Proceedings of the 13th International Congress of Phonetic Sciences Stockholm*, vol. II. Stockholm: Stockholm University, pp. 210–213.

Liljencrants, J. & Lindblom, B. (1972). Numeric simulation of vowel quality systems: the role of perceptual contrast. *Language*, 48, 839–862.

Lindblom, B. (1975). Experiments in sound structure. Paper read at the 8th International Congress of Phonetic Sciences in Leeds. (Ms.)

(1984). Can the models of evolutionary biology be applied to phonetic problems? In Van den Broecke, M. P. R. & Cohen, A. (eds.) *Proceedings of the 10th International Congress of Phonetic Sciences Utrecht*. Dordrecht: Foris, pp. 67–81.

(1986). Phonetic universals in vowel systems. In Ohala, J. J. & Jaeger, J. J. (eds.) *Experimental Phonology*. Orlando, FL: Academic Press, pp. 13–44.

(1990a). Explaining phonetic variation: a sketch of the H and H theory. In Hardcastle, W. J. & Marchal, A. (eds.) *Speech Production and Speech Modelling*. Dordrecht: Kluwer, pp. 403–439.

(1990b). On the notion of 'possible speech sound'. *Journal of Phonetics*, 18, 135–152.

& Maddieson, I. (1988). Phonetic universals in consonant systems. In Hyman, L. M. & Li, C. N. (eds.) *Language, Speech and Mind*. London and New York: Routledge, pp. 62–78.

MacNeilage, P. F. & Davis, B. L. (1990). Acquisition of speech production: the achievement of segmental independence. In Hardcastle, W. J. & Marchal, A. (eds.) *Speech Production and Speech Modelling*. Dordrecht: Kluwer, pp. 55–68.

Maddieson, I. (1984). *Patterns of Sounds*. Cambridge: Cambridge University Press.

Miller, G. A. & Nicely, F. E. (1955). An analysis of perceptual confusions among some English consonants. *Journal of the Acoustical Society of America*, 27, 338–352.

Newman, F. R. (1980). *Mouthsounds*. New York: Workman Publishing.

Ohala, J. (1983). Cross-language use of pitch: an ethological view. *Phonetica*, 40, 1–18.

(1984). An ethological perspective on common cross-language utilization of F0 of voice. *Phonetica*, 41, 1–16.

Pätzold, M. & Simpson, A. P. (1995). An acoustic analysis of hesitation particles in German. In Elenius, K. & Branderud, P. (eds.) *Proceedings of the 13th International Congress of Phonetic Sciences Stockholm*, vol. III. Stockholm: Stockholm University, pp. 512–515.

Pike, K. L. (1943). *Phonetics*. Ann Arbor: University of Michigan Press.

17 Synonymy avoidance, phonology and the origin of syntax

ANDREW CARSTAIRS-MCCARTHY

1 Background: the oddness of human language as a clue to its evolution

I will argue that certain characteristics of human language which at first sight may seem natural are in fact quite odd. But recognizing what is odd about language renders attractive a novel scenario for its origin. This scenario ties together certain characteristics of grammar, vocabulary and human anatomy which otherwise appear unrelated. At this stage, all I want to suggest is that my scenario has enough *prima facie* appeal to justify serious investigation. I have no space to discuss here its relationship to other factors contributing to language evolution or the issues it raises about logic and the philosophy of language; but that does not mean I regard these as unimportant.

Human beings are at a disadvantage in thinking about how languages originated, simply because, being ourselves all native speakers of a human language, we cannot easily look at them from the outside. Our familiarity with language as it is may tempt us to dismiss alternative patterns of semantic or syntactic organization as self-evidently non-viable, rather than investigate seriously the questions which they provoke about why language has evolved in one direction rather than others. Connected with this prejudice is a temptation to see modern human language as something waiting to be 'discovered' at a certain stage in human evolution, rather like the source of the Nile, with all its fundamental characteristics somehow fixed in advance. If pressed, probably few of us would explicitly uphold such a view. But it is still possible to be unconsciously misled by it into thinking that the way language is is the only way it could conceivably be. I ask readers to bear this in mind when evaluating my suggestions about why syntax has gone down one particular path rather than other conceivable ones.

2 Two linguistic oddities

2.1 *A perverse consequence of synonymy-avoidance*

An aspect of many human languages which frustrates learners and puzzles linguists is inflectional complexity. Anyone who learns German is faced with remembering which of four plural endings (*-e*, *-er*, *-en*, *-s*) belongs with each noun. For example, *Tag* 'day', *Wald* 'forest', *Held* 'hero' and *Park* 'park' form the plurals *Tage*, *Wälder*, *Helden* and *Parks*, respectively. The choice is partly predictable on the basis of gender or the phonological shape of the stem, but there is a large residue of arbitrariness. Thus, the nouns which I have just listed are all masculine, and their plural endings just have to be learned. German nouns are traditionally divided into 'inflection classes' on the basis of the affixes they choose to express the eight 'cells' in the German nominal 'paradigm' – that is, the eight inflectionally relevant combinations of number (singular and plural) and case (nominative, accusative, genitive and dative).

By no means all languages exhibit this sort of complexity. Nevertheless, it is widespread throughout the world, and can be stable over time. One might expect that linguistic complexity which serves no obvious communicative purpose – which does not correlate with anything in the extralinguistic world – would be vulnerable to rapid erosion. Yet languages whose history contains no pidgin or creole phase may retain arbitrary inflection class differences for millennia, even while seemingly more 'useful' aspects of grammar (such as the marking of case in nouns, or person and number in verbs) disappear. Why?

One recent suggestion relates inflection classes to a well-documented characteristic of how vocabulary is acquired in childhood. Encountering a new word, children assume that it means something different from all the words they already know. This assumption, or pragmatic principle of vocabulary acquisition, has been called the Principle of Contrast (E. Clark 1993). (Related to this principle is the stronger Mutual Exclusivity Principle, discussed by Merriman & Bowman (1989).) The Principle of Contrast assists vocabulary acquisition by reducing the hypothesis space of possible meanings for any new word. It is not rigid, for if it were no synonyms would exist; but it does lead us to expect that exact synonyms should be rare and should tend to belong to those areas of vocabulary which are learned in adulthood, after the critical period for rapid learning of vocabulary in early childhood. Both these expectations seem well supported by evidence.

Table 17.1 Inflection classes of German masculine nouns

	Class A	*Class B*	*Class C*	*Class D*	*Class E*	*Class F*
Gen sg	-es	-es	-es	-en	-es	-ens
Nom pl	-e	-er	-s	-en	-en	-en
	Tag	Wald	Park	Held	Dorn	Name
	'day'	'forest'	'park'	'hero'	'thorn'	'name'

Table 17.2 Inflection classes of Pseudo-German masculine nouns

	Class A	*Class B*	*Class C*	*Class D*	*Class E*	*Class F*
Gen sg	-en	-es	-ens	-en	-es	-ens
Nom pl	-e	-er	-s	-en	-e	-er

To show how the Principle of Contrast impinges on the phenomenon of inflection classes, I will use some evidence from German. The four plural endings mentioned above are distributed among six inflection classes for masculine nouns, as shown in Table 17.1. This table also shows the endings for the genitive singular, the most inflectionally various of the other case–number cells. A crucial characteristic of this distribution is that all the endings fall into one of two types. Some are peculiar to one inflection class, like *-en* and *-ens* in the genitive singular (peculiar to classes D and F respectively) and *-e*, *-er* and *-s* in the nominative plural (peculiar to classes A, B and C respectively). Let us call these 'class-identifiers'. The other type consists of the sole genitive singular ending and the sole nominative plural ending shared by more than one inflection class, namely *-es* and *-en*. Let us call these 'class-defaults', because they can be thought of as the endings which appear automatically where no appropriate class-identifier is available.

The fact that all these endings are either class-identifiers or class-defaults is not logically necessary. Compare their distribution in German and in an imaginary Pseudo-German, illustrated in Table 17.2. Pseudo-German resembles actual German in its inflectional endings and in having six inflection classes, but it is unlike German in that all the endings except nominative plural *-s* and *-en* fall between stools: they are not class-identifiers (because they are shared by more than one class), but they are not class-defaults either (because in each cell there are at least two endings shared by more than one class). It has been suggested on the basis of a variety of evidence that all languages with inflection class systems resemble actual German rather than Pseudo-German in that all their inflectional affixes are either class-identifiers or class-defaults (Carstairs-McCarthy 1994).

Why should this be, and how is it related to Clark's Principle of Contrast? If young children are assisted in learning vocabulary by the reliability of the assumption that any new word will have a new meaning, it is reasonable to investigate whether the same assumption can be relied on for learning inflectional affixes too. The fact that all inflectional affixes are either class-identifiers or class-defaults seems to confirm this. At first sight, the existence of a range of affixes for one morphosyntactic cell, as for nominative plural in Table 17.1, constitutes violation of the Principle of Contrast. But the fact that each of the nominative plural endings *-e*, *-er* and *-s* is a class-identifier entitles us to say that their 'meanings' are all different: not just 'nominative plural' but 'nominative plural, class A', 'nominative plural, class B' and 'nominative plural, class C'. By contrast, *-en* means simply 'nominative plural'. In the genitive singular, the 'meanings' of the class-identifiers *-en* and *-ens* and the class-default *-es* are distinguished similarly.

I have put the words 'mean' and 'meaning' in scare quotes. Many readers may suspect that if we allow a purely intralinguistic notion such as inflection class to constitute part of the 'meaning' of an affix for the purpose of testing compliance with the Principle of Contrast, then the Principle is rendered vacuous; but no. The intralinguistic inflection-class 'meanings' which we need to invoke differ in a crucial respect from 'meanings' that we would need to invoke if the pattern of affix distribution illustrated in Table 17.2 ever occurred. There the 'meanings' would have to include disjunctions. For example, *-es* would have to 'mean' 'genitive singular, class B *or* E', *-er* would have to 'mean' 'nominative plural, class B *or* F', and so on. But if an affix is always either a class-identifier or a class-default, inflection-class 'meanings' never include disjunctions. Not only is this a striking restriction in itself, but it cries out to be related to the fact that disjunctive concepts, such as the meaning of the baseball term *strike*, are hard to learn (Bruner, Goodnow & Austin 1956).

Any objection to counting inflection class membership as a 'concept' which may count as part of the 'meaning' of an affix must therefore be based on an *a priori* insistence that meanings must be extralinguistic. Such insistence, however, is unwise. As Lass (1990) puts it, linguistic 'junk' can be 'exapted' to perform new functions, even if these functions are purely intralinguistic, with no correlate in the 'real world'. When two linguistic forms (words or affixes) undergo historical changes which risk rendering them synonymous, one way of reconciling the situation with the Principle of Contrast is to create a meaning difference to distinguish them, even if this is only an intralinguistic 'meaning' difference, such as restricting one affix to a single inflection class. So the Principle of Contrast operates not only to facilitate vocabulary acquisition but also, perversely, to facilitate the learning of inflection class systems organized in such a way that the 'meanings' concerned are clearcut.

Let us introduce the term 'information content' to subsume both extralinguistic meaning and intralinguistic 'meaning'. The Principle of Contrast thus operates on the basis of differences in information content rather than differences in meaning. Given what language is for, it is not surprising that most differences of information content should be differences of meaning in the traditional, extralinguistic, sense; but the behaviour of inflection classes (along with evidence of the kind cited by Lass) shows that this is not always so.

2.2 *The distinction between sentences and noun phrases*

Languages vary considerably as to what they express syntactically, but no language has been reported as lacking a syntactic distinction between sentences, such as at (1), and noun phrases, such as at (2):

(1) John arrived yesterday.

(2) a John
b John's arrival
c John's arrival yesterday

The reason for this may at first seem obvious. A central feature of human language, one which differentiates it from most, if not all, animal communication systems, is that it enables us to make statements; and the sentence is, you may think, the syntactic device which crucially underlies this feature. By contrast, noun phrases are not typically used to make statements; rather, they identify things, people and events in the world. To put it another way, sentences are used to assert (truly or falsely) whereas noun phrases are used to refer; and these functions are distinct.

Although this distinction is taken for granted in most philosophical writing on language from Aristotle to the present day, I will question the need for syntax to express it. The following thought-experiment illustrates why. Imagine that you are listening to someone (call her the Earthling) explaining human language to a Martian – an intelligent extraterrestrial creature who communicates by some means quite unlike human language. The Earthling might start by explaining that syntactic units called 'noun phrases' are typically used to refer to things in the world, and are typically combined with other units called 'verb phrases' to form 'sentences' which make statements about the things referred to. She might add that statements can be true or false, according to whether they fit the world or not, and that reference too can be either successful or unsuccessful, according to whether the referent exists or not. (A noun phrase with no referent in the twentieth century is *the present King of France*; logical characteristics of sentences containing such noun phrases are discussed by Russell (1905) and Strawson (1950).) The Martian might now reply: 'OK, I get the idea. A noun phrase has one kind of relationship to the world: successful or unsuccessful reference. A noun phrase is combined with a second kind of syntactic unit called a verb phrase to form a third kind of unit called a sentence. A sentence has a second kind of relationship to the world: truth or falsity. Presumably, then, a sentence is combined with some fourth kind of syntactic unit to form a fifth kind of unit, which in turn will have a third kind of relationship to the world, and so on up. In fact, each odd-numbered syntactic unit will have its own kind of relationship to the world, and these relationships can be seen as forming an ordered set such that any odd-numbered syntactic unit n will have relationship $(n+1)/2$ to the real world.' At this point the Earthling interjects: 'No! Nothing so elaborate! We stop at sentences. We can indeed combine sentences in various ways, but combinations of sentences just make more elaborate statements, which are still either true or false.' The Martian now replies: 'I'm confused! Why does your language allow precisely two syntactic units to have their own special kind of relationship to the world? If you don't like overelaboration, why don't you make do with just one? What's so special about the number two?' This is a good question. How is the Earthling to reply?

We may be tempted to see it as inevitable that a communication system which does what human language does should distinguish between mentioning and asserting. But this simply postpones the crucial question, which now becomes: why should humans have evolved a communication system which does what language does? Even if we grant for argument's sake that the mentioning–asserting distinction is important, it does not follow that it must be reflected in syntax. To our hypothetical Martian it will seem just as natural that there should be a distinction in syntactic category between plain assertions on the one hand and higher-order constructs in which sentences figure as arguments, and so on up. The Martian might even argue that this syntactic distinction would serve the useful purpose of signalling the potential presence of 'opaque contexts' (Quine 1960), i.e. contexts where the substitution of one expression for another with the same reference (e.g. *Venus* for *the Morning Star*) can change the truth-value of what is said; for example, *Alex believes that Venus is inhabited* may be true even while *Alex believes that the Morning Star is inhabited* is false, if Alex is ignorant of astronomy. Yet the syntax of actual languages, while permitting sentences to be embedded within larger units, does not assign these larger units to a new syntactic category. Why not?

A short answer to this question is that there are many distinctions which grammar might conceivably express but which it consistently neglects. One distinction familiar to philosophers but neglected by grammar is that between tokens and types. There is no language (so far as I know) whose grammar expresses this distinction consistently. Consider (3) and (4):

(3) John's lecture on existentialism was interrupted by a fire alarm yesterday.

(4) John's lecture on existentialism is popular with audiences of all sorts.

In (3) *John's lecture on existentialism* denotes an event token, located in space and time; in (4) it denotes an event type, not so located. Most people do not find this distinction hard to grasp once it is pointed out to them. Yet it is not expressed in the grammar of English or of any other language, so far as I am aware. A further distinction, intersecting with the type–token distinction, is illustrated in (5) and (6):

(5) John's lecture on existentialism was used by Joan to light the fire yesterday.

(6) John's lecture on existentialism can be found on the philosophy shelves in any good bookshop.

In (5) and (6) *John's lecture on existentialism* denotes a token and a type respectively, just as in (3) and (4), but this time they relate to physical objects, not events. So the phrase has four clearly distinct interpretations which are not reflected in the grammar of English or, perhaps, of any language.

Noticing this should sound a warning for anyone who thinks it self-evident that syntax must encode the distinction between mentioning and asserting. It is easy to imagine a world in which all languages encode consistently the distinction between tokens and types and also that between events and physical objects. To language users in such a world it would probably appear scarcely conceivable, at first, that languages could function without reflecting those distinctions in their grammar. Yet our own world shows that they can. Conversely, languages in that same world might fail to encode the distinction between mentioning and asserting. The fact that languages in our own world have a mechanism for encoding this does not entail that any communication system which does roughly what human languages do must have one also. I will show this by comparing two dialogues, one in ordinary English and the other in a pseudo-English which lacks the syntactic distinction between sentences and noun phrases, and in which all English sentences appear in nominalized form. I will call this pseudo-English 'Nominalized English'.

Here is the first dialogue, in ordinary English:

(7) BILL Hello. I was sorry to hear you had been ill. You're certainly looking a lot better now!

ALICE Yes, I had a nasty bout of bronchitis for three weeks, but I've got over it, fortunately. Just as well, because we've got to get ready for Bridget's wedding next month.

BILL Oh, I didn't even know she was engaged!

ALICE Yes, he's someone she met in Spain last year. It's going to be a very quiet ceremony, because they're desperately saving money to buy a house. If they can't afford one in Fendalton, they're thinking of moving to a cheaper suburb.

Now here is a Nominalized English counterpart:

(8) BILL Greetings. My regret about news of your earlier illness. A definite improvement in your present appearance.

ALICE Yes, my three weeks' endurance of a nasty bout of bronchitis, but my fortunate recovery. Timeliness due to the urgency of preparation for Bridget's wedding next month.

BILL Oh, my surprising ignorance of her engagement!

ALICE Yes, her encounter with him in Spain last year. A very quiet projected ceremony due to their desperate money-saving for house purchase. An entailment by eventual non-affordability in Fendalton of thoughts about relocation to a cheaper suburb.

This dialogue sounds quaint. But once one has got over its strangeness, it is hard to find any reason why we could not communicate through Nominalized English just as effectively as through actual English. The objection which one is at first inclined to make – that it does not distinguish between mentioning and asserting – cannot be regarded as fatal. If Grice's maxims of conversation (1989) are assumed to apply to the interpretation of dialogues in Nominalized English, then there will be no difficulty in practice in distinguishing between what is asserted and what is not. After all, even in actual English a noun phrase on its own may be interpreted as an assertion. If, on hearing me exclaim 'Gosh! A helicopter!', you rush to the window but find no helicopter in sight, you are entitled to be indignant if I insist that I was merely mentioning a helicopter, with no intention of asserting the presence of one. If you are educated in the literature of pragmatics you may well accuse me of behaving in a perversely un-Gricean fashion.

Nominalized English is not categorially uniform throughout because it still distinguishes nominal, prepositional, adjectival and adverbial phrases. A thorough-going 'Uniformitarian' language might have the following characteristics:

(9) a There are simple expressions (or 'calls') and complex ones.
b A complex call is formed by combining an appropriate number of calls (simple or complex) with an operator (one-place, two-place, three-place, . . .).
c All calls have the same syntactic status.

The term 'call' is deliberately intended to recall a term used by students of animal communication for the vocalizations of primates. A fragment of a vocabulary for a hypothetical Uniformitarian consistent with (9) might be as in (10):

(10) Simple calls: snake, you
One-place operators: YESTERDAY, DISAPPEAR, SEEM
Two-place operator: SEE
(Capitals distinguish operators from simple calls.)

Examples of complex calls formed with this vocabulary are in (11), where operators are consistently placed after their arguments:

(11) a you snake SEE YESTERDAY
'You saw a snake yesterday.'
'the snake you saw yesterday'
'your having seen a snake yesterday'
b you snake SEE YESTERDAY DISAPPEAR SEEM
'The snake you saw yesterday seems to have disappeared.'
'the apparent disappearance of the snake you saw yesterday'

The multiple glosses in (11) may at first seem strange. They are intended to indicate the kind of 'ambiguity' which would naturally accompany consistent grammatical uniformitarianism. The reader may be inclined to think that these ambiguities, so unlike any we find in English, would be intolerable. But the reader should also be able by now to anticipate my reply. Would these ambiguities be any more intolerable in practice than those between type and token and between object and event, which are so effectively resolved in nearly all contexts of unselfconscious language use that one does not even notice them? To assume that the ambiguities of (3)–(6) are acceptable while those of (11) are not is to assume that human language as it is, with its own particular preferences about which distinctions to encode and which to ignore, is the only conceivable outcome of linguistic evolution.

Uniformitarian, as outlined here, does not represent a random choice among the infinite range of nonhuman linguistic possibilities. It is intended to represent a possible direction for linguistic evolution which is arguably more likely than the direction actually taken. The work of Cheney & Seyfarth (1990) and other animal ethologists has shown that some of the vocal calls of some primates have a meaning which deserves to be called in part 'referential' rather than just 'motivational' or 'affective'; for example, vervet monkeys have distinct calls for three different kinds of predator: snakes, leopards and eagles. It does not make sense, however, to ask whether the vervets' snake call (for example) is nominal in nature ('A snake!') or sentential, whether declarative ('There's a snake over there!') or imperative ('Get away from the snake!'). These categories are just not appropriate for the vervet call system. But is there a stage in human linguistic evolution when such categories would inevitably become appropriate? The answer indicated by Nominalized English and Uniformitarian is 'no'. One can envisage the possibility that a call system something like the vervets' might increase in elaboration so as to allow complex calls in which operators and arguments (or 'modifiers' and 'heads') are distinguished, but without ever developing a category distinction between sentences and noun phrases. The fact that all human languages encode this distinction syntactically, so far from being a self-evident necessity, is a central puzzle for any account of language evolution.

This conclusion is reinforced if one imagines what questions would arise in debates on language origins if all humans spoke some version of Uniformitarian. Many of the questions which currently puzzle us would puzzle Uniformitarian speakers too: how to interpret fossil and archaeological evidence, how language relates to primate vocalizations, and so on. But it is hard to see why speakers of Uniformitarian would ever see a reason to be puzzled over their languages' failure to encode differences akin to that between sentences and noun phrases. Their reaction to the idea that that distinction somehow 'ought' to be encoded syntactically would be like our immediate reaction to the Martian's suggestion that our languages 'ought' to distinguish syntactically between sentences whose main argument is an 'ordinary' nonsentential noun phrase and 'sentences' whose main argument is a sentence. 'We get along perfectly well without such syntactic complexity', we would tell the Martian – and that is also what the Uniformitarians would tell us.

3 A scenario which may explain the oddities: the impact of vocal tract changes

The evolution of language has involved two kinds of change which distinguish humans from other animals. On the one hand are the technological, social and cultural advances which have accompanied it, whether as causes or effects. On the other hand are the anatomical changes which make human speech possible, especially the descent of the larynx so as to create the characteristically human L-shaped vocal tract. Which of these came first? That question oversimplifies the issue; behavioural and anatomical changes must have taken place in parallel over a long period. Nevertheless the question is worthwhile because of its link to another: in the sound–meaning partnership that constitutes human spoken language, which is the senior partner? This is another oversimple question, but an answer to it is stated or assumed in much thinking and writing about language, namely: meaning. To be sure, language could not exist without some medium of expression, but the existence of deaf sign languages shows that the vocal medium is not the only one available. Quite apart from that, the medium of expression must surely be subordinate to what is expressed (it is generally thought), so that what was really essential for the evolution of human language must have been the cognitive developments which gave humans something to say.

The anatomical drawbacks of the adult human vocal tract may seem to support this view. In adult humans the larynx is relatively lower in the neck than in other mammals, so that the pharynx carries both food to the stomach and air in and out of the lungs. Consequently, adult humans can choke more easily than other mammals, and cannot breathe while swallowing. What compensated for this double disadvantage? To many scholars the answer has seemed obvious: the facilitation of spoken language. But where did the drive for language come from? One answer sometimes given is: increased brain size. But that simply postpones the problem further. Even if we suppose that a bigger brain brought nonlinguistic benefits – greater skill in tool manufacture or in hunting techniques, say – it is not clear why it should have led to the development of a system for communication or mental representation with precisely the characteristics which human language has. In particular, two aspects of human language remain mysterious: its lexical elaboration and the nature of its syntactic structure. I commented on the second mystery in section 2.2; I will now say something about the first.

3.1 *An impetus for lexical elaboration*

We have seen that a perverse consequence of the Principle of Contrast is the maintenance of arbitrary inflection class distinctions. The principle is clearly useful in vocabulary acquisition, but its surprising consequences elsewhere in grammar suggest that it is not just a handy tool which children coincidentally happen upon when learning their first language; rather, it seems likely to be ingrained as part of our innate cognitive endowment. This is supported by observations of chimpanzees in artificial communication experiments: they assume that any one 'meaning' (such as a food reward) will be associated with only one signalling device (such as a plastic token or keyboard character), and show puzzlement when trained in ways which contradict this expectation (Piattelli-Palmarini 1980: 229; Savage-Rumbaugh 1986).

It is easy to see why such a principle might have become ingrained. Provided that a linguistic or quasi-linguistic code does not contain rampant synonymy, individuals whose genetic endowment contains the Principle of Contrast will learn the code faster than other individuals who waste time exploring the possibility that every new 'word' may be synonymous with some familiar 'word'. Conversely, individuals who are closely related and who therefore share much of their genetic endowment will be likely to develop a code in which synonymy is rare or nonexistent, provided that their genetic endowment contains the principle. So, assuming that rapid learning of a linguistic or quasi-linguistic code confers an advantage within a group which shares that code, a Principle-of-Contrast gene (or allele) ought to spread. The only apparent disadvantage of this spread (that it might favour the development of a code with some purely code-internal 'meanings') would be a disadvantage only from the point of view of some tidy-minded outside observer.

Consider now the sort of vocal communication system which our hominid ancestors possessed before the lowering of the larynx and the concomitant changes in the vocal tract. We can be pretty confident that they did communicate vocally, since all apes and most monkeys do. In view of the evidence for the ingrained character of the Principle of Contrast, it also seems likely that our ancestors' vocalizations were governed by the principle, that is, that distinct calls had different meanings.

Now incorporate into this picture a new ingredient: the reconfiguration of the vocal tract so as to produce the full range of modern articulatory possibilities. A nonlinguistic impetus for larynx lowering may well have been upright posture and the consequent reconfiguring of the skull and jaw (Du Brul 1977). Obviously this reconfiguration took time. Our present purpose, though, is to explore its consequences rather than when it happened, as Lieberman (1984) does. An immediate consequence is tension with the Principle of Contrast. If our ancestors had a small, finite vocabulary of distinguishable calls (perhaps 20 or so, like some contemporary apes), they could easily comply with the principle by assigning a distinct meaning to each call. But with a modern human vocal tract one is not limited to 20 calls. Even on a single exhalation of breath from the lungs, the number of distinguishable calls (if we now take 'call' to mean 'phonologically permissible combination of speech sounds') is enormous. In a language with only 60 distinct syllables (which is at the low end of the range of possibilities in actual human languages), the number of distinguishable calls with 6 or fewer syllables is 47, 446, 779, 660. If we assume a bigger syllable inventory or more syllables per exhalation, the number of distinguishable calls increases accordingly. How can a call system of that size be reconciled with observance of the Principle of Contrast? Clearly, memory limitations militate against storing so many calls individually, each with a distinct meaning! So, in the scenario which I am presenting, the changes in the vocal tract interact with the Principle of Contrast to pose a serious dilemma.

One way of resolving the dilemma would be to leave the new articulatory possibilities unexploited. The fact that millions of calls are distinguishable does not entail that they must be distinguished. But the way in which the Principle of Contrast operates in the grammar of contemporary languages suggests that, despite the common view that meaning is the senior partner in the sound–meaning relationship, sound differences can be the driving force in the creation of 'meanings'. This suggests the beginnings of an answer to the mystery of lexical elaboration. Even without any prior cognitive advance, a reconfiguration of the vocal tract combined with the Principle of Contrast may have been enough to set human language on the road toward acquiring vocabularies vastly larger than any primate call system. New calls could be produced; therefore they might as well be made to mean something – necessarily something different from all pre-existing calls. A group of humans with a larger vocabulary would clearly have an advantage, no matter how slight, over a group with a smaller vocabulary, so the impetus provided by the vocal tract changes would be spurred on by selective pressures.

No matter how large the expansion in the vocabulary of calls, however, the astronomical numbers cited earlier make it inevitable that the expansion process would run up against memory limitations before the fund of phonologically distinguishable calls was exhausted. Inevitably, it seems, many of the distinguishable calls would go to waste. But that presupposes that our ancestors had to store in their memory whole calls (that is, whole strings of syllables produced on one exhalation). There was an alternative, however: to store just short calls (perhaps one or two syllables long), and analyse longer calls as composites of these. That way, the resources for call-construction provided by the vocal apparatus could be exploited to a much greater extent than if whole calls had to be memorized individually. But what will these strings of short calls, or call-parts, mean? A call system of that kind needs a syntax to govern how individual call-parts contribute to the interpretation of the whole. This brings us back to the second mystery: the origin of syntax.

3.2 *A model for syntax*

We have already seen that the way that syntax is is not the only way it could have been. It is time now to suggest a reason for the distinction between sentences and noun phrases, whose pervasiveness is so mysterious. My suggestion is that the model adopted for syntax was that which had evolved independently for syllable structure.

The syllable is not a unit which figures in descriptions of nonhuman primate calls. The need for it arose with the reconfiguration of the vocal tract. This affected not only the kinds of sound which humans could

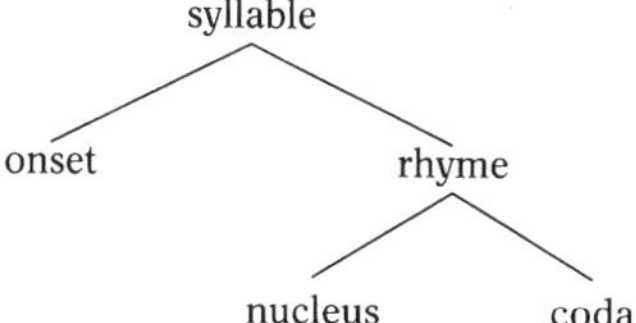

Figure 17.1 Syllable structure.

produce but also the way in which the new, more elaborate, calls were structured. The adult human vocal apparatus facilitates a type of vocalization different from that of other primates, involving successive widenings and narrowings of the vocal tract, with accompanying alternations in the perceived loudness, or sonority, of the sound produced. Peaks of sonority are salient for ordinary speakers in that regular patterns of them constitute the basis for verse and for formulaic uses of language in cultural traditions everywhere. Moreover, relatively less sonorous sounds (consonants) are felt to 'belong with' neighbouring sonority peaks, but in an asymmetrical fashion: a consonant attaches itself for preference to the following sonority peak rather than the preceding one. Phonetic reasons for this asymmetry are not entirely obvious (Laver 1994; J. Clark & Yallop 1995), but may perhaps have to do with ease of neuromuscular control. The asymmetry is reflected in phonology, in that some languages forbid syllable-final consonants but no languages forbid syllable-initial ones (Clements & Keyser 1983). All this has led most phonologists to view the syllable as having an asymmetrical hierarchical structure on the lines of Figure 17.1 (Blevins 1995), with the sonority peak constituting an obligatory nucleus, the less sonorous elements constituting margins (designated 'onset' and 'coda'), and the nucleus and coda forming a 'rhyme' constituent alongside the onset.

We are told by evolutionary biologists that evolution proceeds in an *ad hoc* fashion, making do with what is available rather than designing ideal solutions for the problems which organisms face. Accordingly, I suggest, when faced with the problem of finding a syntax for strings of call-parts (let's call them 'words'), our ancestors (or rather, our ancestors' brains) made do with a pattern of syntax which had evolved for the quite different purpose of organizing strings of speech sounds. The distinction in status between the margins and the syllable was the model for that between the noun phrase and the sentence. The special status of the syllable onset, by contrast with the coda, provided a model for the privileged status which most languages accord to one noun phrase within the sentence, usually called the subject; and the rhyme, with its obligatory nucleus and optional coda, formed a model for the verb phrase, with its obligatory verbal element and optional complements and adjuncts.

The idea that syntactic structure derives from brain mechanisms evolved for speech production has already been put forward by MacNeilage, Studdert-Kennedy & Lindblom (1984) and Lieberman (e.g. 1992). Resemblances between syllable structure and syntactic structure have also been noticed by Levin (1985) and by Kaye, Lowenstamm & Vergnaud (1990). But neither MacNeilage and colleagues nor Lieberman remark on the possible significance of the close parallel between sentence, verb phrase and noun phrase on the one hand and syllable, rhyme and onset on the other; and Levin and Kaye and colleagues, while noticing such parallels, attribute them to aspects of linguistic structure which are neutral between syntax and phonology rather than to a historical carry-over from phonology into syntax.

I am not suggesting that the syntax of human languages conforms universally to the pattern of Figure 17.1. If that were true, we would expect that all languages should have rigid Subject–Verb–Object order, and that sentences should never be embedded as arguments in sentences or as modifiers in noun phrases, any more than syllables can function as margins within larger syllables. I am not even suggesting that any one language must adopt exactly parallel patterns of syntactic and syllabic structure, so that (for example) languages which ban syllable codas would also be rigidly verb-final. Rather, the neural control mechanisms which govern syllable structure, having been co-opted for syntax, evolved independently in that role, but left traces of their origin in certain otherwise mysterious characteristics of human language syntax.

If this scenario is correct, the control of phonological structure within the brain should be located close to that of syntactic structure. If articulatory dysfluency has any correlation with some other kind of speech malfunction, therefore, we would expect it to be with syntactic disturbances rather than with difficulties in word recognition or suchlike; and that seems to be true. Lesions in Broca's area typically cause not only fractured syntax but also dysarthric or slurred articulation, while lesions in other areas do not affect articulatory fluency so generally (Kohn 1993).

4 Questions remaining

There is then *prima facie* evidence that certain apparently independent characteristics of human language may be related historically as consequences of interaction between vocal tract changes and an innate Principle of Contrast. But, even bearing in mind my warning that this scenario is not meant to represent the whole story, questions will arise about two aspects of the scenario in particular. Firstly, how does it fit in with what we know about the timing of vocal tract changes with respect to other developments, such as brain enlargement and cultural innovation? Secondly, some readers may think that my questioning of the need for the distinction between sentences and noun phrases implies an attempt to subvert the philosophical distinction between reference and truth. No such implication follows, however. The truth–reference distinction could be of genuine fundamental importance but one which Uniformitarian languages would just fail to encode, rather as the type–token distinction is not encoded by English. I must admit, however, that, for me, one of the most exciting aspects of this scenario is the hint that certain fundamental aspects of language, not only syntactic but semantic, may be mere byproducts of a change in vocal tract anatomy. This hint alone makes it seem worthwhile to test the scenario's implications further.

Acknowledgments
For discussion of ideas underlying this chapter, I am grateful to David Armstrong, Derek Bickerton, Robert Bull, Jack Copeland, Dan Dennett, Mike Dukes, Jim Hurford, Kate Kearns, Alan Montefiore, Andy Spencer, Stephen Stich, Michael Studdert-Kennedy and members of the Cognitive Science Discussion Group at the University of Canterbury. None of these people should be assumed to agree with anything I say, however. The work was supported by a grant from the Marsden Fund in New Zealand.

References

Blevins, Juliette (1995). The syllable in phonological theory. In Goldsmith, John A. (ed.) *The Handbook of Phonological Theory*. Oxford: Blackwell, pp. 206–244.

Bruner, Jerome S., Goodnow, Jacqueline J. & Austin, George A. (1956). *A Study in Thinking*. New York: Wiley.

Carstairs-McCarthy, Andrew (1994). Inflection classes, gender and the Principle of Contrast. *Language*, 70, 737–788.

Cheney, Dorothy L. & Seyfarth, Robert M. (1990). *How Monkeys See the World: Inside the Mind of Another Species*. Chicago: University of Chicago Press.

Clark, Eve (1993). *The Lexicon in Acquisition*. Cambridge: Cambridge University Press.

Clark, John & Yallop, Colin (1995). *An Introduction to Phonetics and Phonology*. (2nd edition) Oxford: Blackwell.

Clements, George N. & Keyser, Samuel J. (1983). *CV Phonology*. Cambridge, MA: MIT Press.

Du Brul, E. Lloyd (1977). Origins of the speech apparatus and its reconstruction in fossils. *Brain and Language*, 4, 365–381.

Grice, H. P. (1989). *Studies in the Way of Words*. Cambridge, MA: Harvard University Press.

Kaye, Jonathan, Lowenstamm, J. & Vergnaud, Jean-Roger (1990). Constituent structure and government in phonology. *Phonology*, 7, 193–231.

Kohn, Susan E. (1993). Segmental disorders in aphasia. In Blanken, Gerhard, Dittmann, Jürgen, Grimm, Hannelore, Marshall, John C. & Wallesch, Claus W. (eds.) *Linguistic Disorders and Pathologies: An International Handbook*. Berlin: Walter de Gruyter, pp. 197–209.

Lass, Roger (1990). How to do things with junk: exaptation in language evolution. *Journal of Linguistics*, 26, 79–102.

Laver, John (1994). *Principles of Phonetics*. Cambridge: Cambridge University Press.

Levin, Juliette (1985). A metrical theory of syllabicity. Ph.D. dissertation, MIT.

Lieberman, Philip (1984). *The Biology and Evolution of Language*. Cambridge, MA: Harvard University Press.

(1992). On the evolution of human language. In Hawkins, John A. & Gell-Mann, Murray (eds.) *The Evolution of Human Languages*. Santa Fe Institute Studies in the Science of Complexity. Redwood City, CA: Addison-Wesley, pp. 21–47.

MacNeilage, Peter F., Studdert-Kennedy, Michael G. & Lindblom, Björn (1984). Functional precursors to language and its lateralization. *American Journal of Physiology*, 246, R912–R914.

Merriman, William E. & Bowman, Laura L. (1989). The mutual exclusivity bias in children's word learning. *Monographs of the Society for Research in Child Development*, serial no. 220, volume 54, nos. 3–4.

Piattelli-Palmarini, Massimo (ed.) (1980). *Language and Learning: The Debate between Jean Piaget and Noam Chomsky*. London: Routledge & Kegan Paul.

Quine, Willard Van Orman (1960). *Word and Object*. Cambridge, MA: MIT Press.

Russell, Bertrand. (1905). On denoting. *Mind*, 14, 479–493.

Savage-Rumbaugh, E. Sue (1986). *Ape Language: From Conditioned Response to Symbol*. New York: Columbia University Press.

Strawson, Peter. (1950). On referring. *Mind*, 59, 320–344.

Part III The emergence of syntax

18 Introduction: the emergence of syntax

JAMES R. HURFORD

Capacity for language is what makes humans unique, as generations of scholarship have repeatedly stated. Since the 1950s, Linguistics has placed syntax at the heart of the human language capacity. Theoretical syntax has held centre stage more than any other subfield of the subject, and the twin themes of the autonomy of syntax and the centrality of syntax have become virtually axiomatic. Syntactic theorists have emphasized the great complexity and abstractness of syntactic structure and have largely accepted the view that much of this structure had no obvious functional motivation. The rather isolationist stance of syntactic theory has been in tension with the obvious fact that this complex syntactic capacity *did* emerge in the human evolutionary context. Pinker & Bloom's 1990 article in *Behavioral and Brain Sciences* began to break the deadlock and argued for the compatibility of generative syntactic theory and Darwinian evolution. The evolution of the human *syntactic* capacity can be seen as constituting the central challenge for any theory of the evolution of language. The challenge can be distributed, however, by a recognition that not all complex structure need be accounted for by phylogenetic evolution, as the last three chapters in this volume show.

Linguists have left an 'influence vacuum' in the area, having been slow to take up evolutionary concerns; two notable exceptions, linguists who have been closely associated with the dominant paradigm in theoretical syntax, and who take the evolution of language seriously, are Frederick Newmeyer and Robert Berwick. Newmeyer's chapter provides a ready summary of the arguments of those who, like Chomsky, dismiss the possibility of any enlightening account of the evolution of linguistic structure. Newmeyer's own vigorous refutation of these arguments, from the standpoint of one well acquainted with the intricacies of generative syntactic theory, serves a classic bridging function in an interdisciplinary volume. Through his chapter, non-linguists can see that the anti-evolutionary stance is not a necessary concomitant or consequence of the generative approach to language; the door for meaningful communication (and argument) between theoretical syntax and the disciplines more traditionally concerned with evolution is open.

No sooner is the door open than someone walks through it; generative syntactic controversy moves into evolutionary linguistics. Observers of the succession of revolutions and counterrevolutions in generative syntax over the last few decades will have noted with a certain irony the radical new position adopted by Chomsky in his 'Minimalist Program'. The Minimalist Program offers the prospect of language structure being far less complex than previous versions of Chomsky's theories (e.g. Chomsky 1965, 1981) have indicated. This simplification of theory (while it still needs to be reconciled with the massively recalcitrant data provided by languages) is methodologically welcome. But the new simplicity is a two-edged weapon. Both Berwick and Newmeyer discuss the implications of the Minimalist Program for evolutionary accounts of syntax; they emphasize rather different aspects.

If the universal principles of human syntax are basically simple, then there is less for any evolutionary account of human syntactic capacity to explain, and so presumably more hope of success for an evolutionary account of syntax. Berwick's chapter outlines in some detail the basic operations of a version of Minimalist syntax, giving a comparison with previous theories. Although he deals mainly with matters of syntactic theory, Berwick does so with a view to showing how: 'a pre-existing substrate of words (a lexicon) *qua* conceptual relations and categorical perception . . . coupled with the appearance of a *single* combinatorial operation of *hierarchical concatenation*, . . . leads directly to many of the distinguishing human syntactic properties'. Berwick argues that a version of Minimalism provides a way of seeing syntax not as a collection of principles, each of which had to evolve separately, but as arising from a single principle, which he labels 'Merge'.

The new simplicity of Minimalism is a matter of simplicity of representation (by the grammarian, as a describer, or by the native speaker, as a storer, of competence). Newmeyer discusses Chomsky's arguments that the simplicity of the Minimalist Program has enormously dysfunctional implications for performance – the actual online mental processing of sentences in perception and production. This, in turn, would make any adaptationist account of human syntax less plausible, if the Minimalist Program turns out to give correct accounts of our grammatical competence. Berwick is more optimistic about the implications of Minimalism for performance, arguing that it automatically builds structures amenable to the most general, and already well-understood, parsing strategy. It is interesting to see how even in discussions of the evolution of syntax, of which he basically disapproves, Chomsky's models stir up controversy. The specificity and explicitness of the models are enough to support detailed interpretations, but not so explicit as to rule out alternative views. The differences between Newmeyer's and Berwick's interpretations of the promise that the Minimalist Program holds out for evolutionary accounts of syntax will take time to resolve. Newmeyer concentrates on the computational effort required as a result of the economy principles, which would necessarily invoke comparisons with many other possible sentences during the processing of a single sentence. Berwick concentrates, on the other hand, on the 'Merge' operation for building syntactic trees out of lexical entries.

Berwick's chapter, refreshingly for a chapter so clearly stemming from theoretical syntax, and in contrast to the 'isolationist' tendencies of the past, makes clear links to works basing linguistic capacities in non-linguistic capacities (e.g. Worden, Studdert-Kennedy and Bickerton, this volume). There is a suggestive formal similarity between Berwick's 'Merge' operation and the unification appealed to by Worden. Only a few pages of Berwick's chapter say anything explicitly about evolution, but this introduction does set the scene for a debate about one of the crucial debated points in the theory of the evolution of language. How could the emergence of language have been anything but gradual? This is the principal point made by Pinker & Bloom in their seminal article, and this question now begins to get an interestingly uniform kind of answer from three very different styles of theorist (Bickerton, Berwick and Worden) in their contributions to this volume. Berwick's proposal is massively reductionist and will be resisted by many traditional syntacticians whose style of theorizing tends away from such 'big picture', grandly unified theories.

In dialogues between linguists and nonlinguists, there is a tendency for linguists to emphasize the *special* richness of linguistic structure, and to be wary of accounts which would seem to reduce this structure to a case of general cognitive structure or of simple emergence from rich social interactions. Derek Bickerton's contribution to this volume is an interesting combination of emphasis on the richness of syntactic structure with a reductionist strategy. In common with Worden and Berwick,

Bickerton puts the conceptual structure associated with lexical items at the basis of syntax. Syntactic organization is largely projected from information stored in individual lexical items. In Bickerton's evolutionary scenario, there was one crucial neuroanatomical change which made syntax possible, the establishment of a connection between two pre-existing systems. The two pre-existing systems were a system of 'one-word' signs, with a *signifiant* and a *signifié*, but restricted to vocabulary only, and a 'theta-role' system, linking general conceptual analysis of the world with social understanding of the 'who did what to whom' variety. These suggestions are well in tune with other contributions to this volume which have stressed *preadaptation* for language, as well as with Bickerton's own seminal work on creolization and the concept of protolanguage. Bickerton's contribution is strident and challenging; he has not shown the detailed mechanisms by which the set of syntactic structures came to be constrained to just the complex set of cases we actually find in languages.

Simon Kirby's chapter is aptly placed between those of linguists who, like Newmeyer, Berwick and Bickerton, emphasize the phylogenetic evolution of humans as a language-possessing species, and the chapters of roboticists and cognitive scientists, like Luc Steels and John Batali, whose works emphasize the emergence of syntax-like structure, without biological evolution, in communicating groups of agents. Kirby's training is in Artificial Intelligence and Linguistics, and he is in a position to span some of the gap between linguists and cognitive scientists and roboticists. Kirby takes up a theme that preoccupies syntacticians, generativist and non-generativist alike, that of syntactic universals. By detailed analysis of some well-known cases, including computer simulations of agents interacting in a historically developing language community, he shows how the emergence of some complex patterns of syntactic structure can be accounted for in terms of the historical movement of languages in response to pressures of use. Kirby does not dismiss the nativist program. But he does show that there can be non-biological evolution (in a broad sense) of languages (the plural is important). This reminds us of something we should never forget, that languages evolve, and the human language capacity evolved, and that the two kinds of evolutionary process are distinct in their mechanisms, but intertwined in their effects.

Implicit in the arguments of linguists like Newmeyer and Pinker, when they propose an integration of generative linguistics with

Darwinian evolutionary theory, is the assumption that the main story is a phylogenetic one. For this, they take criticism of the sort embodied in Lightfoot's gibe: 'the Subjacency Condition has many virtues, but I am sure that it could not have increased the chances of having fruitful sex' (Lightfoot 1991: 69). Kirby's timely reminder that languages themselves evolve, by non-genetic mechanisms, takes much of the sting out of such criticism.

Because of its pivotal role in any account of the evolution of human language, the evolution of syntax has attracted not only linguists, but others with an interest in the evolution of human communication, for example roboticists, such as Luc Steels, and cognitive scientists, such as John Batali. Cognitive scientists and roboticists tend to have more experience than linguists in the general theory of complex adaptive systems; they may be in a position to see wider generalizations about complex systems that can be profitably used in an account of the evolution of syntax.

Luc Steels' chapter is a concise summary of an alternative explanatory paradigm to the Darwinian phylogenetic one. Steels' research programme is an effort to minimize the amount of domain-specific genetic information one needs to postulate in order to account for the structure of language. In common with Kirby and Batali, he uses computer (even robotic) simulations to demonstrate the coherence of his explanatory mechanisms. This work is largely unknown to the linguistic community and has much to offer. It shows that some aspects of the co-ordinated communication behaviour of individuals interacting in a group can be accounted for simply as emerging from the very fact of interaction. Clearly, this work starts from very different assumptions about language from those of the generativists. This genre of work assumes that language *is essentially* co-ordinated communication behaviour, rather than an individual's tacit knowledge of rules of grammar. Nevertheless, as all contributors would agree, what is needed is theories which account both for the detailed competences acquired by human children and the fact that these competences are co-ordinated and used successfully for communication. Steels' proposals about the emergence of syntax are at this stage still programmatic.

John Batali's chapter reports simulations independent of Steels' work, but showing the same kind of emergence of structure from social interaction as Steels emphasizes. Batali's simulation, the first of its kind, is impressive. In it, a set of agents are equipped initially with a shared set of meaningless gestures and a shared set of unexpressed concepts, and only random, unshared, associations between these gestures and concepts. These agents are made to 'try' to express meanings to each other as best they can, which initially involves randomly gesturing at each other. But they learn from one another, via a general-purpose learning algorithm (a neural net) and begin to behave according to what they have learned. A surprisingly elegant and language-like shared code, pairing sequences of gestures with meanings, emerges. The emerging system is still, from a linguist's point of view, simple, and probably better described as morphology than as syntax, but this is, nevertheless, a striking demonstration of how a language-like subsystem can emerge from nothing, given a population of individuals intent on communicating with, and able to learn from, each other.

In the chapters presented here, then, there is clear progress toward a better understanding of the evolutionary processes involved in the emergence of syntactic structure. Four particularly promising themes, many stretching to chapters in other sections of this volume, can be identified in the section as a whole:

1 plausible appeal to preadaptations for syntactic structure (Bickerton, Berwick).
2 the distinction between phylogenetic evolution of syntax-acquisition capacity in the species (mainly addressed by Newmeyer, Berwick and Bickerton) and the emergence of structure as a consequence of communicative interaction between individuals in a group (Steels, Batali). Kirby emphasizes that the two processes are not mutually exclusive, and may interact.
3 the incremental progression from simple lexical systems (protolanguage) to syntactic structure (Bickerton, Steels), or its generative counterpart, the role of the lexicon in projecting syntactic structure (Berwick, Bickerton).
4 the use of computational simulations as a tool in exploring the working of complex adaptive systems (Kirby, Steels, Batali).

References

Chomsky, N. (1965). *Aspects of the Theory of Syntax*. Cambridge, MA: MIT Press.
(1981). *Lectures on Government and Binding: The Pisa Lectures*. Dordrecht: Foris.
Lightfoot, David (1991). Subjacency and sex. *Language and Communication*, 11 (1–2), 67–69.
Pinker, Steven & Bloom, Paul (1990). Natural language and natural selection. *Behavioral and Brain Sciences*, 13, 707–784.

19 On the supposed 'counterfunctionality' of Universal Grammar: some evolutionary implications

FREDERICK J. NEWMEYER

1 Chomsky and natural selection

I feel strongly that generative grammarians have an obligation to address the question of the evolution of language. A central tenet of the principal approach within generative grammar, that associated with Chomsky and his co-thinkers, is that our biological endowment embodies an innately determined universal grammar (UG) that accounts for the major structural properties of the world's languages and helps to shape the acquisition by children of particular grammars. A persistent criticism of this UG position has centred on the absence of any account of its phylogenesis. What forces, it is often asked, could have led these hypothesized universal properties of language to become incorporated into the human genome? One must concede that the absence of even the rudiments of an answer to this question has conferred a rhetorical advantage on those opposing the idea of an innate UG.

Chomsky has, in general, been extremely reluctant to point to *any* external forces shaping the design of UG, suggesting, in fact, that its properties are actually *dysfunctional*. He suggests that we look instead to 'physical principles' for an explanation of its phylogenesis. The purpose of this paper is to present and criticize Chomsky's position. I hope to demonstrate that he fails to make an adequate case for a nonadaptationist origin for UG. Space limitations prevent me from developing an alternative account of language origins here; the reader is referred to my book now in preparation, *Language Form and Language Function*, for such an account.

One might think that Chomsky, as the leading exponent of the idea that we are endowed with an innate 'language organ', would be at the forefront of the attempt to provide a reasonable account of its evolution in the species. Indeed, one would think that a plausible account of language origins and evolution would be one avenue to take in the long route to *confirming* the idea that our genetic inheritance includes a richly articulated universal grammar.

I doubt, however, that if one added up all of the passages from Chomsky's writings devoted to the topic of language evolution, even ignoring the extensive overlap among their contents, one would come up with as much text as there is in an average-sized chapter of *Syntactic Structures*. One theme unifies all of these passages: nothing is to be gained by searching for any external factors that, in the course of evolution, might have shaped the structural properties of language.[1] He also makes it crystal clear why such a search would likely prove fruitless. Rather than being 'simply a more complex instance of something to be found elsewhere in the animal world, [language] is an example of true "emergence" – the appearance of a qualitatively different phenomenon at a specific stage of complexity of organization' (Chomsky 1972: 70). Furthermore: 'Evolutionary theory appears to have very little to say about speciation, or about any kind of innovation. It can explain how you get a different distribution of qualities that are already present, but does not say much about how new qualities can emerge' (Chomsky 1982: 23). 'It would be an error, then', Chomsky concludes, 'to suppose that all properties, or the interesting properties of the [linguistic] structures that have evolved, can be "explained" in terms of natural selection' (Chomsky 1975: 59).

Chomsky appears to be perfectly willing to regard UG as unique in the natural world, immune, it would seem, from the set of forces that shape other biological systems. For example, in the course of a discussion of attempts to diminish the high degree of redundant overlap among UG principles, he notes that 'it has often proven to be a useful guiding intuition in research that if some property of language is "overdetermined" by proposed principles, then probably the principles are wrong, and some way should be found to reconstruct them so as to avoid this redundancy' (Chomsky 1991a: 49). He goes on to write: 'Typically, biological systems are not like this at all. They are highly redundant, for reasons that have a plausible functional account. Redundancy offers protection against damage, and might facilitate overcoming problems that are computational in nature. Why language should be so different from other biological systems is a problem, possibly even a mystery' (pp. 49–50).

1 In very recent work he seems to have modified this point slightly (see section 3 below).

As we will see in section 3 below, he feels that a solution to the problem (or mystery) might lie in the unique origins of UG – not as a product of natural selection, but rather as a mathematical consequence of physical laws that govern what happens when more and more brain cells get packed together.[2]

To be sure, Chomsky, stating what any thinking person in the world must consider to be a truism, has noted that 'there is an obvious selectional advantage in the ability to discover the language of one's speech community' (Chomsky 1975: 252) and that the capacity for language 'has an obvious selectional value' (Chomsky 1982: 19). And in at least one case, he was willing to speculate (with Lasnik) that *some specific* aspect of the language faculty might have been selected for, remarking that if there is a functional explanation for a particular filter, it might hold 'at the level of evolution of the species' (Chomsky & Lasnik 1977: 437). Nevertheless, he has in general shied away from speculations of this sort, opting instead for a scenario of language evolution that maximizes its differences from other biological systems.

Chomsky attempts to undercut the idea that UG has functional roots by calling attention to the fact that:

> Parsability – that is, the ability of the mind/brain to assign a structural analysis to a sentence – is not a requirement that must be met by a language, contrary to what is often claimed. In this case, in fact, we know that the claim is false: every language permits many different categories of expressions that cannot be used or understood, a fact that in no way impedes communication. [Chomsky 1992: 16]

But the fact that some sentences are unusable has no damaging consequences for the hypothesis that parsing demands helped to shape language as long as 'enough' sentences produced by the grammar *are* usable and as long as the ones that are not usable do not result in communication being significantly impeded. An analogy might be helpful here. The component parts of the digestive tract evolved over the course of evolutionary time to facilitate the ingestion, processing and metabolization of nourishment. Could one imagine an evolutionary biologist putting forward an argument parallel to Chomsky's, such as the following?

2 Johnson & Lappin (1997) report that Chomsky speculated at a public lecture that the reason grammar might appear to be unique among biological systems in displaying optimal design is that current biological theories may have misconstrued biological phenomena and failed to discover the underlying principles which govern them. Johnson and Lappin 'take this [position] to be a *reductio ad absurdum*' (p. 41).

> A role in digestion – that is the ability of the human body to metabolize food – is not a requirement that must be met by the esophagus, contrary to what is often claimed. In this case, in fact, we know that the claim is false: every esophagus permits many objects to pass through it that cannot be digested, a fact that in no way impedes the metabolization of food.

Hence, if UG arose in part from pressure to enable human communication, it no more follows that the principles that govern it should be 'optimal' (in some engineering sense) for this task than that the fact that our lungs evolved for respiration should lead them to be 'perfect' breathing machines. It takes more than a casual observation that some innate structure is not particularly efficient at carrying out some task to disqualify it from contention for having been shaped by natural selection.

There surely are properties of the language faculty that are consequences of extra-adaptive mechanisms. One such property was the focal point of debate between Searle and Chomsky twenty years ago. Searle (1972/1974) made the sensible observation that although 'we don't know how language evolved in human prehistory, . . . it is quite reasonable to suppose that the needs of communication influenced the structure' (p. 16). Chomsky replied:

> Consider, again, the principle of structure-dependence discussed earlier. This seems to be a general property of an interesting class of linguistic rules, innate to the mind. Following what I take to be Searle's suggestion, let us try to account for it in terms of communication . . . But a language could function for communication (or otherwise) just as well with structure-independent rules, so it would seem. [Chomsky 1977: 57–58]

But no one taking an adaptationist view of the origins of the language faculty is *obligated* to demonstrate that structure-dependence was an adaptation. A more plausible account, in fact, is that it is a consequence of design pressure to make *all* information-bearing complex systems structured hierarchies (Abler 1989; Simon 1962). If so, the property of structure-dependence is irrelevant to whether UG as a whole was shaped by selection.[3]

3 See Abler for interesting remarks comparing natural language grammar with chemical compounding and the genetic code. He calls all three 'Humboldt systems' because they make infinite use of finite means. Sampson (1978) regards the fact that structure-dependence is not limited to grammar as an argument against there being any UG at all. But as I pointed out in Newmeyer (1983: 103), the particular characteristics of grammatical structure-dependence are so different from those of structure-dependence in other domains that Sampson's argument loses its force.

Furthermore, it takes more than showing that some proposed principle of UG has a *dysfunctional* consequence to rule out an adaptive explanation for UG as a whole. Consider, for example, Lightfoot's (1995) attempt to demonstrate that the human capacity for language was shaped 'only to a very limited extent and perhaps not at all' (p. 1) by natural selection. His only substantive argument is based on the subpart of the Empty Category Principle (ECP) that demands that traces be lexically governed. He first motivates the innateness of this principle by means of a poverty of the stimulus argument. Since children receive no evidence that (1b), an ECP violation, is impossible, in contrast to grammatical (1a), he concludes that the ECP is innate:

(1) a That Kay left was obvious to all of us.
b *Kay left was obvious to all of us.

But one consequence of the ECP, Lightfoot argues, is to prevent extraction of subjects, even when it is communicatively desirable to be able to do so. Speakers have to resort to cumbersome strategies to convey information that could have been conveyed straightforwardly by violating the ECP. Hence, the ECP is, to a degree, dysfunctional and therefore in Lightfoot's view unlikely to have been shaped by selection.

The main problem with Lightfoot's reasoning is that it is hyper-selectionist: he equates 'functionally useful' with 'likely to have been shaped by natural selection'. But natural selection drives evolutionary change by favouring individuals who, by the luck of the genetic draw, are endowed with a trait that increases their chances of surviving to the age where they can reproduce and pass that trait on to their descendants. Nobody, and surely not Lightfoot, would argue that being forced to delete a complementizer in order to extract a tensed subject might impact one's chances for reproductive success! Hence, whether the ECP slows down the conveying of a proposition by a few milliseconds or not is quite irrelevant to whether this principle was shaped by natural selection.

Darwin himself was adamant in rejecting hyper-selectionism. As he emphasized, organisms are integrated systems, so an evolutionary change that has beneficial consequences in one domain might have detrimental effects in another. Interestingly, one of his examples involved language. He called attention to 'the strange fact that every particle of food and drink which we swallow has to pass over the orifice of the trachea, with some risk of falling into the lungs' (Darwin 1859/1964: 191). His conclusion was that the vocal tract, which had originally evolved for respiration, was co-opted for language, with detrimental effects for the former. Thus the fact that our respiratory system is 'nonoptimal' does not refute natural selection. Rather, its component structures were shaped by selective forces to assume a different – and, to a degree, conflicting – function.

It seems reasonable to speculate that certain features of UG are 'nonoptimal' for precisely the same reason. The needs of communication place conflicting demands both on the anatomical apparatus enabling communication to take place and on the communicators themselves. What is easy for the brain to conceive might be difficult for the vocal tract to execute. What is optimal for the speaker might cause problems for the hearer. Thus it is totally within the realm of possibility that UG is an evolutionary compromise, nonoptimal from the point of view of any subtask that it has to perform, but nevertheless shaped by selection to carry out the ensemble of tasks as well as evolution could 'arrange' for it to do.

Another point to keep in mind is that no trait is an evolutionary adaptation in the abstract, but only with respect to the point in time that it was incorporated into the organism's genome. With the passage of time, what was once highly adaptive could end up being much less so or even maladaptive. Berwick & Weinberg (1984), citing Moore (1981), give an example of such a circumstance based on plant photosynthesis. Wheat would grow 20% more if the oxygen content of the air were 2% instead of 20%. Why the 'inefficiency'? Because the photosynthetic system evolved hundreds of millions of years ago when the oxygen content of the air was around 2%. 'Certain plants have evolved clever ways to sidestep this defect by getting rid of the excess oxygen, but there is apparently no way at this late date to redirect the enzymatic pathways to a completely different system' (p. 267).

Therefore to ask whether the ECP, Subjacency, or whatever increases our survival possibilities today is to ask the wrong question. Rather, we need to ask what their evolutionary antecedents were and, most importantly, to investigate their interaction with other innate principles at the time of their incorporation into the human genome. The fact that we do not have this understanding now and, for all we know, may never have it in full, does not alter the point of principle.

2 The Minimalist Program and language evolution

Chomsky's conception of the structure of UG has changed considerably since the mid 1980s. The leading idea of the Government-Binding model of the 1980s was that the internal structure of the grammar is modular. That is, syntactic complexity results from the interaction of grammatical subsystems, each characterizable in terms of its own set of general principles. The central goal of syntactic theory was thus to identify such systems and characterize the degree to which they may vary (i.e. be 'parameterized') from language to language. Among such principle-governed subsystems were Binding Theory, Bounding Theory, Government Theory and so on.

In the Minimalist Program (MP), however, the computational system consists of a set of unparameterized principles of a 'least-effort' sort that discard all but the most 'economical' derivations involving the same lexical resources (see Chomsky 1995 and, for a general overview, Marantz 1995). Without getting into unnecessary technical detail, a derivation involving a short move might be preferred over one involving a long move, a derivation involving a later application of movement might be preferred over one involving an earlier, and so on. What this means is that a grammar involves what have been called 'transderivational' principles: the derivation of one sentence involves globally scanning other possible derivations from a given set.

Parametric variation in the MP is localized in the lexicon, where entries contain 'morphological' features such as strong vs weak, overt versus covert, on versus off, and so on. Features need to be checked and erased in the course of a derivation; otherwise the derivation 'crashes'. The cross-linguistic variation in feature settings leads to the different surface properties that we find among the world's languages.

Chomsky on several occasions has characterized the least-effort principles as being 'counter-functional':

> Least effort principles such as these induce extreme problems of computational intractability, since they imply that the structural description of an expression must satisfy highly 'global' properties. Therefore if language design really satisfies these conditions, then languages are unusable in a far-reaching sense . . . There are computational tricks that will overcome the problem of intractability. [Chomsky 1991a: 49]

> As discussed elsewhere . . . , these properties of UG, if indeed they are real, are rather surprising in a number of respects. For one thing, they are the kinds of properties that yield computational difficulties, since structural descriptions

> have to meet 'global' conditions. From the point of view of parsing, suppose that we have a process recovering an S-Structure representation *s* from the PF representation *p*.[4] Then to determine the status of *s*, we have to carry out a number of operations. We have to determine whether *s* is derived from a properly formed D-Structure representation *d* licensed by the lexicon, and whether the derivation from *d* through *s* to the LF representation *l* is minimal in the required sense, less costly than any other derivation from *d*. Furthermore, we have to determine whether *l* satisfies the conditions of external licensing, FI, and other properties of LF. In general, these computations may be nontrivial. In these respects, language design appears to be problematic from a parsing-theoretic perspective, though elegant regarded in isolation from considerations of use. [Chomsky 1991b: 447–448][5]

Many have found such comments to be nothing less than astonishing. Chomsky appears to be equating the computations involved in providing the optimal characterization of a grammar with the procedures required for the on-line parsing of sentences. In other words, he appears to be assuming a model of language use that was abandoned by most psycholinguists in the 1970s, namely the Derivational Theory of Complexity (DTC), under which the steps of a grammatical derivation are matched one-for-one in real-time speech production and comprehension (for discussion of the DTC and why it is untenable, see J. A. Fodor, Bever & Garrett 1974). How else might one interpret his taking as the null hypothesis the idea that the steps of a derivation match up with the steps carried out by the parser? It would be unreasonable to conclude that language design is 'problematic from a parsing-theoretic perspective' if parsing operations were not necessarily in lock-step with grammatical operations. Indeed, Chomsky's virtually equating the task of the grammar and that of the processor has led Johnson & Lappin (1997) to remark that 'the global economy metric seems to threaten the distinction between competence and performance in that it incorporates considerations of efficiency of computational implementation into the characterization of grammaticality' (p. 40).

4 Chomsky was soon to propose that the levels of D-Structure and S-Structure can be dispensed with. However, that fact is immaterial to the essential content of the point he is making here (and to my response to it below).

5 A corollary of such a view is the denial that parsing is a rapid process. Chomsky & Lasnik (1993) write: 'It has sometimes been argued that linguistic theory must meet the empirical condition that it account for the ease and rapidity of parsing. But parsing does not, in fact, have these properties' (p. 375). I do not know of any psycholinguists who would agree with Chomsky & Lasnik on this point. Indeed, J. A. Fodor (1983) has called parsing a 'reflex'. For remarks devoted to the speed of parsing, see especially J. D. Fodor (1991).

The only sense that I can make out of Chomsky's position is that he feels that the MP would be seriously compromised if the null hypothesis were not that the speaker–hearer's task is to construct a reference set of legitimate derivations and then to choose from this set the most economical one.[6] Nobody disputes the idea that there is some nonrandom relationship between the grammar and the parser, nor that the discovery that the parser makes use of some central theoretical construct would count as confirmation of the necessity of that construct. Since it is uncontroversial that it is the global economy principles that distinguish the MP from all alternative approaches to grammar, Chomsky seems to feel that they *must* be implicated in parsing if this theory is to have any claim to represent the speaker's internalized model of grammar. And hence the need to appeal to (never elaborated) 'computational tricks', which allow the speaker to short-cut the extraordinary amount of computation that the MP would commit one to perform.

Now then, how does the move from the systems of principles of GB to the economy principles of the MP impact the matters that concern us here? Assuming, following Chomsky, that grammatical principles are directly implemented in parsing, GB and the MP have opposite implications. A plausible case can be made that many principles of GB aid this process, in that their filtering function has the effect of reducing the set of possible candidate structures that the hearer of a sentence has to posit online. For example, Subjacency will lead the hearer to throw out potential antecedents that are 'too far' from their associated gaps, the Binding principles will lead the hearer to throw out potential antecedents that are in the wrong structural configuration, and so on.

But the economy principles, as Chomsky is surely correct in pointing out, have precisely the opposite effect. Far from being local filters, they require, as we have seen, an immense amount of computation just to determine what derivations *might* be possible, followed by a cumbersome procedure of comparison of derivations and rejection of all but the one that is most economical. Furthermore, the set of parameterized morphological features also lacks any plausible functional roots. It is hard to imagine how or why language might have evolved to drive children to 'want' to learn whether a particular feature is checked off before or after Spell Out.

6 This interpretation is based on discussion with Shalom Lappin, though my interpretation and his are not necessarily congruent.

In sum, the principles of GB have a plausible (though, of course, not necessary) origin in communication, insofar as they speed up the identification of structure (and hence meaning). The economy principles of the MP, however, have precisely the opposite effect. Their 'dysfunctionality' (Chomsky 1991a: 50), along with the nonfunctionality of the parameterized morphological features, provides Chomsky with additional wedges to insert against an adaptationist account of the origins and evolution of language.

But those wedges threaten to topple such an account, of course, only if the MP is a well-motivated theory of grammar. If Johnson & Lappin (1997), for example, are correct in maintaining that the global economy conditions can either be replaced by a local restriction on movement or simply be discarded without any loss in empirical coverage for the theory, then it hardly matters whether they are dysfunctional or not. The next few years should clarify whether we need to consider principles of the sort envisaged by the MP to occupy a prominent place in linguistic competence.

3 'Physical principles' and language evolution

Chomsky has not, in fact, been entirely loath to speculate about the origins of language. As early as 1975, he raised the possibility that the evolution of UG might be attributed to a solution to what is, essentially, a 'packing problem':

> We know very little about what happens when 10^{10} neurons are crammed into something the size of a basketball, with further conditions imposed by the specific manner in which this system developed over time. It would be a serious error to suppose that all properties, or the interesting properties of the structures that evolved, can be 'explained' in terms of natural selection. [Chomsky 1975: 59]

More recently:

> Evolutionary theory is informative about many things, but it has little to say, as of now, of questions of [language evolution]. The answers may well not lie so much in the theory of natural selection as in molecular biology, in what kinds of physical systems can develop under the conditions of life on earth and why, ultimately because of physical principles . . . It may be that at some remote period a mutation took place that gave rise to the property of discrete infinity, perhaps for reasons that have to do with the biology of cells, to be explained in terms of the property of physical mechanisms, now unknown. [Chomsky 1988: 167–170]

> Perhaps these [properties of language] are simply emergent physical properties of a brain that reaches a certain level of complexity under the specific conditions of human evolution. [Chomsky 1991a: 50]

Lightfoot (1991) elaborates on Chomsky's remarks by suggesting that key properties of language might have been determined by general constraints on the physical form of complex systems, such as those discussed so eloquently by D'Arcy Thompson (1961). Piattelli-Palmarini (1989) agrees, arguing that UG is a 'spandrel' (Gould & Lewontin 1984), in other words a trait that has arisen as a necessary structural, physical or architectural consequence of some pre-existing trait. Two arches side-by-side yield a spandrel. Analogously, in the opinion of Chomsky, Lightfoot and Piattelli-Palmarini, enough neurons side-by-side in the pre-human brain yielded UG.

I find a Thompsonian/spandrel explanation for the design features of any significant aspect of the language faculty to be utterly implausible. The hexagonal cell aggregates, the equiangular spirals, and so on found repeatedly in nature, and determined by the same laws of physics that suggest the optimal design for a bridge or the arrangement of packing crates, have no counterpart in the language faculty. Indeed, perhaps the most salient (and, at times, frustrating) aspect of UG is its lack of symmetry, the irregularity and idiosyncrasy that it tolerates, the widely different principles of organization of its various subcomponents and consequent wide variety of linking rules relating them.

The idea that UG is a by-product of the physical properties of big brains seems incompatible with what has always been taken to be one of its most characteristic properties – its autonomy. According to the autonomy thesis there exists a self-contained 'grammar module', i.e. a system governed by a set of formal, discrete and interacting principles and rules. That is, underlying linguistic behaviour there is a separate component of our knowledge, the grammar, which is not reducible to other forms of knowledge. But we have a contradiction here. UG cannot be derivative and autonomous at one and the same time. What are the chances of UG emerging as an automatic consequence of *any* set of external principles, but having an internal algebra totally independent of those principles? Absolutely none, I would venture to say. That would be analogous to claiming that the geometrical properties of the spandrels of San Marco Cathedral are independent of the geometrical properties of the arches that yielded them as an inevitable consequence.

The view that UG is simply a consequence of efficient packaging of neurons in a brain reaching a certain size is consistent with – if not entailed by – the idea that the brain is an all-purpose learning device. Not surprisingly, then, Gould, who does have such a view of the brain, heartily endorses Chomsky's position on this matter:

> I can't prove that language was not the selected basis of increasing brain size; but the universals of language are so different from anything else in nature, and so quirky in their structure, that origin as a side consequence of the brain's enhanced capacity, rather than as a simple advance in continuity from ancestral grunts and gestures, seems indicated. (I lay no claim to originality for this argument about language. The reasoning follows directly as an evolutionary reading for Noam Chomsky's theory of universal grammar.) [Gould 1993: 321]

Chomsky, of course, has nothing but contempt for the idea that the mind is a system of general intelligence in which specific cognitive faculties are 'side consequences' (see for example Chomsky 1991a: 50–51). But, unlike Gould, who is at least consistent, Chomsky wants to have it both ways. He wants language, at one and the same time, to be an epiphenomenon and an 'organ', the latter by definition a product of a dedicated genetic blueprint. But it cannot be an 'organ', even in a metaphorical sense, if it is simply an inevitable consequence of a big brain. If it were, we could speak perspicuously about a 'culture organ', a 'planning-for-the-future organ', an 'automobile-driving organ' and an organ for any other attribute that our big brains allow us to manifest.

Furthermore, there are a million steps – and, no doubt, a million years – between possessing the property of discrete infinity (a central, but surely not exclusive, feature of UG, according to Chomsky) and the systems of principles of GB and their possible parameter settings or the economy principles of the MP and the innately given parameterized feature values that interact with them in a derivation. Would Chomsky maintain that we had a continuing series of physically induced mutations that gave us all of that? That is what the logic of his position would commit him to, it would seem. I find it wholly implausible.

In recent work, Chomsky (1995) has come to agree that certain aspects of UG may have been imposed as a result of external pressure. One is the existence of a phonological component; another, that of movement operations that displace elements from the position at which they appear at LF (and thereby violate the strictest minimalist scenario). These may well exist by virtue of the fact that 'the information provided by L[anguage] has to be accommodated to the human sensory and motor apparatus' (p. 221); that is, they involve 'considerations of language use' (p. 317). While I can only agree with this point, it leads to an ambiguity in the interpretation of Chomsky's position that was missing in previous accounts. By opening the door to a functional explanation for the phonological component and for the existence of transformational rules, he pulls the rug out from his oft-repeated implication that UG 'just happened'. These aspects of language are not some marginal features of the periphery – they are central to grammatical architecture.

Chomsky now seems to be holding the line against functionalist (i.e. adaptationist) explanations of UG only with respect to the economy principles themselves, which lead language to the seemingly paradoxical state of being '"beautiful", but in general unusable' (Chomsky 1991a: 49). In other words, Chomsky no longer conceives his unexplicated physical principles to have engendered all of the messy parameterized and often complex principles that were once attributed to UG – only their residue subsumed by the economy principles. This position at least has the virtue of not forcing us to analogize somebody's 27-line-long definition of government or c-command to the hexagonal honeycombs of a beehive. But it still leaves us with the problem of accounting for the origins of the vast amount of grammatical properties that are still arguably provided by an innate UG, yet in no way reflect economy principles. To take just one example, consider the rich inventory of substantive universals of the theory. Among these are the large and still growing number of categorial projections and the seemingly open-ended number of morphological features, each acted upon in a different way by the economy principles. To what would Chomsky attribute their existence? If not physical principles, then what other evolutionary factor might have shaped them? One awaits a discussion of this question by Chomsky and others who, in the past, were willing to regard the design features of UG as spandrels.

4 Conclusion

Noam Chomsky's ideas have, quite properly, set the research agenda for linguistic theory for several decades. Such ideas lead inexorably to the postulation of genetically determined aspects of grammar, which, in turn, naturally invite inquiry as to their phylogenesis. Unfortunately, Chomsky has either disparaged the value of such inquiry or advanced ideas that seem, at one and the same time, generally inadequate and mutually contradictory. I hope to have demonstrated successfully that his published remarks on language evolution can and should be evaluated independently of his theory of language *per se*; advocacy of the latter in no way invites acceptance of the former.

References

Abler, William (1989). On the particulate principle of self-diversifying systems. *Journal of Social and Biological Structures*, 12, 1–13.

Berwick, Robert C. & Weinberg, Amy (1984). *The Grammatical Basis of Linguistic Performance: Language Use and Acquisition*. Cambridge, MA: MIT Press.

Chomsky, Noam (1972). *Language and Mind*. (Enlarged edition) New York: Harcourt Brace Jovanovich.

(1975). *Reflections on Language*. New York: Pantheon.

(1977). Questions of form and interpretation. In Chomsky, N. *Essays on Form and Interpretation*. Amsterdam: North Holland, pp. 25–59. Originally in *Linguistic Analysis*, 1 (1975), 75–109.

(1982). *The Generative Enterprise: A Discussion with Riny Huybregts and Henk van Riemsdijk*. Dordrecht: Foris.

(1988). *Language and Problems of Knowledge: The Managua Lectures*. Current Studies in Linguistics 16. Cambridge, MA: MIT Press.

(1991a). Linguistics and cognitive science: problems and mysteries. In Kasher, Asa (ed.) *The Chomskyan Turn: Generative Linguistics, Philosophy, Mathematics, and Psychology*. Oxford: Blackwell, pp. 26–55.

(1991b). Some notes on economy of derivation and representation. In Freidin, Robert (ed.) *Principles and Parameters in Comparative Grammar*. Cambridge, MA: MIT Press, pp. 417–454.

(1992). On the nature, use, and acquisition of language. In Pütz, Martin (ed.) *Thirty Years of Linguistic Evolution: Studies in Honor of René Dirven on the Occasion of his Sixtieth Birthday*. Amsterdam: John Benjamins, pp. 3–30.

(1995). *The Minimalist Program*. Cambridge, MA: MIT Press.

& Lasnik, Howard (1977). Filters and control. *Linguistic Inquiry*, 8, 425–504.

& Lasnik, Howard (1993). Principles and parameters theory. In Jacobs, J., Von Stechow, A., Sternefeld, W. & Venneman, T. (eds.) *Syntax: An International Handbook of Contemporary Research*. Berlin: Walter de Gruyter.

Darwin, Charles (1859/1964). *On the Origin of Species*. (Facsimile edition) Cambridge, MA: Harvard University Press.

Fodor, Janet D. (1991). Sentence processing and the mental grammar. In Sells, Peter, Shieber, Stuart M. & Wasow, Thomas (eds.) *Foundational Issues in Natural Language Processing*. Cambridge, MA: MIT Press, pp. 83–113.

Fodor, Jerry A. (1983). *The Modularity of Mind*. Cambridge, MA: MIT Press.

Bever, Thomas G. & Garrett, Merrill F. (1974). *The Psychology of Language: An Introduction to Psycholinguistics and Generative Grammar*. New York: McGraw-Hill.

Gould, Stephen Jay (1993). *Eight Little Piggies: Reflections in Natural History*. New York: W. W. Norton.

& Lewontin, R. C. (1984). The spandrels of San Marco and the Panglossian paradigm. In Sober, E. (ed.) *Conceptual Issues in Evolutionary Biology*. Cambridge, MA: Bradford Books.

Johnson, David & Lappin, Shalom (1997). A critique of the minimalist program. *Linguistics and Philosophy*, 20, 273–333.

Lightfoot, David W. (1991). Subjacency and sex. *Language and Communication*, 11, 67–69.

(1995). Empty categories, adaptationism, and the spandrels of San Marco. Unpublished paper, University of Maryland.

Marantz, Alec (1995). The minimalist program. In Webelhuth, Gert (ed.) *Government Binding Theory and the Minimalist Program: Principles and Parameters in Syntactic Theory*. Oxford: Blackwell, pp. 349–381.

Moore, P. (1981). The varied ways plants tap the sun. *New Scientist* (12 February), 394–397.

Newmeyer, Frederick J. (1983). *Grammatical Theory: Its Limits and its Possibilities*. Chicago: University of Chicago Press.

Piattelli-Palmarini, Massimo (1989). Evolution, selection and cognition: from 'learning' to parameter setting in biology and in the study of language. *Cognition*, 31, 1–44.

Sampson, Geoffrey (1978). Linguistic universals as evidence for empiricism. *Journal of Linguistics*, 14, 183–206.

Searle, John (1972/1974). Chomsky's revolution in linguistics. In Harman, Gilbert (ed.) *On Noam Chomsky: Critical Essays*. Garden City, NY: Anchor Books, pp. 2–33. Originally published in *New York Review of Books* (29 June 1972), pp. 16–24.

Simon, Herbert (1962). The architecture of complexity. *Proceedings of the American Philosophical Society*, 106, 467–482.

Thompson, D'Arcy W. (1961). *On Growth and Form*. (Abridged edition edited by J. T. Bonner) Cambridge: Cambridge University Press.

20 Language evolution and the Minimalist Program: the origins of syntax

ROBERT C. BERWICK

1 Introduction: language origins, syntax and discontinuity

Ever since Darwin and long before, the species-specific human language faculty has captured the imagination of evolutionary thinkers. The reason is simple: for evolutionists, novelties or new traits in a single lineage – 'autapomorphies' – have always posed a challenge. For instance, we can much more easily explain why *Homo* has hair by standard comparative reasoning: (a) all primates have hair; (b) hair is a shared character, derived from early mammals; (c) by comparison with functional analogies in other lineages (such as feathers), early mammals had hair because it served for warmth – that was the functional property that was selected for. The key point is that we can bring selection into the picture only because it gains explanatory power via comparison – similar circumstances result in similar (functional) responses. But when a unique trait appears in a single evolutionary line, comparison becomes impossible. If we have only one example, then we lose the ability to sort out what features are historical contingencies, what features are developmental or intrinsic constraints, and what features were truly selected for.

Without a comparative crutch, one is logically driven to invent one: in order to resolve the obvious discontinuity between humans and other hominoids, one must therefore first adduce some trait similarity between the two – to assert that something that primates do 'is like', perhaps 'just like', what humans do, be it language, communication, gossip, or whatever. The result is a proliferation of stories (Landau 1991) in all possible permutations: terrestrialism, bipedalism, encephalization/language, civilization; or bipedalism, terrestrialism, civilization, language; or language, bipedalism, terrestrialism, then civilization, and so forth.

Even Darwin tried. In his remarkable follow-up to *Origin of Species*, the two-volume *Descent of Man and Selection in Relation to Sex* (1871), Darwin wrote that

> the large size of the brain in man, in comparison with that of the lower animals, relatively to the size of their bodies, may be attributed in chief part . . . to the early use of some simple form of language, – that wonderful engine which affixes signs to all sorts of objects and qualities, and excites trains of thought which would never arise from the mere impression of the senses [for then] the continued use of language will have reacted on the brain, and produced an inherited effect; and this again will have reacted on the improvement of language. [pp. 390–391]

It is the very model of a modern evolutionary story – a coevolutionary 'arms race' forged language, driven by sexual selection. (A few pages later, Darwin rhapsodizes with some eloquence over the possibility that our male ancestors' singing played the role of the peacock's tail, leading to female selection for mates, and true language.)

Has anyone been able to best Darwin's selectionist account? Not really. In some cases, the terminology has been updated: one can argue that all the special properties of language have been specifically selected for as directly adaptive, with gradual changes leading from non-language-using ancestors to speaking/gesturing hominoids, a 'pan-selectionist' evolutionary stance in the R. A. Fisher (1930) reductionist, marginalist tradition, where the smallest atomic traits are gradually and individually selected for. Such a view is apparently advocated by some modern authors like Szathmáry (1996) or Pinker & Bloom (1990). In other cases, the locus of sexual selection has shifted: so we find Dunbar (1996) arguing that grooming in conjunction with larger group size forced the coevolutionary need for a communicative replacement.

A third scenario calls for pre-adaptation – actually 'exaptation' in the sense of Gould & Vrba (1982) – that human language has hitchhiked on the back of a related, already-adaptively advantageous cognitive subsystem, such as motor-gesture articulation, or possibly, as in some proposals, hierarchical tool-making. Bootstrapping also embraces so-called 'Big-Bang' alternatives like Bickerton's bioprogram hypothesis, a protolanguage-to-human-syntax jump (1990, 1995, this volume; Aitchison, this volume). Whatever the evolutionary scenario, one must strike a balance between language's singularity and evolutionary continuity: how can one account for the striking specificity of human syntactic constraints and at the same time retain a Darwinian-style explanation for language's emergence?

In this chapter I show how to resolve this discontinuity paradox in a new way – appealing to the recent linguistic syntactic theory dubbed the 'Minimalist Program' (Chomsky 1995). As a direct extension to Studdert-Kennedy's chapter in this volume, I demonstrate that, once the fundamental property of *generativity* has emerged, then Minimalism forces much of the rest of human syntax to follow. All we need in addition is what Bickerton (1990, 1995) has argued for: a pre-existing substrate of words (a lexicon) *qua* conceptual relations and categorical perception. Coupled with the appearance of a *single* combinatorial operation of *hierarchical concatenation*, this leads directly to many of the distinguishing human syntactic properties:

Digital infinity or recursive generative capacity – language 'makes infinite use of finite means', in the familiar sense that sentences can be arbitrarily long, recursive and novel;

Displacement – phrases may be dislocated from their natural argument positions, as in *this student, I want to solve the problem* where the subject of the verb *solve*, namely *the student*, appears at the front of the sentence instead of in its normal position before the verb;[1]

Structure dependence – grammatical operations like question formation manipulate phrase structure rather than counting words – 'move the first auxiliary verb (like *will*) after the subject noun phrase to the front' is a possible grammatical rule for question formation, but not 'move the first auxiliary verb to the front';

Core grammatical relations like subject-of and object-of (and including the less well-known but just as important grammatical relation known as *c-command*);

Locality constraints that prevent displacement from acting over unbounded domains – one can say, *What did the guy drink* or *How do you know what the guy drank?*, but not, *What did you know how the guy drank?*, where *what* as the object of *drank* has been displaced 'too far'.[2]

Put another way, while it is surely true that natural language, like the vertebrate eye, is in some sense an 'organ of extreme complexity and perfection', in Darwin's terms, we shall argue that one does not need to advance incremental, adaptationist arguments with intermediate steps to explain much of natural language's specific syntactic design.

1 Note that displacement is one property that does not seem to occur in some proposed 'parasitic' bootstrapping scenarios, such as tool-making.

2 I highlight constraints like these because Maynard Smith & Szathmáry (1995) have recently discussed a similar example in the context of 'simplicity' and natural selection. I demonstrate that similar constraints are *derivable* from the generative properties of language.

For syntax, what is this design? Natural languages apparently deploy only a handful of syntactic relations and predicates out of the potentially infinite variety of logically possible relations: for example, human languages often invoke syntactic relations that link verbs and objects, or inflection/tense/verb and the subject, as with agreement in English or the selection of particular verbs – the familiar *John admires honesty* but not *Honesty admires John*. But there is no relational analog to 'object-of', say 'subobj', that relates subject and object bidirectionally.[3] If our account is on the right track, the explanation for why human syntax looks this way rather than some other way – why languages have 'object-of' but not 'subobj-of' – is not for an adaptationist story to tell, but rather follows from the more basic principles of syntactic combination itself.

As to the origins of the fundamental hierarchical combinatory ability itself – the origins of generativity – this may have arisen via any number of plausible routes, perhaps along the lines suggested by Studdert-Kennedy (this volume), or via Bickerton's bioprogram model (this volume), or possibly by motor-gesticulatory bootstrapping (Aitchison, this volume). Our proposal is consistent with any of these scenarios. However, one scenario that seems to fit less well is the trait-by-trait evolution of human language – picking up a particular locality constraint at one step, for example, and the relation of subject to verb at another. As we discuss below, the origin of evolutionary novelties, especially autapomorphies, more generally seems to take a route other than selectional gradualism (Raff 1996): expanded developmental alternatives are opened up perhaps by gene (even whole genome) duplication and a period of neutral drift, followed by co-option, and this is seemingly the rule rather than the exception. Of course, each case must be taken on its own biological merits, as I suggest in the conclusion. Further, on the view presented here, one need not appeal to notions of 'communicative efficiency' to account for its *initial* emergence, though such factors may perfectly well have been operative, for all that we know.[4] Rather, along

3 There is of course a familiar link between subject and object if the object is a pronoun like *her* or a reflexive pronoun like *herself* – in the first case the object may or may not refer to the subject, while in the second case the object *must* refer to the subject. As we shall see, this kind of directional, 'linking' relation is possible.

4 I note that it is more difficult than usually supposed to give a purely 'functional' account for some of the properties of natural language syntax. For instance, it is sometimes suggested that recursive generative capacity is somehow *necessary* for communication, thus bridging the gap between protolanguage and recursive human syntax. However, this argument is more difficult to make than one might think, because of examples of existing human languages that evidently possess the ability to form recursive sentences but that

with the evolutionary theorist G. C. Williams (1992: 77), I speculate that the hierarchical combinatorial ability appeared as other evolutionary novelties do: 'new structures arise in evolution in one of two ultimate ways, as redundancies or *spandrels*' [a structure arising as an incidental consequence of some evolutionary change].

In sum, if our overall approach is correct then we can then answer, turning Linnaeus' famous dictum on its head: *syntax facit saltum*, 'syntax makes jumps', because language's syntactic structure, its 'outer form' or phenotype, follows from rich interactions amongst components of its 'inner form', its genotype, rather than via the gradual accumulation of surface traits or rules.

2 The Minimalist Program

To begin, I outline the bare essentials of the Minimalist Program, putting to one side many important details not germane to the argument. The essence of Chomsky's Minimalism is to eliminate syntactic entities and principles not absolutely necessary for linguistic explanation. Syntax mediates form and meaning in a classical Saussurean sense, constrained only by so-called 'bare output conditions' – empirical legibility conditions at the articulatory–perceptual and conceptual–intentional interfaces, with the first interface, *phonological/phonetic form* or *PF*, interacting with the systems of parsing and sentence production (essentially articulatory, perhaps entirely in the motor domain in the case of signed languages), and the second interface, *logical form* or *LF*, interacting with other cognitive systems of intentionality, interpretation and inference. The bare output conditions thus act as 'impedance matching' readability constraints, dictating that what is passed to PF

apparently do not make use of such power: a well-known example is the Australian language Warlpiri, where a sentence that would be recursively structured in many other languages, such as *I think that John is a fool* is formed via linear concatenation, *I ponder it. John is a fool*, or to take a cited example, *Yi-rna wita yirripura jaru jukurrpa-warnu wiinyiinypa*, lit., 'little tell-present-tense story dreaming hawk', translated as 'I want to tell a little dreaming story about a hawk' (Swartz 1988; Nash 1986). Evidently then, recursion is not 'essential to express the beliefs about the intentional states of others', contrary to what Pinker & Bloom (1990) and others have claimed. Note that the Warlpiri do *possess* the ability to construct recursive sentence forms. Apparently the same was true of Old English, if the data and linguistic arguments presented in O'Neil (1977) are correct.

must be 'pronounceable', or perhaps in a certain sense parsable (one cannot pronounce both a high and a low vowel at the same time), and what is passed to LF must be interpretable (one cannot have the same object being both the agent and the affected object of an action).

To build syntactic objects and relations, Minimalism invokes only the notion of a 'word' as a list of features plus a generalized hierarchical concatenation operator, called 'Merge'. Let us consider a concrete example that we will follow through the remainder of this chapter. The following two figures illustrate this, with Figure 20.1 providing a conceptual overview and Figure 20.2 the details. Figure 20.1 shows how Merge works: we start from an initial (unordered) word multiset {the, guy, drank, the, wine}. Following a chemical analogy, words have formal (F), phonological/sound (P) and semantic (S) features, which we depict as F, P and S features in an initial word soup; the formal syntactic features have both + and – tags. The core idea of sentence derivation in Minimalism is that Merge combines words into larger, hierarchical superwords as shown, in the process 'cancelling' +F and –F features. Each Merge operation either combines two words into a new 'superword', with one of the two being selected as the 'functor' or 'head' of the new structure, as shown via the combination of two grey lines into a triangle, or else Merge combines a word or superword with another superword. (Note that Merge operates only on *adjacent* items, by analogy with the notion of string concatenation. Also note that every hierarchical 'superword' must ultimately be grounded on some particular word, its *word base*.) After all possible Merges, any features that remain are copied or *projected* to the top of the new hierarchical structure. Then the process repeats itself until no more features can be cancelled. In our example, this is what happens after a sequence of four Merges: we derive a (sound, meaning) pair, in which all *F* features are gone, and only sound and meaning features remain – a syntactic object traditionally represented as a phrase structure tree, as shown.

Merge thus builds new hierarchical structure from old – in this example, the sentence *The guy drank the wine.*[5] In short, Merge is the very heart of generative combination in Studdert-Kennedy's sense – the hierarchical analog of linear concatenation.

5 For now we put to one side precisely why we have chosen this particular merger sequence out of 5! possibilities. In fact, other derivation orders are possible: we could have Merged first *the* and *guy*, for example.

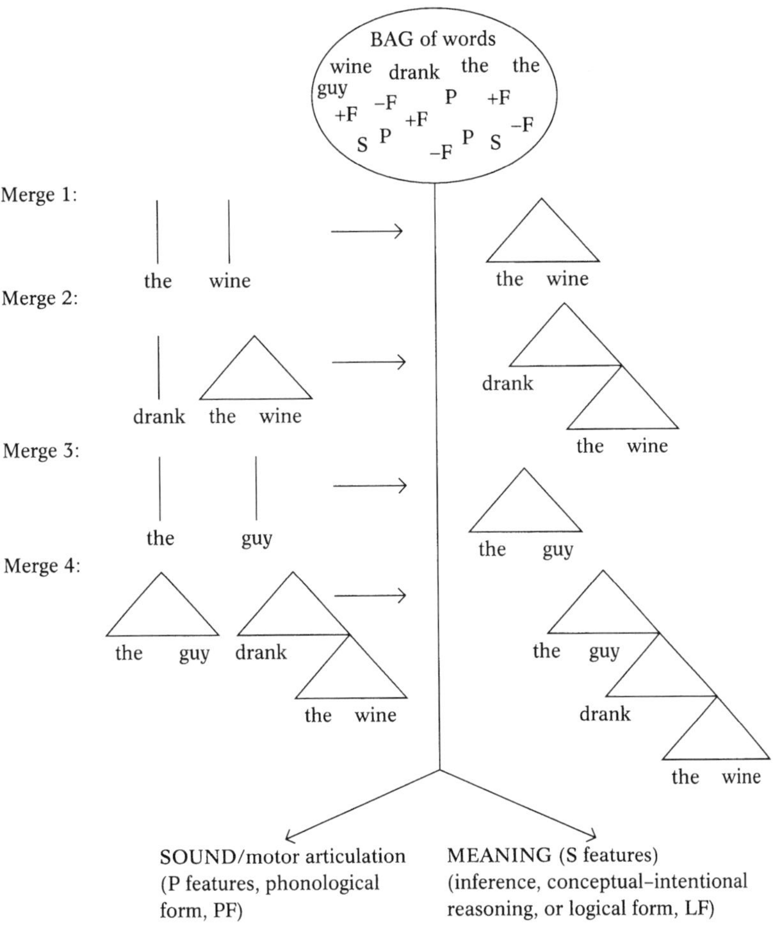

Figure 20.1 The basic derivational operator in the minimalist framework, Merge. This figure sketches how a sequence of Merge operations derivationally generates a sentence, starting with an unordered set of words. Each Merge combines either two words, indicated by grey straight lines, into a hierarchical superword, indicated by a triangle, or else combines two words/hierarchical superwords into a new hierarchical combination.

The elements entering into a Merge operation are precisely those that can be syntactically related to each other. Merge thus defines the 'atoms' visible for combination, as shown on either side of the grey derivational arrow in Figure 20.1. At the sound–meaning interfaces,

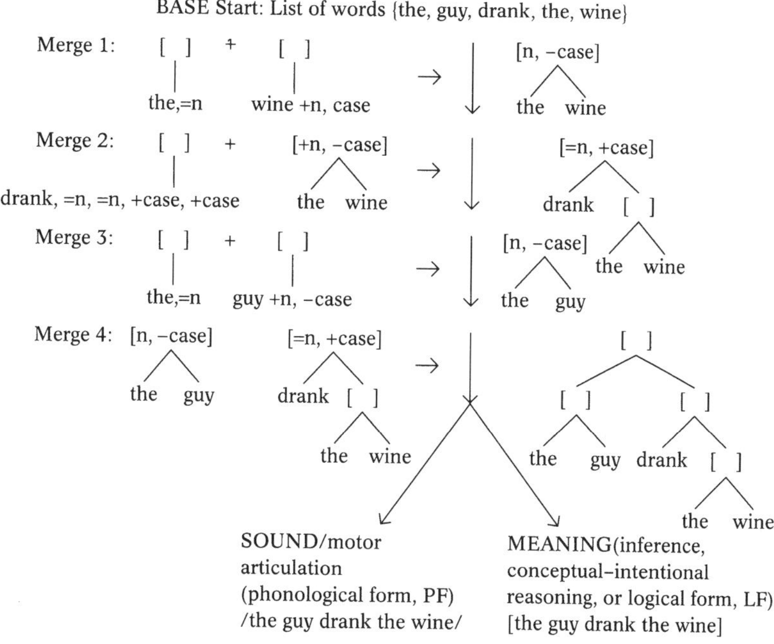

Figure 20.2 The basic derivational operator in the minimalist framework, Merge, maps from an initial word sequence to a sound, meaning pair. A sequence of Merges – a *derivation* – generates sentences from an initial unordered word set. Merge takes two elements, either two words, a word and an already-combined 'superword', or two superwords, and hierarchically concatenates them, in the process eliminating one or more syntactic features, moving toward the sound and meaning interfaces. Merge is feature-driven. For example, in the figure, the 'case' feature +case attached to *drank* is eliminated by combining *drank* with the 'case receiving' element *the wine*, marked with –case. If all goes well, only phonological (sound/articulatory) features are left at the sound or phonological form (PF) interface, and only semantically interpretable features remain at the meaning or logical form (LF) interface. Some word features are omitted for clarity.

the only available entities are syntactic objects and the syntactic structure(s) these objects form. These entities contain inherent word features that impose constraints on articulatory generation or parsing and conceptual–intentional interpretation.

Figure 20.2 provides more detail: Merge takes as input any two **adjacent** syntactic objects, here *drink* and *the wine*, **selects** one of them as a 'functor' (importantly, without regard for left or right order) – in this case, *drink* – and **projects** that functor to be the head of a new hierarchical structure, a kind of 'superword' as shown in the figure. The other element, *the wine*, acts as an argument to the 'functor' *drink*. The functor *drink* has certain formal features to assign or check – it requires an object with the 'semantic' (actually thematic) role of something to be drunk – while the argument *the wine* has certain features to absorb – it can be something that is drunk. Merge does not operate otherwise.

In our example, we can picture the 'mutual attraction' that drives Merge as a set of features attached to the word *drink*: =**n,** +**case**, standing for 'checks that there is an adjacent item with the feature of a n[oun], and assigns an (objective) case feature' and a corresponding feature set attached to *the wine*: **n,** –**case** standing for 'has the feature n(oun), and can receive case'. (Case is an abstract feature analog of the familiar Latinate case system whose residue can still be heard in some English words like *she/her*, with *she* being assigned nominative case and *her*, objective case.) We further simplify the picture by adding to *drink* a second set of **case** and **n** features to check, corresponding to the Subject noun phrase. In a more linguistically realistic picture, this would be done in a more complex way via the 'tensed' form of *drink*, *drunk*, but this is not relevant to our main point here.

When Merge takes place, the + and – or = and + features cancel (the latter indicating feature agreement), with any remaining features passed on up to the root of the new hierarchical structure. An entire sentence is generated by first selecting an (unordered) list of words from the dictionary, where words are simply feature bundles, and then applying Merge over and over, building ever larger 'superwords' until no further applications are possible. The result is passed off to be pronounced and semantically interpreted, as shown in Figure 20.2.[6]

Figure 20.3 relates the minimalist picture to a more traditional transformational one (the 'Extended Standard Theory' of the 1970s or 'Government–Binding theory' of the 1980s). It depicts the 'traditional' view of sentence formation in transformational generative grammar. In the traditional view, two additional representational levels help generate sentences: first, D-structure, a canonical way to represent predicate–argument thematic relations and basic sentence forms

6 I will not cover the clear resemblance between this approach and classical categorial grammar; this connection is explored in Berwick & Epstein 1995.

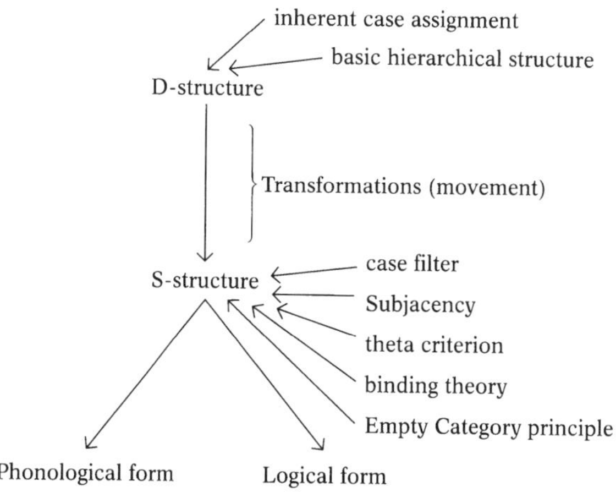

Figure 20.3 A conceptual picture of the 'traditional' (Extended Standard Theory, Government–Binding) transformational generative grammar framework. *Black* arrows indicate restrictions that possible sentence forms must satisfy, like the case filter. I do not describe all the listed constraints in this chapter.

– essentially, 'who did what to whom', as in *The guy ate the ice-cream* where *the guy* is the eater and *ice-cream* is what is eaten; and second, S-structure, essentially a way to represent argument relations *after* 'displacement' – what are called transformations, more broadly 'movement' – has taken place.

Since the late 1960s – since the publication of Chomsky's *Aspects of the Theory of Syntax* (1965) – the general evolution of generative grammar has been to *eliminate* particular transformational rules, unifying them under a central operator like 'Move any phrase' or 'displacement'. There is no longer a *particular* rule of passive formation, but rather the interaction of a single general displacement operator with other, more fundamental grammatical operations, that gives rise to the surface appearance of a passive rule. This is the central insight developed in the so-called 'Government and Binding' grammatical theory of the late 1970s and early 1980s, and, more lately, in the Principles-and-Parameters grammatical framework, as discussed in Chomsky (1981) and many other works.

After the application of 'transformations' (movement), S-structure splits, feeding PF and LF representations to produce (sound, meaning) pairs. Overall then, on the traditional picture, sentences are *derived* by starting with a canonical thematic representation that conforms to the basic tree for a particular language, and then mapping to S-structure via a sequence (possibly empty) of displacement operations. For instance, we might start with *The guy ate the ice-cream* in hierarchical form with thematic structure, as shown in Figure 20.3; via displacements this can get mapped into *the ice-cream, the guy ate* – by moving *ice-cream* up front.

Conceptually then, we can picture sentence generation as starting at D-structure and then 'running a gauntlet' through a set of constraint boxes placed at D-structure and S-structure, as shown in the figure. A sentence is completely well formed if it passes all the constraints and emerges at the other two interfaces of PF and LF with one (or more) pronunciation and interpretation pairing(s).

D-structure constraints dictate possible hierarchical sentence 'tree shapes' for a language and output constraints on S-structure. In English, these state that phrases come in 'function–argument' order: a predicate or verb phrase like *ate the ice-cream* divides into a verb followed by an object, *the ice-cream*; a prepositional phrase such as *with a spoon* consists of a preposition followed by the object of the preposition, and so forth.

Other constraints prescribe legal S-structures. A basic constraint is the so-called *theta criterion*: if one thinks of a verb taking some number of arguments – its thematic roles, such as *drink* requiring something to be drunk – then at the end of play, all of the verb's arguments must have been 'discharged' or realized in the sentence, and every possible argument in the sentence must have received some thematic role. A second constraint is the *case filter*: any noun phrase like *the guy* that one 'hears' – that is pronounced – must be assigned the feature called *Case*. One can show that approximately thirty such constraints suffice to describe much of syntax's core.

In the minimalist picture, D-structure and S-structure are gone. What replaces them? What plays the role of constraints like the theta criterion or the case filter?

To replace D- and S-structure we again begin with a base set – any (unordered) set of words, such as {the, guy, drank, the, wine} and then apply a derivational operator over and over again to yield sentences. But we do not begin with a 'canonical' thematic structure. Rather, we simply select all possible combinations allowed by feature compatibility to drive the construction of all possible predicate–argument structures.

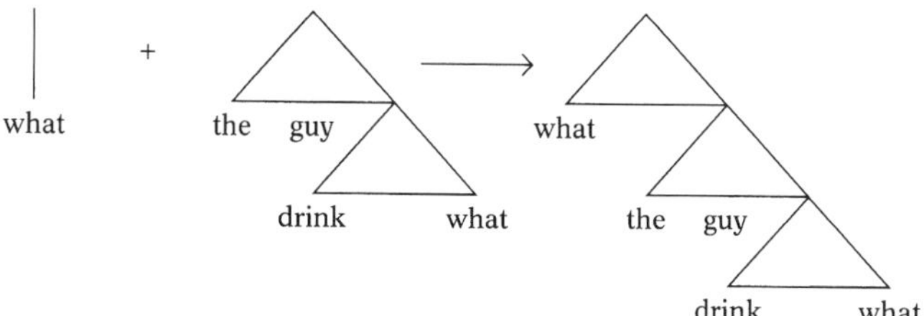

Figure 20.4 Phrase displacement can be considered a subcase of Merge. Here, *wh*-question formation for *What did the guy drink?* is shown as the Merger of two elements, *what* and a (traditionally named) sentence phrase, *the guy drink what.*

Some combinations will not be allowed in the first place – to a first approximation, one cannot directly merge two functors, two verbs; other combinations will be blocked by later constraints; still others may yield alternative, valid derivations, accounting for other derivations as well as syntactic ambiguity – for example, Merge can certainly combine *drank* and *the guy* as the object of *drank*, ultimately yielding the syntactically well-formed but semantically anomalous sentence *the wine drank the guy*. Presumably, the anomaly here is detected by some conceptual–intentional component.

It is easy to see that the feature elimination requirement reproduces the effect of the theta criterion and the case filter: if we do not go far enough in our derivation and leave a feature like **n** unchecked or have a residual noun phrase that does not have case, as in *the guy drank the wine the ice-cream* or *the guy hit*, then the derivation 'crashes'. Further, we cannot merge *any* two objects, unless they are 'chemically compatible' – one must have a feature +f that the other can receive, –f. Finally, to repeat an earlier point, by the end of a derivation, all *formal* features must have been cancelled, so that PF and LF can properly 'read' the result.

With this definition of Merge constraint in place, we now have all the required machinery for minimalist syntax. What about displacement, or phrase movement? Following Kitihara as described in Epstein (1995), displacement is actually a subcase of Merge as we have defined it; Figure 20.4 exhibits a picture where we form the question *What did the guy drink?* by moving *what* from its canonical object position after the verb *drink*. We may define Merge as *Merge* (*X*, *Y*), where *X* and *Y* are either words or superwords (traditional phrases). If *X* is a hierarchical subset of *Y* (approximately a subtree), then this is a case of movement, as illustrated in Figure 20.4: *X=what* is a subtree of *Y=the guy drink what*. As usual, the Merge forms a new hierarchical object, selecting and projecting one of the items – here, *what* – as the root of the new 'tree'. Note that this approach amounts to *copying* the displaced element to its new position, leaving behind a copy of *what*: *what the guy drink what*. A general phonological principle at PF avoids 'pronouncing' the copied *what* a second time, yielding the form that is actually heard.[7]

This formulation also accounts for several of the stipulated properties of movement. Even more surprisingly, the notion of merge-as-derivation suffices to fix *all* and *only* the syntactic relations appearing in natural languages. In other words, we can answer the question: why do some syntactic relations and constraints exist in natural languages and not others? We turn next to these key results.

3 Deriving syntactic relations and constraints

Syntactic relations obtain only among certain syntactic elements, under certain circumstances. Returning to our list at the beginning of this chapter, let us now see what properties are actually forced by the minimalist framework, in particular, Merge.

Recursive generative capacity: this is an inherent property of Merge. Since Merge applies recursively to its own output, infinitely large hierarchical structures can be generated. (Of course, this potential competence does not imply that a particular language will necessarily *use* such recursion, as the Warlpiri example cited earlier demonstrates.)

Structure dependence. Algebraically, Merge works by concatenation of two (structured) objects, either words or superwords. It is therefore a *noncounting* function: its inputs can be any two *adjacent* elements, but by definition it cannot locate the first auxiliary verb *in* a string of elements (unless that element happened to appear at the left edge of a phrase), nor, *a fortiori*, can it locate the third or seventeenth item in a string. Note that given a 'conceptually minimal' concatenative apparatus, this is what we should expect: clearly, Merge would not work on a *single* object (what would it merge with?), so the minimal meaningful arguments to Merge are two syntactic objects, not one or three.

Displacement. Given Merge, the previous section showed that a mechanism to implement displacement exists. Again, whether and how a particular human

7 I omit detailed discussion here of the *tense* feature that forces the appearance of the word *did* in the English sentence, as well as the traditional 'Q-marker' for questions that is prompting the feature-checking Merger in the first place.

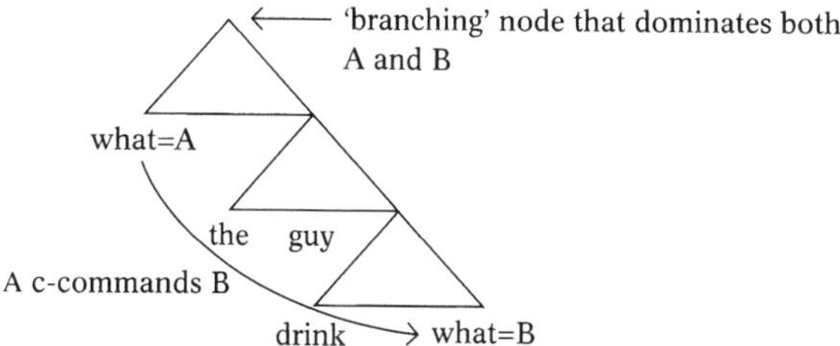

Figure 20.5 C-command is an asymmetrical grammatical relation between two hierarchical nodes in a sentence structure. This example shows that displaced elements always c-command their original locations.

language chooses to use displacement is an option dependent on the properties of particular words (up to the constraints enforced by Merge); for example, English uses displacement to form *wh*-questions, but Japanese does not. If displacement is a subcase of Merge, then the following constraints on displacement follow. These properties are all attested.

(a) Displaced items *c-command* their original locations. C-command is the basic syntactic relation of 'scope' in natural language; for our purposes, c-command may be defined as follows (Reinhart 1983).

 (i) A c-commands B iff
  - the first branching node dominating A dominates B
  - A does not dominate B
  - A does not equal B.

 Figure 20.5 illustrates this. As one can see, in our displaced question sentence the first *what* (=A) c-commands the second *what* (=B), the object of the verb, because the lowest 'branching node' above *what* dominates (lies above) the second *what*. Note that the relation is asymmetric: the second *what* does not c-command the first.

 The c-command relation between displaced elements and their original locations follows from a general property of Merge: given any two inputs to *X*, *Y*, where *X* is the selected and projected element, *X* c-commands *Y* and all the subcomponents of *Y*, because, by the definition of Merge, we form a new hierarchical structure with a new root element dominating both *X* and *Y*. In particular, for displacement, when *X* is a subcomponent of *Y*, *X* will dominate the original location that is a subpart of *Y*. Below, we show how to derive the *form* that c-command takes, from more primitive properties of Merge.

(b) Locality conditions: displacement is not totally free. Returning to our example from the introduction, we now have an answer to what blocks question-formation such as *What do you know how the guy drank?*, while allowing *How do you know what the guy drank?* This too has a direct answer, given Merge. Note that any phrase such as *How the guy drank what* is *locally convergent*

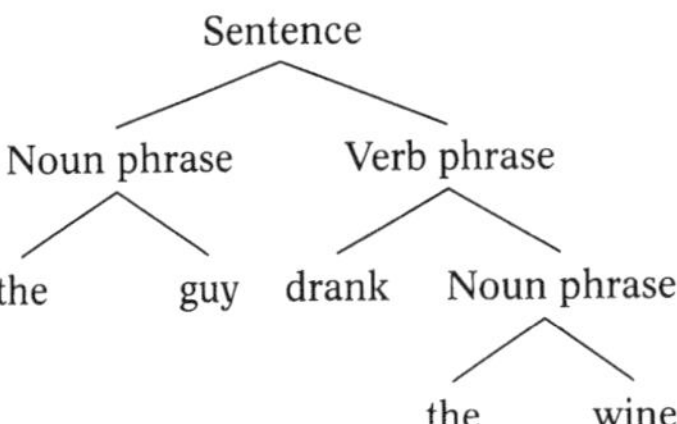

Figure 20.6 A traditional picture of the hierarchical structure corresponding to *The guy drank the wine*.

> in the sense that all its case and other feature-checking requirements have already been satisfied – this is what is called in linguistics an *adjunct phrase*. (*How* satisfies any feature-checking requirement for the full sentence's 'aspect'.) Another way to think of the same situation is that at this point, only phonological and semantic features remain in this subphrase; therefore, this phrase may be shipped off for semantic interpretation, and is rendered opaque to further syntactic manipulation. If this is so, then there is nothing that allows *what* to be further Merged – that is, displaced or moved. In contrast, the hierarchical object corresponding to *did the guy drink what* is still 'open', because (in English) the aspectual/question feature associated with the full sentence has yet to be satisfied – and in fact, can be satisfied by Merging *what* with the sentence, moving *what* to the front: *what did the guy drink what*. Finally, this sentence may be combined as an argument with *How do you know* to yield *How do you know what the guy drank?* Note that this is *roughly* the answer that Maynard Smith & Szathmáry (1995) give, with one difference, namely, fewer stipulations: we do not have to invoke a separate locality principle that *what* cannot be moved too far; rather, we simply state the constraint in terms of the convergent 'barrier' that *how* places in the way. In other words, given the feature-checking properties of Merge, plus its operation on simply adjacent syntactic domains, we would expect, and we do find, roadblocks like the one illustrated.

To conclude our 'Cook's tour' of syntax and how its basic properties are *derivable* from the fundamental generative operator, following Epstein (1995), we can show that natural languages use a limited set of relations like subject-of, object-of and c-command, rather than any *arbitrary* relation between the hierarchical components in, say, the last structure shown in Figure 20.1, repeated in Figure 20.6.

For example, the c-command relation holds between *the guy* and *the wine*, but not vice versa. In so-called representational theories of syntax, such as Government–Binding theory, the notion of c-command is usually given by definition (Reinhart 1983). But consider the following conceptual puzzles: why must c-command be defined this way, not some other way, between some other arbitrary pairs of syntactic objects? Indeed, why are the key syntactic relations (seemingly) just subject-of, object-of, c-command and only these?

To see why, consider again the Merge operation. Casting it this time in a set-theoretic notation, Merge takes a pair of syntactic objects α and β, sometimes directly lexical items, concatenating them and projecting α, forming a compound object $\gamma = \{\alpha, \{\alpha, \beta\}\}$. Syntactic structure is thus a temporal sequence of Merges, as we have seen. Given a derivational history and the syntactic structure it forms, we obtain the set of syntactically possible relations among syntactic objects. Our notion of a possible syntactic object and relation can be expressed via the following definitions, that formalize the notion of 'made visible' that I alluded to earlier.

Definition 1 *Let* α *be a* **syntactic object** *if and only if it is a selected word or a syntactic object formed by Merge.*

Definition 2 *A syntactic object is said to be* **in the derivation** *iff it has been paired with another object via Merge.*

Definition 3 *We say* α *and* β *are* **connected** *if they are parts of another (larger, common) syntactic object* γ.

From these definitions we know that a word's presence in the initial 'bag of words' does *not* imply it is already in the derivation. Rather, only when it undergoes Merge and is built into a larger structure does it enter into the derivation.

We can now deduce c-command from Merge:

Theorem 1 *Let* α *and* β *be syntactic objects;* α **c-commands** β *if* α *is connected to* β *at the moment* α *enters into derivation.*

Let us see how this works. When *the* and *wine* are Merged, they enter into the derivation, and thus either may c-command the other, as is required. The Merge creates a new hierarchical object, essentially the projection of *the*. Similarly, because they are Merged, the verb *drank* and the object (the traditional object noun phrase) *the wine* will c-command each other. Importantly, we can now derive the asymmetry of c-command: the verb *drank* will also c-command all the *subparts* of *the*

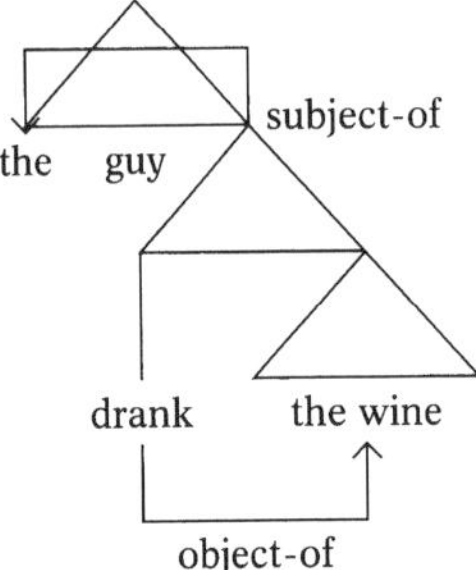

Figure 20.7 The core syntactic relations are fixed by Merge. This figure depicts the subject-of and object-of relations, with the 'selected' or functor-like pair of the Merger drawn as the source of the arrow.

wine, namely, *the* and *wine*, because **at the moment *drank* entered the derivation** via Merge, *drank*, *the* and *wine* were all subparts of a larger, common structure (what is conventionally called the entire verb phrase, *drank the wine*). However, *the* and *wine* **do not** c-command *drank*, because at the moment that *the* and *wine* entered the derivation – at the time they were Merged to form a phrase – then *drank* was not even in the derivation (Figure 20.1).

Similarly, the subject phrase *the guy* c-commands *drank the wine* and vice versa – because these two objects are Merged. Letting α=*the guy* and β=*drank the wine*, we see that α is by definition **connected** to all the subparts of *drank the wine* because it is connected to β at the time it enters the derivation. Therefore, the subject c-commands all the *subparts* of *drank the wine*, namely, *drank*, *the* and *wine*. The converse is not true – neither *drank*, nor *the*, nor *wine* c-commands the subject – because, for α=*wine* for instance, *wine* was not connected to the subject at the time *wine* entered into the derivation (was Merged for the first time).[8]

All other cases of syntactic relations reduce to subcases of this same 'visibility' criterion, that is, to relations between elements related at the time of a Merge. Figure 20.7 illustrates this.

8 We can now return to the question posed at the outset of this chapter: while there is indeed no 'subobj' relation, there *is* an asymmetric relation between subject and object, namely, that of c-command. It is this relation that blocks a co-reference link between subject and object, forcing *herself* to appear in English.

Object-of is the relation: Merge and select a word base (functor) with either another word or a hierarchical structure.

Subject-of is the relation: Merge a previously-merged hierarchical structure with a second hierarchical structure, selecting the first as the new hierarchical root, and the second as the 'subject'.

Head-of is the relation: copy base lexical features after a Merge.

C-command is the relation as it has been described above.

No other (natural) syntactic relations are possible, e.g., relating, say, *guy* with *wine*, since these items are *not* connected at the time of their participation in Merge.

4 Conclusions: evolution from Merge to language

Taking stock, we see that Merge covers much ground that formerly had to be assumed in transformational generative grammar. Many fundamental syntactic particulars are derivative: basic skeletal tree structure; movement rules; grammatical relations like object-of; locality constraints; even sentence phrase by sentence phrase grammatical operations – all these fall into place once the fundamental generative operation of Merge is up and running. These are the broad-brush outlines for human language – nothing here has to be specifically 'selected for' in the gradualist, pan-selectionist sense.

How might an evolutionary novelty like Merge actually arise? While we of course cannot actually know, in general it seems that one major route for new evolutionary possibilities is the development of 'slack' biological resources, ultimately deriving from the expression of new developmental genes via some method of duplication (unequal crossing over, tandem repeats and the like). If an existing gene is duplicated, its paralog retains the function of the old gene. Such a gene is now released from selection and free to 'drift' under neutral selection, thereby prompting a race between entropic decay by random mutation and the chance uncovering of a new developmental role. Since the probability of such a gene ultimately driving to fixation *without* selection is $1/2N$, where N is the population size, in small populations in the tens of thousands, such as those believed characteristic of ancestral hominoids, the role of drift is greatly enhanced: if there are 1,000 individuals, one in every 2,000 neutral mutations that occur will be fixed and retained as evolutionary change (Kimura 1983). If such a regulatory mutation is even slightly advantageous – perhaps for other reasons – then its chance of fixation is proportional to $2s(N_e/N)/1/(2N)$, or $4sN_e$, where s is the selective advantage and N_e is the so-called 'effective' population size (usually smaller than N). Thus, for s equal to 1 per cent we get an order-of-magnitude increase in the likelihood of fixation. In short, even if the fraction of properly regulatory mutations is 10 times lower than that of functionally degenerate mutations, there is still a 10 times greater chance that the drifting gene will wind up with an advantageous regulatory mutation. In this way, genetic resources that are 'freed up' from selection can carve out new functional domains. To be sure, such a scenario for evolutionary innovation is speculative, but it is at least one that can be tested and is currently being tested in living organisms (Li & Graur 1993).

In this context, it is important to recognize the difference between individual and population-level changes: for example, consider the famous textbook case of industrial melanism in the moth *Biston betularia* (see Bishop & Cook (1980) for a modern review). While the *B. betularia* population changed gradually from white to darker shades over a period of roughly 100 years, *for each individual moth* the change was a true saltation – that is, some developmental switch (a dominant gene) that altered its colouration radically from white to dark; no intermediates were required. Much the same could have happened with natural language – or rather, there is little direct evidence to choose against this view and some direct evidence (the unique appearance and properties of human language) in favour of it.

Returning then to natural language, Merge cannot tell us everything we need to know. It does not say how words came to be, and will have little to say about the word features particular to each language – why English has a question word that sounds like *what*, or why such a word in English has features that force it to agree with an abstract question marker, while this is apparently not so in Japanese. Similarly, Chinese has no overt markings for verbal tense. The different words and associated features each language chooses ultimately lead to different possibilities for combinations, hence different sentence types. But there is no need to invoke an array of distinct rules for each language, just as there is no need to invoke different laws of chemistry, once the basic principles are known. As Chomsky (1995) has remarked, echoing the structuralists, while 'Universal Grammar' has a long history, nobody has ever assumed there would be a 'universal morphology'. Different languages will have different words with different features, and it is precisely here, where variation has been known all along, that languages would be expected to vary. In this sense, there is no possibility of an 'intermediate' *syntax* between a non-combinatorial one and full natural language – one either has Merge in all its generative glory, or one has no combinatorial syntax at all. Rather, one would see what looks like agrammatic aphasia: alternative cognitive strategies for assigning thematic roles to word strings. Naturally, in a system that gives pride-of-place to word features, one would expect that deficits in feature recognition or processing – the 'feature blindness' described by Gopnik (1990) – could lead to great cognitive difficulties; many important details remain to be explored here. But if the account here is on the right track, while there can be individual words, in a sense there is only a single grammatical operation: Merge. Once Merge arose, the stage for natural language was set. There was no turning back.

Acknowledgment

This research was supported by NSF grant 9217041-ASC and ARPA under the HPCC program. Noam Chomsky, Jim Hurford, Morris Halle and an anonymous reviewer provided many valuable comments; all remaining errors are my own.

References

Berwick, R. C. & Epstein, S. (1995). Merge: the categorial imperative. In Nijholt, Anton (ed.) *Proceedings of AMAST Conference*. Twente, Netherlands: University of Twente.

Bickerton, D. (1990). *Language and Species*. Chicago and London: University of Chicago Press.

(1995). *Language and Human Behaviour*. Seattle, WA: University of Washington Press.

Bishop, J. A. & Cook, M. (1980). Industrial melanism and the urban environment. *Advances in Ecological Research*, 11, 373–404.

Chomsky, N. A. (1965). *Aspects of the Theory of Syntax*. Cambridge, MA: MIT Press.

(1981). *Lectures on Government and Binding*. Dordrecht: Foris.

(1995). *The Minimalist Program*. Cambridge, MA: MIT Press.

Darwin, C. (1871). *The Descent of Man, and Selection in Relation to Sex*. (Facsimile 1981) Princeton: Princeton University Press.

Dunbar, R. (1996). *Grooming, Gossip, and the Evolution of Language*. London: Faber & Faber.

Epstein, S. D. (1995). Un-principled syntax and derivational relations. Ms., Harvard University, Cambridge, MA.

Fisher, R. A. (1930). *The Genetical Theory of Natural Selection*. New York: Dover Publications.

Gopnik, Myrna (1990). Feature-blind grammar and dysphasia. *Nature*, 344, 715.

Gould, S. & Vrba, E. S. (1982). Exaptation – a missing term in the science of form. *Paleobiology*, 1, 4–15.

Kimura, M. (1983). *The Neutral Theory of Molecular Evolution*. Cambridge: Cambridge University Press.

Landau, M. (1991). *Narratives of Human Evolution*. New Haven: Yale University Press.

Li, W. & Graur, D. (1993). *Fundamentals of Molecular Evolution*. Sunderland, MA: Sinnauer Associates.

Maynard Smith, J. & Szathmáry, E. (1995). *The Major Transitions in Evolution*. Oxford: W. H. Freeman.

Nash, D. (1986). *Topics in Warlpiri Syntax*. New York: Garland Press.

O'Neil, W. (1979). Clause adjunction in Old English. *General Linguistics*, 17, 199–212.

Pinker, S. & Bloom, P. (1990). Natural language and natural selection. *Behavioral and Brain Sciences*, 13, 704–784.

Raff, R. (1996). *The Shape of Life*. Chicago: University of Chicago Press.

Reinhart, T. (1983). *Anaphora and Semantic Interpretation*. Chicago: University of Chicago Press.

Swartz, S. (1988). Constraints on zero anaphora and word order in Warlpiri narrative text. MS thesis, Pacific Center for Graduate Studies, with William Carey College.

Szathmáry, E. (1996). From RNA to language. *Current Biology*, 6(7), 764.

Williams, G. C. (1992). *Natural Selection: Domains, Levels, and Challenges*. Princeton: Princeton University Press.

21 Catastrophic evolution: the case for a single step from protolanguage to full human language

DEREK BICKERTON

1 The initial implausibility of catastrophic syntax

The idea that full human language could have emerged, if not from an alingual state, at least from a primitive and unstructured protolanguage in a single step – or in other words, that a single evolutionary development could account for all the major mechanisms of syntax – seems so counterintuitive that most students of evolution have been content to brush it aside without even considering it. I hope to show not merely that this idea is worthy of consideration, but that every substantive fact and cogent argument supports it.

Two factors alone might seem to argue against it. One is evolutionary: all evolutionary events are (more or less) gradual and mosaic, and the evolution of complex organs, like the eye (or, by implication, language), must therefore be more gradual and mosaic still. One is linguistic: syntax, at least according to some currently popular schools of thought (see e.g. Chomsky 1986), is a very complex thing, arising through the interaction of a number of independent task-specific modules which, according to some students of language evolution, must have evolved independently of one another, and presumably in some sequence (Newmeyer 1991; Pinker & Bloom 1990). The formidable combination of these lines of argument makes it difficult even to get a hearing for a catastrophic scenario for the emergence of modern human language.

Certainly, arguments will not make any headway against this combination unless one can tell a sensible story about how language *could* have emerged catastrophically. Accordingly I shall do that first, and then briefly summarize several independent lines of argument that support the story.

2 Two models of a neural circuit for syntax

Curiously enough, the general outline of the proposals to be made here do not, at an appropriate level of abstraction, differ all that much from the proposals of Lieberman (1991, 1992). Both accounts emphasize preadaptation, with modern language resulting from the operations of a task-specific neural circuit formed relatively late (possibly being itself the speciation event that produced *Homo sapiens sapiens*). The accounts differ only in the relative importance they place on syntax and phonology, and in the conclusions they draw with respect to the innateness and autonomy of the language faculty.

To Lieberman, phonology is primary, and syntax results automatically from pre-existing motor processes once there is an adequate vocal channel in place. To me, syntax is primary, and the birth of syntax as we know it was precisely what selected, very rapidly and efficiently, for an improved vocal apparatus even at the cost of maladaptive effects on ingestion.

Lieberman argues that motor control circuits which developed to facilitate primitive speech became responsible for the organization of syntax. He produces no explicit argument as to how this process could have come about, and presumably relies on an implied analogy between phonological and syntactic processes, supported by the frequent (but by no means universal) co-occurrence of phonological and syntactic deficits among victims of Parkinson's disease and Broca's aphasia. Although again quite inexplicit on this point, he appears to share the belief, apparently all but universal among non-syntacticians, that syntax consists merely in placing words in some regular serial order. Indeed, in language evolution circles generally, the belief seems widespread that once you have progressed as far as *John loves Mary* and *The cat sat on the mat*, syntax is off and running and nothing stands in the way of it gradually expanding to embrace all of the many complexities found in contemporary languages.

Every serious syntactician knows that this is untrue. Serial sequencing is the least important aspect of syntax. Crucial relationships are vertical, not horizontal: for instance, command (the capacity of a syntactic constituent in a 'higher' position to influence one in a 'lower', but not vice versa); control (the capacity of a phonologically overt syntactic constituent to determine the referential content of a phonologically null constituent); and containment (factors creating limited domains

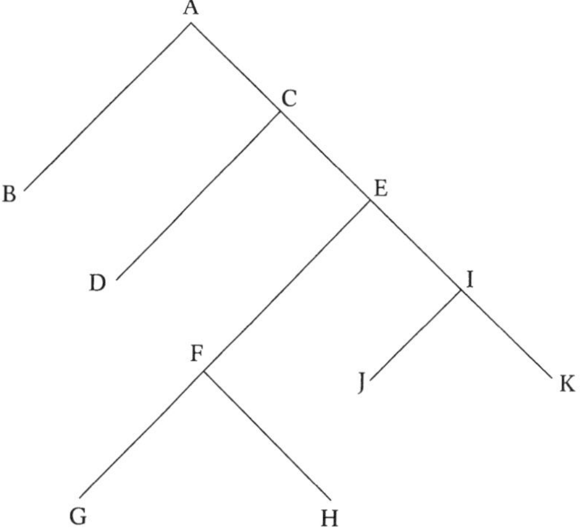

Figure 21.1 Command, containment and control. In this figure, terminal node D commands terminal nodes G, H, J and K, but not B. G and H, and J and K, reciprocally command one another, but neither G nor H commands J or K, or vice versa. Nonterminal node A contains all other nodes; nonterminal node C contains all nodes except A and B; nonterminal node E contains nodes F–K but no others. An overt noun at node H controls the identity of a non-overt noun at node J, by virtue of the fact that E contains both H and J, and that there is no node outside I that is closer to J than H; though equidistant, D cannot control J because D is not contained by E.

which prevent co-reference between constituents within those domains and constituents outside them, sometimes referred to in the linguistic literature as 'barriers', 'islands' or 'Subjacency effects'). See Figure 21.1 for illustration.

Furthermore (as will be shown below) the development of true language out of a prior protolanguage would have involved processes of *expansion* and *extension*. It is unrealistic to suppose that any development of speech motor control could have yielded command, control, containment, expansion and extension: no mechanisms that could have facilitated such a development have even been hypothesized, and indeed it is impossible to imagine what such mechanisms would be like. It is equally unrealistic to suppose that the development of a modern phonological capacity could ever have selected for syntactic capacity, since, as the foregoing paragraphs should have made clear, syntax is exclusively a computational mechanism, and moreover one that must deal with units (words, phrases, clauses, sentences) which cannot (unlike phonemes, nuclei, syllables, etc.) be defined in phonological terms (that is, terms that are articulatory, acoustic or depend on mental representations of articulatory or acoustic units).

On the other hand, if syntax developed while phonology was still primitive, the capacity to produce long and complex sentences and thus to arrange and communicate much longer and more complicated pieces of information – a highly adaptive capacity that would surely have enhanced the relative fertility of those possessing it – would have selected very strongly for improvements in clarity (involving among other things much finer-grained distinctions between speech sounds) and speed of speech. For these reasons we may conclude that modern phonology and modern syntax are partially disjoint in their neural infrastructure (even though that infrastructure must be partially shared, or speech as we know it would be impossible) and that the emergence of syntax must have preceded the emergence of a fully modern vocal tract, rather than vice versa.

The second difference between the two approaches, that concerning autonomy and innateness, is much less substantive, and may indeed amount to nothing more than a semantic one. Lieberman (1992), in common with Müller (1996) and others, seems to suppose that an autonomous system must be modular, rather than a circuit that links several modules. There is, of course, no logical basis for this assumption. One commentary on Müller (Bickerton 1996) points out that

> No theory of language . . . has ever claimed . . . strict modularity or localisation of brain functions . . . (T)he infrastructure of language [could consist of] a dedicated network of cells (any of which might also do other jobs) linking several disparate brain areas . . . But why does this refute autonomy? If a bricklayer moonlights as a plumber, does that mean he's not really a bricklayer? Or that he must therefore lay bricks the same way he plumbs? The network, qua network, handles nothing but language. The cells in it, qua cells, do language when they are doing language and something else when they are doing something else.

In other words, as will be shown below, a number of discrete areas of the brain could engage in a variety of tasks, some protolanguage-related, some not, all of which would have been required, for one reason or another, prior to the emergence of syntax. Such an ensemble could be regarded collectively as a preadaptation for syntax. However, syntax could not function until all the areas were linked in a single circuit, and as any practical electrician will tell you, a circuit will not function even if only a single link is required to complete it. To claim that such a dedicated circuit – dedicated *as* a circuit, dedicated only while it *functions* as a circuit – does not constitute an autonomous language organ is simply to juggle with words.

The two foregoing issues apart (only one of which has any substance), our two accounts match. Lieberman notes that the model in Bickerton (1990) is restricted to neocortical structures, but this is certainly not true of the revised model (in Bickerton 1995), which explicitly mentions subcortical involvement (see especially pp. 82, 144). Indeed, leaving aside the degree of importance Lieberman attaches to Broca's area, and the failure of his model to incorporate any function of the brain that would impose syntactic structure on utterances, there seems to be little substantive difference between the models, although in previous work neither model has been sufficiently elaborated to determine accurately the degree of similarity.

3 Neural prerequisites for the establishment of syntax

I begin by assuming that there were, in the brains of alingual hominid predecessors (australopithecines, *habilis*), a number of areas adapted for purposes having nothing to do with language that were, however, potential preadaptations for language. The relevant areas are shown in Figure 21.2, which is obviously schematic and not at all intended as a structural map of the brain. For present purposes it does not matter where the various functions were located, the point being that they had to be performed somewhere, somehow. What I have called the 'neo-cerebellar speeder-upper' relates to the immense expansion of the cerebellum which appears to have taken place after the hominid–pongid evolutionary split (Braitenberg & Atwood 1958; Passingham 1975), apparently utilized first to automate and expedite execution of motor functions, but subsequently becoming involved in many so-called 'higher' activities, including linguistic and cognitive ones (Leiner, Leiner & Dow 1989, 1991). The broken line from this area merely indicates uncertainty as to exactly when it became operative.

The potential role of what I have called the theta-analysis component may require some explanation. Recent literature has stressed the significance of 'Machiavellian intelligence' (Byrne & Whiten 1988) in

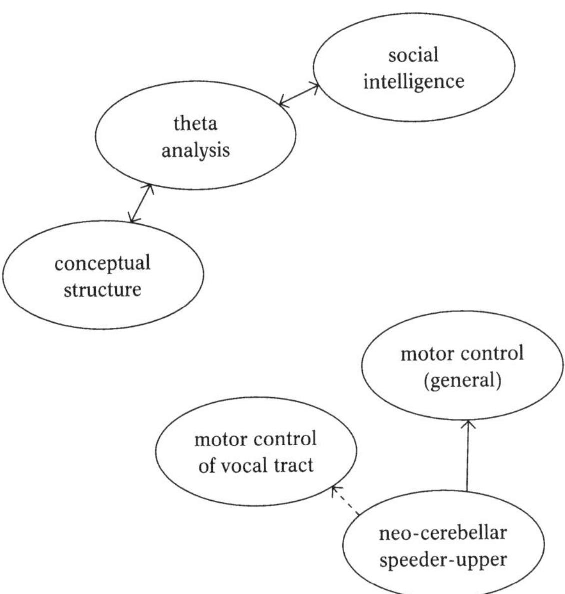

Figure 21.2 Prelinguistic functional brain units.

primate development in general; in particular, several studies (Dunbar 1995, this volume; Knight, Worden, this volume) have claimed direct links of one sort or another between primate social intelligence and the evolution of language. Since syntax is a computational mechanism, a link might seem dubious at first. However, the intuitions of these researchers are essentially along the right lines. Even though the way in which social intelligence influenced the development of language is much subtler and more complex than has so far been suggested, it turns out to be at least as far-reaching, as will be shown shortly.

First, however, we must consider the minimal changes in the brain that came about with the emergence of protolanguage (Figure 21.3). All that was required was for an area of the brain to develop which would represent the phonetic shapes of words, and for this area to become linked to the areas involved in conceptual structure – those which determine what categories inhabit the world – and to the motor organs controlling the vocal channel, which now added speech to their prior calling and ingesting capacities. This novel area may be identified with Broca's area (Wilkins & Wakefield 1995) but, as noted, identification

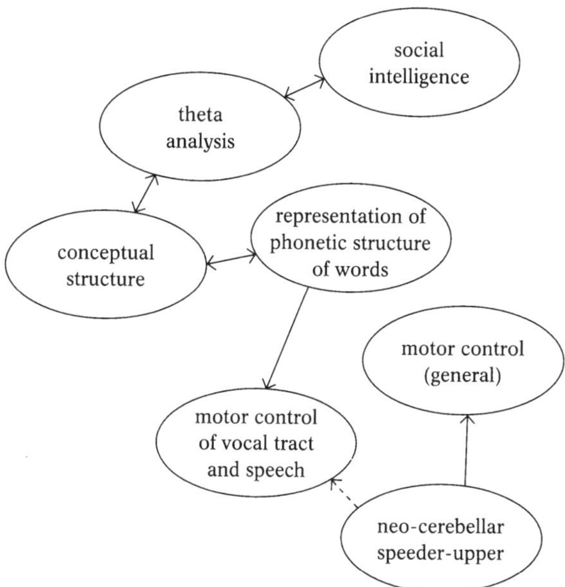

Figure 21.3 Protolinguistic functional brain units.

of specific neural areas is irrelevant to the present schematic and functional account. Note that in production, information would travel downstream from conceptual structure to phonetic representation to motor control, with no mechanism for imposing any formal structure on the sequential linkage of individual words.

Note that the absence of formal structure imposes narrow limits on the possible length of utterances. Protolanguage utterances of a few (say, a maximum of three to five) words in length could have been uttered and interpreted largely without computational problems, since pragmatic and semantic factors could have been used to resolve problems of interpretation without excessive loss of time – especially if, as seems likely, the speed of protolinguistic speech was noticeably slower than that of modern speech. However, problems of interpretation increase exponentially as sentence length increases, since one has to determine whether each word is a head or a modifier of a head; where phrases and clauses begin and end; which words (or rather which positions in a sentence) can share a common referent and which cannot; to what extent the distribution of information, or factors such as emphasis or presupposition, can allow the placing of constituents 'away from' their 'expected' positions in the sentence; and countless other factors.

There is no doubt that many (though certainly not all) interpretation problems could be solved by the use of semantic and pragmatic clues. But such procedures, which require some degree of conscious attention, would slow down both speech and understanding to an extent that would severely reduce their efficiency, and probably place an intolerable burden on the immediate memory, since the latter would have to store constantly multiplying alternative interpretations (a sentence with two ambiguities is quadruply ambiguous, a sentence with three ambiguities has eight possible meanings, and so on). For language to function efficiently, it has to be interpreted *entirely unconsciously and automatically*, that is to say without taking any semantic or pragmatic factors into account.

Such interpretation is impossible without an automatic computational mechanism of some kind. As a minimum, such a mechanism must divide the stream of speech into subunits whose boundaries are unambiguous and must distinguish levels – that is to say, in a sentence such as *I gave John a glass of orange juice*, it must be able to determine that although *a glass of orange juice* consists of five words, those five words constitute a unit on the same level as *I* and *John*, while *orange juice*, although consisting of two words, is not on the same level. It is precisely this mechanism of subunits and levels that is presupposed by factors such as command, control and containment, discussed in the previous section, which in turn help to limit (usually to just one) the wide range of possible meanings that strings of merely concatenated words might be interpreted as expressing.

The mechanism in question lies in the way that syntax is organized (Bickerton 1990: ch. 3). The most basic unit of syntax is the clause. The scope of a clause is determined by what is known as the thematic grid of the single verb that each clause obligatorily contains. Every verb subcategorizes for (obligatorily selects) one, two or three *arguments*, that is to say, nouns or noun phrases referring to some necessary participant in the state or action expressed by the verb, and each of these arguments will have a *thematic role*, that is, will stand in a particular semantic relationship to that state or action.

Thus a verb like *think* or *sleep* will have only a single subcategorized argument, and that argument will have the (thematic) role of Theme:

that which experiences, is affected by or results from the state or action of the verb. A verb like *break* or *love* will have two arguments, again a Theme (whoever or whatever is broken or loved), plus this time an Agent that does the breaking or loving. A verb like *give* or *tell* will have three arguments, a Theme, an Agent and a Goal (whoever receives what is given or told). Occasionally other roles may be selected: *put* requires Location, for instance (you cannot say *I put the book*, you have to say something like *I put the book on your desk*). In addition, a very small number of non-subcategorized roles (such as Time, Instrument, Beneficiary. etc.) may be selected.

In language, verbs and their obligatory arguments must be fully represented. This is what differentiates language from protolanguage. In protolanguage, neither verbs nor any of their arguments make obligatory appearances. Any words whatsoever can be put together: strings of nouns, strings of verbs, two- or three-argument verbs with only a single argument, and so on (for abundant examples see Bickerton (1995: appendix A)). If indeed the functional structure of the protolinguistic brain was as indicated in Figure 21.3, then this is exactly what one would expect, since messages travel directly from conceptual structure through phonetic representation to the machinery that executes those messages, with nothing anywhere to impose structure on them.

Protolanguage turned into language when something supplied that structure: when, instead of words being randomly concatenated, they were analysed into units consisting of a verb plus its argument(s) and these units were then mapped onto binary-branching hierarchical structures like that shown in Figure 21.1, so that each verb and each argument had a predetermined position. Note, however, that to say that verbs and their obligatory arguments must be fully represented does not mean that each of these must necessarily have overt representation. Given the mechanisms described, *speaker and hearer know that those obligatory arguments must be there even if they are not evident to the senses*, and additional mechanisms (see the discussion of *John wants someone to work for* in section 5) ensure that we can properly identify every unexpressed constituent.

For instance, take the sentence *John chose to vote for himself*. We know that *vote* as well as *chose* requires an Agent argument and we also know that *John* is that Agent, even though *John* is overtly represented only as Agent of *chose*. You may well think this is trivial, since *chose* and *to vote* are contiguous and there is no other possible voter than

John. If so, then consider *John, despite his promise to Bill, would have erred in not taking advantage of the opportunity provided by Fred to vote for himself*. Here, even though ten words separate the verb *erred* (of which *John* is overt Agent) from the verb *to vote*, and even though two named individuals, *Bill* and *Fred*, are nearer to *vote* than *John* is, and even though *Fred* is actually contiguous to *vote*, we somehow know that it is John, and not Bill or Fred, who voted for himself. A computational mechanism of this power is anything but trivial.

But where could such a mechanism have come from?

4 The origins of syntax

The answer is: the mechanism was there all the time, but it was not being used for language.

Consider the significance, in primate social life generally, of reciprocal altruism (Trivers 1971). De Waal, in stressing the significance of reciprocal altruism as the foundation-stone of human morality, points out that it included the following among its necessary characteristics: 'giving is contingent on receiving' and 'there is a time lag between giving and receiving' (1996: 24).

What mental equipment would primates require to run a system of reciprocal altruism? Let us suppose there are five primates: A, who is an ally of B; C, who is the alpha male of the group; and two others, D and E. A grooms, defends and occasionally shares food with B, who does likewise with A; the two of them together are capable of outwitting and/or facing down C. The effort devoted to this partnership represents a considerable investment on A's part, one he can ill afford to make if he is not getting full reciprocity. How can A know that he is not giving more than he receives? Only if he is able to keep track of all the interactions between himself and B, noting on how many occasions he is the performer or donor (Agent) and B the object or the recipient (Theme or Goal) of his actions, and on how many occasions these roles are reversed. And, as De Waal points out, these computations have to be carried out over considerable time periods.

Suppose that A concludes (quite unconsciously, no doubt) that B has degenerated into a cheater. He now needs another ally, but in whom should he begin to invest effort, D or E? In order not to make the wrong choice, he has had to be able, even while continuing to monitor his relationship with B, to keep track of his interactions with D and E, and theirs with C and other members of their group. Which of the two has acted favourably toward him with the greatest frequency (indicating a likelihood to respond favourably to an offer of alliance)? Which has been most frequently the passive, acted-on participant in interactions with C (indicating an ally of little value, not worth investing in)? Clearly, the more skill a primate has in tracking and analysing interactions and the more interactions he is capable of monitoring, the more successful that primate will be. So thematic analysis must have been selected-for long before the hominid–pongid split, and some functional area of the brain devoted to analysing the thematic roles of event participants may have pre-existed language by several million years.

Yet it may be that for a period of between 1 and 2 million years – a period of 'almost unimaginable monotony', according to Jelinek (1977: 28) – protolanguage and thematic analysis co-existed within hominid brains, yet remained quite unconnected with one another. What would have connected them? Thematic analysis had been built to run in an entirely alingual brain. Such analysis constituted a near-perfect preadaptation for imposing the needed structure on the nascent but formless protolanguage, but this function could not be exercised until the necessary neural links were in place.

How did those links come into existence? We can assume that, as indicated in Figures 21.2–21.4, links had always existed between thematic analysis and conceptual structure; Events, Agents, Themes and Goals could not even have been distinguished, let alone used in the analysis of behaviour, if they had not already formed part of the primate inventory of 'Things that there are in the world'. However, if all information went downstream from conceptual structure to phonetic representation, thematic analysis could not possibly have influenced the processing of that information.

But evolution is, as Monod (1971) remarked, a mixture of genetic chance and adaptive necessity. Chance operates very significantly in ontogenetic (and hence ultimately in phylogenetic) brain development. The brain contains far too many cells and connections for these to be directly specified in the genetic code and, accordingly, epigenetic factors with a sizeable component of randomness determine the detailed distribution of both cell-connection and cells (Benno 1990; Shankland & Macagno 1992). Equally there is marked individual variation in brain areas at the levels of both morpho-anatomy (Kolb & Whishaw 1990:

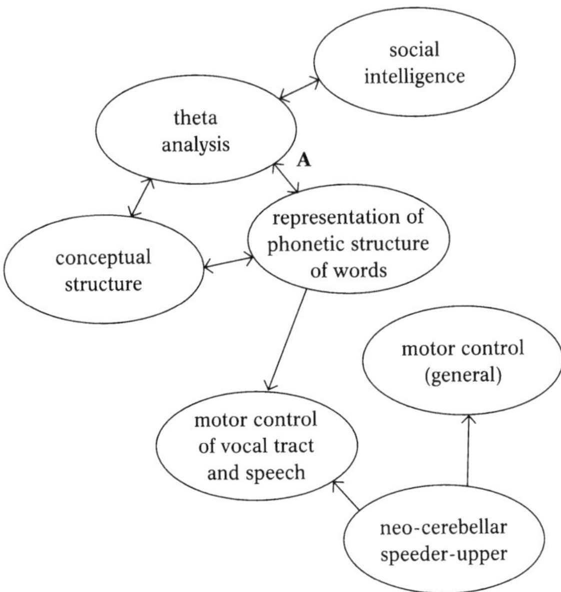

Figure 21.4 Linguistic functional brain units.

75f.) and neurofunctional organization (Schlaug, Knorr & Seitz 1994). What this meant in practice was that in some members of *Homo erectus* the distance between thematic analysis areas and phonetic representation areas would be less than in others, and that in some of those members (perhaps in a relatively small and isolated population in Southern Africa around 120,000 years BP), random, opportunistic connections could have formed between the two areas. Note that such a development needs no mutation or indeed anything beyond the natural and inevitable recombination of genetic material that occurs in all species which reproduce sexually.

The creation of such connections (indicated by the letter A in Figure 21.4) would have enabled information to pass through the theta-analysis component before it reached phonetic representation. Information passing through this area would have been automatically sorted into units consisting of an action and its participants obligatorily represented – exactly those clausal units that constitute the basic units of syntax. Since, in the case of certain verbs (verbs of thinking, believing, reporting and so on), an argument may consist of another such clausal unit (as in *Mary was hoping YOU WOULD BRING HER A PRESENT*) or even two or more such units (as in *Bill told me [MARY WAS HOPING [YOU WOULD BRING HER A PRESENT]]*) it follows that such a system of processing information is infinitely recursive, constrained only by immediate-memory limitations.

Note that the creation of a new neural pathway in no way entails the extinction of the previous one. On the contrary, the fact that we remain capable of functioning in the protolinguistic mode (as for example when forced to speak in a language of which we know no more than a few words) indicates the persistence of the older link. However, those who utilized the new link were immediately capable of longer and more complex exchanges of information, well beyond what their unequipped fellows could utter or comprehend. Sexual selection would then surely have begun to operate – other things being equal (or even if they were to some extent unequal!), females would surely have preferred mates whose communicative capacities so strikingly outclassed those of other available partners. Indeed, under such conditions, a speciation event (presumably, that which gave rise to anatomically modern humans) could well have occurred relatively rapidly.

At the same time, the capacity to produce and understand sentences of indefinite length would have rapidly selected for improvements in the vocal channel to reduce what would otherwise have been an increased risk of phonetic ambiguity. That capacity would also have selected for an increase in the speed of speech, probably mediated by the neo-cerebellar speeder-upper, since there would now be a risk that the beginning of a sentence might be forgotten by the hearer before its end had been spoken. The same capacity would further have provided a selective pressure for the genetic developments surveyed by Gopnik and her colleagues (Gopnik & Crago 1991), which created a component for storage and use of grammatical items that even further reduced possible structural ambiguities and made the production and comprehension of language yet more rapid and automatic. In other words, the linkage of theta analysis with other elements involved in protolanguage would not merely have put in place the basic structure of syntax, but would also have led directly to a cascade of consequences that would, in one rapid and continuous sequence, have transformed protolanguage into language substantially as we know it today.

5 Supplementary arguments for a single-step scenario

The foregoing sections show that syntax could have developed catastrophically without appealing to a macromutation or indeed to any but the best-known and most mundane of genetic events. However, it is one thing to show that this *could have* happened, and something else to show that it *did* happen. Here I shall briefly summarize five independent lines of argument which all point toward catastrophic rather than gradual evolution.

First consider human cognition: it is widely recognized that a significant increment in human cognition resulted from the emergence of language (Davidson & Noble 1989; Donald 1991; Falk 1987). Certainly the fruit of a major increment in cognition is apparent in the avalanche of technological and behavioural developments, unprecedented in any other species, that began only after the emergence of our own species. It is implausible to suppose that cognition grew gradually over the 2-million-plus years of hominid development but had virtually no effect on behaviour or technology. If it had grown thus, we would expect to find that a slow but steady increase in the rate of technological and behavioural change left marks in the fossil record over at least the last million and a half years. Instead a long period of stagnation was followed by a cognitive explosion occurring only *after* the emergence of anatomically modern humans in South Africa about 120,000 years BP. These developments are compatible with the scenario just sketched but not with any other scenario of language evolution.

The second line of argument comes from the absence of any synchronic varieties of language intermediate between protolanguage (apparent in pidgin 'languages', ape 'language', and the language of children under two, see Bickerton (1990, 1995)) and fully developed human language (apparent in the creole languages – Haitian, Papiamentu, Sranan, etc. – that developed from pidgins). There would be a much stronger case for gradual evolution if there existed some kind(s) of 'linguistic fossil', some definable stage(s) through which a syntaxless pidgin had to pass before becoming a syntaxful creole. None, apparently, exists. However, historical research over the last few years in Hawaii has uncovered enormous quantities of empirical data on the pidgin–creole interface (Roberts 1995a, 1995b, to appear) and has confirmed that a novel language was created there (a) by children, (b) in one generation, (c) from radically degenerate, unstructured input, just as had previously been claimed on the basis of comparative linguistic and demographic studies (Bickerton 1981, 1984).

In addition it is surely significant that, across the wide range of aphasic and dysphasic syndromes, cryptolects, stages of first and second language acquisition, and all other atypical manifestations of the human language faculty, we do not find any stable level between language and protolanguage. Either syntax is fully present, or fully absent, or else it is fairly evenly degraded across its entire structure. (Note that the component affected by the language-specific deficit discussed in Gopnik & Crago (1991), though an essential part of language, is not properly speaking a part of syntax *per se* but rather a morphological component designed to improve the processing of syntax.) Here is a third line of argument in favour of a catastrophic origin. If syntax had developed gradually, whether by the addition of quasi-independent modules, as some generativists might suppose, or by the progressive attainment of higher levels of complexity, we would expect to find somewhere, somehow, in all this broad gamut, that at least one condition involved the absence of some particular aspect of syntax, or allowed stable levels of complexity below the level of normal language to exist. Indeed the gradualist models proposed by Newmeyer (1991) and by Pinker & Bloom (1990) directly predict (even though the latter explicitly denies this) that such selective syntactic deficits should occur. The fact that no such deficits appear in the clinical literature suggests that syntax is indeed a single independent module and that language as we know it emerged from an *erectus* protolanguage as abruptly as a creole emerges from a pidgin.

One could of course argue that intermediate stages might have permanently self-destructed and be irrecoverable today. Were that so, it would still surely not be beyond human ingenuity, since we know the initial state (protolanguage) and the final state (language), to determine what those intermediate stages would have been like. But a fourth line of argument comes from the apparent impossibility of this feat. Several varieties suggested by Premack (1985) and Pinker (1994) fail in light of reasonable constraints that must be placed on hypothetical intermediates (Bickerton 1986, 1995: 72–73): an intermediate must constitute a viable system in its own right, it should be derivable from protolanguage by logical and consistent process, and one should in turn be able to derive language from such an intermediate by a similar process.

A fifth line of argument stems from the apparent indissociability of those properties that distinguish language from protolanguage.

For instance, one feature of natural language is that it contains empty categories and that these categories can be interpreted automatically, systematically, without regard for semantics, pragmatics or anything else. We know for instance that the Agent argument of *work for* in *Bill wants someone to work for* is *Bill*, even though *Bill* is not expressed as that argument and *someone* is nearer to the argument position than *Bill* is. We know equally that in *Bill wants someone to work for him*, *someone*, not *Bill*, is now the Agent of *work for*. The processes by which we automatically know this are computations defined over units consisting of a verb and its arguments generated automatically when the products of thematic analysis are mapped onto a hierarchical tree structure.

In the example in question, a property of phonetically null elements like the Agent of *to work for* is that any such element must co-refer with an overt referential element within the same sentence (unless there is no such element, as in *It's hard to find work nowadays*, when the null element takes a general reference). However, two null elements in the same clause cannot co-refer; this follows from the broader fact that no two constituents of a clause can co-refer unless one of them is marked as reflexive (in English, by substitution of *himself* or some similar form). Thus in the version *Bill wants someone to work for*, in which both Agent and Theme arguments of *work for* are null, one element must refer to *Bill* and one to *someone*. Since the most deeply embedded null argument is the Theme, this must be interpreted first and must co-refer with the nearest available referent, which is *someone*. Therefore, the null Agent of *work for* here is *Bill*.

However, in the alternative version *Bill wants someone to work for him*, the overt pronoun *him* replaces the null element as Theme and the most deeply embedded null argument is the Agent. Thus this time it is the Agent that must be interpreted first (as *someone*). But the two arguments cannot co-refer, and in any case *him* is barred from referring to anything within its own clause. This time, therefore, the Theme of *work for* is *Bill*.

Thus the identity of empty categories is derived by simple algorithmic processes. But these processes are defined over, and indeed could not exist without, the structure of thematic mappings onto hierarchical tree structures whose origins the present chapter has sought to determine. And this relationship between process and structure represents but one of countless interdependencies between the various aspects of syntax. These interdependencies are so widespread, persistent and robust as to suggest that syntax could not possibly work as a computational device unless its major defining properties were intimately linked and had emerged simultaneously.

Of the five foregoing lines of argument, none, perhaps, is conclusive in itself. What is impressive is the conjunction of all five, and the fact that (leaving aside the prejudices mentioned in the opening section) no line of argument points in a contrary direction. The burden of proof therefore lies squarely upon the shoulders of those who would claim the emergence of syntax as a gradual process or a series of several events, rather than a single, catastrophic process.

References

Benno, R. H. (1990). Development of the nervous system: genetics, epigenetics and phylogenetics. In Broman, S. H. & Grafman, J. (eds.) *Atypical Cognitive Deficits in Developmental Disorders*. London: Erlbaum.

Bickerton, D. (1981). *Roots of Language*. Ann Arbor: Karoma.

(1984). The language bioprogram hypothesis. *Behavioral and Brain Sciences*, 7, 173–221.

(1986). More than nature needs? A reply to Premack. *Cognition*, 23, 73–79.

(1990). *Language and Species*. Chicago and London: University of Chicago Press.

(1995). *Language and Human Behavior*. Seattle: University of Washington Press.

(1996). An innate language faculty needs neither modularity nor localization. *Behavioural and Brain Sciences*, 19, 631–632.

Braitenberg, V. & Atwood, R. P. (1958). Morphological observations on the cerebellar cortex. *Journal of Comparative Neurology*, 109, 1–34.

Byrne, R. W. & Whiten, A. (eds.) (1988). *Machiavellian Intelligence. Social Expertise and the Evolution of Intellect in Monkeys, Apes, and Humans.* Oxford: Clarendon Press.

Chomsky, N. (1986). *Barriers*. Cambridge, MA: MIT Press.

Davidson, I. & Noble, W. (1989). The archaeology of perception: traces of depiction and language. *Current Anthropology*, 30, 125–155.

De Waal, F. (1996). *Good-natured: The Origin of Right and Wrong in Humans and Other Animals*. Cambridge, MA: Harvard University Press.

Donald, M. (1991). *Origins of Modern Mind: Three Stages in the Evolution of Culture and Cognition.* Cambridge, MA: Harvard University Press.

Dunbar, R. I. M. (1996). *Grooming, Gossip and the Evolution of Language*. London: Faber & Faber.

Falk, D. (1987). Hominid paleoneurology. *Annual Review of Anthropology*, 16, 13–30.

Gopnik, M. & Crago, M. B. (1991). Familial aggregation of a developmental language disorder. *Cognition*, 39, 1–50.

Jelinek, A. J. (1977). The lower paleolithic: current evidence and interpretations. *Annual Review of Anthropology*, 6, 11–32.

Kolb, B. & Whishaw, J. (1990). *Fundamentals of Human Neuro-psychology.* (3rd edition) New York: Freeman.
Leiner, H. C., Leiner, A. L. & Dow, R. S. (1989). Reappraising the cerebellum: what does the hindbrain contribute to the forebrain? *Behavioral Neuroscience*, 103, 998–1008.
(1991). The human cerebro-cerebellar system: its computing, cognitive and language skills. *Behavioural Brain Research*, 44, 113–128.
Lieberman, P. (1991). *Uniquely Human. The Evolution of Speech, Thought and Selfless Behavior.* Cambridge, MA: Harvard University Press.
(1992). Could an autonomous syntax module have evolved? *Brain and Language*, 41, 768–774.
Monod, J. (1971). *Chance and Necessity.* New York: Knopf.
Müller, R.-A. (1996). Innateness, autonomy, universality? Neurobiological approaches to language. *Behavioral and Brain Sciences*, 19, 611–675.
Newmeyer, F. J. (1991). Functional explanation in linguistics and the origins of language. *Language and Communication*, 11, 3–28.
Passingham, R. E. (1975). Changes in the size and organization of the brain in man and his ancestors. *Brain, Behavior and Evolution*, 11, 73–90.
Pinker, S. (1994). *The Language Instinct.* New York: Morrow; London: Penguin.
& Bloom, P. (1990). Natural language and natural selection. *Behavioral and Brain Sciences*, 13, 707–784.
Premack, D. (1985). Gavagai, or the future history of the animal language controversy. *Cognition*, 19, 207–296.
Roberts, J. M. (1995a). Pidgin Hawaiian: a sociohistorical study. *Journal of Pidgin and Creole Languages*, 10, 1–56.
(1995b). A structural sketch of Pidgin Hawaiian. *Amsterdam Creole Studies*, 12, 97–126.
(to appear). The role of diffusion in creole genesis. To appear in *Language.*
Schlaug, G., Knorr, U. & Seitz, R. (1994). Inter-subject variability of cerebral activations in acquiring a motor skill. *Experimental Brain Research*, 98, 523–534.
Shankland, M. & Macagno, E. R. (eds.) (1992). *Determinants of Neuronal Identity.* San Diego: Academic Press.
Trivers, R. L. (1971). The evolution of reciprocal altruism. *Quarterly Review of Biology*, 46, 35–57.
Wilkins, W. K. & Wakefield, J. (1995). Brain evolution and neurolinguistic preconditions. *Behavioral and Brain Sciences*, 18, 161–226.

22 Fitness and the selective adaptation of language

SIMON KIRBY

1 Introduction

The question that is at the centre of this chapter is: how can we go about explaining the observed constraints on variation across languages – in other words, language universals?[1] What makes many of these constraints interesting is that they appear to have 'evolved' in that they are adaptive; a point that is made repeatedly in the functionalist literature. What I will argue here, however, is that we should not rush into a biological evolutionary explanation for such universals. Where language is concerned, adaptation may be the result of several different interacting dynamic systems. It is important to note that this paper is wholly concerned with the origins of constraints on linguistic variation, not the origins of language itself. I look to answer the question 'Why do languages pattern the way they do?', not 'How did language emerge from non-language?' In a sense this chapter looks at the last stages of adaptation in a complete picture of language evolution.

The order of presentation will be as follows. The next section is an introduction to what it means for something to be adaptive. The following two sections will illustrate this with two processing and typological asymmetries connected with word order and relative clauses. A potential biological explanation will be put forward and rejected in favour of a historical explanation in the next two sections. This alternative explanation will be tested using a computational model of interacting agents using language over several generations. Finally, the implications of this

1 Much of the material for this chapter is covered in more detail in Kirby (1996), although the analysis of the relation between glossogenetic and phylogenetic adaptation is new. This research was supported by ESRC grant R000236551 and a visiting fellowship at the Collegium Budapest Institute for Advanced Study.

approach for the phylogenetic evolution of language will be sketched in the concluding section.

The novel contribution of this chapter is the suggestion that languages evolve *historically* to be optimal communicative systems, and that the innately specified human language learning mechanisms have evolved in order to learn these systems more efficiently. In other words, human language has *not* evolved (in the phylogenetic timescale) directly in response to communicative needs, even though the cross-linguistic evidence is that language is well adapted for communication.

2 The fitness of universals

I have suggested that many of the constraints on cross-linguistic variation found in the typological literature (see e.g. Comrie 1981; Croft 1990; Greenberg 1963; Hawkins 1988) are adaptive. By this I mean that they have a striking *appearance of design*. Cziko (1995) refers to this feature of systems as the 'puzzle of fit'. Many attempts at explaining universals have pointed out the fit of universals to the communicative functions of language. Although these observations are important and insightful, I believe they leave the real mystery unsolved. Rather than explaining the origin of universals, this fit is in itself puzzling. Assuming that languages do not have a designer, how do they end up looking as though they have been crafted with a particular purpose in mind? Why is it that, as we shall see, the constraints on relative clauses give an optimal balance between speakers' and hearers' needs in communication, for example?

Before answering these questions, we need to review briefly what we mean by 'fitness'. In general, the term can be used to describe the appearance of design in some structure whose formal properties correlate with its function. So, an umbrella's fitness derives from the fact that its canopy shields its user from rain and its handle and stem are arranged so that it can be easily carried. The formal and functional elements of the umbrella so neatly dovetail that we are led to expect that it has been designed.

Similarly, the term 'typological fitness' can be used to describe the property of universals whose formal structure dovetails with the functions of language. In this chapter I will concentrate on one aspect of this fitness: the match of cross-linguistic asymmetries with asymmetries in language processing. Just as umbrellas cannot weigh more than a few pounds in order to be carried by their users, languages appear to be constrained cross-linguistically to be efficiently processed in real time.

There are many explanations for language universals given in the literature that make reference to this kind of fitness. For example, Cutler, Hawkins & Gilligan (1985) aim to explain the cross-linguistic preference for suffixes (as opposed to prefixes) in terms of the way in which language is processed by hearers in real time. The crucial feature of this processing is that it is constrained by the left-to-right, serial nature of speech. The start of a word is clearly received by the processor before the end, and the assumption is that work starts on processing input as soon as it arrives. Simplifying their argument somewhat, Cutler *et al.* point out that early lexical access is preferred by hearers because placing of salient information early in the word aids processing. If lexical access is stem-based – as they argue from experimental evidence – then the tendency for languages to be suffixal matches the preference of the processor.

3 Processing asymmetries

For the examples in this chapter I will be using the general theory of processing complexity put forward in Hawkins (1994a). This is useful since Hawkins is primarily concerned with using his theory to explain language universals, and so it provides us with an ideal opportunity to explore the origin of typological fitness.

Hawkins' theory is based on the idea of defining a measure of tree-complexity associated with a particular node in a constituent that is relative to a particular psycholinguistic operation. Any processing operation involves a subset of the tree structure of an utterance that is relevant to the operation – a *structural domain* in Hawkins' terminology. The assumption is that processing mechanisms that have to operate as quickly as possible prefer *minimal structural domains*. Two applications of this idea are discussed here: minimal constituent recognition domains, and minimal relativization domains.

3.1 *Immediate constituent attachment*

One of the most important jobs of the parser is to attach constituents to mother nodes in the left-to-right processing of an utterance. Hawkins

(1990, and the bulk of 1994a) is concerned with the implications of assuming that the parser will prefer constituent orders whose immediate constituents (ICs) are attached as rapidly as possible to a particular mother once attachment starts.[2] Importantly, it is possible to attach all ICs to a mother, based on a subset of the words dominated by that mother. This structural domain is the set of words that starts from the point in the string where the first IC dominated by the mother is constructed and ends where the last IC is constructed.

The relevant feature of the string of words presented to the parser thus becomes the order of the categories that construct immediate constituents. One type of category (and the most important for Hawkins) that is involved in construction is the mother-node constructing category (MNCC). These are categories which *uniquely determine* a mother node. These MNCCs are similar to heads in traditional syntactic theory, but may also include some closed-class function words such as determiners which uniquely construct noun phrases. So, for example, in the verb phrase *watched the cricket*, *watched* can construct VP, and *the* and *cricket* can both construct NP. A simple demonstration of the impact of reordering such categories can be had from some examples of Particle Movement in English. In the sentences below, there are three MNCCs which construct categories that are immediately dominated by the verb phrase: *looked*, *the* and *up*. As the distance between the first of the MNCCs and the last increases so too does the awkwardness of the construction. The last sentence is the most acceptable since the three MNCCs are adjacent.

(1) John **looked the** number **up**.

(2) John **looked the** number of the pub **up**.

(3) John **looked the** number of the pub on Rose Street **up**.

(4) John **looked up the** number of the pub on Rose Street.

This example gives a flavour of Hawkins' approach, although the details of his metric are rather more complex than there is room for here. We will return to IC attachment later when we compare this processing asymmetry with the cross-linguistic data.

2 Attachment of ICs to a mother does not necessarily happen straight away. A constituent may be recognized on its right boundary, for example, in which case a look-ahead buffer for non-attached constituents is used. For the details of Hawkins' approach refer to one of the cited texts.

3.2 *Relativization*

Of course, IC attachment is not the only problem posed to the parser in attempting to build a representation of the structure of an input string. One of the other problems that Hawkins looks at is that of associating a trace or resumptive pronoun with the head noun in a relative clause. Just as IC attachment involves a subset of nodes in the tree, the size of the structural domain for relativization will vary depending on the type of relative clause and will typically be less than the whole of the clause.

Hawkins' (1994a: 28–31) definitions for relativization domains are given below:

The *structural complexity of a relative clause* is calculated by counting the nodes in the *relativization domain*.
The *relativization domain* consists of that subset of nodes within the NP dominating relative clause that structurally integrate the trace or pronoun.
The set of nodes which *structurally integrate X in C* are:
all nodes dominating X within C (including C itself)
all sisters of X[3]
all sisters of the nodes dominating X within C.

These definitions capture the idea that relating a trace (or pronoun) with a head noun becomes more complex the more that trace (or pronoun) is embedded within the subordinate clause. Figures 22.1 and 22.2 show how the relativization domain is larger in an object relative than in a subject relative, since the trace is more deeply embedded.

Just as the complexity predictions for the order of MNCCs are reflected in examples such as Particle Movement, the prediction that subject relatives should be easier to process than object relatives is borne out by the psycholinguistic literature on the subject (see e.g. Keenan & Hawkins 1987).

4 Typological asymmetries

In the previous section two processing asymmetries have been reviewed. The evidence that universals are fit comes when we compare processing with the cross-linguistic data. For both the processing asymmetries above (and many others), there are corresponding typological asymmetries.

3 In fact, some sisters may be excluded if the language has a flatter configurational structure. See Hawkins (1994a: 27–28) for discussion.

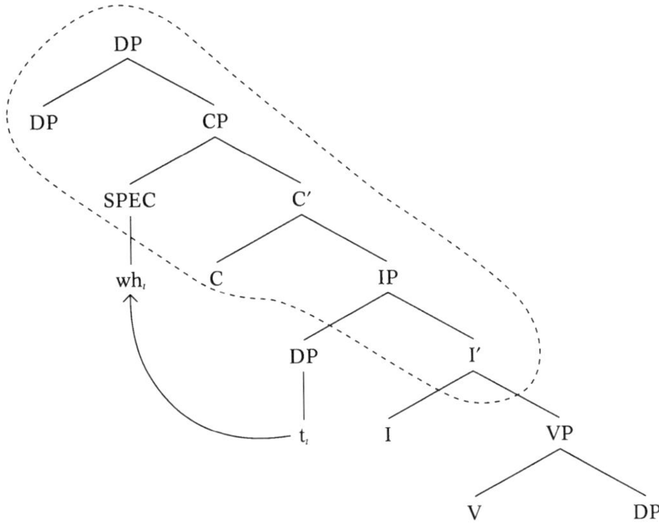

Figure 22.1 Subject relative with domain circled.

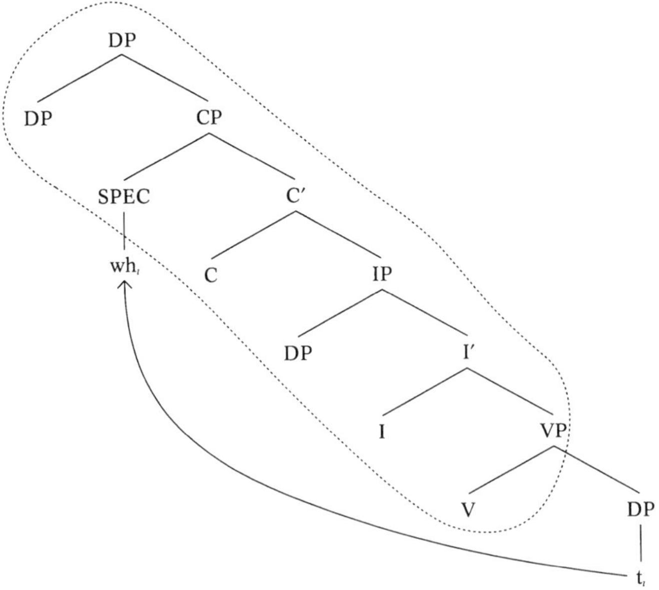

Figure 22.2 Object relative with domain circled.

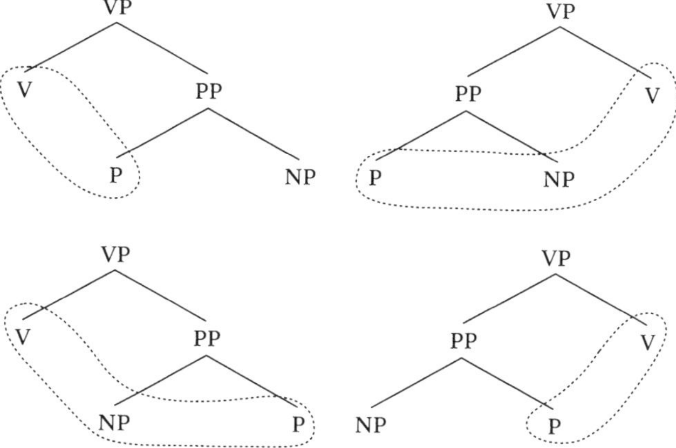

Figure 22.3 Four VP-internal PPs.

4.1 *Consistent branching direction*

On the basis of a large sample of languages and using a method intended to compensate for biases in the sample due to historical relatedness of languages and areal groupings, Dryer (1992) formulates the following universal: 'a pair of elements X and Y will employ the order XY significantly more often among OV languages if and only if X is a nonphrasal category and Y is a phrasal category' (p. 89). One of the features of this *Branching Direction Theory* is that it predicts that heads will tend to order consistently on one side or another of non-heads cross-linguistically – a general tendency that has long been recognized.

One of the clearest predictions that Dryer's universal makes and that was recognized earlier by Greenberg (1963) is the correlation of the order of verb and object and the order of adposition and NP:

VO ↔ PrNP

Figure 22.3 shows the basic structures of VP-internal PPs in the four possible language types defined by this typology. The nodes that have been circled are the ones involved in immediate constituent attachment for the mother VP. Just as in the Particle Movement examples, the parser prefers the MNCCs to be close together. In this case, the relevant MNCCs are the verb and adposition. Clearly the structures that are easier to process are the ones that are more common cross-linguistically. A similar argument can be made for other predictions of Dryer's universal if non-branching categories tend to be MNCCs.[4]

This, then, is an example of typological fitness. The Branching Direction Theory, a statement about the distribution of languages in the world, dovetails with the minimal attachment domain theory, a statement of the processing complexity of particular utterances.

4.2 *Object relativization*

A similar fit of universal and function can be found if we look at the cross-linguistic distribution of relative clause types. The well-known implicational hierarchy of Keenan & Comrie (1977) puts noun-phrase types in order of accessibility to relativization:

> Subject>Direct Object>Indirect Object>Oblique>Genitive>Object of Comparison
>
> **Accessibility Hierarchy Constraint** 'If a language can relativise any position on the AH with a primary strategy [a strategy for forming relatives that is used for subjects], then it can relativise all higher positions with that strategy' (Comrie & Keenan 1979: 653).

This hierarchy unpacks as a series of chained implicational statements:

> (Object of Comparison → Genitive) &
> (Genitive → Oblique) &
> (Oblique → Indirect Object) &
> (Indirect Object → Direct Object) &
> (Direct Object → Subject)

For this chapter, we will concentrate on the fourth of these: if a language relativizes indirect objects with a primary strategy, then it will relativize direct objects with a primary strategy.

Hawkins argues that this typological asymmetry reflects a psycholinguistic asymmetry in terms of the minimal structural domain for relativization: 'The minimal SD [structural domain] of a DO [direct

4 This will not always be the case, which is why Dryer's statement goes further than consistent head ordering. For example, Dryer notes that the order of adjective and noun does *not* correlate with VO/OV order. These discrepancies between Hawkins' processing theory and the cross-linguistic data may be the result of a problem with either the processing theory or the sampling method. Another possibility, however, is that the match between typology and processing may not always be one-to-one for some other reason (see Kirby, in press, for discussion of problems like this). I will not go into these mismatches here, although it is important that they be a focus of future typological and psycholinguistic research.

object] is properly included in that of an IO [indirect object], since a clause with an IO generally requires an accompanying DO and also a SU [subject], whereas a DO can occur both with and without an IO, i.e. Min SD(DO)⊂Min SD(IO)' (Hawkins 1994a: 39). This is also backed up by the psycholinguistic literature as noted earlier (e.g. Keenan & Hawkins (1987) in their experiments on a repetition task with English-speaking children).

Once again, there is a clear fit of the typological facts and the preference of the parser as predicted by Hawkins' theory and backed-up by psycholinguistic experiments. The explanation for this fit is the focus of the remainder of this chapter.

5 A phylogenetic explanation?

The appearance of design is a characteristic of biological structures whose evolution is mediated by natural selection. Since language is a product of a biological organism – part of our *extended phenotype* in Dawkins' (1982) terms – then a phylogenetic explanation for the adaptive nature of its universals seems the obvious place to look.

5.1 *Natural selection and the LAD*

It is widely believed that the human ability to acquire language is at least in some part innately given, and that the Chomskyan Universal Grammar (UG) is embodied in this ability. Since we may assume that on the whole this biological endowment is shared by all members of our species, then we have a ready explanation for universals – they are simply the result of idiosyncratic properties of the innate mechanism for acquisition (see e.g. Hoekstra & Kooij 1988).

Various authors (e.g. Hurford 1989, 1991; Pinker & Bloom 1990) have argued that a complex innately specified language acquisition device (LAD) must have evolved through natural selection.

> All we have argued is that human language, like other specialized biological systems, evolved by natural selection. Our conclusion is based on two facts that we would think would be entirely uncontroversial: Language shows signs of complex design for the communication of propositional structures, and the only explanation for the origins of organs with complex design is the process of natural selection. [Pinker & Bloom 1990: 726]

In particular, the LAD is claimed to have evolved through selection *for the function it now fulfils*. This relies on the assumption that human language confers a survival or reproductive advantage on the organisms that have it. This assumption is to be fairly well accepted, although when we get to specific features of UG there seems to be greater unease. Lightfoot (1991: 69), for example, pours scorn on this argument, suggesting: 'the Subjacency Condition has many virtues, but I am sure that it could not have increased the chances of having fruitful sex'. We shall return to the Subjacency and Sex problem in the concluding section, but for the moment let us continue following the logic of the phylogenetic argument.

5.2 *Selection for parsability*

In order to solve our problem of the origin of typological fitness all we need to do now is argue that different possible LADs could be selected for on the basis of the parsability of the output of the grammars they allow to be acquired. Newmeyer (1991) has made precisely this argument with respect to features of the LAD specific to the Government and Binding theory of syntax (see e.g. Haegeman 1991): 'It is quite plausible that the design of the grammatical model as a whole or *some particular grammatical principle* might have become encoded in our genes by virtue of its being so successful in facilitating communication that the survival and reproductive possibilities of those possessing it were enhanced' (Newmeyer 1991: 5; emphasis my own).

One such feature of UG that Newmeyer approaches in this fashion is the Subjacency Condition (the object of Lightfoot's scorn as mentioned above). Briefly, the Subjacency Condition is a universal that constrains the structural distance between two elements that are related by some rule of the grammar (Riemsdijk & Williams 1986: 62, cited in Newmeyer 1991: 12):

> Subjacency Condition No rule can relate X, Y in the structure
>
> $$\ldots X \ldots [_{\alpha} \ldots [_{\beta} \ldots Y \ldots$$
>
> or
>
> $$\ldots Y \ldots]_{\beta} \ldots]_{\alpha} \ldots X \ldots$$
>
> where α and β are bounding nodes.

In English, the bounding nodes are IP and NP, hence the ungrammaticality of the sentences below, where *who* has moved over two bounding nodes (with no intermediate 'landing site'[5]):

5 See, for example, Haegeman 1991: §6.2 for further details of the applicability of the Subjacency Condition.

(5) a *I met the fan who$_i$ we played $_{NP}$[the song which$_j$ $_{IP}$[t_i liked t_j]]
b *Who$_i$ did $_{IP}$[Matt tell you when$_j$ $_{IP}$[he had met $t_i t_j$]]

The standard assumption is that the Subjacency Condition is one of a set of constraints on the application of the transformation move-α that form part of our innate knowledge of language. Although there is some cross-linguistic variability in the inventory of bounding nodes, the constraint can, in principle, be applied to any language. How can the existence of this constraint be explained? Berwick & Weinberg (1984) point out that the Subjacency Condition tends to rule out sentences in which the distance between the *wh*-element and its co-indexed gap is long. As already discussed above, there is a pressure from the parser to keep this distance to a minimum (although clearly there is not a direct parallel between the formulation of the Subjacency Condition and minimal relativization domains). Newmeyer's argument is that this parsing pressure led to the biological selection of a language acquisition device that had some way of eliminating the worst *wh*-extractions from the language.

6 A glossogenetic explanation

Although the argument presented in the previous section is persuasive, there is an alternative that should be considered – one which will allow us to approach the specific examples of typological fitness that were reviewed earlier. It will be argued in this section that languages *themselves* adapt to aid their own 'survival' in the transmission from speaker to speaker. In this view, selection for parsability acts on a historical rather than biological timescale, or in Hurford's (1990) terms, this is a *glossogenetic* as opposed to *phylogenetic* explanation. A glossogenetic explanation for fitness relies on a theory of linguistic selection. Such a theory is set out in more detail elsewhere (e.g. Kirby 1994, 1996, 1997), but a sketch of its main components will be given here.

Selection takes place whenever there is differential replication of information through a dynamic system. Gell-Mann's (1992) treatment of complex adaptive systems treats the objects over which selection is made as *schemata*. In his view, schemata 'unfold' in the environment to produce effects or behaviour which have consequences for the viability of the schema in terms of survival to a later generation. There is therefore a cycle of:

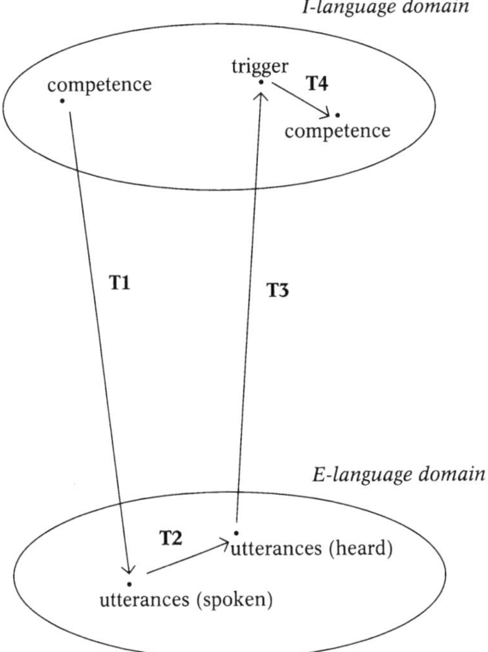

Figure 22.4 Transformations within and between I- and E-language domains.

(a) unfolding of schemata to produce environmental effect,
(b) differential selection of schemata based on that effect,
(c) compression of information in environment to produce next generation of schemata.

Notice that this cycle involves two different types of object: the schema itself, and its 'external' effects. It is the transformations between these objects that give rise to the selective effect. Lewontin (1974) (cited in Sober (1984)) talks about biological evolution in exactly these terms, highlighting the importance of transformation between genotype and phenotype in biology. Kirby (1997) adapts Lewontin's map of the transformations for linguistics, replacing genotypes with *I-language* and phenotypes with *E-language* (Figure 22.4).

For us the important transformations on this diagram are the ones that map between the I- and E-language domains: production (**T1**) and parsing (**T3**). If we assume that the transformations are not perfect mappings from competence to performance (and vice versa), then we have selection. To put it another way: as long as the only way for language to be transmitted from generation to generation is through being repeatedly produced and parsed, then the form of the language that survives this process will naturally be adapted to being produced and parsed. This is what I mean by saying that languages adapt to aid their *own* survival.

7 Computer simulations

Now that there is a basic framework in which to think about linguistic selection, we need some way of seeing what effect various possible processing pressures have on the eventual distribution of languages. The methodology employed here is to use computational simulations of populations of language users. This allows us to test exactly what effect changing the selection criteria over utterances has on the languages spoken. In this way, the computer provides us with an excellent tool for testing the behaviour of complex adaptive systems whose behaviour is the *emergent* result of the interactions of many individuals.

7.1 *General set-up of the simulations*

The simulations are made up of three central components, each of which consists of a two-dimensional toroidal surface or array of elements arranged so that each element has four neighbours (above, below, to the left, and to the right). The first array of elements represents speakers, the second represents utterances and the third, acquirers. What form each of these kinds of element can take depends on the particular processing metric being tested.

Each generation, all the speakers randomly produce utterances in line with their particular grammars. At this point, the choice of which utterances to produce may be biased according to some measure of production complexity – this is the kind of selection associated with transformation **T1** in Figure 22.4. After the production phase has taken place, all the acquirers take a sample of the utterances produced by the speakers closest to their position in the array (the speaker in the same position, and the four neighbours). Again, this sample may be biased according to some measure of parsing complexity – the selection in **T3** in Figure 22.4. The resultant sample of utterances is used to set the acquirer's grammar. Finally, the acquirers become the speakers of the next iteration of the simulation (see Figure 22.5).

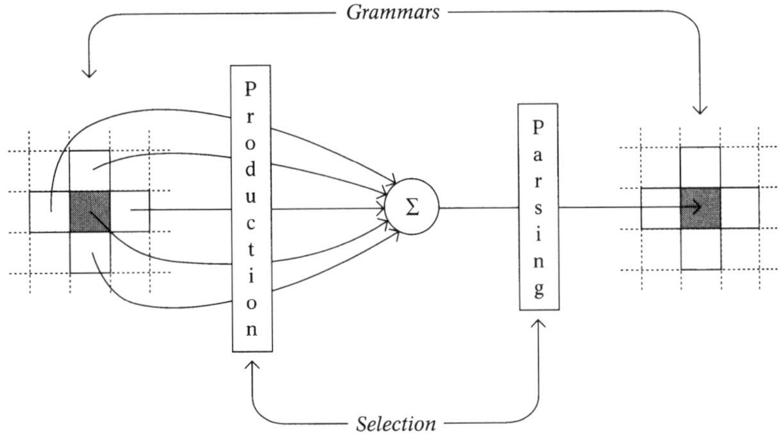

Figure 22.5 Computer simulation of glossogenetic adaptation.

7.2 *The S-shaped curve*

Kroch (1994) refers to situations where languages change the relative frequency of variants as *grammar competition*. Under his formulation, two or more broadly syntactic doublets behave in the same way as morphological doublets in competition for a paradigm slot. This view follows from a move in syntactic analysis to treat cross-linguistic variation as a reflection of variation in the properties and inventories of functional heads.

> If we take this view seriously, we are led to the conclusion that syntactic variation should be governed by the same principles as variation in morphology, since the locus of the variability in the two cases is the same – the formative. Just as morphological variants which are not functionally distinguished are disallowed, so we should not expect to find variation between semantically non-distinct syntactic heads. To the extent that such variability is found, it poses the same theoretical problem as the appearance of doublets does in morphology. [1994: 5]

Kroch points out that the 'blocking effect' in morphology (whereby the presence of an irregular form in a paradigm slot blocks the occupation of that slot by a regular form) is a central tenet of modern morphology. Doublets *are* in fact often observed in languages; however, if the doublets are functionally equivalent, speakers 'learn either one or the other form in the course of basic language acquisition, but not both' (p. 6). Later on, the same speakers may recognize the existence of the variant form, which 'for them has the status of a foreign accent' (p. 6). Finally, one of these two doublets will tend to win out in a particular community or the two forms will become functionally differentiated.

The first example of the simulation in action looks at the time course of change where there are two such variants in competition. This is the simplest possible example, with only two possible grammars and two possible utterances. Furthermore, for the run displayed here, the spatial organization of the population described in the last section is 'switched off' so that all speakers can potentially contribute to all acquirers' trigger experience.

Imagine a situation where there is a language with basic VO order and postpositions. This type of language is sub-optimal with regard to rapid IC attachment in constructions such as $_{VP}[V\ _{PP}[NP\ P]\ ]$ since the structural domain for attachment of the ICs to the VP stretches from the initial verb to the postposition (over the noun phrase). Now, if prepositions were to be introduced as a minor variant, perhaps during language contact, then this variant will be selected more frequently by the parser than the postpositional variant to trigger acquisition.

In the simulation of this scenario, the initial speech community is made up of 450 speakers with the postpositional variant, and 50 speakers with prepositions. Each utterance is assigned a 'parsability score' which is based on Hawkins' suggested metric for VO languages (Hawkins 1990: 238).[6] In general, for an individual acquirer, the probability of a particular variant v being acquired is:

$$P(v) = \frac{\sum_{i \in I_v} w_i}{\sum_{j \in (I_v \cup I_{v'})} w_j}$$

where I_v is the set of utterances in the input that can trigger the acquisition of v; w_i is the parsing complexity of an utterance; and v' is the competitor for v. The result of this simulation run is given in Figure 22.6.

The striking feature of this result is its similarity to the S-shaped curve that Kroch (1989a, b) finds in his data for the rise of periphrastic *do* in English – a case of the replacement by competition of one variant by another. This result is also found by Niyogi & Berwick (1995) in their analysis of the dynamics of parameterized grammatical change, although in their case, the complexity of parsing is not considered. Research is

6 This means that $W_{prepositions} = 1$ and $W_{postpositions} = 0.79$ in the following equation.

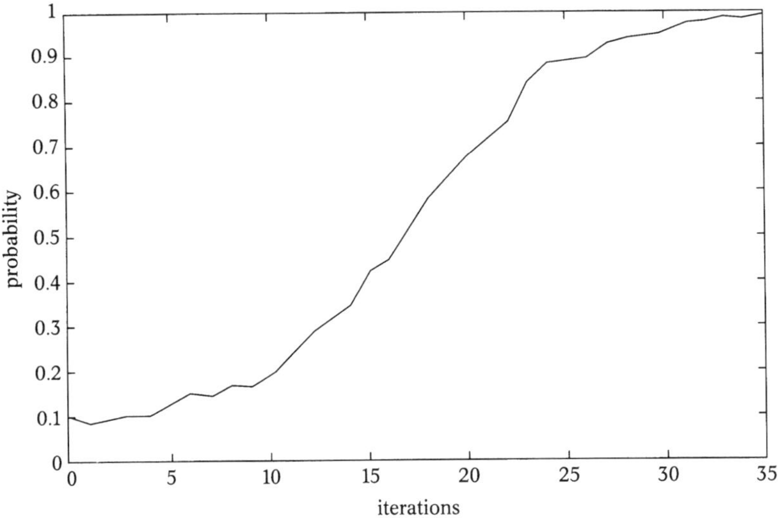

Figure 22.6 The S-shaped curve.

currently underway to analyse more carefully the dynamic properties of parametrically specified grammars under the influence of parsing pressures (Clark 1996). For the moment, however, the closeness of the time course of change resulting from the simulation to that observed in the historical data is certainly encouraging.

7.3 *Emergence of branching direction*

The previous example simply demonstrated one form taking over another in a community. In order to show how typological fitness can emerge, the simulation should give rise to more than one 'winning' language type in a multi-dimensional typology. Consider the case of consistent branching direction; the minimum we need to show this emerging is two variable orthogonal typological parameters, such as verb/object order and adposition/noun order. In the previous example, only adposition order was variable. If both are variable, then we should see the emergence of a correlation between VO and prepositions *and* OV and postpositions.

In this more complex example, the parsability of a particular variant is dependent on the proportions of the orthogonal variant in the input. This is modelled by the following complexity functions:

Figure 22.7 Initial state of the simulation.

$$w_{i \in I_{prep}} = \alpha|I_{vo}| + (1 - \alpha)|I_{ov}|$$
$$w_{i \in I_{postp}} = \alpha|I_{ov}| + (1 - \alpha)|I_{vo}|$$
$$w_{i \in I_{vo}} = \alpha|I_{prep}| + (1 - \alpha)|I_{postp}|$$
$$w_{i \in I_{ov}} = \alpha|I_{postp}| + (1 - \alpha)|I_{prep}|$$

where $|I_v|$ is the number of utterances in the input that trigger the acquisition of v, and α is a measure of relatedness of verb/object order and adposition order varying from 0 to 1. With α less than 0.5, VO and postpositions are correlated in terms of complexity; with α greater than 0.5, VO and prepositions are correlated. For the run shown here, α is 0.6.

For this simulation, a 40×40 grid of speakers was set up so that each speaker initially had a random grammar corresponding to either VO&Prep, VO&Postp, OV&Prep, or OV&Postp. This initial condition is shown in Figure 22.7. Each shade of square corresponds to a different grammar. After 30 iterations of the simulation, consistent branching direction emerges (Figure 22.8). The language types have organized themselves into two major groups spatially, corresponding to left- and right-branching. These groups shift slowly over time, both in size and position. The inconsistently branching languages remain in the minority, occurring as transitional types as a particular area switches from one order to another where two language groups are in contact.

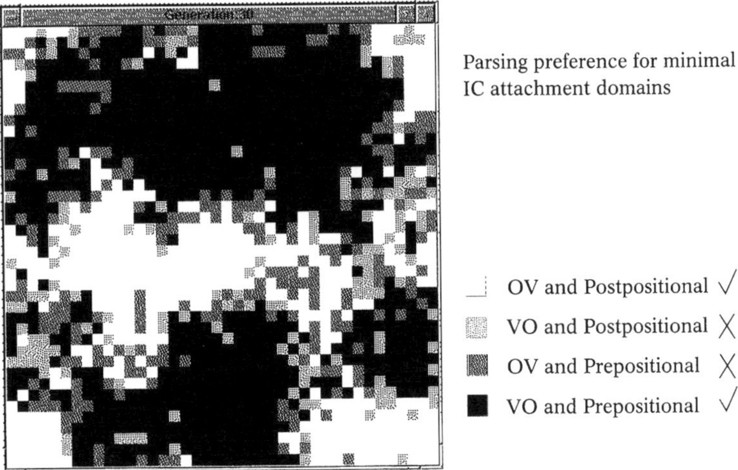

Figure 22.8 The emergence of branching direction.

This simulation shows that large sub-groupings in a speech community can emerge and remain stable even though only *individuals* are being modelled. More importantly, typological fitness also emerges. The language groups organize themselves so that they allow a particular variant only if it makes utterances easy to parse, given the other variants in the language. This global property appears to be inevitable given the large number of individuals interacting on a purely local basis, as long as this interaction is differentially successful for particular variants.

7.4 *Emergence of the object relative universal*

The final example shows how an implicational hierarchy may emerge given two types of selection in conflict. Consider the object relative universal presented earlier:

Indirect Object → Direct Object

In order to test if this emerges from the simulation we need to set up the complexity of indirect and direct object relatives:

$$0 < w_{IO} < w_{DO} < 0.5$$
$$w_{v'} = (1 - w_v)$$

This means that indirect object relatives are more complex to parse than direct object relatives (as shown in section 3.2), and both are more complex than a competing variant that does not involve object relativization. Such a non-object relative variant might be a subject relative in which the object has been promoted by a passive, for example. See Keenan & Hawkins (1987) for some discussion of the complexity of promoted and non-promoted relatives.

The problem with this set-up is that, given any set of values of w_{IO} and w_{DO} that conform to the inequality above, the end result is always solely languages with no object relativization. However, what we find cross-linguistically are:

(a) languages with no object relatives,
(b) languages with only direct object relatives, and
(c) languages with both direct and indirect object relatives.

What seems to be happening is that languages are adapting to fit the only processing pressures that are about in the simulation – in other words, the pressures relating to the complexity of object relatives. The inevitable result of this is that these relatives will be avoided altogether.

On the other hand, it is possible object relatives are not rejected wholesale since *the alternative is also complex*. The sentences below show an object relative, and its derived-subject variant:

(6) The batsman who Atherton dropped got a century.

(7) The batsman who was dropped by Atherton got a century.

The second example has a lower parsing complexity because it relativizes the subject of the subordinate clause.[7] Counteracting this, it involves extra morphemes to support the passivization of *the embedded clause*. Kirby (1997) argues that the speaker (as opposed to the acquirer) will select from variant forms on the basis of the morphological (as opposed to parsing) complexity. This means that there is a *competing motivation* involved in the selection of relative clause types in the cycle of acquisition and use.

If this is the case, we need to include a distinction in the simulation between the two types of complexity:

p-complexity The complexity of the utterance from the point of view of the acquirer (parsing-complexity):
$0 < w^p_{IO} < w^p_{DO} < 0.5$

7 This is not exactly what Hawkins (1994b) predicts; however, it seems to be consonant with the data from repetition tasks in Keenan & Hawkins (1987).

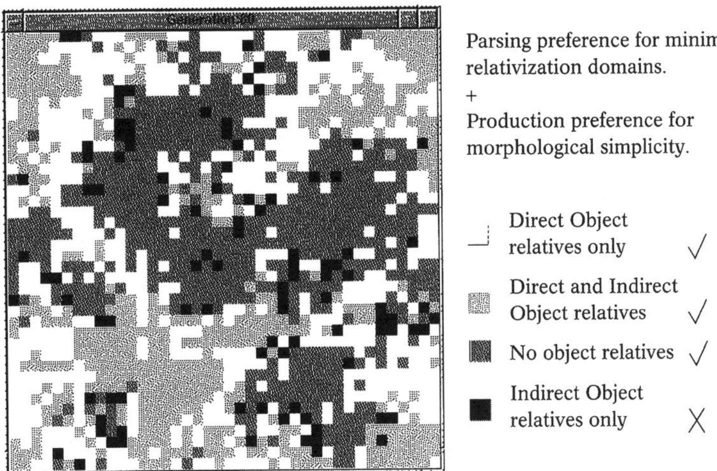

Figure 22.9 The emergence of an implicational universal.

m-complexity The complexity of the utterance from the point of view of the speaker (morphological-complexity):
$0 < w^{m}_{IO'} = w^{m}_{DO'} < 0.5$

The result of running the simulation with these complexity considerations is shown in Figure 22.9. The actual settings of the various complexity measures is rather more complex than in previous simulations since the relative prominence of p- and m-complexity in the selection of utterances varies dependent on other features in the language, which are assumed to be random with respect to relativization possibilities. For further details see Kirby (1997).

The result shows clearly that the implicational universal emerges out of the conflict between hearer- and speaker-related processing considerations. This, then, is a paradigm example of the emergence of typological fitness. An individual language may 'decide' to impose zero, one or two object relatives upon its hearers (in response to the needs of speakers), but the relatives it allows will always be the ones which hearers find easier to parse. All this emerges once again solely from individual language users interacting on a purely local basis without any teleological motivation.

8 Conclusion: language evolution as the interaction of adaptive systems

In this chapter, I have shown that the occurrence of typological fitness does not necessarily mean we should immediately conclude that there is a phylogenetic explanation for that fitness. The other possibility is that languages may adapt themselves on a glossogenetic timescale simply by virtue of their need to propagate themselves through the medium of communication. The computer simulation results show that, even with very simple assumptions, complex adaptive behaviour emerges, with stable end states which show a characteristic 'appearance of design'. None of this rules out the phylogenetic explanation, however, and in this final section I will conclude with some speculative remarks about how this glossogenetic perspective may solve some problems that beset any potential account for the evolution of the human language faculty.

The problems with the phylogenetic account outlined in section 5 are to do with the need to assume that a cross-linguistic constraint could evolve by giving a survival advantage to an individual who has a mutated LAD that gives rise to that constraint. Even if that particular constraint will in the long run give rise to languages that have constructions that are easy to parse, it is still difficult to see how the individual's survival chances are increased. The classic problems (which Pinker & Bloom (1990) attempt to solve) are:

(a) How is the selfish individual better off if her output is easier to parse?
(b) How is an innovation in a single individual any use when language is a shared activity?
(c) Even if the previous two points are not problems for evolution given enough time, does that mean language could not have evolved as quickly as it seems to have?
(d) Does the Subjacency Condition really increase the chances of fruitful sex by making sentences easier to parse?

In view of the glossogenetic approach, we can say that these questions become irrelevant. Languages evolve orders-of-magnitude faster than their users' species, and they appear to do so in order to increase the survival chances of the rules with which they are made up. This just happens to make things easier for us as speakers and hearers.

Where does this leave innateness? Well, we can simply say that the branching direction universal and the Accessibility Hierarchy are not innate. In other words, they are not hard-wired into whatever part of our brain carries out language acquisition. But what about other universals, such as the Subjacency Condition, that have been argued by many – and for reasons other than their usefulness for parsing – to be part of our innate endowment?

In the view set out in this chapter, there is absolutely no need to reject innateness. Instead we need to realize that the LAD has evolved for the specific (and totally selfish from the individual's point of view) purpose of *learning language quickly*. Even if language were to prove to be acquirable using some kind of general-purpose learning mechanism, there is no particular reason why it should be acquired this way. If certain features of the languages that humans need to learn show up again and again, it makes sense for these features to be part of our innate endowment so that we are not forced to learn them from scratch. The Baldwin Effect (see e.g. Baldwin 1896; Hinton & Nowlan 1987; Kirby & Hurford 1997a) predicts that just this sort of nativization will arise wherever learning and evolution interact.

If languages have adapted glossogenetically to avoid some type of construction consistently because it is hard to parse, then an individual will be at an advantage who does not need to learn this fact and instead has it given innately. In other words, the Subjacency Condition may be an innate 'fossil' of a glossogenetic adaptation to avoid long-distance dependencies. In this way, the LAD does not evolve to constrain languages to be better communicative tools – this is simply a by-product of the evolution of faster and better ways of learning a cultural artifact that is itself an adaptive system.

Future research into the evolution of the language faculty must take this interaction of adaptive systems seriously. We can imagine a type of bootstrapping process where a particular stage in the phylogenetic evolution of language licenses certain kinds of glossogenetic adaptation. If the fitness of individuals is related to their ability to acquire the language around them, then any universals that emerge from this glossogenetic adaptation will in turn alter the fitness of the language faculties around at the time. If this leads to the evolution of those faculties, then the types of glossogenetic adaptation that are possible will also change. In this way, phylogenetic evolution may 'track' glossogenetic evolution solely through selection pressure to learn quickly.

This view of the evolution of language raises many questions, and challenges our understanding of complex adaptive systems. In this chapter, I have not *shown* that glossogenetic adaptation interacts with phylogenetic evolution – simply that wherever there is adaptation, natural selection is not the only explanation. Further modelling work is needed to marry the type of simulation discussed in this chapter and those that look at the evolution of learning (e.g. Ackley & Littman 1991). This will require an interesting synthesis of functionalist accounts of diachrony and universals on the one hand and generative/innatist accounts of language acquisition on the other (see Kirby & Hurford 1997b for an approach to this kind of modelling). Perhaps the biggest challenge facing those studying the evolution of language is finding common ground between the two.

References

Ackley, David & Littman, Michael (1991). Interactions between learning and evolution. In Langton, C. G., Taylor, C., Farmer, J. D. & Ramussen, S. (eds.) *Artificial Life II*. Redwood City, CA: Addison-Wesley, pp. 487–509.

Baldwin, J. M. (1896). A new factor in evolution. *American Naturalist*, 30, 441–451.

Berwick, R. C. & Weinberg, A. S. (1984). *The Grammatical Basis of Linguistic Performance: Language Use and Acquisition*. Cambridge, MA: MIT Press.

Clark, Robert (1996). Internal and external factors affecting language change: a computational model. Master's thesis, University of Edinburgh.

Comrie, Bernard (1981). *Language Universals and Linguistic Typology*. Oxford: Basil Blackwell.

& Keenan, Edward (1979). Noun phrase accessibility revisited. *Language*, 55, 649–664.

Croft, William (1990). *Typology and Universals*. Cambridge: Cambridge University Press.

Cutler, A., Hawkins, J. & Gilligan, G. (1985). The suffixing preference: a processing explanation. *Linguistics*, 23, 723–758.

Cziko, Gary. (1995). *Without Miracles: Universal Selection Theory and the Second Darwinian Revolution*. Cambridge, MA: MIT Press.

Dawkins, Richard (1982). *The Extended Phenotype – The Gene as the Unit of Selection*. Oxford: W. H. Freeman and Company.

Dryer, Matthew (1992). The Greenbergian word order correlations. *Language*, 68, 81–138.

Gell-Mann, Murray (1992). Complexity and complex adaptive systems. In Hawkins, J. A. & Gell-Mann, M. (eds.) *The Evolution of Human Languages*. Redwood City, CA: Addison-Wesley.

Greenberg, Joseph (1963). Some universals of grammar with particular reference to the order of meaningful elements. In Greenberg, Joseph (ed.) *Universals of Language*. Cambridge, MA: MIT Press, pp. 73–113.

Haegeman, Liliane (1991). *Introduction to Government and Binding Theory*. Oxford: Blackwell.

Hawkins, John A. (1988). Explaining language universals. In Hawkins, John A. (ed.) *Explaining Language Universals*. Oxford: Basil Blackwell.

(1990). A parsing theory of word order universals. *Linguistic Inquiry*, 21, 223–261.
(1994a). *A Performance Theory of Order and Constituency*. Cambridge: Cambridge University Press.
(1994b). Some issues in a performance theory of word order. Ms., University of Southern California.
Hinton, G. & Nowlan, S. (1987). How learning can guide evolution. *Complex Systems*, 1, 495–502.
Hoekstra, Teun & Kooij, Jan G. (1988). The innateness hypothesis. In Hawkins, John A. (ed.) *Explaining Language Universals*. Oxford: Blackwell.
Hurford, James (1989). Biological evolution of the Saussurean sign as a component of the language acquisition device. *Lingua*, 77, 187–222.
(1990). Nativist and functional explanations in language acquisition. In Roca, I. M. (ed.) *Logical Issues in Language Acquisition*. Dordrecht: Foris Publications, pp. 85–136.
(1991). The evolution of the critical period for language acquisition. *Cognition*, 40, 159–201.
Keenan, Edward & Comrie, Bernard (1977). Noun phrase accessibility and universal grammar. *Linguistic Inquiry*, 8, 63–99.
& Hawkins, Sarah (1987). The psychological validity of the accessibility hierarchy. In Keenan, Edward (ed.) *Universal Grammar: 15 Essays*. London: Croom Helm, pp. 60–85.
Kirby, Simon (1994). Adaptive explanations for language universals: a model of Hawkins' performance theory. *Sprachtypologie und Universalienforschung*, 47, 186–210.
(1996). The emergence of universals: function, selection and innateness. University of Edinburgh. Ph.D. thesis.
(1997). Competing motivations and emergence: explaining implicational hierarchies. *Language Typology* 1(1), 5–32.
(in press). Constraints on constraints, or the limits of functional adaptation. To appear in Noonan, Mickey, Moravcsik, Edith & Newmeyer, Frederick (eds.) *Functionalism Formalism in Linguistics*. Proceedings of the 23rd annual UWM Linguistics Symposium, University of Wisconsin-Milwaukee, 1996.
& Hurford, James (1997a). The evolution of incremental learning: language, development and critical periods. University of Edinburgh Occasional Paper in Linguistics EOPL-97-2.
& Hurford, James (1997b). Learning, culture and evolution in the origin of linguistic constraints. In Husbands, Phil & Harvey, Inman (eds.) *Fourth European Conference on Artificial Life*. Cambridge, MA: MIT Press, pp. 493–502.
Kroch, Anthony (1989a). Function and grammar in the history of English. In Fasold, Ralph & Schiffrin, Deborah (eds.) *Language Change and Variation*. Amsterdam: Benjamins, pp. 133–172.
(1989b). Reflexes of grammar in patterns of language change. *Language Variation and Change*, 1, 199–244.

(1994). Morphosyntactic variation. In Beals, K. (ed.) *Papers from the 30th Regional Meeting of the Chicago Linguistics Society*. Chicago: Chicago Linguistics Society.

Lewontin, R. (1974). *The Genetic Basis of Evolutionary Change*. New York: Columbia University Press.

Lightfoot, David (1991). Subjacency and sex. *Language and Communication*, 11 (1–2), 67–69.

Newmeyer, Frederick J. (1991). Functional explanation in linguistics and the origins of language. *Language and Communication*, 11, 3–28.

Niyogi, Partha & Berwick, Robert (1995). The logical problem of language change. Technical Report AI Memo 1516 / CBCL Paper 115, MIT AI Laboratory and Center for Biological and Computational Learning, Department of Brain and Cognitive Sciences.

Pinker, Steven & Bloom, Paul (1990). Natural language and natural selection. *Behavioral and Brain Sciences*, 13, 707–784.

Riemsdijk, H. Van & Williams, E. (1986). *Introduction to the Theory of Grammar*. Cambridge, MA: MIT Press.

Sober, Elliot (1984). *The Nature of Selection: Evolutionary Theory in Philosophical Focus*. Cambridge, MA: MIT Press.

23 Synthesizing the origins of language and meaning using coevolution, self-organization and level formation

LUC STEELS

1 Introduction

A good way to test a model of a particular phenomenon is to build simulations or artificial systems that exhibit phenomena the same as, or similar to, those one is trying to model. This methodology can also be applied to the problem of the origins of language and meaning. Concretely, experiments with robotic agents and software agents can be set up to test whether certain hypothesized mechanisms indeed lead to the formation of language and the creation of new meaning. This chapter reports on recent work following this approach.

The methodology of computer simulations and experiments with robotic systems is in itself neutral with respect to a theory of the origins and evolution of language. For example, Gillis, Durieux & Daelemans (1995) report on research to test through computational experiments the feasibility of the Chomskyan Principles-and-Parameters hypothesis and Batali (1994) has been investigating how a universal grammar, encoded as recurrent neural networks with prior weights, might result from an evolutionary process. In my own work the following two hypotheses are investigated.

(a) *Language is an emergent phenomenon.* Language is emergent in two ways. First of all, it is a mass phenomenon actualized by the different agents interacting with each other. No single individual has a complete view of the language nor does anyone control the language. In this sense, language is like a cloud of birds which attains and keeps its coherence based on individual behaviours enacted by each bird. Second, language is emergent in the sense that it spontaneously forms itself once the appropriate physiological, psychological and social conditions are satisfied, and it becomes more complex due to its own dynamics and pressure to express an ever-expanding set of conceptualizations and speech acts.

(b) *Language and meaning coevolve.* Language is not a mere complex system of labels for concepts and conceptual structures which already exist prior to language, but, rather, the complexification of language contributes to the ability to form richer conceptualizations which then in turn cause language itself to become more complex.

Given these two hypotheses, the main technical challenge is to identify the basic principles and a possible precise scenario for the origin and progressive build-up of language complexity.

The origins of complexity are currently being studied in many different areas of science, ranging from chemistry (Kauffman 1993) to biology (Maynard Smith & Szathmáry 1993). The general study of complex systems, which started in earnest in the sixties with the study of dissipative systems (Prigogine & Stengers 1984), synergetics (Haken 1983) and chaos (Peitgen, Jurgens & Saupe 1982), is trying to identify general mechanisms that give rise to complexity. These mechanisms include evolution, coevolution, self-organization and level formation. It therefore makes sense to explore these mechanisms for the origins of language as well.

Before starting, an important disclaimer must be made. This work does *not* make any empirical claim that the proposed mechanisms are an explanation of how language actually originated in humans. Such investigations must be (and are) carried out by neurobiologists, anthropologists and linguists studying historical evolutions (McMahon 1994), child language (Halliday 1978) or creolization (Bickerton 1990). Here, I only propose and examine a theoretical possibility. If this possibility can be shown to lead to the formation of language and meaning in autonomous distributed artificial agents, then it is at least coherent and plausible. Thus, if meaning-creation mechanisms enable agents to autonomously construct and ground meaning in perception, action and interaction, then it is no longer self-evident that meaning has to be universal and innate, as claimed e.g. by Fodor (1975). And if the proposed language formation mechanisms enable artificial agents to create their own language, then it is no longer self-evident that 'linguistic knowledge' must for the most part be universal and innate as claimed by Chomsky (1980), or that the origin and evolution of language can only be explained by genetic mutation and selection (Pinker & Bloom 1990).

This chapter does not focus on the origin of co-operation or the origin of communication in itself, although these are obviously prerequisites for language. These topics are being investigated by other researchers, using a similar biological point of view. For example, Dawkins (1976) has argued that two organisms will co-operate if they share enough of the same genes, because what counts is the further propagation of these genes not the survival of the individual organism. Axelrod (1980), Lindgren & Nordahl (1995) and others have shown that co-operation will arise even if every agent is entirely selfish. MacLennan (1991) and Werner & Dyer (1991) have experimentally shown that communication arises as a side effect of co-operation if it is beneficial for co-operation. The emergent communication systems discussed in these papers do not constitute a language in the normal definition of the word, however. The number of agents is small and fixed. The repertoire of symbols is small and fixed. None of the other properties of a natural language, such as multiple levels, synonymy, ambiguity, syntax, etc., are observed. The main target of the research discussed in this chapter is to study the origins of communication systems that do have all these properties.

The remaining sections of the chapter focus on different general principles which are hypothesized to explain the origins and evolution of language: adaptive games (section 2), coevolution (section 3), self-organization (section 4) and level formation (section 5). Each section briefly discusses concrete experimental results.

2 Adaptive language games

Since Darwin, evolution by natural selection has played a key role in attempts to explain the origin and diversity of species. Evolution takes place when there is a source for generating variety and a selective force that retains those variations that are most adapted. Selectionism is not restricted to genetic evolution however. The only requirements are a mechanism of information preservation (i.e. a representation), a source of variation, and a feedback loop between the occurrence of a specific variation and selective 'success'. In the case of genetic evolution, the information is preserved in the genes. Variation is caused by errors in transmission (mutation and crossover). The feedback loop is established through the reproductive success of the organism carrying a particular set of genes. This success will depend as much on the environment in which the organism finds itself as on the genes it has.

I propose that selectionism is a major force in the origin of language as well. However, I do *not* mean selectionism in the genetic sense, but in a cultural sense. Information is preserved in the language memory of individuals. It is transmitted as part of a linguistic interaction because the hearer imitates or adopts the conventions of the speaker to be maximally successful in future interactions. Variation comes from many sources: there is spontaneous variation because of performance errors, overgeneralization because a single individual has no complete overview of the language, the construction of new rules by individuals to fill gaps, changes to existing rules to be more conformed to the group, etc. The feedback loop is based on minimizing cognitive effort and maximizing communicative success. For example, the selectionist criteria for a new phoneme or phoneme combination include: ease of producibility and reproducibility for the speaker – which includes the articulators being able to reach the desired goal states possibly with minimum energy requirements – and ease in understandability for the hearer – which includes that there is enough information in the signal to detect the sound reliably and distinguish it from others in the repertoire (Lindblom 1986).

The whole system bootstraps itself when variation is not only created by adapting of existing rules but by the creation of new rules from scratch. For example, a new gestural phonetic score could be created by assembling a random sequence of articulatory goals, a new word could be created by a random combination of phoneme segments, a new syntactic construction is created when a particular word order becomes conventionalized, etc.

Evolution is often studied in terms of games (Maynard Smith 1982). A game is an interaction between two agents or between an agent and an environment. A game has a certain outcome which determines the course of evolution. For language games, the outcome can directly be used by the agents to adapt the structures governing their linguistic behaviour. For example, if a certain association between a word and a meaning is not effective, then the agent should potentially review whether this association is to be part of his lexicon. If a certain phoneme cannot be recognized reliably by the hearer, the producing agent should reconsider whether it is to be part of his phonetics. Language games thus become adaptive, and the evolution of language becomes a kind of cultural evolution. This may explain why language evolution occasionally takes place very rapidly.

Figure 23.1 Physical robots used in the experiments. The robot has on-board computational resources, a battery, left and right motors, and about thirty sensors, including vision. The robot 'lives' in a robotic ecosystem together with other robots. There is a charging station as well as competition for the available energy.

2.1 *Meaning creation through discrimination games*

In our Brussels laboratory, we have built a variety of robots (Figure 23.1) that execute dynamical behaviours in a robotic ecosystem. These robots, which are the ultimate hardware platform for our language experiments, have a wealth of data channels (Figure 23.2) resulting from internal or external sensors, internal motivational states, actuator states, etc. Perceptually grounded meaning creation operates over these data channels.

One way in which meaning creation can take place is through *discrimination games*: the agent attempts to distinguish two objects or situations using a repertoire of categorizers which transform the continuous values produced by feature detectors into discrete categories. For example, a value from a continuously varying intensity scale for left visible light is divided into regions, which could be lexicalized as strong, medium and weak. When a particular value falls within one of these

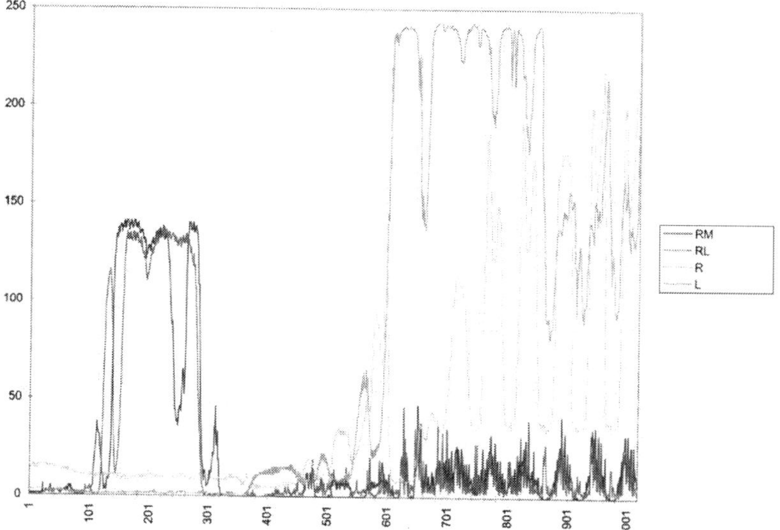

Figure 23.2 The graph shows the dynamical sensory states of a robot. RM and RL are right and left modulated light (detecting objects competing for energy) and R and L are right and left visible light (detecting the charging station). The data is for a 25-sec. time interval. The robot is engaged in phototaxis first to modulated light and then to visible light. Data channels such as these are the starting point of discrimination games that attempt to distinguish one situation from another.

regions a discrete category is output by the categorizer. When the game fails, i.e. an object cannot be distinguished from a set of other objects, the agent creates new categorizers by refining existing ones or by creating a new one for an unexplored sensory channel. As shown in another paper (Steels 1996c) this leads indeed to the build-up of a repertoire of features adequate for distinguishing objects. Moreover, the repertoire is adaptive. When new objects are to be considered or new data channels become available, the repertoire of categories expands if necessary.

A typical example of a discrimination game (from Steels (1996c)) is the following: an agent (a-5) tries to distinguish an object called the topic (o-6) from other objects making up the context (o-2 and o-5). The game is successful because the feature obtained for one object sc-5-2 with value v-0 either does not apply or results in a different value for the other objects:

Discrimination by a-5: o-6 ↔ {o-2 o-5}
Existing features:
  o-6 = ((sc-5-2 v-0))
  o-2 = NIL
  o-5 = ((sc-5-2 v-1))
Distinctive: ((sc-5-2 v-0))
Success

The following game is not successful because the topic o-7 has the same value for attribute sc-1-2 as o-2. The agent therefore creates a new feature detector sc-3-2. Whether this feature detector will do the job will only become clear in later discrimination games.

Discrimination by a-5: o-7 ↔ {o-1 o-2}
Existing features:
  o-7 = ((sc-1-2 v-1))
  o-1 = NIL
  o-2 = ((sc-1-2 v-1))
Distinctive: NIL
Failure
No distinctive features but new ones possible on channels: (sc-2 sc-3 sc-8)
New attribute created: sc-3-2

Figure 23.3 shows an experiment where an agent builds up a repertoire of feature detectors, starting from scratch. The graph shows the increasing discrimination success as experienced by the agent in discrimination games. It also shows the total success with the features so far, i.e. all objects are compared to all other objects and it is calculated which percentage can be distinguished. Average success during a certain time period is higher than total success because not all objects are encountered within each period.

Many other kinds of meaning creation games can be imagined. For example, an agent can attempt to classify an object against a list of classes and extend the feature repertoire or change the definitions of classes in order to be successful. An agent can attempt to predict aspects of a situation by formulating some features and deducing other features from them. Success in a game then equals predictive success and failure leads to the construction of more refined features or the revision of prediction rules.

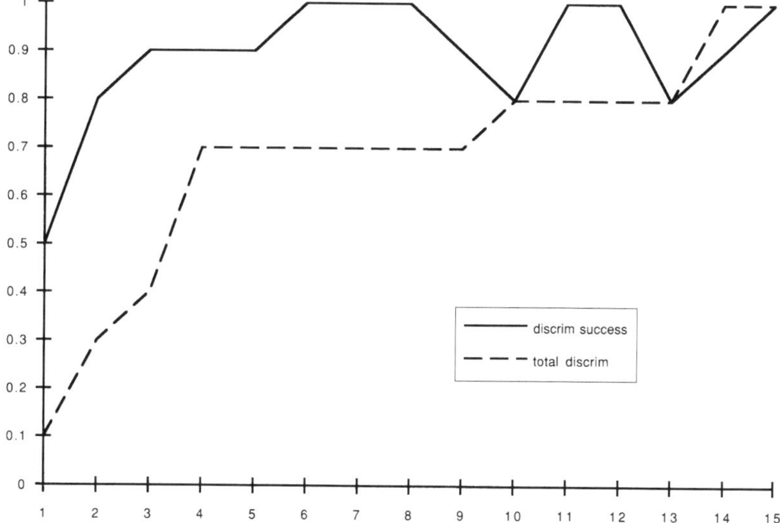

Figure 23.3 The graph shows the evolution of the discriminatory capacities of a single agent. The total number of objects (10) is fixed. There are 5 data channels. The average success in discrimination games as well as the total success is shown on the y-axis. The number of discriminations is mapped on the x-axis (scale 1/10). All objects can be discriminated after 150 discrimination games.

2.2 *Lexicons through language games*

We now turn to the lexicon. As discussed in other papers (Steels 1996a, b, d), adaptive language games can be set up that lead to the formation of a lexicon. In each game, there is a speaker and a hearer and a set of objects making up a context. The speaker identifies one object (the topic), for example by pointing. Both then find a feature set discriminating the topic with respect to the other objects in the context by playing discrimination games of the sort discussed in the previous subsection. The speaker attempts to code this feature set into language by using words in a lexicon that relates words to meanings. The hearer decodes the resulting expression using his lexicon and the game succeeds if the distinctive feature set decoded by the hearer matches with the expected distinctive feature set. When the game fails, the speaker or the hearer change their lexicon. For example, if the speaker does not have a word yet for the distinctive feature set that he wants to express, he may create a new word and add a new association to his lexicon; if the feature set

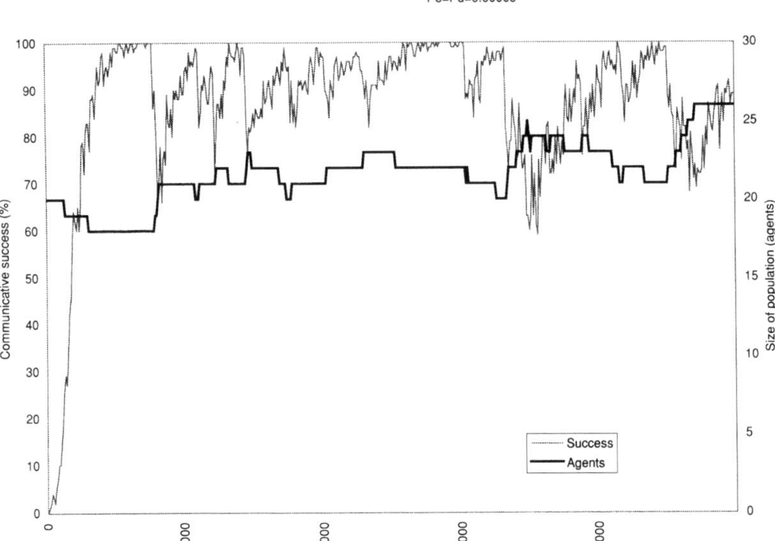

Figure 23.4 The figure shows the evolution of the communicative success (left y-axis) in a fluctuating population of agents (right y-axis) as it develops over time (x-axis). The population starts with the formation of a lexicon from scratch and quickly reaches total communicative success. The experiment shows that the communication remains stable even though the population renews itself. New agents enter with a probability 0.00005 and depart with the same probability. 50,000 language games are shown.

decoded by the hearer is more general than the one expected, then the hearer can refine his associations between words and meanings, etc. There is additional complexity because one word may have multiple meanings and one meaning may be expressed by multiple (competing) words.

A typical experiment shows a rapid creation of a lexicon which is adequate to reflect the meanings that are necessary for discrimination among a certain set of objects (see Figure 23.4). There is again adaptivity. When new meanings need to be expressed or new agents enter the group, the lexicon expands with new lexicalizations or contracts when ambiguity gets resolved.

Here are two examples from simulated adaptive naming games. The agents talk about themselves. The speaker (a-1) is describing himself to the hearer (a-3). The context includes a-2, a-3 and a-6. There are two possible distinctive feature sets that distinguish a-1 from the context. One is chosen, namely ((*size tall*) (*color white*)). It is translated to the sentence '(*k a*) (*v o*)' and subsequently decoded correctly by the hearer. The language game succeeds because the resulting feature set was expected by the hearer.

```
Dialog 2301 between a-1 and a-3 about a-1.
    Context: {a-2 a-3 a-6}
    Distinctive:
        ( ( (size tall) (color white) )
         ( (weight light) (color white) ) )
a-1: ( (size tall) (color white) )
        → ( (k a) (v o) ) →
a-3: ( ( (size tall) ) ( (color white) ) )
Success
```

Here is another language game where the hearer does not know the word and extends his lexicon. Because there is uncertainty (both (*size tall*) and (*weight light*) are possible discriminating features), an ambiguity enters into the hearer's lexicon:

```
Dialog 423 between a-3 and a-1 about a-2.
    Context: {a-3 a-2 a-5}
    Distinctive:
    ( ( (size tall) ) ( (weight light) ) )
a-3: ( (size tall) ) → ( (z u) ) ← a-1: nil
Failure
new word: a-1: ( (size tall) ) → (z u)
new word: a-1: ( (weight light) ) → (z u)
```

When later the word '(*z u*)' is used to identify the same object within the same context, the communication succeeds and so no disambiguation is possible. Disambiguation only takes place when a-1 uses '(*z u*)' in a situation where one of the descriptions is not appropriate.

2.3 *Shared sounds through imitation games*

In another series of experiments, conducted together with Bart de Boer, I have shown that a *shared sound repertoire* can evolve through imitation games. The repertoire consists of phonemes and phoneme segments which are admissible and distinctive in the language. Agents must develop both the capacity to produce the phonemes and the capacity to recognize them from acoustic signals. This is achieved by engaging in adaptive imitation games. An imitation game works as follows: a speaker

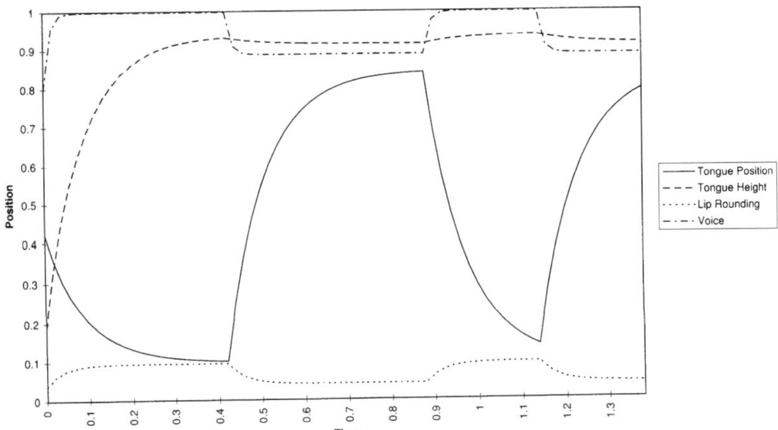

Figure 23.5 A gestural score based on two phonemes is generated by a speaker as part of an imitation game. The score sets articulatory targets which are to be reached dynamically at specific timings.

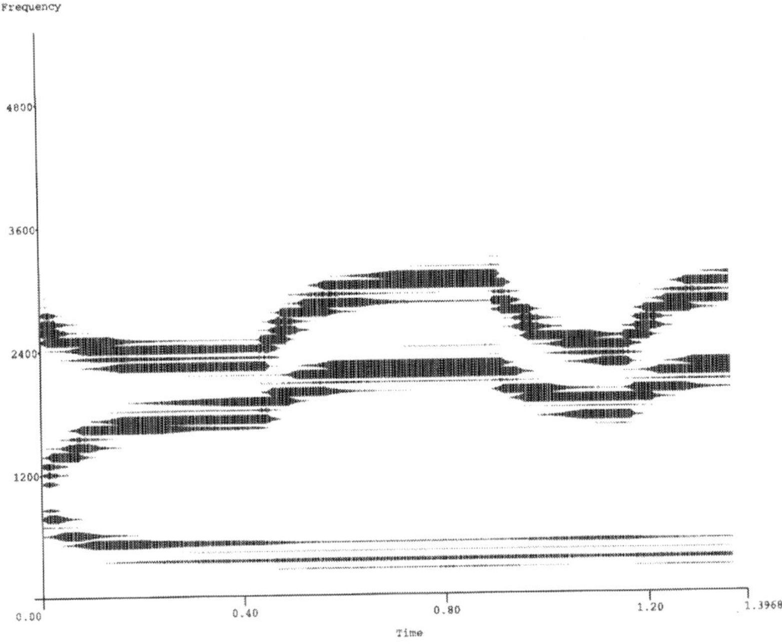

Figure 23.6 Frequency diagram corresponding to the gestural score produced in Figure 23.5. The hearer applies feature detectors to this signal in order to recover the phoneme sequence.

picks a phoneme or phoneme sequence from his repertoire, or possibly creates a new phoneme or phoneme sequence by producing a random gestural score. A gestural score is a sequence of articulatory targets. An example of such a score from our simulations is shown in Figure 23.5. The hearer then applies low-level feature detectors to the signal (Figure 23.6) in order to recognize the phonemes. When this recognition is successful, the hearer attempts to reproduce the phonemes again. The speaker now attempts recognition and can provide feedback on whether the result is compatible with the originally produced phoneme sequence.

Our experiments show that a common phoneme and phoneme sequence (syllable) repertoire indeed develops and, under the demands of the lexicon, expands. These experiments confirm hypotheses, formulated by Lindblom, among others, that selectionist criteria such as distinctiveness, minimization of articulatory energy, etc., explain the characteristics of natural phonetic systems (Lindblom 1986).

3 Linguistic coevolution

In genetic evolution the selectionist criteria are not fixed but derive from an environment which is constantly changing due to coevolution. For example, one species, acting as a prey, is evolving to become better at escaping its predator. But this causes the predator to evolve again toward becoming better at catching the prey. Whereas evolution in itself causes an equilibrium to be reached, coevolution causes a self-enforcing spiral toward greater complexity.

Also in the case of language, coevolution appears to play a crucial role for pushing a language toward greater complexity. The ultimate pressure comes from the growing complexity of agent–agent and agent–environment interaction, partly enabled by an increasingly more powerful linguistic ability. Thus language complexity feeds on itself and escalates. The lexicon puts pressure on phonetic creation to create an adequate repertoire of phonemes. If there are not enough phonemes, new ones will be generated through imitation games. The language game puts pressure first on the meaning creation modules, for example, to have enough distinctions. When there are more different types of objects, more distinctions are needed. It also puts pressure on the lexicon to lexicalize the meanings that need to be communicated. Thus the more meanings are used in language games, the bigger the lexicon will have to be.

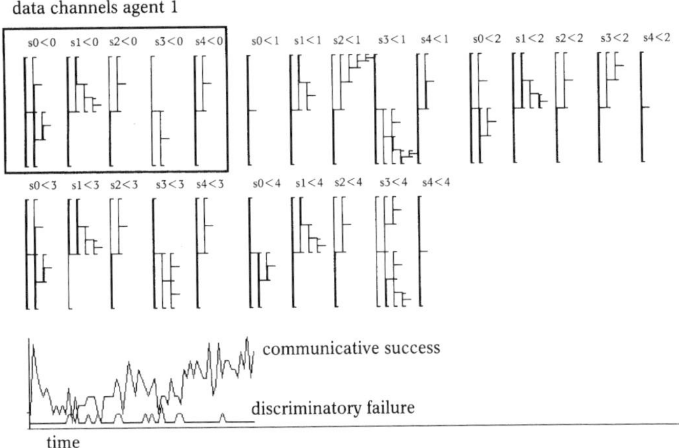

Figure 23.7 Experiment in the co-evolution of words and meanings. The top window shows evolving binary discrimination trees operating on 5 different data channels (s-0 through s-4) for 5 agents. The bottom window shows on the one hand the failure in discrimination (descending) and on the other the success in communication (ascending) after 500 language games (and consequently 1,000 discrimination games).

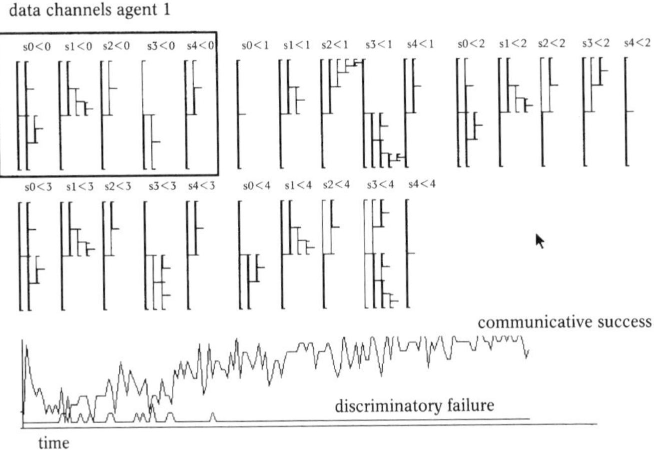

Figure 23.8 Continuation of the experiment given in Figure 23.7 after 5,000 language games. We see that the discrimination trees have grown further and that more categories have become lexicalized. The communicative success reaches its absolute value (1.0) and discriminatory failure has fallen to 0.0.

We can investigate these phenomena by coupling the different adaptive games in two ways: the output of one is used as input by the other, and conversely the 'user' provides feedback to the producing module. For example, a category used in discrimination is more appropriate in a language game if it has also been lexicalized. When one agent uses a word and thus certain categories, the other agent may have to expand his category repertoire accordingly before being able to decode the word. Thus there are two selectionist pressures on categories: (a) are they adequate for discrimination? and (b) do they have or are they needed for lexicalization? Similarly a phoneme is not appropriate as part of the phonetic repertoire when it can only be produced and understood – it must also be used by the lexicon.

Another paper (Steels 1997a) illustrates this in more detail based on experiments for the coevolution of words and meanings by a combination of discrimination games (discussed in 2.1) and language games (discussed in 2.2). The agents engage in a series of language games and as part of each language game each agent performs one discrimination game. Figures 23.7 and 23.8 illustrate these experiments which show a coevolution of distinctions and words to lexicalize them, driven by an expanding set of objects. The top shows the binary discrimination trees for each channel and each agent. The continuous space of each channel (between 0.0 and 1.0) is first divided into two regions (resulting in one attribute with two possible values and thus two categories). Each of these may be further refined. The lines are thicker when there is a lexicalization of a particular category. Not all meanings are lexicalized.

Interestingly enough, each agent develops its own repertoire of categories. Nevertheless a relative coherence emerges between the agents because they are in the same environment and thus encounter the same objects. This can be seen by comparing the trees of the different agents for each respective channel. We see for example that agent 1 has fewer refinements on channel 3 than the agent below it (agent 3). What counts however is communicative success. Differences in word meaning may go unnoticed by the agents until a situation arises that forces disambiguation.

4 Self-organization

Evolution and coevolution are in themselves not enough. Usually there are many possible structures which are equally plausible from the viewpoint of the selectionist criteria operating for language. But out of the many possibilities usually only one is selected and adopted by the linguistic population. Language and meanings are *shared*. This is a big puzzle for anyone who seeks a non-nativist theory of language and meaning. If meaning and language is innate, then it is genetically shared and coherence comes for free. But if language and meaning are not innate, we must explain how coherence may arise without central control and with agents having access to each other's states only through localized interactions.

The origins of coherence in a distributed system with many interacting elements have been studied in biology and other sciences under the heading of self-organization. A typical example is a cloud of birds or a path formed by ants. Examples of self-organization are also found at lower levels. For example, regular temporal or spatial patterns in the Bhelouzow-Zhabotinsky reaction or the sudden appearance of coherent light in lasers are chemical and physical examples of self-organization (Nicolis & Prigogine 1985).

The principle of self-organization prescribes two necessary ingredients: there must be a set of possible variations and random fluctuations that temporarily may cause one fluctuation to gain prominence. Most of the time these fluctuations are damped and the system is in a (dynamic) equilibrium state. However, if there is a positive feedback loop causing a certain fluctuation to become enforced, then one fluctuation eventually dominates. The feedback loop is typically a function of the environment so that the self-organization only takes place for specific parameter regimes. When these parameters are in a lower regime they leave the system in equilibrium. When the parameters are in a higher regime, they bring the system into (deterministic) chaos. Structure arises and is maintained on the edge of chaos (Langton 1995).

In the computational experiments, self-organization has proven to be an effective way to arrive at coherence (see Figure 23.9). The positive feedback loop is based on success in games that involve multiple agents. Those rules are preferred that are the most used and the most successful in use. For example, for each word–meaning pair, a record is kept of how many times this pair has been used and how many times the use of the pair in a specific language game was successful. The (speaking) agent always prefers the most successful word. This causes the positive feedback effect: the more a word is used, the more successful it will be and the more it will be used. Initially there will be a struggle between the

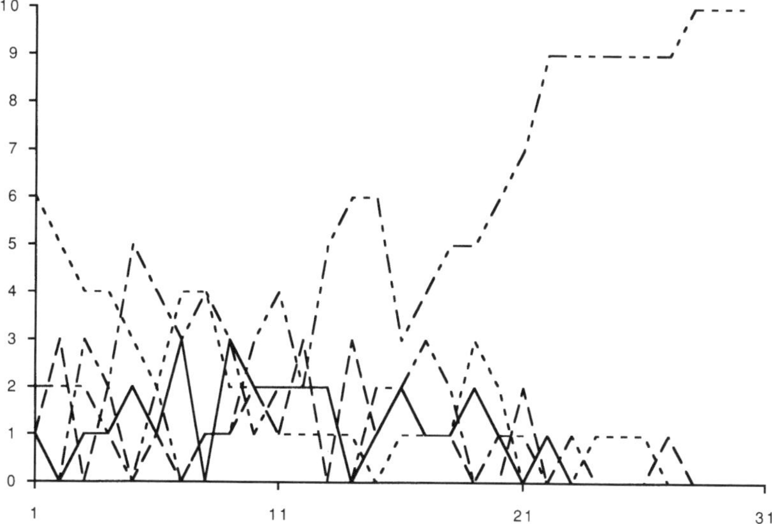

Figure 23.9 This figure plots the results of a computational experiment in lexicon formation with 10 agents, 5 competing words and 1 meaning. It plots the communicative success of each word (y-axis) over time (x-axis). We see a search period in which different words compete to express the same meaning until one gains complete dominance.

different word–meaning pairs until one dominates. Coherence crystallizes quite rapidly once a word starts to dominate, similar to a phase transition.

5 Level formation

Many linguists argue that a representation system is only a language when it also features a complex syntax. In the experiments discussed so far, there was no syntax yet, although there is a steadily increasing lexicon, sound and meaning repertoire. All the ingredients are therefore in place for a protolanguage (Bickerton 1995). Although syntax is obviously important, these other aspects of language are just as crucial and no theory of the origins of language is complete without explaining how they might evolve. Nevertheless the origin of syntax is an essential part of the problem and it must be addressed. I hypothesize that level formation is the key to solving it. Level formation is not exclusively restricted to syntax but is most pertinent to explain it.

Level formation is very common in biosystems. It occurs when a number of independent units develop a symbiotic relationship due to co-occurrence, eventually making the units no longer independent. Level formation has, for example, been used to explain the formation of cells (De Duve 1996) and the origin of chromosomes which group individual genes (Maynard Smith & Szathmáry 1993). In the case of the cell, there were initially free-floating organisms and structures which came to depend on each other, for example because one organism produces products for another one or destroys lethal products. Gradually the relationship between these organisms and structures becomes so strong that they give up some of their independence to become a fixed part of the whole.

As shown in another paper (Steels 1997b), the emergence of grammar may start as soon as there are multiple-word sentences (which arise naturally from the meaning creation and naming games discussed in the previous sections). The different words are grouped in a *schema* which is initially completely word/situation-specific. When one of the words re-occurs, it triggers the same schema so that expectations are set up about the other elements and their constraints. From this humble basis, the formation of grammatical complexity takes off through a variety of operations.

Schemas may be fused to give larger schemas. For example, when w1 and w2 were grouped in f1, and w2 and w3 in f2, a new schema could be created by fusing f1 and f2.

Semantic and syntactic classes form on what can fill a slot in an existing schema, i.e. the constraints on a frame may generalize. The generalization could be based on semantic criteria (features of the objects or situations concerned) but could also be based on tagging words as belonging to certain syntactic classes.

Hierarchical structures emerge because the elements in a schema themselves become schemas. These hierarchical structures co-evolve with the emergence of the hierarchical structures implicit in more complex language games.

Constraints in the form of additional syntactic devices are added to distinguish one schema from another, to enable more rapid recognition, etc. The addition takes place by a variety of operators. One of them is overinterpretation. Observed properties of a schema application, such as word order, are taken to be obligatory as opposed to a mere side effect.

Here is an example of an implementation of these mechanisms at work. A language game takes place in which the speaker uses two words. A schema is created with slots for the parts of the semantic structure and slots for the parts of the syntactic structure. These slots are filled by members of newly created classes. Both semantic and syntactic constraints are recorded.

```
Game 297. Speaker: head-40 Hearer: head-41
    Topic: im-37 Context: im-36 im-39 im-42 im-38
++> head-40 #<FUNCTION-FRAME #x605A91E>
Distinctive: ((feature-1 v-221) (feature-7 v-227) (feature-5 v-230))
             ((feature-11 v-234))
Meaning: ((feature-7 v-227) (feature-5 v-230) (feature-1 v-221))
Lemmas: (#<SCHEMA #x5EB9E96> #<SCHEMA #x5E8FFB6>)
++> head-40 #<FORM-FRAME #x605B8FE>
Failure: MISSING-SYNTAX-SPEAKER
⇒ Extend grammar:
Schema: #<SCHEMA #x5ED026E>
    Function: ((slot-26 cl-26) (slot-28 cl-28))
        ((conjunction (>> slot-26) (>> slot-28)))
    cl-26 = {(feature-1 v-221)}
    cl-28 = {(feature-5 v-230), (feature-7 v-227)}
    Form: ((slot-25 cl-25) (slot-27 cl-27))
          ((ordering (>> slot-25) (>> slot-27)))
          cl-25 = {(E D)} cl-27 = {(D E)}
```

Later on this schema is re-used, which includes the imposition of a certain word order:

```
Game 356. Speaker: head-40 Hearer: head-41
    Topic: im-37 Context: im-36 im-42 im-39 im-38
++> head-40 #<FUNCTION-FRAME #x605A91E>
++> head-40 #<FORM-FRAME #x605B8FE>
Distinctive: ((feature-1 v-221) (feature-7 v-227)) ((feature-3 v-234))
Meaning: ((feature-7 v-227) (feature-1 v-221))
Lemmas: (#<SCHEMA #x5EB9E96> #<SCHEMA #x5E8FFB6>)
Syntax: (#<SCHEMA #x5ED1686>
        (slot-27 #<SCHEMA #x5E8FFB6>)
        (slot-25 #<SCHEMA #x5EB9E96>))
Expression: ((E D) (D E))
```

The following is a step in the process of accommodating a new situation by expanding an earlier-created schema:

```
Game 347. Speaker: head-40 Hearer: head-41
    Topic: im-39 Context: im-36 im-38 im-42
++> head-40 #<FUNCTION-FRAME #x61DF806>
++> head-40 #<FORM-FRAME #x61E080E>
Failure: MISSING-SYNTAX-SPEAKER
⇒ Expansion synt class cl-27 with (A F) for #<SCHEMA #x5ED2AB6>
⇒ Expansion sem class cl-28 with #<SPEC #x5E8FB0E>
  for #<SCHEMA #x5ED2AB6>
```

Current research is focusing on a large-scale application of these schema-forming processes coupled with the meaning-creation and lexicon formation processes, themselves coupled to visually grounded sensory stimuli.

6 Conclusions

This chapter proposed a number of mechanisms that together might explain the origins of language: adaptive games, coevolution, self-organization and level formation. Each of these mechanisms is known to play a critical role in the origins of complexity in biosystems (Maynard Smith & Szathmáry 1993), which justifies their application to the origins and evolution of language. A key point of the present chapter is that these mechanisms are not applied to biological structures (for example genes or neural networks), but rather to language itself. For example, no 'catastrophic' genetic mutation is proposed, as in Bickerton (1995), to explain the origins of syntax, rather syntax is hypothesized to originate spontaneously through level formation based on the pressure to express more meanings with limited resources of time, memory and processing power.

An analogy can be seen between language and species and between an individual's language rules (at different linguistic levels) and genes. Evolutionary processes operate on the individual rules causing the language to boot-strap and evolve. Selectionist criteria are not in terms of reproductive success (as in the case of genetic evolution) but rather success, ease and efficiency in linguistic communication. Coherence emerges through self-organization.

Of course, the individual brain must have the appropriate capabilities to engage in the operations necessary to represent and enact the linguistic rules. This includes fine motor control of the articulatory system, frequency analysis of the speech signal, associative memory, discretization of continuous sensory data channels, set operations over feature structures, monitoring and establishment of feedback loops between use and success, planning and recognition of sequences, etc. But none of these functions is unique for language. The fine motor control needed for the articulatory system is similar to the one needed for controlling a hand. The frequency analysis of the speech signal is identical to that needed for recognizing other kinds of sounds. Set operations, associative memory, planning and recognition of action sequences are all needed for daily survival and can be found in lower animals, albeit with much less sophistication.

Testing the adequacy of mechanisms for the origins of language by building software simulations and robotic agents has proven to be a very effective methodology although it requires a large amount of work. So far, concrete positive results have been obtained for meaning, lexicons and phonology. Much more research needs to be done, particularly in the area of syntax and in the evolution of language games and speech acts. But many exciting new insights are clearly within reach.

Acknowledgments

The research and writing of this chapter has been financed by the Belgian Federal Government FKFO project on emergent functionality (FKFO contract no. G.0014.95) and the IUAP 'Construct' Project (no. 20) of the Belgian Government, with additional support from the external researcher programme of the Sony Computer Science Laboratory in Tokyo. The contributions of Angus McIntyre of Sony CSL to the simulation of language games are gratefully acknowledged, as well as the contributions of several members of the VUB AI Laboratory, particularly Paul Vogt on grounding the language games in mobile robots, and Bart de Boer on the phonetics experiments.

References

Axelrod, R. (1984). *The Evolution of Cooperation*. New York: Basic Books.

Batali, J. (1994). Innate biases and critical periods: combining evolution and learning in the acquisition of syntax. In Brooks, R. & Maes, P. (eds.) *Proceedings of the Fourth Artificial Life Workshop*. Cambridge, MA: MIT Press, pp. 160–171.

Bickerton, D. (1990). *Language and Species*. Chicago: Chicago University Press.

(1995). *Language and Human Behaviour*. London: University College London Press.

Chomsky, N. (1980). *Rules and Representations*. New York: Columbia University Press.

Dawkins, R. (1976). *The Selfish Gene*. Oxford: Oxford University Press.

De Duve, C. (1996). The birth of complex cells. *Scientific American*, 274(4), 38–45.

Fodor, J. A. (1975). *The Language of Thought*. Scranton, PA: Crowell.

Gillis, S., Durieux, G. & Daelemans, W. (1995). A computational model of P and P: Dresher and Kaye (1990) revisited. *Amsterdam Series in Child Language Development*, 5, 135–173.

Haken, H. (1983). *Advanced Synergetics: Instability Hierarchies of Self-Organising Systems and Devices*. Berlin: Springer-Verlag.

Halliday, M. A. K. (1978). *Learning How To Mean*. Cambridge: Cambridge University Press.

Kauffman, S. (1993). *The Origins of Order*. Oxford: Oxford University Press.

Langton, C. (ed.) (1995). *Artificial Life. An Overview*. Cambridge, MA: MIT Press.

Lindblom, B. (1986). Phonetic universals in vowel systems. In Ohala, J. J. & Jaeger, J. J. (eds.) *Experimental Phonology*. Orlando, FL: Academic Press, pp. 13–44.

Lindgren, K. & Nordahl, M. G. (1995). Cooperation and community structure in artificial ecosystems. *Artificial Life*, 1/2, 15–37.

MacLennan, B. (1991). Synthetic ethology: an approach to the study of communication. In Langton, C., Taylor, C., Farmer, D. & Rasmussen, S. (eds.) *Artificial Life II*. Redwood City, CA: Addison-Wesley, pp. 631–658.

Maynard Smith, J. (1982). *Evolution and the Theory of Games*. Cambridge: Cambridge University Press.

& Szathmáry, E. (1993). The origin of chromosomes I. Selection of linkage. *Journal of Theoretical Biology*, 164, 437–66.

& Szathmáry, E. (1995). *The Major Transitions in Evolution*. Oxford: W. H. Freeman.

McMahon, A. (1994). *Understanding Language Change*. Cambridge: Cambridge University Press.

Nicolis, G. & Prigogine, I. (1985). *Exploring Complexity*. Munich: Piper.

Peitgen, H.-O., Jurgens, H. & Saupe, D. (1992). *Chaos and Fractals. New Frontiers of Science*. Berlin: Springer-Verlag.

Pinker, S. & Bloom, P. (1990). Natural language and natural selection. *Behavioural and Brain Science*, 13, 707–784.

Prigogine, I. & Stengers, I. (1984). *Order Out of Chaos*. New York: Bantam Books.

Steels, L. (1996a) The spontaneous self-organisation of an adaptive language. In Muggleton, S. (ed.) *Machine Intelligence 15*. Oxford: Oxford University Press.

(1996b). A self-organizing spatial vocabulary. *Artificial Life Journal*, 2(4).

(1996c). Perceptually grounded meaning creation. In Tokoro, M. (ed.) *ICMAS-96 Proceedings Second International Conference on Multi-Agent Systems*. Menlo Park, CA: AAAI Press, pp. 338–344.

(1996d). Emergent adaptive lexicons. In Maes, P., Mataric, M., Meyer, J.-A., Pollack, J. & Wilson, S. W. (1996). *From Animals to Animats 4: Proceedings of the Fourth International Conference on Simulation of Adaptive Behaviour*. Cambridge, MA: MIT Press.

(1997a). The coevolution of words and meanings. Constructing and sharing perceptual distinctions. In Van Someren, M. & Widmer, G. (eds.) *Proceedings of the European Conference on Machine Learning*, Prague, April 1997. Berlin: Springer-Verlag.

(1997b). The origins of syntax in visually grounded robotic agents. In Pollack, M. (ed.) *Proceedings of the IJCAI-97 Conference*. Los Angeles: The AAAI Press, Morgan Kaufmann Pub.

Werner, G. & Dyer, M. (1991). Evolution of communication in artificial organisms. In Langton, C., Taylor, C., Farmer, D. & Rasmussen, S. (eds.) *Artificial Life II*. Redwood City, CA: Addison-Wesley, pp. 659–687.

24 Computational simulations of the emergence of grammar

JOHN BATALI

1 Introduction

Human language makes it possible to express a vast number of different and complex meanings with sequences composed of a relatively small number of relatively simple elements – and to interpret such sequences as the meanings they express. A traditional sense of the word 'grammar', and the one I adopt here, refers to the systematic regularities between meanings and their expression as sequences of sounds or gestures in a language.

In particular, the grammars of human languages incorporate systematic regularities involving the *structures* of the meanings and the sequences that express them. For example the morphological structure of an inflected verb conveys information about the person, number, and gender of one or more of the participants in the event or situation the verb describes.

The structural regularities of a language constitute a resource that a speaker can use to express novel meaning combinations, provided that the elements out of which the new meaning is constructed and the relations constituting that structure are consonant with the language's grammar. The hearer can accurately interpret the utterance as involving those familiar structural constituents and relations, even though that specific combination may never have been used before. Thus the system can be used to express meanings tailored to the specific occasion of their use, and can be extended as the need to express new meanings arises. Learning is relatively easy because the novice has to master only the structural regularities and basic elements of a language, instead of memorizing all of its meaning/expression pairs.

The ability to communicate by exploiting a system of structural regularities therefore represents an invaluable achievement of a species for which co-ordinated social activity is vital to survival, and for which the accurate exchange of information often provides adaptive benefit. Given this benefit, it is tempting to explain the achievement as the result of natural selection.

However, it is important to distinguish between the evolution of language itself – in particular the emergence, modification and enrichment of the grammatical resources in human languages – and the biological evolution of articulate hominids. Clearly they are related: lacking appropriate anatomical and neurological endowment, an animal will be unable to produce or perceive complex signals, and without sufficiently powerful cognitive abilities, it cannot entertain meanings worth communicating in the first place. But the adaptive benefits of such traits are not specific to communication, and it is not clear how communication alone could provide sufficient selection pressure for their development.

In this chapter, I explore the idea that some of the grammatical regularities manifest in human language could emerge as a result of non-genetic cultural processes among a population of animals with the cognitive capacities required for communication, but who do not initially share a co-ordinated communication system. Whether or not this is what really happened in our species is unknown, but the possibility seems worth investigating, to understand better both its plausibility and its limitations.

Speculation about the origins and early development of human language must perforce originate in intuitions based on experience with its modern versions. Though these intuitions can be tested methodologically, with the resources of linguistics, psychology, anthropology, neuroscience, literary studies and other disciplines, we are for the most part limited to the one class of exemplars. There is obviously no way to go back and observe what has happened since the Pliocene epoch, and the differences between the regularities exhibited by the grammars of human languages and those of other animal communication systems seem profound.

Mathematical and computational models provide a way to explore alternative accounts of the emergence of systems of communication. If the consequences of a model are consistent with expectations based on intuitions or speculation, they might obtain some small measure of support. But more interestingly (and, as it happens, more often), the consequences of a model may deviate from expectations. In working out the reasons for the differences, one can potentially develop a richer set of intuitions. Models are thus valuable to the degree that they explicitly illustrate the consequences of the set of assumptions they embody. This may be even more important than whether those assumptions are correct.

The computational simulations described in this chapter involve populations of simple agents that can produce sequences of tokens to encode structured meanings, and can assign interpretations to sequences of tokens. Initially the agents' communication systems are almost totally uncoordinated: few, if any, agents send the same sequence for the same meaning, and none of the agents is able to interpret sequences sent by others correctly. During the simulation runs, each agent alternates between learning to interpret sequences sent by the other members of the population and sending sequences that other agents learn to interpret. Such populations eventually develop systems that support highly accurate communication, even of novel meaning combinations. As the cognitive skills of the simulated agents are possessed by some primate species, and no language-specific innate capacities are required, the simulations might model the emergence of some of the grammatical regularities in human languages.

2 Communicative agents

The simple model of communication explored in the computational simulations is illustrated in Figure 24.1. Each agent contains a 'meaning vector' that stores ten real numbers between 0.0 and 1.0, and a simple

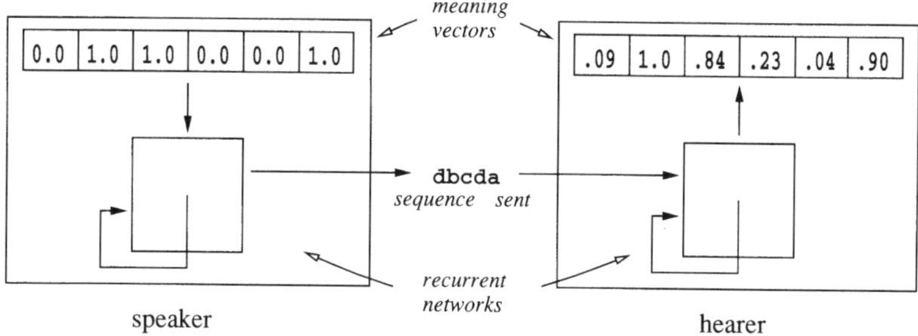

Figure 24.1 Communicative agents. The values in the speaker's meaning vector are used by the speaker's recurrent network to determine a sequence of characters to send. The hearer's recurrent network processes that sequence to determine the values stored in the hearer's meaning vector.

recurrent network that is used to send and receive sequences of characters from the set {a, b, c, d}.

In an episode of communication between a pair of agents, each value in the speaker's meaning vector is first set to either 0.0 or 1.0, depending on which of the set of meanings described in section 3 is to be conveyed. The values in the speaker's meaning vector are used by the speaker's recurrent network to determine the sequence of characters it sends. This sequence is processed by the hearer's network to determine the hearer's meaning vector.

The accuracy of a communicative episode is assessed by comparing the values in the speaker's meaning vector with those in the hearer's after the sequence sent by the speaker for a given meaning has been processed by the hearer. A value in the hearer's vector will be called 'correct' if it is within 0.5 of the value in the corresponding position of the speaker's vector. A more sensitive measure of the accuracy of the hearer's interpretation is obtained by computing the root mean square of the difference between the values in the meaning vectors of the speaker and the hearer, after processing the sequence. This value will be referred to as the hearer's 'error' for the sequence.

Treating meaning as a pattern of binary values is wildly simplistic of course, but is at least straightforward and explicit, and is consistent with the approach of information theory. A more subtle assumption underlying this model is that the agents are capable of producing and recognizing tokens from some finite set, and of mapping sequences of such tokens to and from meanings. While there is evidence that humans perceive and produce speech sounds as tokens of discrete categorical types, and that this ability is partly innate, it is also at least partly learned (Eimas, Siqueland, Juscyk & Vigorito 1971). Even if innate, the ability to perceive such categories must have developed along with other linguistic abilities, as opposed to being present in fully developed form before the emergence of grammar, as this model assumes.

The architecture of the recurrent network in each agent is illustrated in Figure 24.2. The networks have three layers of units, with feed-forward connections between the units of the input layer and those of the hidden layer, and between the hidden layer and the output layer. The logistic activation function was used for all of the units in the network (see Haykin 1994: ch. 6). Each network has one input unit for each of the characters, thirty context input units, thirty units in its hidden layer, and ten output units (corresponding to the number of values in the agents' meaning vectors).

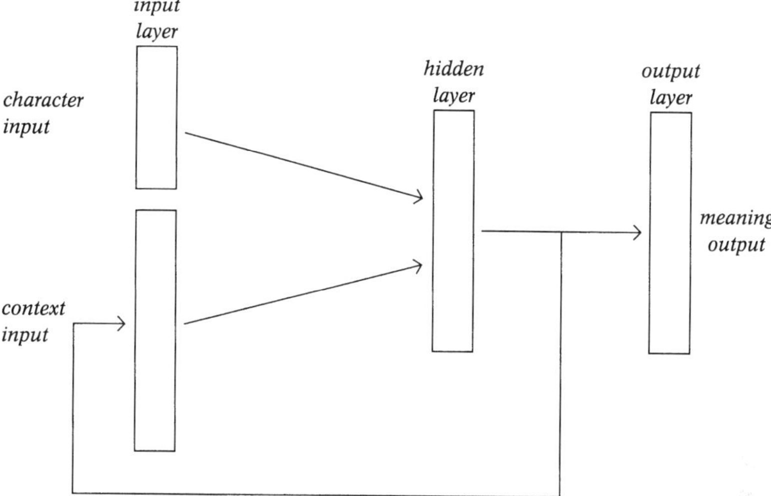

Figure 24.2 Recurrent neural networks used in the communicative agents. Each layer contains a set of units whose activation values are determined by units in the previous layer and the values of connection weights between the units. Activation values of the character input units in the input layer are set externally. Activation values of the context input units are copied from the activation values of the units in the hidden layer after each character is processed.

h.1 Set all network inputs to zero.
h.2 Process each character:
- **h.2.a** Set the input corresponding to the character to 1.0; set the rest of the inputs to 0.0.
- **h.2.b** Feed activation values forward through the network.
- **h.2.c** Copy the values of the hidden units to the context input units.

h.3 When the sequence is complete, copy the values of the output layer of the network to the agent's meaning vector.

Figure 24.3 Operation of the recurrent networks shown in Figure 24.2, when receiving a sequence of characters.

When receiving a sequence of characters (i.e. when used inside the 'hearer' of Figure 24.1), the networks are operated as described in Figure 24.3. After initializing the network, each character in the sequence is processed by activating the input unit corresponding to that character, feeding activation values forward through the network, and then copying the activation values of the hidden layer to the network's context input units. These values can thus encode temporal properties of the sequence that has been processed so far. After the last character of the sequence has been processed, the output of the hearer's network represents the hearer's interpretation of the sequence.

Recurrent neural networks can be trained to associate specific output vectors with specific sequences, or with sequences that satisfy various formal constraints (Batali 1994; Cleeremans, Servan-Schreiber & McClelland 1989; Elman 1990; Jordan 1986; Siegelmann 1993).

To train a network to interpret a sequence as a given meaning vector, the network is operated as shown in Figure 24.3, except that, after step h.2.b, the back-propagation algorithm (Rumelhart, Hinton & Williams 1986) is used to modify the weights of the network. The error of each output unit is determined by the difference between the value of the meaning vector at the position corresponding to the unit, and the unit's actual value. A backpropagation learning rate of 0.01 is used.

The network is trained after each character in the sequence is processed, even the first character. Though, in general, it will not be able to correctly interpret sequences so early, this method of training forces the networks to develop representations of temporal properties of the sequences in their hidden layers that will enable the networks to produce the correct output after more characters are processed.

The agents' networks are used to send sequences according to the algorithm described in Figure 24.4. As the speaker generates a sequence of characters, its network processes those characters as if it were receiving them. To choose which character to send at each point in the sequence, the speaker determines which of the four characters would bring its own output closest to the meaning being conveyed. That character is then sent, and processed, by the speaker. If, after doing so, all the speaker's output units are correct for the meaning being conveyed (or if the sequence has reached a cutoff length of twenty characters), the speaker stops sending. Otherwise the process is repeated.

Networks are not trained to send sequences for meanings. However, being trained to interpret sequences will also modify a network's sending behaviour by changing the network's connection weight values.

The mechanism for sending characters was designed with the results of Hurford (1989) in mind. His simulations involve a simpler model of communication, in which unitary signals are used to convey meanings.

s.1 Set all network inputs to zero.
s.2 Choose a character to send:
  s.2.a For each character, determine how many output values would be correct, were that character processed.
  s.2.b Choose the character for which this value is highest.
  s.2.c If more than one character would give the same number of correct outputs, choose from them the one whose error is lowest.
s.3 That character is sent to the hearer.
s.4 That character is processed by the network, as described in step h.2 in Figure 24.3.
s.5 After the character is processed:
  s.5.a If each value in the network's output layer is correct, stop sending characters.
  s.5.b Otherwise if the total length of the sequence sent exceeds a maximum value, stop sending characters.
  s.5.c Otherwise continue at step s.2.

Figure 24.4 Operation of the recurrent networks shown in Figure 24.2, when used to send a sequence of characters.

Hurford investigates a learning procedure he calls 'Saussurean', where an agent uses its own learned responses to signals to determine what to send, and shows that Saussurean learners often develop highly co-ordinated signalling systems.

While the complexity of the current model precluded using Hurford's learning procedure directly, the sending mechanism was designed to enforce a relation between an agent's transmission and reception behaviour. Since the agent's network processes each character in a sequence as it is sent, the network's units will have identical activation values after processing each character when sending a sequence and when receiving that same sequence. Therefore, if it stopped sending according to step s.5.a, when each of its output activation values was correct, the network will, after hearing the sequence, also have the correct meaning. Thus the agent will correctly interpret sequences that it sends. (This will not be true, on the other hand, for sequences terminated because the cutoff length is reached.)

The assumption that agents can use their own responses to characters as a means to predict the responses of others is crucial to the present model, and must be satisfied in any animals to which it could be applied. The ability to use one's own cognitive and emotional responses to potential situations to predict or understand those of others is of great value for animals with rich social interactions. It appears to be present to some degree in the primates, and is relatively developed in apes, though not nearly to the degree it is in humans. (See the papers in Whiten (1991)).

3 An interpretation of the meaning vectors

The meanings transferred between the agents are just vectors of numerical values. The mnemonic interpretation of the meaning vectors described in this section will be used in the analysis of the sequences used to convey them. Although the interpretation is motivated by speculation about the emergence of grammar in humans, and involves a model of properties of natural language pronouns, I am *not* claiming that results of the computational simulations constitute any sort of justification for either. The simulations are intended to explore whether agents can develop co-ordinated systems for conveying structured meanings. The following interpretation of the meaning vectors is intended only to facilitate the analysis of whether and how they do.

A crucial event in the emergence of grammar occurred when discrete signals, perhaps like those used as alarm calls by vervet monkeys (Cheney & Seyfarth 1990), began to be treated as being composed of relatively independent meaningful segments that could be systematically combined to produce new signals. For this to happen, their users must have been capable of comprehending meanings whose content could be analysed into more or less independently meaningful components, perhaps as involving a group of one or more individuals that manifest some property or relation, or are participating in some type of process or event. Given the capacity to comprehend such meanings, it might then have been useful to express them.

In human languages such meanings are expressed with a clause, headed by a verb whose inflectional form often conveys information about one or more of its thematic arguments, as well as about the process or situation involving the individuals those arguments refer to. In some languages, the information conveyed by its inflection enables a single verb form to function as a complete utterance.

The interpretation of the meaning vectors is therefore motivated by the possibility that the grammar of an early communication system might have resembled the inflectional morphology of verbs in modern

Predicates

values	
011001	*happy*
011100	*sad*
101001	*angry*
100011	*tired*
110001	*excited*
100101	*sick*
100110	*hungry*
000111	*thirsty*
010101	*silly*
010011	*scared*

Referents

sp	*hr*	*ot*	*pl*	
1	0	0	0	*me*
1	0	0	1	*we*
1	0	1	1	*mip*
0	1	0	0	*you*
0	1	0	1	*yall*
0	1	1	1	*yup*
1	1	0	1	*yumi*
0	0	1	0	*one*
0	0	1	1	*they*
1	1	1	1	*all*

Example Meanings

values	
0010101001	*(one angry)*
1101010101	*(yumi silly)*
1111100101	*(all sick)*
0111100110	*(yup hungry)*
1011010101	*(mip silly)*
0111100101	*(yup sick)*
0100100011	*(you tired)*
0011000111	*(they thirsty)*
1001011100	*(we sad)*
1000110001	*(me excited)*

Figure 24.5 Meaning vectors for the predicates (left), referents (centre), and 10 example meanings (right).

languages. The values in the meaning vectors are partitioned into 2 groups: 6 of the values are taken as encoding a predicate, and the remaining 4 are taken as encoding a referent to which the predicate applies. There are 10 patterns each for the predicates and referents, and therefore 100 different meanings that can be represented. The meaning vectors corresponding to the predicates and referents are shown in Figure 24.5, in addition to 10 example meanings.

The meaning vectors for the predicates are randomly chosen, such that each has 3 positions whose value is 1 and 3 whose value is 0. The word assigned to each of them is entirely arbitrary. (For example, there is no intended relationship between the pattern representing *happy* and that representing *sad*.)

As with the set of predicates, the names used for the referent have no significance other than the vector of values they stand for. However, the names are related to the values in the meaning vectors according to a simple model of natural language pronouns. Each position in the referent vector indicates whether a certain property is true of the set of one or more referents. The first position represents whether the set includes the speaker (*sp*) or not. The second position indicates whether the hearer (*hr*) is included. The third position indicates whether any other (*ot*) individuals are included. The fourth position indicates whether the set of referents is plural (*pl*) or not.

Given this set of properties, there are ten combinations that are logically consistent. The names assigned to them are based on words of English and the English-based Creole language Tok Pisin, spoken in Papua New Guinea. The features of the referents *me*, *you* and *they* correspond to those of the English pronouns. The referent *one* is third-person singular. *Mip* and *yup* (based on Tok Pisin 'mipela' and 'yupela') refer to groups containing either the speaker or the hearer, respectively, but not both, in addition to at least one other individual. The referent *yumi* (also from Tok Pisin) designates a group containing only the speaker and hearer. The referents *we* and *yall* designate the speakers, or hearers, respectively, when construed as a group. The referent of *all* is a group including the speaker, the hearer and others.

4 Negotiation of co-ordinated communication

To communicate successfully, the members of a population of agents must all send more or less the same sequence of characters for each of the meanings, and must be able to interpret correctly most of the sequences sent by the other members. Co-ordinated communication is achieved in the simulation runs as each agent in the population alternates between learning to interpret the sequences sent by others, and sending sequences for others to emulate. I characterize this process as 'negotiation' because all of the agents both contribute to, and conform to, the population's communication system as it develops.

A simulation run is begun by creating a population of agents and initializing the connection weights of their networks to random values chosen from a uniform distribution between −0.5 and +0.5. The simulation run then proceeds as a sequence of 'rounds' of negotiation, performed as described in Figure 24.6. Quantitative measures of the degree of co-ordination of the population's communication, described in Figure 24.7, are recorded after each round of the simulation. Figure 24.8 presents the record of a simulation run of a population of 30 agents.

In the first round of the simulation illustrated, the randomly initialized agents have a correctness value near 0.0,[1] their error is approximately 0.5, their distinctness is low and the average length of their sequences is high. All of these values indicate that the members

1 Its expected value is 2^{-n}, where n is the number of values in the meaning vectors.

n.1 Choose an agent at random from the population to act as the 'learner'.
n.2 Repeat 10 times:
  n.2.1 Choose an agent other than the learner at random from the population to act as the 'teacher'.
  n.2.2 Train the learner's network to interpret correctly the sequences sent by the teacher, each presented once, in random order.
  n.2.3 Return the teacher to the population.
n.3 Return the learner to the population.

Figure 24.6 A negotiation round.

correctness The fraction of communicative episodes observed in which each value in the hearer's meaning vector is correct.
error The average root mean square error between the hearer's meaning vector and that of the speaker after a communication episode.
distinctness The average fraction of sequences an agent sends for exactly one meaning.
length The average total length of the set of sequences sent by each agent for the set of meanings. A value 1.0 indicates that the length of each sequence equals the cutoff value of 20.

Figure 24.7 Quantitative measures for assessing the degree of co-ordination of communication in a population. Each value is based on a sample of communicative episodes observed after a round of a simulation run.

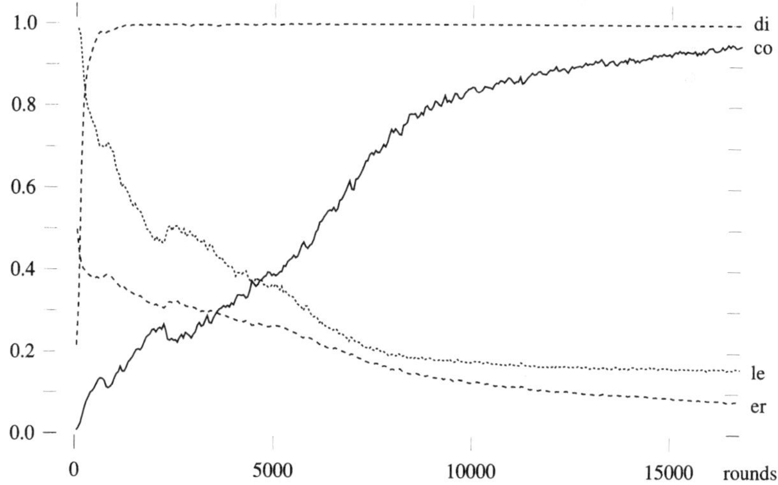

Figure 24.8 Record of a simulation run of a population of 30 agents. Plotted each round are the population's correctness (co), error (er), distinctness (di) and length (le) values. (See Figure 24.7.)

of the initial population do not succeed very well in their communicative attempts; indeed the fact that the average length of the languages is near the maximum indicates that the agents are unable to interpret their own sequences accurately.

In the early rounds of the negotiation, the distinctness value rises sharply, from near 0.20 at round 1 to above 0.90 by round 300. This happens because each learner observes the sequences sent by ten other agents for each meaning. Its training input is therefore almost certainly different for each meaning, even though no individual agent sends a different sequence for each meaning.

By round 300, each agent sends more than 90 different sequences for the 100 meanings, but the agents are still not interpreting them very accurately. Each learner will see, in general, 10 different sequences for each meaning as it is trained. This contradictory input makes it unlikely that after training it will correctly interpret any of them very well. Still, slight statistical fluctuations do occur, and increase the likelihood that certain sequences will be sent for a given meaning. Such fluctuations are amplified as each agent is trained, and the population starts to converge toward agreement about the sequence to be sent for each meaning.

As this agreement develops, the agents are exposed to increasingly less contradictory training input. They are therefore able to learn the developing system with greater accuracy, as shown by the increase in correctness and the decrease in error. The average length of the sequences sent steadily decreases, as an agent need only send enough characters to differentiate one meaning from the others.

By round 15,000, the population has achieved a very high level of communicative accuracy. Over 92% of the meanings are being interpreted accurately. The error has dropped to below 0.1, and the agents send different, and short, sequences for each meaning. This run was continued for a total of 35,670 rounds, at the end of which 97.6% of the meanings were being interpreted correctly, with an average error of 0.044.

Figure 24.9 presents the sequences that an agent sends for some of the meanings before, and after, a simulation run. The initialized agent's sequences are all the maximum length, and the agent sends only 34 different sequences for the set of 100 meanings. After the simulation run, the network's sequences are significantly shorter, and it sends a different one for each meaning.

meaning	sequence
(yumi scared)	cccccccccccccccccccc
(mip hungry)	dbddddbdddbbdbddddbd
(yall sad)	ccbaccccacaadbcabcac
(they scared)	dbddccdccccccccccccc
(mip silly)	aaaaaaaaaaaaaaaaaaaa
(yall angry)	cccccccccccccccccccc
(yup sad)	dddddddddddddddddddd
(me angry)	aaaaaaaaaaaaaaaaaaaa
(yup silly)	adddddcdddddddddadcd
(we hungry)	ccddccccccdddccccdcc
(they sad)	cccccccccccccccccccc

meaning	sequence
(yumi scared)	cacd
(mip hungry)	dbd
(yall sad)	acb
(they scared)	caad
(mip silly)	ada
(yall angry)	bcdbbbbbb
(yup sad)	abac
(me angry)	bdd
(yup silly)	adba
(we hungry)	ddc
(they sad)	abab

Figure 24.9 Sequences sent by an agent for some of the meanings when its connection weight values are initialized to random values (left), and after it has participated in a simulation run (right).

Figure 24.10 illustrates that the agents in a population after a simulation run can interpret each other's sequences accurately. For several of the meanings, the sequence sent by one agent is shown, as well as the meaning vector of another agent after processing the characters in the sequence. Note that almost all of the values are 'correct' in the sense of being within 0.5 of the value in the speaker's meaning vector, but, for the most part, they are much closer than that, consistent with the low error value the population achieved.

5 Analysing the systems

While the agents can evidently interpret each other's sequences correctly, this ability does not necessarily require that any systematic regularities exist between the meaning patterns and the sequences that convey them. The agents might have just settled on a set of short and distinct, but unrelated, sequences to convey the meanings. In this section I describe some of the languages that emerged in simulation runs and seek to elucidate whatever systematicity they possess.

At the end of the simulation that involved the agents whose performance is illustrated in Figures 24.9 and 24.10, the languages produced by each agent in the population were compared. For 65 of the meanings, each agent in the population produced exactly the same sequence. For 14 of the meanings, all of the agents but one produced the same

(me happy)	ba								
1	0	0	0	0	1	1	0	0	1
0.97	0.02	0.05	0.19	0.00	1.00	0.99	0.00	0.00	0.98

(yumi scared)	cacd								
1	1	0	1	0	1	0	0	1	1
0.98	0.97	0.00	0.98	0.00	0.99	0.00	0.01	0.99	1.00

(you scared)	caca								
0	1	0	0	0	1	0	0	1	1
0.00	0.97	0.00	0.01	0.02	0.99	0.00	0.00	0.99	1.00

(mip hungry)	dbd								
1	0	1	1	1	0	0	1	1	0
0.97	0.00	0.99	0.92	0.98	0.00	0.00	0.99	0.99	0.02

(yall sad)	acb								
0	1	0	1	0	1	1	1	0	0
0.05	1.00	0.00	0.95	0.00	0.99	0.96	0.99	0.00	0.02

(they scared)	caad								
0	0	1	1	0	1	0	0	1	1
0.10	0.00	0.99	0.83	0.00	0.97	0.00	0.00	1.00	1.00

(mip silly)	ada								
1	0	1	1	0	1	0	1	0	1
0.49	0.07	0.99	0.92	0.00	0.99	0.00	0.99	0.00	0.99

(yall angry)	bcdbbbbbb								
0	1	0	1	1	0	1	0	0	1
0.26	1.00	0.03	1.00	0.99	0.00	0.99	0.00	0.00	1.00

Figure 24.10 One agent interprets sequences sent by another. Two agents that participated in a simulation run were chosen, one to act as the speaker, the other as the hearer. Each box above shows, for one of the meanings, the sequence sent by the speaker. Below that is shown the correct pattern of 1's and 0's corresponding to that meaning. The last line in each box shows the hearer's meaning vector after processing the sequence.

sequence, and for 17 of the meanings, all of the agents but two produced the same sequence. For the remaining meanings, most of the population produced the same sequence, though there were more alternatives produced, usually by one or two agents each.

	one	*they*	*you*	*yall*	*yup*	*me*	*we*	*mip*	*yumi*	*all*
tired	cda	cdab	cdc	cdcb	cdba	cd	cdd	cddb	cdcd	cdb
scared	caa	caab	cac	cacb	caba	ca	cad	cadb	cacd	cab
sick	daa	daab	dac	dacb	daba	da	dad	dadb	dacd	dab
happy	baa	baab	bca	bcab	baac	ba	badc	bab	bac	babc
sad	aba	abab	ac	acb	abac	a	abdc	abb	abc	abbc
excited	cba	cbab	cca	ccab	cbca	c	ccdc	cb	ccb	cbc
angry	bb	bbb	bc	bcb	bbc	b	bddc	bdb	bdc	bdbc
silly	aa	aaab	aca	acab	adba	add	addc	adad	adc	adbc
thirsty	dbaa	dbab	dca	dcba	dbca	dda	ddac	dbad	dcad	dbacd
hungry	dbb	dbbd	dc	dcb	dbc	dd	ddc	dbd	dcd	dbcd

	one	*they*	*you*	*yall*	*yup*	*me*	*we*	*mip*	*yumi*	*all*
tired	--a	--ab	--c	--cb	--ba	--	--d	--db	--cd	--b
scared	--a	--ab	--c	--cb	--ba	--	--d	--db	--cd	--b
sick	--a	--ab	--c	--cb	--ba	--	--d	--db	--cd	--b
happy	--a	--ab	-c-	-c-b	--ac	--	--dc	--b	--c	--bc
sad	-ba	-bab	-c	-cb	-bac	-	-bdc	-bb	-bc	-bbc
excited	-ba	-bab	-ca	-cab	-bca	-	-cdc	-b	-cb	-bc
angry	-b	-bb	-c	-cb	-bc	-	-ddc	-db	-dc	-dbc
silly	(aa)	(aaab)	(aca)	(acab)	--ba	--d	--dc	--ad	--c	--bc
thirsty	-b-a	-b-b	-c-	-cb-	-bc-	-d-	-d-c	-b-d	-c-d	-b-cd
hungry	-bb	-bbd	-c	-cb	-bc	-d	-dc	-bd	-cd	-bcd

Figure 24.11 Sequences used by a majority of the population for each of the given meanings (top). A potential analysis of the system in terms of a root plus modifications (bottom). Sequences in parentheses cannot be made to fit into this analysis.

5.1 *A paradigmatic analysis*

The sequences sent by a majority of the population for each of the meanings are arranged as a paradigm, in accord with the motivation behind the interpretation of the meaning vectors, at the top of Figure 24.11. The agent whose sequences are shown in Figures 24.9 and 24.10, as it happens, does not follow the majority exactly, most strikingly in the sequence it sends for (*yall angry*).

While not completely regular, the sequences do exhibit some systematicity. A quasi-linguistic analysis of the system is shown at the bottom of Figure 24.11. Each sequence is analysed as a root that expresses the predicate, plus some modification to the root that expresses the referent. The analysis is illustrated by replacing the characters of the supposed root with the symbol '–', followed by, or interspersed with, the modifier characters. The predicates are ordered so that the most regular part of the paradigm is at the top.

For the predicates *tired*, *scared* and *sick*, all of the sequences can be analysed as a root plus a suffix that determines the referent. For the referent *me*, the suffix is empty.

Sequences expressing the predicate *happy* do not completely conform to this pattern. Instead of adding the character c to the end of the root form to express the referent *you*, the character c is inserted between the two characters of the root. A similar internal change, also with c, occurs when the referent is *yall*. Instead of ending with ba for the pronoun *yup*, the suffix ac appears. For *we* and *all*, sequences whose predicate is *happy* add an extra c, compared with the first three predicates; and for *mip* and *yumi*, the suffix does not include the final d that sequences for the first three predicates use.

The sequences for *sad* and *excited* also deviate from the regularities exhibited by the first three predicates, but at least some of the differences might be due to the fact that the root forms for these two predicates consist of a single character, as opposed to two for those above them. The root is followed by b for the pronouns *one* and *they*, but otherwise the sequences for those referents are consistent with the predicates above them. For *you* and *yall,* the suffixes are the same as the first three predicates, except that sequences whose predicate is *excited* have an a following the initial c in the suffix. The rest of the paradigms for these two predicates differ substantially from those of the first three predicates shown, but seem to be more similar to the one for *happy*, and this similarity continues to the sequences for the predicate *angry*, whose root form also has one character.

The first four entries in the paradigm for *silly* cannot easily be analysed as a root form with modifications as with the predicates above it. In particular, the sequence for *me* is certainly not the bare root. Still, many of the entries in this row are similar to those of the other predicates.

Sequences for *thirsty* and *hungry*, while also showing some similarities to those of the other predicates, do not completely conform to any of their patterns.

5.2 *Shared trajectories through activation space*

Like any linguistic analysis, the one just outlined would be open to question on a number of issues were it proposed to account for the inflectional system of a newly described human language. However, the analyses would be at least provisionally justified by the fact that similar analysis techniques are known to apply to other human languages, and seem to express deep regularities among them. Of course this is not a human language, and so the plausibility of the analysis has no such support. The existence of partial regularities in the system can be used as a convenient way to group the sequences, but may be entirely artifactual, and certainly does not entail that any sort of analysis in terms of those regularities is involved in the agents' interpretation of the sequences.

A more plausible account, more consistent with the operation of recurrent neural networks, is that characters and short sequences encode trajectories through the vector space of network activation values. To express each of the meanings with a distinct sequence, and to be able to interpret sequences correctly, the weights of an agent's network must be such that for each meaning there is a sequence of characters that moves the network's output activations through a trajectory to that meaning vector.

For the members of a population of agents to communicate successfully, the trajectory followed by each agent's network output activations on an identical sequence must be roughly similar. If they were to diverge substantially at some point in the sequence, there would be little chance that the sequence of remaining characters would bring them back together, such that they will both end up at the same vector of output values.

It is therefore likely that the systematicity observed in the communication systems that emerge in the simulation runs is due to the networks acquiring a shared set of mappings from partial sequences to transformations of their output values. If this set of transformations can be composed to span the set of meanings, the agents will be able to assemble sequences of characters that will guide each other's networks through trajectories in activation space that will terminate in the correct meaning vectors.

This explanation is consistent with the sort of partial regularity seen in the negotiated systems. For example, in the system shown in Figure 24.11, the supposed roots for the top predicates guide the agents' output values to vectors corresponding to the meaning corresponding to that predicate applied to the referent *me*. The subsequences corresponding to the suffixes then move the activation values slightly, changing only the values corresponding to the referent.

On the other hand, this is not the only way that the output activation values of the network can be guided to their correct values. Other partial sequences will also move the activation values along specific paths, and the agents will use them if the regular sequence does not quite work. For example, the sequences bad and bab would have fit more consistently into the system shown in Figure 24.11 to express *(we happy)* and *(all happy)*, respectively. Apparently the former sequence does not quite bring the output activation vector to the correct values, and so an additional c is added, indeed this final c is used for all of the entries in the column except the three supposedly regular entries. The sequence bab cannot be used to express *(all happy)* because it is used for *(mip happy)*. The additional c is needed to adjust the output vector to add a 1 in the position corresponding to the *ot (other)* feature. (See Figure 24.3.) The *ot* feature also needs to be 1 in meanings whose referent is *we*, and this seems to be the effect of the final c in most of those entries.

It is also possible that specific sequences used to guide the network activation values to correct values might be used for only a small set of the meanings, or that meanings involving different predicates or referents would use different sets of sequences. For example, the sequence aa is used to express *(one silly)*, and while this cannot be seen as conforming to the 'root plus suffix' analysis in much of the rest of the paradigm, the sequence ab can still be used, as it is for other predicates, to adjust the meaning vector to express the referent *they*. In the entries for the referent *yup*, four of the predicates end with ba, and four of the remaining predicates use a sequence that includes bc, indicating that at least two routes to this referent are available to the agents. About half of the predicates use one, and most of the rest use the other.

This explanation also accounts for one aspect of the systems that emerge in the simulations that is certainly an artifact, namely that most of them, including the one just discussed, tend to express the predicate portion of the meaning with the first few characters of the sequences. Recall from section 3 that the predicate involves six of the values in the meaning vector with the remaining four used to express the predicate. Since the networks generate sequences by determining which character would bring their outputs closest to the meaning being expressed, as determined by counting the number of correct values, characters that modify the output values to get the predicate correct will tend to be chosen. Even so, a few systems have emerged in which the referent is expressed first. Simulations are currently being performed in which predicates and referents are expressed with equal numbers of meaning vector values.

5.3 *Conveying novel meaning combinations*

To determine whether the regularities in a population's communication system enable members of that population to convey novel meaning combinations, a simulation run was performed in which ten of the meanings were omitted. The communication system that emerged in this simulation is shown in Figure 24.12, with blank spaces indicating the omitted meanings.

	one	*they*	*you*	*yall*	*yup*	*me*	*we*	*mip*	*yumi*	*all*
happy		dbad	dac	dcc	bba	dab	dcb	dbd	dbc	bbad
sad	dada		da	dca	dda	dad	dcd	ddd	dd	ddad
angry	abba	cbba		cba	bbba	abb	cbb	bbbd	bbcb	bbba
tired	aa	ca	ac		ba	acd	ccd	bcd	bc	bad
excited	aab	cab	ab	cbc		abd	cbd	bbd	bbcd	bbda
sick	aabb	cabb	acb	ccb	bab		ccbd	bcbd	bcb	babd
hungry	aacb	cacb	accb	ccc	bacb	acdb		bcdb	bccb	bacd
thirsty	aaa	caa	aca	cca	baad	acad	ccda		bdca	badad
silly	aaab	caab	ada	cda	baaa	adb	cdb	bdbd		baabd
scared	aad	cad	ad	cd	baac	add	cdd	bdd	bd	

(yall tired)			cc						
0	1	0	1	1	0	0	0	1	1
0.01	0.98	0.00	0.99	0.88	0.00	0.00	0.44	0.99	0.92

(yup excited)			bbdaccca						
0	1	1	1	1	1	0	0	0	1
0.01	1.00	0.97	1.00	0.99	0.53	0.00	0.06	0.00	1.00

(me sick)			abdbd						
1	0	0	0	1	0	0	1	0	1
0.99	0.02	0.00	0.00	0.99	0.17	0.22	0.06	0.00	0.99

(we hungry)			cccdbdc						
1	0	0	1	1	0	0	1	1	0
0.91	0.00	0.15	1.00	0.99	0.00	0.00	0.99	1.00	0.18

(mip thirsty)			bddba						
1	0	1	1	0	0	0	1	1	1
1.00	0.29	1.00	1.00	0.00	0.00	0.00	0.76	0.98	0.95

(yumi silly)			bbaa						
1	1	0	1	0	1	0	1	0	1
1.00	1.00	0.03	1.00	0.00	0.70	0.23	0.99	0.00	1.00

Figure 24.12 Negotiated communication system of a population for 90 of the meanings (top). Blank spaces in the paradigm indicate meanings not used in the negotiation. Sequences sent by a member of the population and the meaning vectors of another member of the population when shown those sequences, for some of the meanings left out of the original negotiation (bottom).

After the simulation run was complete, one of the agents from the population was used to generate sequences for each of the omitted meanings, and another agent was used to interpret them. The results are shown at the bottom of Figure 24.12.

Even though the agents have never sent sequences for these meanings before, nor have they ever (correctly) interpreted a sequence as one of them, the agents are able to convey them with reasonably good accuracy, using sequences that seem to obey the regularities of the negotiated system. The fact that several of the sequences used for the new meanings are longer than the entries in the paradigm supports the idea that the systematicity observed in the systems is due to the agents making use of a shared set of mappings from partial sequences to trajectories in the space of output vectors. Since the agents have never conveyed these meanings before, the mappings they have acquired do not enable them to guide each other's outputs directly to the desired values in all cases. But since the mappings that they possess are shared, the agents are able to compose longer sequences that are correctly interpreted.

6 Conclusions

The negotiation model used in the simulations was arrived at after a number of different approaches, based on evolutionary simulations in which the reproductive fitness of agents depended on their communicative accuracy, failed to achieve anything like the results described above. While the precise reasons for these failures, and their significance, are unclear, the fact that complex adaptive co-ordination can emerge from social interactions among a population of agents is an important lesson, independent of any specific relevance to language. The co-ordination is achieved in the simulations as a result of a distributed process in which individuals learn by observing the behaviour of others, with no external guidance over how the system ought to develop.

I have argued elsewhere (Batali 1993) that other representational and intentional phenomena can be understood as the result of processes of social activity among populations of animals, whose details are influenced by the animals' cognitive abilities, by the external media in which their interactions occur, and often by arbitrary historical contingencies. Such processes leave enduring traces, for example as modifications to the external environment, or as systematic regularities in the animals' behaviour, that can then become a cognitive resource for the animals, enabling even more co-ordination of their activity.

The most crucial assumption underlying the model involves the procedure used to send sequences. As discussed in section 2, the procedure requires that an animal use its own cognitive responses to predict those of others. While such abilities are rare among animals, the fact that existing hominoids possess them suggests that early hominids did too. The increasing complexity of social organization seen during hominid evolution was most likely accompanied by enhancement of all of the cognitive abilities that underlie social activity.

As the hominids began to develop the abilities to use their own responses to predict and influence those of others, situations might have arisen in which such abilities could have been used to communicate information. With the support of shared context, such communicative attempts could often have been successful, even without any co-ordinated system.

If they were capable of learning from each other's communicative behaviour, however, the simulations described in this chapter suggest that early hominids could develop systems to express structured meanings without any innate language-specific traits. Their communicative behaviour would have exhibited systematic regularities from which some of the grammatical resources of modern human languages might have emerged.

References

Batali, John (1993). Trails as archetypes of Intentionality. In *Proceedings of the Fifteenth Annual Conference of the Cognitive Science Society*, pp. 220–225.

(1994). Innate biases and critical periods: combining evolution and learning in the acquisition of syntax. In Brooks, Rodney & Maes, Pattie (eds.) *Proceedings of the Fourth Artificial Life Workshop*. Cambridge, MA: MIT Press, pp. 160–171.

Cheney, Dorothy L. & Seyfarth, Robert M. (1990). *How Monkeys See the World: Inside the Mind of Another Species*. Chicago: University of Chicago Press.

Cleeremans, A., Servan-Schreiber, D. & McClelland, J. L. (1989). Finite state automata and simple recurrent networks. *Neural Computation*, 1, 372–381.

Eimas, P. D., Siqueland, E. R., Juscyk, P. & Vigorito, J. (1971). Speech perception in infants. *Science*, 171, 303–306.

Elman, Jeffrey L. (1990). Finding structure in time. *Cognitive Science*, 14, 179–211.

Haykin, Simon (1994). *Neural Networks: A Comprehensive Foundation*. New York: Macmillan.

Hurford, J. R. (1989). Biological evolution of the Saussurean sign as a component of the language acquisition device. *Lingua*, 77, 187–222.

Jordan, Michael (1986). Serial order: a parallel distributed processing approach. Technical Report ICS Report no. 8604, Institute for Cognitive Science; University of California at San Diego.

Rumelhart, D. E., Hinton, G. E. & Williams, R. J. (1986). Learning internal representations by error propagation. In Rumelhart, D. E. & McClelland, J. L. (eds.) *Parallel Distributed Processing*, vol. I. Cambridge, MA: MIT Press.

Siegelmann, H. T. (1993). Foundations of recurrent neural networks. Ph.D. thesis, Rutgers University, Graduate Program in Computer Science.

Whiten, Andrew (ed.) (1991). *Natural Theories of Mind: Evolution, Development and Simulation of Everyday Mindreading*. Oxford: Basil Blackwell.

Index

Made in the USA
Lexington, KY
09 May 2011